GATEWAY *to* *The* FRENCH REVOLUTION

Select Writings by Edmund Burke, Friedrich Gentz, and Joseph de Maistre

Edited by
ANNA VINCENZI

GATEWAY
EDITIONS

Translation of "Revolutions Compared" by John Quincy Adams.

Published in the United States by Regnery Gateway, an imprint of Skyhorse Publishing, Inc.

Regnery Gateway™ is a trademark of Skyhorse Publishing, Inc.,® a Delaware corporation.

10 9 8 7 6 5 4 3 2 1

Library of Congress Cataloging-in-Publication Data is available on file.

Print ISBN: 978-1-68451-450-2
eBook ISBN: 978-1-68451-467-0

Printed in the United States of America

Cover design by John Caruso

I thank Bradley Birzer, Matthew Gaetano, Wilfred McClay, and David Stewart for their kind suggestions on the essay that opens this volume, and Patrick Griffin for (among other things) letting me in that seminar that, in the fall 2012, first exposed me to Burke's writings.

This work is dedicated to my parents, Lucia and Massimo.

Preface

The French Revolution and Varieties of Conservatism: A Study in Contrasts

The texts republished here—about seven decades after Regnery first released an edition of each—are more a gateway into conservative reflections on the French Revolution than to the revolution itself. They undoubtedly demonstrate the major impact the French Revolution had on modern political thought, and they also expose the variety and complexity of modern conservatism. As Elisha Greifer argued in his 1959 introduction to the Regnery edition of Joseph de Maistre's *Essay*, the conservatism of Burke (and, I would add, Gentz) differed greatly from that of Maistre, in ways and with legacies that can still provoke readers today.

One could say that modern conservatism itself was a product of the French Revolution, born in reaction to the watershed that the events of the French 1790s represented in European and Western history. Certainly, most of the representatives of the Third Estate who, on June 20, 1789, swore on a tennis court at Versailles that the newly created National Assembly would keep meeting until France had received a constitution, could have never imagined the turn that events would take in Paris in the years that followed. In that summer of 1789, many of those representatives thought (and hoped) that France would develop into a constitutional monarchy on the English model. The National Assembly, however, promptly began passing deeply transformative reforms, such as the abolition of all feudal dues and privileges. In the summer of 1790, the Civil Constitution of the Clergy put the confirmation of new bishops under state control, made secular clergymen salaried employees of the state and subject to popular election, and required all French clergy to swear allegiance to the Revolutionary government. The "refractory" priests who refused to swear had to leave their posts.

The situation escalated in the summer of 1791. The king—who in the first phases of the Revolution had (however reluctantly) approved the reforms passed by the Assembly and had been celebrated as the "Restorer of French liberties"—was caught in Varennes with the royal family while attempting to reach the border and flee France. This event, which many interpreted as proof that he had secretly been plotting with foreign allies against the National Assembly, contributed to the growth of republican sentiments in France. The most radical political clubs in Paris managed to take the reins of the revolutionary process. Jean Paul Marat, one of the leaders of the Cordelier Club, wrote in his newspaper *L'Ami du people* that the Revolution had not gone far enough: "the same actors, the same masks, the same plots, the same forces" were still ruling over the French nation; "the people" were being crushed by those who wanted to stop the revolutionary process, whose true aims "had been missed completely."[1]

At the end of 1792, the king was put on trial. In the previous weeks, some, including Jacobin club leaders Maximilien Robespierre and Louis Antoine Saint-Just, had argued that the king should not even be afforded a trial: as an enemy of the natural rights of man, he—just like any brigand or pirate—had betrayed the fundamental contract of society and therefore was not entitled to the protection of the law. But the king was eventually put on trial for treason and condemned to death. He died at the guillotine on January 21, 1793. Queen Marie Antoinette suffered the same fate in October.

A republican constitution was approved but tacitly suspended after only two months, in October 1793, as the government was proclaimed to be "revolutionary until peacetime"—that is, until the counterrevolutionary threat had been neutralized. In the meantime, on September 5, 1793, the Terror had been proclaimed "the order of the day," so that the work of punishing repression of the enemies of the Revolution could be carried out more effectively and speedily. Thousands of people were executed in Paris, and many thousands more died elsewhere in France, especially in Lyon and other centers of federalist insurrections (provincial revolts against the centralization of power in the hands of the Parisian institutions), and in the Vendée, where Catholicism and royalism were the main inspirations for rebellion. The repression was accompanied by an intense dechristianizing campaign and attempts to fill the void by introducing new religious practices. Important churches and sculptures were destroyed; the Gregorian calendar was replaced by a revolutionary one; revolutionary "catechisms" were issued; the government sponsored massive, impressively choreographic and symbolic festivals to Nature, to "the unity and Indivisibility of the Republic," and to the "Cult of the Supreme Being," in an attempt to reeducate the French citizenry.

Eventually, the Revolution started devouring its own children. In June 1793 the Girondins (one of the main clubs that had supported the republican turn) were purged from the National Convention and tens of their leaders ended up on the guillotine; Cordelier leaders Georges Danton and Camille Desmoulins were also executed in April 1794. The climate of paranoia eventually led the National Convention to rise up against Robespierre and Saint-Just, who were arrested and executed on 9 Thermidor, year II (July 28, 1794), and executed the next day.

Over the four years that followed, under the republican constitution of 1795, France was governed by the Directory—a five-member committee—which tried to bring back some semblance of order and also continued the war that France had been fighting against half of Europe since 1792 both as an attempt to protect the Revolution from its enemies and to export it abroad. The war saw the rise of the skilled Corsican commander Napoleon Bonaparte. Under his leadership, France came to dominate much of continental Europe (including Maistre's Kingdom of Savoy—today in northern Italy—and Gentz's Prussia). Claiming to be securing the fruits of the Revolution, in 1800 Napoleon was nominated consul for life and, in 1804, Emperor of the French. After his fall in 1814, the Congress of Vienna, under the leadership of the Austrian statesman Klemens von Metternich, attempted to restore as much of the pre-Revolutionary order as possible, dismantling the empire and putting most traditional dynasties back on European thrones.

But the clock could not be turned back. The French Revolution represented an unprecedented political and ideological watershed in European and Western history. Most of the -isms we employ today (liberalism, conservatism, individualism, to name just a few) did not exist before the French Revolution. The very meaning of the word "revolution" changed. A word that, up to that moment, dictionaries had presented as a synonym of "vicissitude," "disturbance," and "sudden change" was now charged with millenarian and universal significance. Revolution came to signify a "collective political act ushering in the birth of a new world."[2]

Each of the three writers represented in this volume firmly condemned the palingenetic project of the Jacobins. The stance they took on the French Revolution in their writings was a major reason why later interpreters would label all three them "conservative."

Edmund Burke (1729–1797)—sometimes called "the father of conservatism"—probably needs less of an introduction than the other authors in this collection. Born in Ireland, he initially became famous both in and outside of England for his arguments defending the rights of the American colonists, the emancipation of Irish Catholics, and the impeachment of the corrupt governor-general of India,

Warren Hastings. Famous for these "liberal causes" (to use Kirk's words),[3] which he championed as a Whig member of the House of Commons, an office he held from 1766 to 1794, Burke surprised many (most notoriously Thomas Paine) when, in 1790, he published his rebuttal of what he saw as the principles and aspirations that had inspired the recent events of France. Yet Burke saw no inconsistency between his earlier positions and those presented in the *Reflections*. One could defend the rights of American, Irish, and Indian subjects and reject the French Revolution because, he argued, what those subjects were protesting and pursuing was radically different from what the revolutionaries had overthrown.

This point was also one of the core arguments of Friedrich Gentz's long article on the *Origin and Principles of the American Revolution, Compared with the Origin and Principles of the French Revolution*. A Prussian civil servant and man of letters of non-noble origins—he was only granted the "von" by virtue of a decoration awarded by the King of Sweden in 1804 for his writings—in his youth Gentz (1762–1832) had studied under Immanuel Kant in Königsberg. He had originally looked with excitement to the Parisian upheavals of 1789 and the early 1790s.

Then he encountered Burke's work. Reading the *Reflections* represented something of a conversion for the young Gentz, whose own translation of Burke's book was published in 1793 in Berlin. Gentz—who spoke excellent English and had a greater appreciation and understanding of British politics and administration than most continental Europeans, also read several of Burke's speeches, including those on America. They all informed the essay here reproposed to readers, initially published in 1800 in the *Historisches Journal* that Gentz himself had founded. John Quincy Adams, American plenipotentiary in Prussia from 1797 to 1801, read the article, translated it, and had it published in Philadelphia. Eventually—unlike Burke himself, who died in 1797—Gentz got to see the fulfillment of Burke's prediction that "some popular general" would manage to become "the master of your Assembly, the master of your whole republic."[4]

By the time Napoleon's army passed triumphally through the Brandenburg Gate in Berlin in 1806, Gentz had already moved to Vienna, was employed by the Austrian emperor, and was growing into a determined advocate for a European coalition against Napoleon. Gentz would later be one of the secretaries of the Congress of Vienna and a close advisor to Metternich, the architect of the post-Napoleonic restoration. And yet he has been said to have cultivated a modern (rather than a nostalgic) view of the state, and to have looked favorably on reforms that would make the state more efficient and rational and overcome some of the feudal survivals that were a heritage of the Middle Ages. After all, Gentz was a son of Frederick II's Prussia and its enlightened absolutism. He had been trained under one of the fathers of the Enlightenment—Kant—and he never entirely recanted that background. He was convinced of the social and political value of religion for the state and considered converting to Catholicism, but remained a nominal Lutheran his whole life, though not practicing regularly.[5]

Joseph de Maistre (1753–1821) was born in Savoy, at that time part of the Kingdom of Piedmont-Sardinia, which was ruled as an independent monarchy by the House of Savoy, which in the eighteenth century had, like Frederick of Prussia, attempted to implement its own experiment in enlightened despotism. Maistre served as a magistrate and then as a senator in the Senate of Savoy. He then worked as Piedmontese ambassador in Lausanne between 1793 and 1797, and in Saint Petersburg from 1803 to 1817 (after Piedmont was annexed to France in 1802). He concluded his career back in his native kingdom, with a high post in the Piedmontese judicial system.

Maistre was incredibly well read—in the classics as well as in the most influential texts of the Enlightenment—having inherited a rich library from his mother and having received a classical education at a Jesuit school and a royal *collège*. Like Gentz, he reacted enthusiastically to Burke's *Reflections*, and in 1797 he published his own first work on the French Revolution, *Les Considérations sur la France*. In 1817, he published his influential *Du Pape* (which Gentz read with interest and commented on), in which he argued for papal infallibility, presenting it as the foundation of order in Europe. The *Essay on the Generative Principle of Political Constitutions and Other Human Institutions*, republished in this volume, was (significantly) written from a Russian post in 1807 and published in 1814.

Each of the three texts here proposed to readers was published by Regnery in 1950s, with introductions by Russell Kirk and Elisha Greifer that are also reprinted in this volume. Both of these scholars spent most of their lives in Michigan and both served in World War II. Russell Kirk (1918–1994) studied at Michigan State and Duke before being awarded a D.Litt. by the University of St. Andrews in Scotland. His landmark work, *The Conservative Mind*, which was published by Regnery in 1953, traced the genealogy of a trend of conservative thought that went from Burke to T. S. Eliot through Alexis de Tocqueville, John Quincy Adams, and Nathaniel Hawthorne (among others), and that Kirk identified as the most influential strand of British and American conservatism in his day and key to the American Founding. Kirk produced more than twenty books over the course of his career, which he spent mostly working as an independent scholar, writing about intellectual history, cultural criticism, and education. A few years younger than Kirk, Elisha Greifer (1924–2010) earned his PhD in political science from Harvard in 1958 with a dissertation on "Varieties of Conservative Thought," and went on to teach at Wheaton College, Vassar College, and Northern Michigan University.

Greifer's and Kirk's introductions offer wonderfully insightful biographies of Burke, Gentz, and Maistre and overviews of their main arguments, so in the remainder of this essay I will focus on developing a comparison among them and their conservatisms. These critics of the French Revolution, indeed, were not all of one mind, and they did not draw from the revolutionary years the same lessons on history, politics, and human nature.

What Burke, Gentz, and Maistre did share was that they were all important European critics of the French Revolution. All three of them attacked the dismissal of (if not contempt for) traditional morality and ancient wisdom and the nearly unlimited faith in progress that animated the revolutionary leaders; the fact that the hasty ambition of the revolutionaries was inspired and guided by abstract, universal principles rather than political prudence and a careful consideration of the social circumstances and history of France; that this ambition led the French revolutionaries to act in defiance of the laws of their country and to demolish century-old political institutions almost overnight; that the final purpose of the Revolution was indefinite at the beginning and kept changing. Burke, Gentz, and Maistre all deplored the rationalism, irreligiosity, and anticlericalism they had seen growing in European culture during the second half of the eighteenth century; the presentiment (for Burke) and rearward judgment (for Gentz and Maistre) was that these features were destined to make the revolutionary process deeply destructive, so that it would inevitably degenerate into Terror.

On all of these points, the three writers agreed, and their agreement has led many later interpreters—with good reasons—to label them "conservative."[6] I would add that the three possibly underestimated the significance of more moderate, reformist protagonists of the early, pre-1791 phases of the French Revolutionary process, such as the Marquis de Lafayette and the Feuillants Club, who, though sympathetic to change, thought it should be carried out in tandem with the monarch, and should lead to an English-type constitutional monarchy.

Let us now address their differences.[7] Through the writings of Burke and Gentz, we are exposed to a conservatism that was deeply appreciative of the value of tradition, but did not perceive tradition as antithetical to reform and did not deny that there were problems in the Old Regime which called for change. Burke rejected the French Revolutionaries' aspirations for total change, but he also argued that "a state without the means of some change is without the means of its conservation." He insisted that "conservation" and "correction" (or "improvement") are not to be conceived as at odds with each other, and warned that a state rejecting any reform "might even risk the loss of that part of the constitution which it wished the most religiously to preserve."[8]

Both Burke and Gentz praised Louis XVI (arguably with some idealization of the figure of the king) precisely for his openness to reforming the French state. Both recognized, moreover, the licentiousness of the French clergy and nobility. Both acknowledged that the government of France was "full of abuses," and that "when the deputies of the states assembled together in the year 1789, they had beyond all doubt the *right* to undertake great reforms in the government."[9] The great fault of the French revolutionaries had not been inventing problems that did not exist, but rather making those real defects and abuses the pretexts for pursuing a total refashioning of the French society and government.

Burke's and Gentz's attitude toward tradition and reform was grounded in a notion of the human being as an "intricate" mixture of good and evil, by nature made to live in society. Liberty, they believed, could accompany "wisdom and justice" and become a "rational" and "noble freedom," leading men to the cultivation of a virtuous life, but it could also easily lead one to choose a life of misrule and excess.[10]

Both Burke and Gentz, moreover, thought men to be endowed with rights. As examples, Burke listed the "right to live by [the rule of law]"; the "right to do justice"; the "right to the fruits of their industry; and to the means of making their industry fruitful"; the "right to the acquisitions of their parents; to the nourishment and improvement of their offspring; to instruction in life, and to consolation in death"; and the right "to a fair portion of all which society, with all its combinations of skill and force, can do in his favour." Burke clarified that having "equal rights" did not mean having "equal things," and that individual rights were not to be understood as absolute, but always as rights of a "social civil man," and therefore to be carefully balanced with the needs of the specific community and political order in which the individual was living. These, which Burke called the "real rights of men," he regarded as worth defending.[11] Gentz, who criticized the French Revolution for its "violation" and "contempt of rights," would probably have largely agreed with him, though possibly seeing rights as originating from one's status as a citizen and from constitutions rather than natural law.[12]

From their view of human nature stemmed also their view of government as naturally necessary but also limited. Because "the causes of evil . . . are permanent," Burke wrote, "a certain *quantum* of power must always exist in the community, in some hands, and under some appellation."[13] That a governing power must exist, however, did not mean it should be arbitrary or absolute. Neither Burke nor Gentz denied that resistance to authority could be—in the face of serious abuse—legal, and they believed that, even in normal times, the people and the government should limit and temper each other. One of the great dangers that the French were incurring was that, by making the power of the people unrestrained, the state might become "all in all."[14] That danger was a product of the revolutionary leaders' disregard for the law and for the legality of their actions. Both Burke and Gentz had a very high view of the English constitution and law—both unwritten and written—regarding them as a guarantee of order and also of the rights and liberties of the people.

In Burke's and Gentz's view, the American Revolution, unlike the French one, had been respectful of all these premises, and for this reason deserved their respect. Gentz made the argument more explicitly than Burke, but he was arguably elaborating a comparison that was already implicit in Burke's speeches on America and in the

Reflections.[15] Gentz celebrated the prudence of the American Founders, their determination not to break with the English crown except as a last resort after all attempts at conciliation had failed, their respect for English law, and their concern with the lawfulness of their resolutions. He praised the fact that, after declaring independence, "they allowed to . . . speculative ideas, no visible influence upon their practical measures and resolves."[16]

In presenting these arguments, Gentz displayed great attention to the various steps of the Anglo-American controversy and offered a very detailed disquisition on tea, monopolies, assemblies, taxes, prices, and the respective rights that the English constitution attributed to the colonial assemblies, the Parliament, and the monarchy. One finds the same careful consideration of history and its twists and turns—for example, the character of French society and its orders, and the conduct of the French king in the early phases of the Revolution—in Burke's *Reflections*. This shared attention to history stemmed from the two men's conceptions of the intricate nature of humanity and politics, and of the prudence, moderation, and attention to the innumerable facets of history and human experience that the arts of legislation and government require.

Historical awareness is only one of the many ways in which Burke's and Gentz's texts differ from Maistre's. The main difference is arguably the consequence of different theoretical premises. Maistre did not feel any need to consider whether the specific social and political circumstances of eighteenth-century France could have offered reasonable hope that a path of reform could be undertaken, because he simply rejected that the French Old Regime needed reform. He regarded "reform" itself as a word to be looked upon with suspicion and saw even Jacques Necker's proposal that France should take the English constitution as an example as foolish and pitiful.

Maistre, indeed, denied that human reform could produce improvements of any kind and endorsed Origen's view: "*Nothing . . . can be altered for the better among men* WITHOUT GOD."[17] In his lack of consideration for the specific circumstances of French government and society on the eve of 1789, Maistre totally disregarded and implicitly dismissed the possibility that real problems within the French Old Regime might have played a part in creating the premises for the French Revolution. If abuses had existed, he argued, they should be regarded as an "unavoidable dissonance in the great keyboard [of the universe]" and as divinely ordained; man should not dare judge the faults of rulers or correct them, because God's Providence might use them as instruments of his inscrutable designs.

The Old Regime thus emerges from Maistre's writings (as from those of another influential conservative intellectual, the French Viscount de Bonald) as a time of order and harmony, when the French people were guided to embrace divine truth by God's own emissaries on earth—the pope and king.[18] From this totally idealized view of prerevolutionary France, the French Revolution naturally looked like the deranged product of the folly and propaganda of a group of impious conspirators. Maistre's rejection of what Burke saw as the very legitimate principles of "correction" and "improvement" led Elisha Greifer, in his introduction to Maistre's *Essay*, to label his conservatism as "*intransigeance*" and to ask whether the intransigents' resistance to reform and disregard of the flaws of the Old Regime might have even "invite[d] decay and destruction."[19]

Maistre's intransigence was inspired by a much more negative view of human liberty and reason than Burke's and Gentz's. Though he did state that "doubtless, man is a free, intelligent and noble creature," the rest of the *Essay* did not leave the door open to any possibility that individual human efforts and human reason could ever produce improvement or lead one closer to the truth. In another text, he talked about dogmas, prejudices, individual abnegation, submission, and belief as key to the health of a nation and argued that individual "reason should be curbed under a double yoke; it should be frustrated."[20] In light of the French Revolution, Maistre concluded that if human reason was left free to wonder and explore it would likely come up with dangerous follies such as the Jacobins' ideas of natural liberty and the rights of men. Maistre, on the contrary, regarded liberty and rights as concessions made by kings to their subjects, only *if* the ability of the state to control those subjects allowed.

In a seeming paradox, in some passages Maistre talked of a "primitive common sense" and "practical wisdom" as naturally able to perceive the falsity of Jacobin fancies. He also seemed to envision the possibility of a society in which people would naturally obey the word that God had spoken to the prophets and Christ's disciples and that was communicated to all faithful by the Church and the kings that the Church consecrated.

Thus Maistre's view of human nature seems to fluctuate between two extremes: on one hand, the confidence that man's primitive common sense, when shielded from the pernicious influence of impious, rebellious minds, will naturally obey godly commands and follow the revealed truth; on the other, the conviction that individual human reason should never be left free to wander without guidance or critically evaluate, debate, or judge the truth transmitted by popes and kings—or else impious minds will rise and the "conspiracy" will grow. The common denominator between these two extremes is, ultimately, the submission of the individual to authority. Significantly, the earliest known use of the word "individualism" is by Maistre in 1820, in his account of a conversation in which he expressed his concern about the "deep and frightening division of minds, this infinite fragmentation of all doctrines, political protestantism carried to the most absolute individualism."[21]

Since leaving the individual free to reason alone led to frightening confusion, it was good for men—Maistre believed—to be completely subjected to the political authority of kings. While he praised the English constitution for not being "made *a priori*," and for having developed over time through the "work of circumstances" and "good sense," he did not have much appreciation for mixed government; he thought that English "experience and moderation" were the only reasons such a messy, inherently transient constitution had survived for centuries. It seemed clear to him that "history . . . demonstrates that a hereditary monarchy is the government most stable, appropriate, and natural to man," that people should never be allowed to choose their rulers, and that a state should direct people's conduct "by every possible means."[22] Maistre believed monarchies and empires had been divinely established in primitive, immemorable times and that it was God himself who ruled by the hands and decrees of Catholic kings, consecrated by the Church. A king's power, therefore, should be absolute. Burke, in contrast, would have abhorred the idea that the state might become "all in all"—be it a Jacobin democracy or a Catholic sacral monarchy. Maistre would have seen the latter as ideal.

Maistre went so far as to argue against the need for positive, written law—another point on which he departed from conservatives such as Burke and Gentz, and also from much of Western legal tradition (although he tried to show continuity between his ideas and Greek and Roman jurisprudence).[23] Indeed, much of his *Essay* was occupied with building the argument that laws are weakened by being written down. Putting something into writing makes it a possible object of evaluation and discussion. Maistre seemed to regard it as worthwhile to put something in writing only when a certain truth was suffering serious attack. In his essay, the signing of the English Magna Carta (which Burke celebrated as a fundamental moment in the development of the English constitutional tradition), the Council of Trent, and even Scripture (!) were presented as somewhat unfortunate necessities.[24] The English mixed constitution, Maistre suggested, had survived for so long only because it had *not* been written and had therefore remained somewhat malleable, leaving room for monarchs, for example, to suspend habeas corpus with frequency. Ultimately, what Maistre was calling for was a kind of government where the law would be dictated by the *spoken* word of the king.

The causes of the difference we noted earlier, in the role that history plays in these conservative writers' positions, thus become clear. For Maistre, dogma should be communicated, stated, believed, and obeyed; it should not be explained. History should be interpreted by those chosen by God for the task, and they should translate the wisdom coming from the past into law and speak it to the people. As much as the *Essay* might have stressed the value of history, experience, and the past, the text was much more concerned with building an argument for the spoken word against the written one rather than with a careful consideration of the experience of the past. With his approach to history and his notion of language as the natural expression of the soul of a nation (but also with his vision of a healthy nation, where all would be of one mind and naturally embrace the truth), Maistre came closer to the arguments that, more or less in the same months, the German philosopher Johann Gottlieb Fichte was presenting in a series of addresses given at the University of Berlin than to political thinkers such as Burke and Gentz.[25]

Finally, everything suggests that Maistre, who wrote little about the American Revolution, would have disagreed with Burke and Gentz on that too and judged the American project as insanity, doomed to failure. On top of his arguments against written constitutions, Maistre maintained that an "assembly of men . . . form[ing] a nation" would be "ranked among the most memorable follies." And one can guess, based on his argument that "by the very nature of things, monarchy becomes more necessary in proportion as an association increases in size" and that "the [geographical] size of the French nation precludes even the thought of [a] form of government [other than the monarchical one],"[26] that he would never have thought that the American constitutional order would stand the test of time.

It seems clear, then, that these three witnesses of the French Revolution drew very different lessons from it, and thus contributed to the genesis of different kinds of conservative thought. In Burke and Gentz, on the one hand, we see a reformist kind of conservatism committed to recovering aspects of premodern moral and political traditions without idealizing premodern social structures and institutions, a conservatism that held hierarchies in society as somewhat inevitable but did not see them as antithetical to notions of rights and equality—notions rooted in a biblical view of man and natural law, and recognized by centuries of Christian tradition. In Maistre, on the other side, we see exemplified a more intransigent version of conservative thought, which did not admit any possibility of acceptance of or even coexistence with the postrevolutionary order and condemned ideals of rights and equality as the product of the rebellious mind of a century that had refused to submit to authority and chased the fallacies of individual reasons. Thus, if we want to keep calling Burke the "father of conservatism," we should at least clarify to what kind of conservatism we are referring. The divergences between Maistre's conservatism and Burke's seem at least as important as their points of agreement.

What is the value of reading these texts and comparing these different trends of conservative thought today? Seven decades ago, Russell Kirk presented these writings as a cautionary tale, a warning against a kind of liberal optimism unable to see that the great liberation of the eighteenth century had also liberated forces that, in the attempt to make a more just world, had inspired the Russian Revolution and the Soviet totalitarian project. The point was particularly timely when Kirk was writing, amid the Cold War and the rise of scholarship such as that of R. R. Palmer, who interpreted the American and French Revolutions as part of one worldwide revolutionary movement for democracy.[27] Kirk's point is as valuable today as it was then.

But maybe there is an additional cautionary tale that we can draw from comparing these texts, one that has more to say to readers today—especially readers of a conservative persuasion—than it would have in the 1950s. We are living in an age when Cold War optimism seems to have died and trust in the Western liberal order itself is collapsing. The culture wars may be no less intense today than in Maistre's times. It might be worth remembering, then, that if Kirk was right (and not alone)[28] in seeing an ideological connection between the forces liberated by the French Revolution and the Soviet project, it is also true that, especially in continental Europe, a lot of conservatives à la Maistre—that is, conservatives who perceived the modern liberal order as a total, existential threat to Christian Europe and who were unable or unwilling to consider any possibility of correction of that order from within—were ultimately drawn to place their hopes in extreme figures such as Adolf Hitler, Benito Mussolini, and Francisco Franco. These leaders promised a return to order and (in some cases) a Christian restoration. Millions of conservative Christians contributed, with their votes, devoted support, or just their resigned acceptance, to those authoritarian leaders' rise to power, and ultimately the new kind of revolution that their regimes represented.[29]

Where might a Burke or a Gentz have placed himself amid the turmoil of the twentieth century? Or today? What of the questions that Greifer asked seventy years ago, about the "cohesiveness of society" and whether "a system of belief which integrates society" can include some aspects of the post–French Revolution liberal order?[30] Those questions seem more urgent than ever. All the more reason to read these texts with the greatest care.

—Anna Vincenzi
Hillsdale, Michigan
April 2024

A note on the texts: The works included in this volume are in all essentials the works as they were published by Regnery in the 1950s. The original spelling and punctuation have been retained, with these exceptions: A very few clear errors in the text have been corrected.

Some silent edits have been made to the punctuation of the texts where the original seemed likely to confuse or distract present-day readers. And the notes have been edited to make the information they contain more readily accessible. Regnery originally published Friedrich Gentz's *The Origin and Principles of the American Revolution, Compared with the Origin and Principles of the French Revolution* under the title *The French and American Revolutions Compared* and Joseph de Maistre's *Essay on the Generative Principle of Political Constitutions and Other Human Institutions* as *On God and Society*. In this edition the original titles of both works are restored.

Reflections on the Revolution in France

Edmund Burke

Introduction

by Russell Kirk

When the Bastille fell, Edmund Burke was sixty years old, a party leader who had been out of office most of his career, an orator celebrated for his espousal of liberal causes. His Irish vehemence of character, which had enabled him to overwhelm George III and his supporters with splendid scornful imagery, at this juncture was directed against Warren Hastings, the conqueror and plunderer of India. Burke never had hesitated to attack the powerful, or to defend the weak, or to oppose the might of his high imagination to established interests, if he thought established interests unjust. His chief constructive measure as a statesman had been the Economical Reform, which mightily amended the structure and operation of the government machine in despite of everything that placeholders and royal influence could do to prevent it. He had been the most outspoken champion of the Irish Catholics, zealous to free them from the cruel disabilities under which they labored. He had insisted, when first he rose to eminence in the House of Commons, that Americans possessed both the rights of Englishmen and the rights which they had acquired in the history of their colonial experience. He had steadfastly opposed all policies calculated to reduce private liberties, to centralize authority, or to diminish the prerogatives of Parliament. His generous sympathies for the ancient rights of civilized men extended far beyond England and Ireland, to Canada and Madras. Incorruptible in private and public life, Burke was not a rich man, nor was he of high birth. Even his own party—let alone the English crown—never had properly rewarded his courage, his brilliance, his scholarship, and his energy. It seemed, therefore, to many of the leaders of liberal opinion in revolutionary France—to Mirabeau and Thomas Paine and "Anacharsis" Cloots and a young gentleman named Dupont—that Burke, more than any other English political leader, was admirably calculated to head in Britain a radical movement of reform on French principles.

But the French liberals reckoned without their man. Paine, Cloots, and Dupont all had visited Burke at Beaconsfield, and had enjoyed his kindnesses; and all three wrote to him, in 1789, in the expectation that he would approve their radical alteration of French institutions. They had mistaken Burke's whole nature. He was not a man of the Enlightenment, but a generous Christian statesman, guided by the wisdom of his ancestors, and imbued with the moral and political convictions of Aristotle, Cicero, the Fathers of the Church, the Schoolmen, and the great English divines. The presumption of the Age of Reason summoned forth Burke's indignation and contempt. Endowed with a prophet's genius, he marvellously foresaw the whole course of events which would follow upon the French attempt to reconstruct society after an abstract pattern. The Revolution, after careering fiercely through a series of stages of hysterical violence, would end in a despotism; but by that time, it would have brought down in ruin most that was lovely and noble in traditional society. Burke resolved that England should not share in France's folly, and that the whole of the civilized world must be awakened to the menace of these abstractions of impractical speculators, which would expose mankind to the terrible cruelty of the brute that lurks beneath our fallen human nature, instead of conjuring up the Noble Savage of romantic literature.

Edmund Burke, much read in history and much practiced in the conduct of political affairs, knew that men are not naturally good, but beings of mingled good and evil, kept obedient to a moral law chiefly by the force of habit and custom, which the revolutionaries would discard as so much ancient rubbish. He knew that all the advantages of the civil social existence are the product of intricate human experience over many centuries, not to be amended overnight by some coffee-house philosopher. He knew religion to be a great benefit to mankind, and established order to be a great benefit, and hereditary possessions, and the mass of prescriptive beliefs which we call "prejudices." He set his face, then, against the revolutionaries like a man who finds himself suddenly beset by robbers.

Burke had defended the rights of the American colonists because they were the traditional and real rights of actual men, developed in the course of history. He attacked the false concept of the Rights of Man expounded by the French speculators because he recognized in this abstract notion of rights an insensate desire to be free of all duties toward the past and toward posterity. Burke never favored revolution; he bitterly regretted the American war, and had labored always for conciliation, neither repression nor revolution. And the American Revolution, after all, was in truth, as Burke said of the triumph of William and Mary, "a revolution not made, but prevented"; it was an act of separation, but it preserved, rather than destroyed, the traditional framework of life in America. The French Revolution, on the other hand, was intended to uproot that delicate growth called society, and, if not impeded both in the realm of mind and the realm of politics, would end by subjecting all men either to anarchy or to a ruthless master. They would have lost all real rights in the pursuit of pretended abstract rights.

In Parliament, Burke's high and solemn denunciation of the French Revolution at first had little effect. His own friend and fellow-leader of the Whigs, Fox, looked upon the upheaval in France as a splendid triumph of progress and liberty; while the younger Pitt, then in power, thought the eclipse of the French monarchy more an opportunity for English advantage than a menace to established English society. Perceiving that he must appeal from St. Stephen's Hall to the sound sense of the English public, Burke set to work writing a tremendous answer to a letter from his young French acquaintance Dupont, which soon became that book which is the foundation of conservative philosophy, *Reflections on the Revolution in France.* Dupont never saw this tremendous epistle until it was published, and then was astounded by it. The immediate effect of the *Reflections* was titanic. The Tories, the Portland Whigs, and some other persons began at once to perceive the terrible danger of revolution, and proceeded to that course of action which, in the long run, would crush Napoleon. Fox's Whigs, on the contrary, cried down Burke as an apostate, and the Duke of Bedford was rash enough to accuse Burke of mere self-seeking, so that he provoked Burke's crushing reply called *A Letter to a Noble Lord.* A flood of pamphlets in answer to Burke's great work appeared throughout Britain and the Continent; in the English language, the two most influential retorts were those of James Mackintosh and Tom Paine. Mackintosh, as the Revolution progressed, confessed that Burke had been wholly right, and became one of Burke's most ardent disciples; and though Paine never disavowed his own radicalism, his narrow escape from the guillotine in Paris was sufficient refutation of his early high hopes for French liberty and justice.

Burke, Paine said, pitied the plumage but forgot the dying bird:

> When we see a man dramatically lamenting in a publication intended to be believed that "*The age of chivalry is gone!* that *The glory of Europe is extinguished for ever!* that *The unbought grace of life* (if anyone knows what it is), *the cheap defence of nations, the nurse of manly sentiment and heroic enterprise is* gone!" and all this because the Quixot age of chivalry nonsense is gone, what opinion can we form of his judgment, or

> what regard can we pay to his facts? In the rhapsody of his imagination he has discovered a world of wind mills, and his sorrows are that there are no Quixots to attack them. But if the age of aristocracy, like that of chivalry, should fall (and they had originally some connection), Mr. Burke, the trumpeter of the order, may continue his parody to the end, and finish with exclaiming: "Othello's occupation's gone!"

This passage is from *The Age of Reason.* In the minds of liberals as well as the minds of conservatives, from Woodrow Wilson to Harold Laski, from Samuel Taylor Coleridge to Paul Elmer More, Burke vanquished Paine in this great debate; and certainly he won the immense majority of his countrymen, so that Britain turned all her immense energies toward the defeat of revolutionary violence. The leadership which is inspired by honor, that love of things established which grows out of a high veneration of the wisdom of our ancestors, that profound sagacity which reconciles necessary change with the best in the old order—these things Burke knew to be infinitely superior to all the pretended Rights of Man that Paine extolled; and British and American society, at least, have been incalculably influenced by Burke ever since the *Reflections* was published in 1790.

On first examination, the *Reflections* may seem to be a chaotic book; but really it is nothing of the sort. Burke "winds into his subject like a serpent," blending history with principle, splendid imagery with profound practical aphorisms. All his life, he detested "abstractions"—that is, speculative notions with no secure foundation in history or in knowledge of true human character. What Burke is doing in this book, then, is setting forth a system of "principles"—by which he meant general truths deduced from the wisdom of our ancestors, practical experience, and a knowledge of the human heart. He never indulges in "pure" philosophy because he will not admit that the statesman has any right to look at man in the abstract, rather than at particular men in particular circumstances.

The first portion of the book is a comparison of the political convictions of Englishmen with those of the French revolutionaries. Burke demolishes a radical Unitarian preacher of London, Dr. Price, and proceeds to show that the Glorious Revolution of 1688 was not a radical break with English traditions, but rather a preservation of prescriptive institutions. Then he passes on to expose the sophistries and fallacies of the Jacobin reformers, and to analyze the rights of men, true and false. He defends the church against the zealots of Reason, and the old constitution of France against the fanatic advocate of turning society inside out. He speaks up for honor and the unbought grace of life. Then, in the latter portion of his pamphlet, he assails the National Assembly, which by presumption has been delivered up to folly and crime, and which will end by destroying justice and its own existence. To understand the greatness of Burke's book, one must read it through, and that with the closest attention. Written at white heat, the *Reflections* burns with all the wrath and anguish of a prophet who saw the traditions of Christendom and the fabric of the civil social state dissolving before his eyes. Yet his words are suffused with a keenness of observation and a high wisdom which are the marks of a great practical statesman. This book is polemic at its most overwhelming strength, an undying work of political philosophy, and one of the most influential tracts in the history of the world.

Today its pertinence is greater for both conservatives and liberals (Burke himself was both) than it was forty years ago. The revolution of our times has dissipated the shallow optimism of the early years of the twentieth century, and we now perceive in the Russian Revolution the counterpart, still more terrible, of the French Revolution; and we behold in the grinding tyranny of the Soviets the full realization of Burke's prophecies. Having broken with all the old sanctions to integrity, Burke knew, revolutionaries must come down to force and terror, the only influences which suffice to govern a society that repudiates the conservative principles of veneration and prudence. The spirit of religion and the spirit of a gentleman, Burke tells us, gave to modern Europe everything generous and lovely in our culture. A speculative system which detests both piety and just order speedily will repudiate even the pretended affection for equality which gives that system its initial appeal to the masses. "To them, the will, the wish, the want, the liberty, the toil, the blood of individuals is nothing," Burke wrote of the Jacobins. "Individuality is left out of their scheme of government. The state is all in all. Everything is referred to the production of force; afterwards, everything is trusted to the use of it. It is military in its principle, in its maxims, in its spirit, and in all its movements. The state has dominion and conquest for its sole objects; dominion over minds by proselytism, over bodies by arms." We know all too well, in the middle of the twentieth century, the dreadful accuracy of this description, which nineteenth-century optimists took for mere distempered fantasy. We, to our sorrow, live in that "antagonist world" of madness and despair which Burke contrasted with the traditional order of civil social existence.

A year after the *Reflections* was published, the ascendancy of that book was not yet complete among Burke's personal friends, though by 1793 the power of Burke's mind, combining with the reaction from the Terror, would turn the overwhelming majority of thinking Englishmen against radical schemes of social alteration. Even Earl Fitzwilliam, the heir of Burke's great friend and patron Lord Rockingham, still hoped, late in 1791, that some might come out of Continental liberalism; he hesitated to endorse a crusade against the revolutionary regime. By '93, however, the pamphlets of Paine and Priestley, the sermons of Dr. Price, the intrigues of the Constitutional Society and the Revolutionary Society, even the eloquence of Fox, all were scattered like chaff in the blast of Burke's whirlwind wrath. "I am come to a time of life," he wrote to Lord Fitzwilliam, "in which it is not permitted that we should trifle with our existence. I am fallen into a state of the world, that will not suffer me to play at little sports, or to enfeeble the part I am bound to take, by smaller collateral considerations. I cannot proceed, as if things went on in the beaten circle of events, such as I have known them for half a century. The moral state of mankind fills me with dismay and horrors. The abyss of Hell itself seems to yawn before me. I must act, think, and feel according to the exigencies of its tremendous reason." Oliver Goldsmith once feared that Burke was giving to his party the noble talents he ought to give to mankind. In the end, it was altogether different, for Burke broke with party and friends and the very climate of opinion, out of "the exigencies of this tremendous reason." Only today are we coming to understand fully the nobility and the wisdom of his act.

Reflections on the Revolution in France and on the Proceedings in Certain Societies in London Relative to That Event: In a Letter Intended to Have Been Sent to a Gentleman in Paris. 1790.

It may not be unnecessary to inform the reader, that the following Reflections had their origin in a correspondence between the Author and a very young gentleman at Paris, who did him the honour of desiring his opinion upon the important transactions, which then, and ever since, have so much occupied the attention of all men. An answer was written some time in the month of October, 1789; but it was kept back upon prudential considerations. That letter is alluded to in the beginning of the following sheets. It has been since forwarded to the person to whom it was addressed. The reasons for the delay in sending it were assigned in a short letter to the same gentleman. This produced on his part a new and pressing application for the Author's sentiments.

The Author began a second and more full discussion on the subject. This he had some thoughts of publishing early in the last spring; but, the matter gaining upon him, he found that what he had undertaken not only far exceeded the measure of a letter, but that its importance required rather a more detailed consideration than at that time he had any leisure to bestow upon it. However, having thrown down his first thoughts in the form of a letter, and, indeed, when he sat down to write, having intended it for a private letter, he found it difficult to change the form of address, when his sentiments had grown into a greater extent, and had received another direction. A different plan, he is sensible, might be more favourable to a commodious division and distribution of his matter.

* * *

Dear Sir,
You are pleased to call again, and with some earnestness, for my thoughts on the late proceedings in France. I will not give you reason to imagine that I think my sentiments of such value as to wish myself to be solicited about them. They are of too little consequence to be very anxiously either communicated or withheld. It was from attention to you, and to you only, that I hesitated at the time when you first desired to receive them. In the first letter I had the honour to write to you, and which at length I send, I wrote neither for, nor from, any description of men; nor shall I in this. My errors, if any, are my own. My reputation alone is to answer for them.

You see, sir, by the long letter I have transmitted to you, that though I do most heartily wish that France may be animated by a spirit of rational liberty, and that I think you bound, in all honest policy, to provide a permanent body in which that spirit may reside, and an effectual organ by which it may act, it is my misfortune to entertain great doubts concerning several material points in your late transactions.

You imagined, when you wrote last, that I might possibly be reckoned among the approvers of certain proceedings in France from the solemn public seal of sanction they have received from two clubs of gentlemen in London, called the Constitutional Society, and the Revolution Society.

I certainly have the honour to belong to more clubs than one, in which the constitution of this kingdom, and the principles of the glorious Revolution, are held in high reverence; and I reckon myself among the most forward in my zeal for maintaining that constitution and those principles in their utmost purity and vigour. It is because I do so that I think it necessary for me that there should be no mistake. Those who cultivate the memory of our Revolution, and those who are attached to the constitution of this kingdom, will take good care how they are involved with persons, who under the pretext of zeal towards the Revolution and constitution too frequently wander from their true principles; and are ready on every occasion to depart from the firm but cautious and deliberate spirit which produced the one, and which presides in the other. Before I proceed to answer the more material particulars in your letter, I shall beg leave to give you such information as I have been able to obtain of the two clubs which have thought proper, as bodies, to interfere in the concerns of France; first assuring you, that I am not, and that I have never been, a member of either of those societies.

The first, calling itself the Constitutional Society, or Society for Constitutional Information, or by some such title, is, I believe, of seven or eight years standing. The institution of this society appears to be of a charitable, and so far of a laudable nature: it was intended for the circulation, at the expense of the members, of many books, which few others would be at the expense of buying; and which might lie on the hands of the booksellers, to the great loss of an useful body of men. Whether the books, so charitably circulated, were ever as charitably read, is more than I know. Possibly several of them have been exported to France; and, like goods not in request here, may with you have found a market. I have heard much talk of the lights to be drawn from books that are sent from hence. What improvements they have had in their passage (as it is said some liquors are meliorated by crossing the sea) I cannot tell: but I never heard a man of common judgment, or the least degree of information, speak a word in praise of the greater part of the publications circulated by that society; nor have their proceedings been accounted, except by some of themselves, as of any serious consequence.

Your National Assembly seems to entertain much the same opinion that I do of this poor charitable club. As a nation, you reserved the whole stock of your eloquent acknowledgments for the Revolution Society; when their fellows in the Constitutional were, in equity, entitled to some share. Since you have selected the Revolution Society as the great object of your national thanks and praises, you will think me excusable in making its late conduct the subject of my observations. The National Assembly of France has given importance to these gentlemen by adopting them: and they return the favour, by acting as a committee in England for extending the principles of the National Assembly. Henceforward we must consider them as a kind of privileged persons; as no inconsiderable members in the diplomatic body. This is one among the revolutions which have given splendour to obscurity, and distinction to undiscerned merit. Until very lately I do not recollect to have heard of this club. I am quite sure that it never occupied a moment of my thoughts; nor, I believe, those of any person out of their own set. I find, upon inquiry, that on the anniversary of the Revolution in 1688, a club of dissenters, but of what denomination I know not, have long had the custom of hearing a sermon in one of their churches; and that afterwards they spent the day cheerfully, as other clubs do, at the tavern. But I never heard that any public measure, or political system, much less that the merits of the constitution of any foreign nation, had been the subject of a formal proceeding at their festivals; until, to my inexpressible surprise, I found them in a sort of public capacity, by a congratulatory address, giving an authoritative sanction to the proceedings of the National Assembly in France.

In the ancient principles and conduct of the club, so far at least as they were declared, I see nothing to which I could take exception. I think it very probable, that for some purpose, new members may have entered among them; and that some truly Christian politicians, who love to dispense benefits, but are careful to conceal the hand which distributes the dole, may have made them the instruments of their pious designs. Whatever I may have reason to suspect concerning private management, I shall speak of nothing as of a certainty but what is public.

For one, I should be sorry to be thought, directly or indirectly, concerned in their proceedings. I certainly take my full share, along with the rest of the world, in my individual and private capacity, in speculating on what has been done, or is doing, on the public stage, in any place ancient or modern; in the republic of Rome, or the republic of Paris; but having no general apostolical mission, being a citizen of a particular state, and being bound up, in a considerable degree, by its public will, I should think it at least improper and irregular for me to open a formal public correspondence with the actual government of a foreign nation, without the express authority of the government under which I live.

I should be still more unwilling to enter into that correspondence under anything like an equivocal description, which to many, unacquainted with our usages, might make the address, in which I joined, appear as the act of persons in some sort of corporate capacity, acknowledged by the laws of this kingdom, and authorized to speak the sense of some part of it. On account of the ambiguity and uncertainty of unauthorized general descriptions, and of the deceit which may be practised under them, and not from mere formality, the House of Commons would reject the most sneaking petition for the most trifling object, under that mode of signature to which you have thrown open the folding doors of your presence chamber, and have ushered into your National Assembly with as much ceremony and parade, and with as great a bustle of applause, as if you had been visited by the whole representative majesty of the whole English nation. If what this society has thought proper to send forth had been a piece of argument, it would have signified little whose argument it was. It would be neither the more nor the less convincing on account of the party it came from. But this is only a vote and resolution. It stands solely on authority; and in this case it is the mere authority of individuals, few of whom appear. Their signatures ought, in my opinion, to have been annexed to their instrument. The world would then have the means of knowing how many they are; who they are; and of what value their opinions may be, from their personal abilities, from their knowledge, their experience, or their lead and authority in this state. To me, who am but a plain man, the proceeding looks a little too refined, and too ingenious; it has too much the air of a political stratagem, adopted for the sake of giving, under a high-sounding name, an importance to the public declarations of this club, which, when the matter came to be closely inspected, they did not altogether so well deserve. It is a policy that has very much the complexion of a fraud.

I flatter myself that I love a manly, moral, regulated liberty as well as any gentleman of that society, be he who he will; and perhaps I have given as good proofs of my attachment to that cause, in the whole course of my public conduct. I think I envy liberty as little as they do, to any other nation. But I cannot stand forward, and give praise or blame to anything which relates to human actions, and human concerns, on a simple view of the object, as it stands stripped of every relation, in all the nakedness and solitude of metaphysical abstraction. Circumstances (which with some gentlemen pass for nothing) give in reality to every political principle its distinguishing colour and discriminating effect. The circumstances are what render every civil and political scheme beneficial or noxious to mankind. Abstractedly speaking, government, as well as liberty, is good; yet could I, in common sense, ten years ago, have felicitated France on her enjoyment of a government (for she then had a government) without inquiry what the nature of that government was, or how it was administered? Can I now congratulate the same nation upon its freedom? Is it because liberty in the abstract may be classed amongst the blessings of mankind, that I am seriously to felicitate a mad-man, who has escaped from the protecting restraint and wholesome darkness of his cell, on his restoration to the enjoyment of light and liberty? Am I to congratulate a highwayman and murderer, who has broke prison, upon the recovery of his natural rights? This would be to act over again the scene of the criminals condemned to the galleys, and their heroic deliverer, the metaphysic knight of the sorrowful countenance.

When I see the spirit of liberty in action, I see a strong principle at work; and this, for a while, is all I can possibly know of it. The wild *gas,* the fixed air, is plainly broke loose: but we ought to suspend our judgment until the first effervescence is a little subsided, till the liquor is cleared, and until we see something deeper than the agitation of a troubled and frothy surface. I must be tolerably sure, before I venture publicly to congratulate men upon a blessing, that they have really received one. Flattery corrupts both the receiver and the giver; and adulation is not of more service to the people than to kings. I should therefore suspend my congratulations on the new liberty of France, until I was informed how it had been combined with government; with public force; with the discipline and obedience of armies; with the collection of an effective and well-distributed revenue; with morality and religion; with the solidity of property; with peace and order; with civil and social manners. All these (in their way) are good things too; and, without them, liberty is not a benefit whilst it lasts, and is not likely to continue long. The effect of liberty to individuals is, that they may do what they please: we ought to see what it will please them to do, before we risk congratulations, which may be soon turned into complaints. Prudence would dictate this in the case of separate, insulated, private men; but liberty, when men act in bodies, is *power.* Considerate people, before they declare themselves, will observe the use which is made of *power;* and particularly of so trying a thing as *new* power in *new* persons, of whose principles, tempers, and dispositions they have little or no experience, and in situations, where those who appear the most stirring in the scene may possibly not be the real movers.

All these considerations however were below the transcendental dignity of the Revolution Society. Whilst I continued in the country, from whence I had the honour of writing to you, I had but an imperfect idea of their transactions. On my coming to town, I sent for an account of their proceedings, which had been published by their authority, containing a sermon of Dr. Price, with the Duke de Rochefoucault's and the Archbishop of Aix's letter, and several other documents annexed. The whole of that publication, with the manifest design of connecting the affairs of France with those of England, by drawing us into an imitation of the conduct of the National Assembly, gave me a considerable degree of uneasiness. The effect of that conduct upon the power, credit, prosperity, and tranquillity of France, became every day more evident. The form of constitution to be settled, for its future polity, became more clear. We are now in a condition to discern, with tolerable exactness, the true nature of the object held up to our imitation. If the prudence of reserve and decorum dictates silence in some circumstances, in others prudence of a higher order may justify us in speaking our thoughts. The beginnings of confusion with us in England are at present feeble enough; but, with you, we have seen an infancy, still more feeble, growing by moments into a strength to heap mountains upon mountains, and to wage war with heaven itself. Whenever our neighbour's house is on fire, it cannot be amiss for the engines to play a little on our own. Better to be despised for too anxious apprehensions, than ruined by too confident a security.

Solicitous chiefly for the peace of my own country, but by no means unconcerned for yours, I wish to communicate more largely what was at first intended only for your private satisfaction. I shall still keep your affairs in my eye, and continue to address myself to you. Indulging myself in the freedom of epistolary intercourse, I beg leave to throw out my thoughts, and express my feelings, just as they arise in my mind, with very little attention to formal method. I set out with the proceedings of the Revolution Society; but I shall not confine myself to them. Is it possible I should? It appears to me as if I were in a great crisis, not of the affairs of France alone, but of all

Europe, perhaps of more than Europe. All circumstances taken together, the French Revolution is the most astonishing that has hitherto happened in the world. The most wonderful things are brought about in many instances by means the most absurd and ridiculous; in the most ridiculous modes; and, apparently, by the most contemptible instruments. Everything seems out of nature in this strange chaos of levity and ferocity, and of all sorts of crimes jumbled together with all sorts of follies. In viewing this monstrous tragi-comic scene, the most opposite passions necessarily succeed, and sometimes mix with each other in the mind; alternate contempt and indignation; alternate laughter and tears; alternate scorn and horror.

It cannot however be denied, that to some this strange scene appeared in quite another point of view. Into them it inspired no other sentiments than those of exultation and rapture. They saw nothing in what has been done in France, but a firm and temperate exertion of freedom; so consistent, on the whole, with morals and with piety, as to make it deserving not only of the secular applause of dashing Machiavelian politicians, but to render it a fit theme for all the devout effusions of sacred eloquence.

On the forenoon of the 4th of November last, Doctor Richard Price, a non-conforming minister of eminence, preached at the dissenting meeting-house of the Old Jewry, to his club or society, a very extraordinary miscellaneous sermon, in which there are some good moral and religious sentiments, and not ill expressed, mixed up in a sort of porridge of various political opinions and reflections; but the Revolution in France is the grand ingredient in the cauldron. I consider the address transmitted by the Revolution Society to the National Assembly, through Earl Stanhope, as originating in the principles of the sermon, and as a corollary from them. It was moved by the preacher of that discourse. It was passed by those who came reeking from the effect of the sermon, without any censure or qualification, expressed or implied. If, however, any of the gentlemen concerned shall wish to separate the sermon from the resolution, they know how to acknowledge the one, and to disavow the other. They may do it: I cannot.

For my part, I looked on that sermon as the public declaration of a man much connected with literary caballers, and intriguing philosophers; with political theologians, and theological politicians, both at home and abroad. I know they set him up as a sort of oracle; because, with the best intentions in the world, he naturally *philippizes*, and chants his prophetic songs in exact unison with their designs.

That sermon is in a strain which I believe has not been heard in this kingdom, in any of the pulpits which are tolerated or encouraged in it, since the year 1648; when a predecessor of Dr. Price, the Rev. Hugh Peters, made the vault of the king's own chapel at St. James's ring with the honour and privilege of the saints, who, with the "high praises of God in their mouths, and a *two*-edged sword in their hands, were to execute judgment on the heathen, and punishments upon the *people;* to bind their *kings* with chains, and their *nobles* with fetters of iron."[1] Few harangues from the pulpit, except in the days of your league in France, or in the days of our solemn league and covenant in England, have ever breathed less of the spirit of moderation than this lecture in the Old Jewry. Supposing, however, that something like moderation were visible in this political sermon; yet politics and the pulpit are terms that have little agreement. No sound ought to be heard in the church but the healing voice of Christian charity. The cause of civil liberty and civil government gains as little as that of religion by this confusion of duties. Those who quit their proper character, to assume what does not belong to them, are, for the greater part, ignorant both of the character they leave, and of the character they assume. Wholly unacquainted with the world in which they are so fond of meddling and inexperienced in all its affairs, on which they pronounce with so much confidence, they have nothing of politics but the passions they excite. Surely the church is a place where one day's truce ought to be allowed to the dissensions and animosities of mankind.

This pulpit style, revived after so long a discontinuance, had to me the air of novelty, and of a novelty not wholly without danger. I do not charge this danger equally to every part of the discourse. The hint given to a noble and reverend lay-divine, who is supposed high in office in one of our universities,[2] and other lay-divines "of *rank* and literature," may be proper and seasonable, though somewhat new. If the noble *Seekers* should find nothing to satisfy their pious fancies in the old staple of the national church, or in all the rich variety to be found in the well-assorted warehouses of the dissenting congregations, Dr. Price advises them to improve upon non-conformity; and to set up, each of them, a separate meeting-house upon his own particular principles.[3] It is somewhat remarkable that this reverend divine should be so earnest for setting up new churches, and so perfectly indifferent concerning the doctrine which may be taught in them. His zeal is of a curious character. It is not for the propagation of his own opinions, but of any opinions. It is not for the diffusion of truth, but for the spreading of contradiction. Let the noble teachers but dissent, it is no matter from whom or from what. This great point once secured, it is taken for granted their religion will be rational and manly. I doubt whether religion would reap all the benefits which the calculating divine computes from this "great company of great preachers." It would certainly be a valuable addition of non-descripts to the ample collection of known classes, genera and species, which at present beautify the *hortus siccus* of dissent. A sermon from a noble duke, or a noble marquis, or a noble earl, or baron bold, would certainly increase and diversify the amusements of this town, which begins to grow satiated with the uniform round of its vapid dissipations. I should only stipulate that these new *Mess-Johns* in robes and coronets should keep some sort of bounds in the democratic and levelling principles which are expected from their titled pulpits. The new evangelists will, I dare say, disappoint the hopes that are conceived of them. They will not become, literally as well as figuratively, polemic divines, nor be disposed so to drill their congregations, that they may, as in former blessed times, preach their doctrines to regiments of dragoons and corps of infantry and artillery. Such arrangements, however favourable to the cause of compulsory freedom, civil and religious, may not be equally conducive to the national tranquillity. These few restrictions I hope are no great stretches of intolerance, no very violent exertions of despotism.

But I may say of our preacher, *"utinam nugis tota illa dedisset tempora sœvitiœ."* All things in this his fulminating bull are not of so innoxious a tendency. His doctrines affect our constitution in its vital parts. He tells the Revolution Society in this political sermon, that his Majesty "is almost the *only* lawful king in the world, because the *only* one who owes his crown to the *choice of his people.*" As to the kings of *the world,* all of whom (except one) this archpontiff of the *rights of men,* with all the plenitude, and with more than the boldness, of the papal deposing power in its meridian fervour of the twelfth century, puts into one sweeping clause of ban and anathema, and proclaims usurpers by circles of longitude and latitude, over the whole globe, it behoves them to consider how they admit into their territories these apostolic missionaries, who are to tell their subjects they are not lawful kings. That is their concern. It is ours, as a domestic interest of some moment, seriously to consider the solidity of the *only* principle upon which these gentlemen acknowledge a king of Great Britain to be entitled to their allegiance.

This doctrine, as applied to the prince now on the British throne, either is nonsense, and therefore neither true nor false, or it affirms a most unfounded, dangerous, illegal, and unconstitutional position. According to this spiritual doctor of politics, if his Majesty does not owe his crown to the choice of his people, he is no *lawful king.* Now nothing can be more untrue than that the crown of this kingdom is so held by his Majesty. Therefore if you follow their rule, the king of Great Britain, who most certainly does not owe his high office to any form of popular election, is in no respect better than the rest of the gang of usurpers, who reign, or rather rob, all over the face of this our miserable world, without any sort of right or title to the allegiance of their people. The policy of this general doctrine, so qualified, is evident enough. The propagators of this political gospel are in hopes that their abstract principle (their principle that a popular choice is necessary to the legal existence of the sovereign magistracy) would be overlooked, whilst the king of Great Britain was not affected by it. In the meantime the ears of their congregations would be gradually habituated to it, as if it were a first principle admitted without dispute. For the present it would only operate as a theory, pickled in the preserving juices of pulpit eloquence, and laid by for future use. *Condo et compono quœ mox depromere possim.* By this policy, whilst our government is soothed with a reservation in its favour, to which it has no claim, the security, which it has in common with all governments, so far as opinion is security, is taken away.

Thus these politicians proceed, whilst little notice is taken of their doctrines; but when they come to be examined upon the plain meaning of their words, and the direct tendency of their doctrines, then equivocations and slippery constructions come into play. When they say the king owes his crown to the choice of his people, and is therefore the only lawful sovereign in the world, they will perhaps tell us they mean to say no more than that some of the king's predecessors have been called to the throne by some sort of choice; and therefore he owes his crown to the choice of his people. Thus, by a miserable subterfuge, they hope to render their proposition safe, by rendering it nugatory. They are welcome to the asylum they seek for their offence, since they take refuge in their folly. For, if you admit this interpretation, how does their idea of election differ from our idea of inheritance? And how does the settlement of the crown in the Brunswick line derived from James the First come to legalize our monarchy, rather than that of any of the neighbouring countries? At some time or other, to be sure, all the beginners of dynasties were chosen by those who called them to govern. There is ground enough for the opinion that all the kingdoms of Europe were, at a remote period, elective, with more or fewer limitations in the objects of choice. But whatever kings might have been here, or elsewhere, a thousand years ago, or in whatever manner the ruling dynasties of England or France may have begun, the king of Great Britain is, at this day, king by a fixed rule of succession, according to the laws of his country; and whilst the legal conditions of the compact of sovereignty are performed by him (as they are performed), he holds his crown in contempt of the choice of the Revolution Society, who have not a single vote for a king amongst them, either individually or collectively; though I make no doubt they would soon erect themselves into an electoral college, if things were ripe to give effect to their claim. His Majesty's heirs and successors, each in his time and order, will come to the crown with the same contempt of their choice with which his Majesty has succeeded to that he wears.

Whatever may be the success of evasion in explaining away the gross error of *fact,* which supposes that his Majesty (though he holds it in concurrence with the wishes) owes his crown to the choice of his people, yet nothing can evade their full explicit declaration, concerning the principle of a right in the people to choose; which right is directly maintained, and tenaciously adhered to. All the oblique insinuations concerning election bottom in this proposition, and are referable to it. Lest the foundation of the king's exclusive legal title should pass for a mere rant of adulatory freedom, the political divine proceeds dogmatically to assert,[4] that, by the principles of the Revolution, the people of England have acquired three fundamental rights, all which, with him, compose one system, and lie together in one short sentence; namely, that we have acquired a right,

1. "To choose our own governors."
2. "To cashier them for misconduct."
3. "To frame a government for ourselves."

This new, and hitherto unheard-of, bill of rights, though made in the name of the whole people, belongs to those gentlemen and their faction only. The body of the people of England have no share in it. They utterly disclaim it. They will resist the practical assertion of it with their lives and fortunes. They are bound to do so by the laws of their country, made at the time of that very Revolution which is appealed to in favour of the fictitious rights claimed by the Society which abuses its name.

These gentlemen of the Old Jewry, in all their reasonings on the Revolution of 1688, have a Revolution which happened in England about forty years before, and the late French Revolution, so much before their eyes, and in their hearts, that they are constantly confounding all the three together. It is necessary that we should separate what they confound. We must recall their erring fancies to the *acts* of the Revolution which we revere, for the discovery of its true *principles.* If the *principles* of the Revolution of 1688 are anywhere to be found, it is in the statute called the *Declaration of Right.* In that most wise, sober, and considerate declaration, drawn up by great lawyers and great statesmen, and not by warm and inexperienced enthusiastis, not one word is said, nor one suggestion made, of a general right "to choose our own *governors;* to cashier them for misconduct; and to *form* a government for *ourselves.*"

This Declaration of Right (the act of the 1st of William and Mary, sess. 2, ch. 2) is the corner-stone of our constitution, as reinforced, explained, improved, and in its fundamental principles for ever settled. It is called "An Act for declaring the rights and liberties of the subject, and for *settling* the *succession* of the crown." You will observe, that these rights and this succession are declared in one body, and bound indissolubly together.

A few years after this period, a second opportunity offered for asserting a right of election to the crown. On the prospect of a total failure of issue from King William, and from the Princess, afterwards Queen Anne, the consideration of the settlement of the crown, and of a further security for the liberties of the people, again came before the legislature. Did they this second time make any provision for legalizing the crown on the spurious revolution principles of the Old Jewry? No. They followed the principles which prevailed in the Declaration of Right; indicating with more precision the persons who were to inherit in the Protestant line. This act also incorporated, by the same policy, our liberties, and an hereditary succession in the same act. Instead of a right to choose our own governors, they declared that the *succession* in that line (the Protestant line drawn from James the First) was absolutely necessary "for the peace, quiet, and security of the realm," and that it was equally urgent on them "to maintain a *certainty in the succession* thereof, to which the subjects may safely have recourse for their protection." Both these acts, in which are heard the unerring, unambiguous oracles of revolution policy, instead of countenancing the delusive, gipsy predictions of a "right to choose our governors," prove to a demonstration how totally adverse the wisdom of the nation was from turning a case of necessity into a rule of law.

Unquestionably there was at the Revolution, in the person of King William, a small and a temporary deviation from the strict order of a regular hereditary succession; but it is against all genuine principles of jurisprudence to draw a principle from a law made in a special case, and regarding an individual person. *Privilegium non transit in exemplum.* If ever there was a time favourable for establishing the principle, that a king of popular choice was the only legal king, without all doubt it was at the Revolution. Its not being done at that time is a proof that the nation was of opinion it ought not to be done at any time. There is no person so completely ignorant of our history as not to know, that the majority in parliament of both parties were so little disposed to anything resembling that principle, that at first they were determined to place the vacant crown, not on the head of the Prince of Orange, but on that of his wife Mary, daughter of King James, the eldest born of the issue of that king, which they acknowledged as undoubtedly his. It would be to repeat a very trite story, to recall to your memory all those circumstances which demonstrated that their accepting King William was not properly a *choice;* but to all those who did not wish, in effect, to recall King James, or to deluge their country in blood, and again to bring their religion, laws, and liberties into the peril they had just escaped, it was an act of *necessity,* in the strictest moral sense in which necessity can be taken.

In the very act, in which for a time, and in a single case, parliament departed from the strict order of inheritance, in favour of a prince, who, though not next, was however very near, in the line of succession, it is curious to observe how Lord Somers, who drew the bill called the Declaration of Right, has comported himself on that delicate occasion. It is curious to observe with what address this temporary solution of continuity is kept from the eye; whilst all that could be found in this act of necessity to countenance the idea of an hereditary succession is brought forward, and fostered, and made the most of, by this great man, and by the legislature who followed him. Quitting the dry, imperative style of an act of parliament, he makes the Lords and Commons fall to a pious, legislative ejaculation, and declare, that they consider it "as a marvellous providence, and merciful goodness of God to this nation, to preserve their said Majesties' *royal* persons, most happily to reign over us *on the throne of their ancestors,* for which, from the bottom of their hearts, they return their humblest thanks and praises." The legislature plainly had in view the act of recognition of the first of Queen Elizabeth, chap. 3rd, and of that of James the First, chap. 1st, both acts strongly declaratory of the inheritable nature of the crown, and in many parts they follow, with a nearly literal precision, the words and even the form of thanksgiving which is found in these old declaratory statutes.

The two Houses, in the act of King William, did not thank God that they had found a fair opportunity to assert a right to choose their own governors, much less to make an election the *only lawful* title to the crown. Their having been in a condition to avoid the very appearance of it, as much as possible, was by them considered as a providential escape. They threw a politic, well-wrought veil over every circumstance tending to weaken the rights, which in the meliorated order of succession they meant to perpetuate; or which might furnish a precedent for any future departure from what they had then settled for ever. Accordingly, that they might not relax the nerves of their monarchy, and that they might preserve a close conformity to the practice of their ancestors, as it appeared in the declaratory statutes of Queen Mary[5] and Queen Elizabeth, in the next clause they vest, by recognition, in their Majesties, *all* the legal prerogatives of the crown, declaring, "that in them they are most *fully,* rightfully, and *entirely* invested, incorporated, united, and annexed." In the clause which follows, for preventing questions, by reason of any pretended titles to the crown, they declare (observing also in this the traditionary language, along with the traditionary policy of the nation, and repeating as from a rubric the language of the preceding acts of Elizabeth and James) that on the preserving "a *certainty* in the SUCCESSION thereof, the unity, peace, and tranquillity of this nation doth, under God, wholly depend."

They knew that a doubtful title of succession would but too much resemble an election; and that an election would be utterly destructive of the "unity, peace, and tranquillity of this nation," which they thought to be considerations of some moment. To provide for these objects, and therefore to exclude for ever the Old Jewry doctrine of "a right to choose our own governors," they follow with a clause containing a most solemn pledge, taken from the preceding act of Queen Elizabeth, as solemn a pledge as ever was or can be given in favour of an hereditary succession, and as solemn a renunciation as could be made of the principles by this Society imputed to them. "The Lords spiritual and temporal, and Commons, do, in the name of all the people aforesaid, most humbly and faithfully submit *themselves, their heirs and posterities for ever;* and do faithfully promise that they will stand to, maintain, and defend their said Majesties, and also the *limitation of the crown,* herein specified and contained, to the utmost of their powers," &c., &c.

So far is it from being true, that we acquired a right by the Revolution to elect our kings, that if we had possessed it before, the English nation did at that time most solemnly renounce and abdicate it, for themselves, and for all their posterity for ever. These gentlemen may value themselves as much as they please on their Whig principles; but I never desire to be thought a better Whig than Lord Somers; or to understand the principles of the Revolution better than those by whom it was brought about; or to read in the Declaration of Right any mysteries unknown to those whose penetrating style has engraved in our ordinances, and in our hearts, the words and spirit of that immortal law.

It is true, that, aided with the powers derived from force and opportunity, the nation was at that time, in some sense, free to take what course it pleased for filling the throne; but only free to do so upon the same grounds on which they might have wholly abolished their monarchy, and every other part of their constitution. However, they did not think such bold changes within their commission. It is indeed difficult, perhaps impossible, to give limits to the mere *abstract* competence of the supreme power, such as was exercised by parliament at that time; but the limits of a *moral* competence, subjecting, even in powers more indisputably sovereign, occasional will to permanent reason, and to the steady maxims of faith, justice, and fixed fundamental policy, are perfectly intelligible, and perfectly binding upon those who exercise any authority, under any name, or under any title, in the state. The House of Lords, for instance, is not morally competent to dissolve the House of Commons; no, nor even to dissolve itself, nor to abdicate, if it would, its portion in the legislature of the kingdom. Though a king may abdicate for his own person, he cannot abdicate for the monarchy. By as strong, or by a stronger reason, the House of Commons cannot renounce its share of authority. The engagement and pact of society, which generally goes by the name of the constitution, forbids such invasion and such surrender. The constituent parts of a state are obliged to hold their public faith with each other, and with all those who derive any serious interest under their engagements, as much as the whole state is bound to keep its faith with separate communities. Otherwise competence and power would soon be confounded, and no law be left but the will of a prevailing force. On this principle the succession of the crown has always been what it now is, an hereditary succession by law: in the old line it was a succession by the common law; in the new by the statute law, operating on the principles of the common law, not changing the substance, but regulating the mode, and describing the persons. Both these descriptions of law are of the same force, and are derived from an equal authority, emanating from the common agreement and original compact of the state, *communi sponsione reipublicæ,* and as such are equally binding on king and people too, as long as the terms are observed, and they continue the same body politic.

It is far from impossible to reconcile, if we do not suffer ourselves to be entangled in the mazes of meta-physic sophistry, the use both of a fixed rule and an occasional deviation; the sacredness of an hereditary principle of succession in our government, with a power of change in its application in cases of extreme emergency. Even in that extremity (if we take the measure of our rights by our exercise of them at the Revolution) the change is to be confined to the peccant part only; to the part which produced the necessary deviation; and even then it is to be effected without a decomposition of the whole civil and political mass, for the purpose of originating a new civil order out of the first elements of society.

A state without the means of some change is without the means of its conservation. Without such means it might even risk the loss of that part of the constitution which it wished the most religiously to preserve. The two principles of conservation and correction operated strongly at the two critical periods of the Restoration and

Revolution, when England found itself without a king. At both those periods the nation had lost the bond of union in their ancient edifice; they did not, however, dissolve the whole fabric. On the contrary, in both cases they regenerated the deficient part of the old constitution through the parts which were not impaired. They kept these old parts exactly as they were, that the part recovered might be suited to them. They acted by the ancient organized states in the shape of their old organization, and not by the organic *moleculæ* of a disbanded people. At no time, perhaps, did the sovereign legislature manifest a more tender regard to that fundamental principle of British constitutional policy, than at the time of the Revolution, when it deviated from the direct line of hereditary succession. The crown was carried somewhat out of the line in which it had before moved; but the new line was derived from the same stock. It was still a line of hereditary descent; still an hereditary descent in the same blood, though an hereditary descent qualified with Protestantism. When the legislature altered the direction, but kept the principle, they showed that they held it inviolable.

On this principle, the law of inheritance had admitted some amendment in the old time, and long before the era of the Revolution. Some time after the conquest great questions arose upon the legal principles of hereditary descent. It became a matter of doubt, whether the heir *per capita* or the heir *per stripes* was to succeed; but whether the heir *per capita* gave way when the heirdom *per stripes* took place, or the Catholic heir when the Protestant was preferred, the inheritable principle survived with a sort of immortality through all transmigrations—*multosque per annos stat fortuna domus, et avi numerantur avorum.* This is the spirit of our constitution, not only in its settled course, but in all its revolutions. Whoever came in, or however he came in, whether he obtained the crown by law, or by force, the hereditary succession was either continued or adopted.

The gentlemen of the Society for Revolutions see nothing in that of 1688 but the deviation from the constitution; and they take the deviation from the principle for the principle. They have little regard to the obvious consequences of their doctrine, though they must see, that it leaves positive authority in very few of the positive institutions of this country. When such an unwarrantable maxim is once established, that no throne is lawful but the elective, no one act of the princes who preceded this era of fictitious election can be valid. Do these theorists mean to imitate some of their predecessors, who dragged the bodies of our ancient sovereigns out of the quiet of their tombs? Do they mean to attaint and disable backwards all the kings that have reigned before the Revolution, and consequently to stain the throne of England with the blot of a continual usurpation? Do they mean to invalidate, annul, or to call into question, together with the titles of the whole line of our kings, that great body of our statute law which passed under those whom they treat as usurpers? to annul laws of inestimable value to our liberties—of as great value at least as any which have passed at or since the period of the Revolution? If kings, who did not owe their crown to the choice of their people, had no title to make laws, what will become of the statute *de tallagio non concedendo?* Of the *petition of right?* Of the act of *habeas corpus?* Do these new doctors of the rights of men presume to assert, that King James the Second, who came to the crown as next of blood, according to the rules of a then unqualified succession, was not to all intents and purposes a lawful king of England, before he had done any of those acts which were justly construed into an abdication of his crown? If he was not, much trouble in parliament might have been saved at the period these gentlemen commemorate. But King James was a bad king with a good title, and not an usurper. The princes who succeeded according to the act of parliament which settled the crown on the Electress Sophia and on her descendants, being Protestants, came in as much by a title of inheritance as King James did. He came in according to the law, as it stood at his accession to the crown; and the princes of the House of Brunswick came to the inheritance of the crown, not by election, but by the law, as it stood at their several accessions of Protestant descent and inheritance, as I hope I have shown sufficiently.

The law, by which this royal family is specifically destined to the succession, is the act of the 12th and 13th of King William. The terms of this act bind "us and our *heirs,* and our *posterity,* to them, their *heirs,* and their *posterity,*" being Protestants, to the end of time, in the same words as the Declaration of Right had bound us to the heirs of King William and Queen Mary. It therefore secures both an hereditary crown and an hereditary allegiance. On what ground, except the constitutional policy of forming an establishment to secure that kind of succession which is to preclude a choice of the people for ever, could the legislature have fastidiously rejected the fair and abundant choice which our country presented to them, and searched in strange lands for a foreign princess, from whose womb the line of our future rulers were to derive their title to govern millions of men through a series of ages?

The Princess Sophia was named in the act of settlement of the 12th and 13th of King William, for a *stock* and root of *inheritance* to our kings, and not for her merits as a temporary administratrix of a power, which she might not, and in fact did not, herself ever exercise. She was adopted for one reason, and for one only, because, says the act, "the most excellent Princess Sophie, Electress and Duchess Dowager of Hanover, is *daughter* of the most excellent Princess Elizabeth, late Queen of Bohemia, *daughter* of our late *sovereign lord* King James the First, of happy memory, and is hereby declared to be the next in *succession* in the Protestant line," &c. &c.; "and the crown shall continue to the *heirs* of her body, being Protestants." This limitation was made by parliament, that through the Princess Sophia an inheritable line not only was to be continued in future, but (what they thought very material) that through her it was to be connected with the old stock of inheritance in King James the First; in order that the monarchy might preserve an unbroken unity through all ages, and might be preserved (with safety to our religion) in the old approved mode by descent, in which, if our liberties had been once endangered, they had often, through all storms and struggles of prerogative and privilege, been preserved. They did well. No experience has taught us, that in any other course or method than that of an *hereditary crown* our liberties can be regularly perpetuated and preserved sacred as our *hereditary right.* An irregular, convulsive movement may be necessary to throw off an irregular, convulsive disease. But the course of succession is the healthy habit of the British constitution. Was it that the legislature wanted, at the act for the limitation of the crown in the Hanoverian line, drawn through the female descendants of James the First, a due sense of the inconveniences of having two or three, or possibly more, foreigners in succession to the British throne? No! They had a due sense of the evils which might happen from such foreign rule, and more than a due sense of them. But a more decisive proof cannot be given of the full conviction of the British nation, that the principles of the Revolution did not authorize them to elect kings at their pleasure, and without any attention to the ancient fundamental principles of our government, than their continuing to adopt a plan of hereditary Protestant succession in the old line, with all the dangers and all the inconveniences of its being a foreign line full before their eyes, and operating with the utmost force upon their minds.

A few years ago I should be ashamed to overload a matter, so capable of supporting itself, by the then unnecessary support of any argument; but this seditious, unconstitutional doctrine is now publicly taught, avowed, and printed. The dislike I feel to revolutions, the signals for which have so often been given from pulpits; the spirit of change that is gone abroad; the total contempt which prevails with you, and may come to prevail with us, of all ancient institutions, when set in opposition to a present sense of convenience, or to the bent of a present inclination: all these considerations make it not unadvisable, in my opinion, to call back our attention to the true principles of our own domestic laws; that you, my French friend, should begin to know, and that we should continue to cherish them. We ought not, on either side of the water, to suffer ourselves to be imposed upon by the counterfeit wares which some persons, by a double fraud, export to you in illicit bottoms, as raw commodities of British growth, though wholly alien to our soil, in order afterwards to smuggle them back again into tins country, manufactured after the newest Paris fashion of an improved liberty.

The people of England will not ape the fashions they have never tried, nor go back to those which they have found mischievous on trial. They look upon the legal hereditary succession of their crown as among their rights, not as among their wrongs; as a benefit, not as a grievance; as a security for their liberty, not as a badge of servitude. They look on the frame of their commonwealth, *such as it stands,* to be of inestimable value; and they conceive the undisturbed succession of the crown to be a pledge of the stability and perpetuity of all the other members of our constitution.

I shall beg leave, before I go any further, to take notice of some paltry artifices, which the abettors of election, as the only lawful title to the crown, are ready to employ, in order to render the support of the just principles of our constitution a task somewhat invidious. These sophisters substitute a fictitious cause, and feigned personages, in whose favour they suppose you engaged, whenever you defend the inheritable nature of the crown. It is common with them to dispute as if they were in a conflict with some of those exploded fanatics of slavery, who formerly maintained, what I believe no creature now maintains, "that the crown is held by divine hereditary and indefeasible right." These old fanatics of single arbitrary power dogmatized as if hereditary royalty was the only lawful government in the world, just as our new fanatics of popular arbitrary power maintain that a popular election is the sole lawful source of authority. The old prerogative enthusiasts, it is true, did speculate foolishly, and perhaps impiously too, as if monarchy had more of a divine sanction than any other mode of government; and as if a right to govern by inheritance were in strictness *indefeasible* in every person, who should be found in the succession to a throne, and under every circumstance, which no civil or political right can be. But an absurd opinion concerning the king's hereditary right to the crown does not prejudice one that is rational, and bottomed upon solid principles of law and policy. If all the absurd theories of lawyers and divines were to vitiate the objects in which they are conversant, we should have no law and no religion left in the world. But an absurd theory on one side of a question forms no justification for alleging a false fact, or promulgating mischievous maxims, on the other.

The second claim of the Revolution Society is "a right of cashiering their governors for *misconduct*." Perhaps the apprehensions our ancestors entertained of forming such a precedent as that "of cashiering for misconduct," was the cause that the declaration of the act, which implied the abdication of King James, was, if it had any fault, rather too guarded, and too circumstantial.[6] But all this guard, and all this accumulation of circumstances, serves to show the spirit of caution which predominated in the national councils in a situation in which men, irritated by oppression, and elevated by a triumph over it, are apt to abandon themselves to violent and extreme courses: it shows the anxiety of the great men who influenced the conduct of affairs at that great event to make the Revolution a parent of settlement, and not a nursery of future revolutions.

No government could stand a moment, if it could be blown down with anything so loose and indefinite as an opinion of "*misconduct*." They who led at the Revolution grounded the virtual abdication of King James upon no such light and uncertain principle. They charged him with nothing less than a design, confirmed by a multitude of illegal overt acts, to *subvert the Protestant church and state*, and their *fundamental*, unquestionable laws and liberties: they charged him with having broken the *original contract* between king and people. This was more than *misconduct*. A grave and overruling necessity obliged them to take the step they took, and took with infinite reluctance, as under that most rigorous of all laws. Their trust for the future preservation of the constitution was not in future revolutions. The grand policy of all their regulations was to render it almost impracticable for any future sovereign to compel the states of the kingdom to have again recourse to those violent remedies. They left the crown what, in the eye and estimation of law, it had ever been, perfectly irresponsible. In order to lighten the crown still further, they aggravated responsibility on ministers of state. By the statute of the 1st of King William, sess. 2nd, called *"the act for declaring the rights and liberties of the subject, and for settling the succession to the crown,"* they enacted, that the ministers should serve the crown on the terms of that declaration. They secured soon after the *frequent meetings of parliament,* by which the whole government would be under the constant inspection and active control of the popular representative and of the magnates of the kingdom. In the next great constitutional act, that of the 12th and 13th of King William, for the further limitation of the crown, and *better* securing the rights and liberties of the subject, they provided, "that no pardon under the great seal of England should be pleadable to an impeachment by the Commons in parliament." The rule laid down for government in the Declaration of Right, the constant inspection of parliament, the practical claim of impeachment, they thought infinitely a better security not only for their constitutional liberty, but against the vices of administration, than the reservation of a right so difficult in the practice, so uncertain in the issue, and often so mischievous in the consequences, as that of "cashiering their governors."

Dr. Price, in his sermon,[7] condemns very properly the practice of gross, adulatory addresses to kings. Instead of this fulsome style, he proposes that his Majesty should be told, on occasions of congratulation, that "he is to consider himself as more properly the servant than the sovereign of his people." For a compliment, this new form of address does not seem to be very soothing. Those who are servants in name, as well as in effect, do not like to be told of their situation, their duty, and their obligations. The slave, in the old play, tells his master, *"Hœc commemoratio est quasi exprobatio."* It is not pleasant as compliment; it is not wholesome as instruction. After all, if the king were to bring himself to echo this new kind of address, to adopt it in terms, and even to take the appellation of Servant of the People as his royal style, how either he or we should be much mended by it, I cannot imagine. I have seen very assuming letters, signed, Your most obedient, humble servant. The proudest denomination that ever was endured on earth took a title of still greater humility than that which is now proposed for sovereigns by the Apostle of Liberty. Kings and nations were trampled upon by the foot of one calling himself "the Servant of Servants"; and mandates for deposing sovereigns were sealed with the signet of "the Fisherman."

I should have considered all this as no more than a sort of flippant, vain discourse, in which, as in an unsavoury fume, several persons suffer the spirit of liberty to evaporate, if it were not plainly in support of the idea, and a part of the scheme, of "cashiering kings for misconduct." In that light it is worth some observation.

Kings, in one sense, are undoubtedly the servants of the people, because their power has no other rational end than that of the general advantage; but it is not true that they are, in the ordinary sense, (by our constitution at least), anything like servants; the essence of whose situation is to obey the commands of some other, and to be removable at pleasure. But the king of Great Britain obeys no other person; all other persons are individually, and collectively too, under him, and owe to him a legal obedience. The law, which knows neither to flatter nor to insult, calls this high magistrate, not our servant, as this humble divine calls him, but *"our sovereign Lord the king;"* and we, on our parts, have learned to speak only the primitive language of the law, and not the confused jargon of their Babylonian pulpits.

As he is not to obey us, but as we are to obey the law in him, our constitution has made no sort of provision towards rendering him, as a servant, in any degree responsible. Our constitution knows nothing of a magistrate like the *Justicia* of Arragon; nor of any court legally appointed, nor of any process legally settled, for submitting the king to the responsibility belonging to all servants. In this he is not distinguished from the Commons and the Lords; who, in their several public capacities, can never be called to an account for their conduct; although the Revolution Society chooses to assert, in direct opposition to one of the wisest and most beautiful parts of our constitution, that "a king is no more than the first servant of the public, created by it, *and responsible to it.*"

Ill would our ancestors at the Revolution have deserved their fame for wisdom, if they had found no security for their freedom, but in rendering their government feeble in its operations and precarious in its tenure; if they had been able to contrive no better remedy against arbitrary power than civil confusion. Let these gentlemen state who that *representative* public is to whom they will affirm the king, as a servant, to be responsible. It will be then time enough for me to produce to them the positive statute law which affirms that he is not.

The ceremony of cashiering kings, of which these gentlemen talk so much at their ease, can rarely, if ever, be performed without force. It then becomes a case of war, and not of constitution. Laws are commanded to hold their tongues amongst arms; and tribunals fall to the ground with the peace they are no longer able to uphold. The Revolution of 1688 was obtained by a just war, in the only case in which any war, and much more a civil war, can be just. "Justa bella quibus *necessaria.*" The question of dethroning, or, if these gentlemen like the phrase better, "cashiering kings," will always be, as it has always been, an extraordinary question of state, and wholly out of the law; a question (like all other questions of state) of dispositions, and of means, and of probable consequences, rather than of positive rights. As it was not made for common abuses, so it is not to be agitated by common minds. The speculative line of demarcation, where obedience ought to end, and resistance must begin, is faint, obscure, and not easily definable. It is not a single act, or a single event, which determines it. Governments must be abused and deranged indeed, before it can be thought of; and the prospect of the future must be as bad as the experience of the past. When things are in that lamentable condition, the nature of the disease is to indicate the remedy to those whom nature has qualified to administer in extremities this critical, ambiguous, bitter potion to a distempered state. Times, and occasions, and provocations, will teach their own lessons. The wise will determine from the gravity of the case; the irritable, from sensibility to oppression; the high-minded, from disdain and indignation at abusive power in unworthy hands; the brave and bold, from the love of honourable danger in a generous cause: but, with or without right, a revolution will be the very last resource of the thinking and the good.

The third head of right, asserted by the pulpit of the Old Jewry, namely, the "right to form a government for ourselves," has, at least, as little countenance from anything done at the Revolution, either in precedent or principle, as the two first of their claims. The Revolution was made to preserve our *ancient,* indisputable laws and liberties, and that *ancient* constitution of government which is our only security for law and liberty. If you are desirous of knowing the spirit of our constitution, and the policy which predominated in that great period which has secured it to this hour, pray look for both in our histories, in our records, in our acts of parliament, and journals of parliament, and not in the sermons of the Old Jewry, and the after-dinner toasts of the Revolution Society. In the former you will find other ideas and another language. Such a claim is as ill-suited to our temper and wishes as it is unsupported by any appearance of authority. The very idea of the fabrication of a new government is enough to fill us with disgust and horror. We wished at the period of the Revolution, and do now wish, to derive all we possess as an *inheritance from our forefathers.* Upon that body and stock of inheritance we have taken care not to inoculate any scion alien to the nature of the original plant. All the reformations we have hitherto made have proceeded upon the principle of reverence to antiquity; and I hope, nay I am persuaded, that all those which possibly may be made hereafter, will be carefully formed upon analogical precedent, authority, and example.

Our oldest reformation is that of Magna Charta. You will see that Sir Edward Coke, that great oracle of our law, and indeed all the great men who follow him, to Blackstone,[8] are industrious to prove the pedigree of our liberties. They endeavour to prove, that the ancient charter, the Magna Charta of King John, was connected with another positive charter from Henry I, and that both the one and the other were nothing more than a re-affirmance of the still more ancient standing law of the kingdom. In the matter of fact, for the greater part, these authors appear to be in the right; perhaps not always; but if the lawyers mistake in some particulars, it proves my position still the more strongly; because it demonstrates the powerful prepossession towards antiquity, with which the minds of all our lawyers and legislators, and of all the people whom they wish to influence, have been always filled; and the stationary policy of this kingdom in considering their most sacred rights and franchises as an *inheritance.*

In the famous law of the 3rd of Charles I, called the *Petition of Right,* the parliament says to the king, "Your subjects have *inherited* this freedom," claiming their franchises not on abstract principles "as the rights of Englishmen, and as a patrimony derived from their forefathers. Selden, and the other profoundly learned men, who drew this Petition of Right, were as well acquainted, at least, with all the general theories concerning the "rights of men," as any of the discoursers in our pulpits, or on your tribune; full as well as Dr. Price, or as the Abbé Sieyes. But, for reasons worthy of that practical wisdom which superseded their theoretic science, they preferred this positive, recorded, *hereditary* title to all which can be dear to the man and the citizen, to that vague speculative right, which exposed their sure inheritance to be scrambled for and torn to pieces by every wild, litigious spirit.

The same policy pervades all the laws which have since been made for the preservation of our liberties. In the 1st of William and Mary, in the famous statute, called the Declaration of Right, the two Houses utter not a syllable of "a right to frame a government for themselves." You will see, that their whole care was to secure the religion, laws, and liberties, that had been long possessed, and had been lately endangered. "Taking into their most serious consideration the *best* means for making such an establishment, that their religion, laws, and liberties might not be in danger of being again subverted," they auspicate all their proceedings, by stating as some of those *best* means, "in the *first place*" to do "as their *ancestors in like cases have usually* done for vindicating their *ancient* rights and liberties, to *declare*"—and then they pray the king and queen, "that it may be *declared* and enacted, that *all and singular* the rights and liberties *asserted and declared*, are the true *ancient* and indubitable rights and liberties of the people of this kingdom."[9]

You will observe, that from Magna Charta to the Declaration of Right, it has been the uniform policy of our constitution to claim and assert our liberties, as an *entailed inheritance* derived to us from our forefathers, and to be transmitted to our posterity; as an estate specially belonging to the people of this kingdom, without any reference whatever to any other more general or prior right. By this means our constitution preserves a unity in so great a diversity of its parts. We have an inheritable crown; an inheritable peerage; and a House of Commons and a people inheriting privileges, franchises, and liberties, from a long line of ancestors.

This policy appears to me to be the result of profound reflection; or rather the happy effect of following nature, which is wisdom without reflection, and above it. A spirit of innovation is generally the result of a selfish temper, and confined views. People will not look forward to posterity, who never look backward to their ancestors.

Besides, the people of England well know, that the idea of inheritance furnishes a sure principle of conservation, and a sure principle of transmission; without at all excluding a principle of improvement. It leaves acquisition free; but it secures what it acquires. Whatever advantages are obtained by a state proceeding on these maxims, are locked fast as in a sort of family settlement; grasped as in a kind of mortmain for ever. By a constitutional policy, working after the pattern of nature, we receive, we hold, we transmit our government and our privileges, in the same manner in which we enjoy and transmit our property and our lives. The institutions of policy, the goods of fortune, the gifts of providence, are handed down to us, and from us, in the same course and order. Our political system is placed in a just correspondence and symmetry with the order of the world, and with the mode of existence decreed to a permanent body composed of transitory parts; wherein, by the disposition of a stupendous wisdom, moulding together the great mysterious incorporation of the human race, the whole, at one time, is never old, or middle-aged, or young, but, in a condition of unchangeable constancy, moves on through the varied tenor of perpetual decay, fall, renovation, and progression. Thus, by preserving the method of nature in the conduct of the state, in what we improve, we are never wholly new; in what we retain, we are never wholly obsolete. By adhering in this manner and on those principles to our forefathers, we are guided not by the superstition of antiquarians, but by the spirit of philosophic analogy. In this choice of inheritance we have given to our frame of polity the image of a relation in blood; binding up the constitution of our country with our dearest domestic ties; adopting our fundamental laws into the bosom of our family affections; keeping inseparable, and cherishing with the warmth of all their combined and mutually reflected charities, our state, our hearths, our sepulchres, and our altars.

Through the same plan of a conformity to nature in our artificial institutions, and by calling in the aid of her unerring and powerful instincts, to fortify the fallible and feeble contrivances of our reason, we have derived several other, and those no small benefits, from considering our liberties in the light of an inheritance. Always acting as if in the presence of cannonized forefathers, the spirit of freedom, leading in itself to misrule and excess, is tempered with an awful gravity. This idea of a liberal descent inspires us with a sense of habitual native dignity, which prevents that upstart insolence almost inevitably adhering to and disgracing those who are the first acquirers of any distinction. By this means our liberty becomes a noble freedom. It carries an imposing and majestic aspect. It has a pedigree and illustrating ancestors. It has its bearings and its ensigns armorial. It has its gallery of portraits; its monumental inscriptions; its records, evidences, and titles. We procure reverence to our civil institutions on the principle upon which nature teaches us to revere individual men; on account of their age, and on account of those from whom they are descended. All your sophisters cannot produce anything better adapted to preserve a rational and manly freedom than the course that we have pursued, who have chosen our nature rather than our speculations, our breasts rather than our inventions, for the great conservatories and magazines of our rights and privileges.

You might, if you pleased, have profited of our example, and have given to your recovered freedom a correspondent dignity. Your privileges, though discontinued, were not lost to memory. Your constitution, it is true, whilst you were out of possession, suffered waste and dilapidation; but you possessed in some parts the walls, and, in all, the foundations, of a noble and venerable castle. You might have repaired those walls; you might have built on those old foundations. Your constitution was suspended before it was perfected; but you had the elements of a constitution very nearly as good as could be wished. In your old states you possessed that variety of parts corresponding with the various descriptions of which your community was happily composed; you had all that combination, and all that opposition of interests, you had that action and counteraction, which, in the natural and in the political world, from the reciprocal struggle of discordant powers, draws out the harmony of the universe. These opposed and conflicting interests, which you considered as so great a blemish in your old and in our present constitution, interpose a salutary check to all precipitate resolutions. They render deliberation a matter not of choice, but of necessity; they make all change a subject of *compromise*, which naturally begets moderation; they produce *temperaments* preventing the sore evil of harsh, crude, unqualified reformations; and rendering all the headlong exertions of arbitrary power, in the few or in the many, for ever impracticable. Through that diversity of members and interests, general liberty had as many securities as there were separate views in the several orders; whilst by pressing down the whole by the weight of a real monarchy, the separate parts would have been prevented from warping, and starting from their allotted places.

You had all these advantages in your ancient states; but you chose to act as if you had never been moulded into civil society, and had everything to begin anew. You began ill, because you began by despising everything that belonged to you. You set up your trade without a capital. If the last generations of your country appeared without much lustre in your eyes, you might have passed them by, and derived your claims from a more early race of ancestors. Under a pious predilection for those ancestors, your imaginations would have realized in them a standard of virtue and wisdom, beyond the vulgar practice of the hour: and you would have risen with the example to whose imitation you aspired. Respecting your forefathers, you would have been taught to respect yourselves. You would not have chosen to consider the French as a people of yesterday, as a nation of low-born servile wretches until the emancipating year of 1789. In order to furnish, at the expense of your honour, an excuse to your apologists here for several enormities of yours, you would not have been content to be represented as a gang of Maroon slaves, suddenly broke loose from the house of bondage, and therefore to be pardoned for your abuse of the liberty to which you were not accustomed, and ill fitted. Would it not, my worthy friend, have been wiser to have you thought, what I, for one, always thought you, a generous and gallant nation, long misled to your disadvantage by your high and romantic sentiments of fidelity, honour, and loyalty; that events had been unfavourable to you, but that you were not enslaved through any illiberal or servile disposition; that in your most devoted submission, you were actuated by a principle of public spirit, and that it was your country you worshipped, in the person of your king? Had you made it to be understood, that in the delusion of this amiable error you had gone further than your wise ancestors; that you were resolved to resume your ancient privileges, whilst you preserved the spirit of your ancient and your recent loyalty and honour; or if, diffident of yourselves, and not clearly discerning the almost obliterated constitution of your ancestors, you had looked to your neighbours in this land, who had kept alive the ancient principles and models of the old common law of Europe meliorated and adapted to its present state—by following wise examples you would have given new examples of wisdom to the world. You would have rendered the cause of liberty venerable in the eyes of every worthy mind in every nation. You would have shamed despotism from the earth, by showing that freedom was not only reconcilable, but, as when well disciplined it is, auxiliary to law. You would have had an unoppressive but a productive revenue. You would have had a flourishing commerce to feed it. You would have had a free constitution; a potent monarchy; a disciplined army; a reformed and venerated clergy; a mitigated but spirited nobility, to lead your virtue, not to overlay it; you would have had a liberal order of commons, to emulate and to recruit that nobility; you would have had a protected, satisfied, laborious, and obedient people, taught to seek and to recognise the happiness that is to be found by virtue in all conditions; in which consists the true moral equality of mankind, and not in that monstrous fiction, which, by inspiring false ideas and vain expectations into men destined to travel in the obscure walk of laborious life, serves only to aggravate and embitter that real inequality, which it never can remove; and which the order of civil life establishes as much for the benefit of those whom it must leave in an humble state, as those whom it is able to exalt to a condition more splendid, but not more happy. You had a smooth and easy career of felicity and glory laid open to you, beyond anything recorded in the history of the world; but you have shown that difficulty is good for man.

Compute your gains: see what is got by those extravagant and presumptuous speculations which have taught your leaders to despise all their predecessors, and all their contemporaries, and even to despise themselves, until the moment in which they became truly despicable. By following those false lights, France has bought undisguised calamities at a higher price than any nation has purchased the most unequivocal blessings! France has bought poverty by crime! France has not sacrificed her virtue to her interest, but she has abandoned her interest, that she might prostitute her virtue. All other nations have begun the fabric of a new government, or the reformation of an old, by establishing originally, or by enforcing with greater exactness, some rites or other of religion. All other people have laid the foundations of civil freedom in severer manners, and a system of a more austere and masculine morality. France, when she let loose the reins of regal authority, doubled the licence of a ferocious dissoluteness in manners, and of an insolent irreligion in opinions and practices; and has extended through all ranks of life, as if she were communicating some privilege, or laying open some secluded benefit, all the unhappy corruptions that usually were the disease of wealth and power. This is one of the new principles of equality in France.

France, by the perfidy of her leaders, has utterly disgraced the tone of lenient council in the cabinets of princes, and disarmed it of its most potent topics. She has sanctified the dark, suspicious maxims of tyrannous distrust; and taught kings to tremble at (what will hereafter be called) the delusive plausibilities of moral politicians. Sovereigns will consider those, who advise them to place an unlimited confidence in their people, as subverters of their thrones; as traitors who aim at their destruction, by leading their easy good-nature, under specious pretences, to admit combinations of bold and faithless men into a participation of their power. This alone (if there were nothing else) is an irreparable calamity to you and to mankind. Remember that your parliament of Paris told your king, that, in calling the states together, he had nothing to fear but the prodigal excess of their zeal in providing for the support of the throne. It is right that these men should hide their heads. It is right that they should bear their part in the ruin which their counsel has brought on their sovereign and their country. Such sanguine declarations tend to lull authority asleep; to encourage it rashly to engage in perilous adventures of untried policy; to neglect those provisions, preparations, and precautions, which distinguished benevolence from imbecility; and without which no man can answer for the salutary effect of any abstract plan of government or of freedom. For want of these, they have seen the medicine of the state corrupted into its poison. They have seen the French rebel against a mild and lawful monarch, with more fury, outrage, and insult, than ever any people has been known to rise against the most illegal usurper, or the most sanguinary tyrant. Their resistance was made to concession; their revolt was from protection; their blow was aimed at a hand holding out graces, favours, and immunities.

This was unnatural. The rest is in order. They have found their punishment in their success. Laws overturned; tribunals subverted; industry without vigour; commerce expiring; the revenue unpaid, yet the people impoverished; a church pillaged, and a state not relieved; civil and military anarchy made the constitution of the kingdom; everything human and divine sacrificed to the idol of public credit, and national bankruptcy the consequence; and, to crown all, the paper securities of new, precarious, tottering power, the discredited paper securities of impoverished fraud and beggared rapine, held out as a currency for the support of an empire, in lieu of the two great recognised species that represent the lasting, conventional credit of mankind, which disappeared and hid themselves in the earth from whence they came, when the principle of property, whose creatures and representatives they are, was systematically subverted.

Were all these dreadful things necessary? Were they the inevitable results of the desperate struggle of determined patriots, compelled to wade through blood and tumult, to the quiet shore of a tranquil and prosperous liberty? No! nothing like it. The fresh ruins of France, which shock our feelings wherever we can turn our eyes, are not the devastation of civil war; they are the sad but instructive monuments of rash and ignorant counsel in time of profound peace. They are the display of inconsiderate and presumptuous, because unresisted and irresistible, authority. The persons who have thus squandered away the precious treasure of their crimes, the persons who have made this prodigal and wild waste of public evils (the last stake reserved for the ultimate ransom of the state) have met in their progress with little, or rather with no opposition at all. Their whole march was more like a triumphal procession, than the progress of a war. Their pioneers have gone before them, and demolished and laid everything level at their feet. Not one drop of *their* blood have they shed in the cause of the country they have ruined. They have made no sacrifices to their projects of greater consequence than their shoe-buckles, whilst they were imprisoning their king, murdering their fellow-citizens, and bathing in tears, and plunging in poverty and distress, thousands of worthy men and worthy families. Their cruelty has not even been the base result of fear. It has been the effect of their sense of perfect safety, in authorizing treasons, robberies, rapes, assassinations, slaughters, and burnings, throughout their harassed land. But the cause of all was plain from the beginning.

This unforced choice, this fond election of evil, would appear perfectly unaccountable, if we did not consider the composition of the National Assembly: I do not mean its formal constitution, which, as it now stands, is exceptionable enough, but the materials of which, in a great measure, it is composed, which is of ten thousand times greater consequence than all the formalities in the world. If we were to know nothing of this assembly but by its title and function, no colours could paint to the imagination anything more venerable. In that light the mind of an inquirer, subdued by such an awful image as that of the virtue and wisdom of a whole people collected into a focus, would pause and hesitate in condemning things even of the very worst aspect. Instead of blameable, they would appear only mysterious. But no name, no power, no function, no artificial institution whatsoever, can make the men of whom any system of authority is composed, any other than God, and nature, and education, and their habits of life have made them. Capacities beyond these the people have not to give. Virtue and wisdom may be the objects of their choice; but their choice confers neither the one nor the other on those upon whom they lay their ordaining hands. They have not the engagement of nature, they have not the promise of revelation, for any such powers.

After I had read over the list of the persons and descriptions elected into the *Tiers Etat,* nothing which they afterwards did could appear astonishing. Among them, indeed, I saw some of known rank; some of shining talents; but of any practical experience in the state, not one man was to be found. The best were only men of theory. But whatever the distinguished few may have been, it is the substance and mass of the body which constitutes its character, and must finally determine its direction. In all bodies, those who will lead, must also, in a considerable degree, follow. They must conform their propositions to the taste, talent, and disposition, of those whom they wish to conduct: therefore, if an assembly is viciously or feebly composed in a very great part of it, nothing but such a supreme degree of virtue as very rarely appears in the world, and for that reason cannot enter into calculation, will prevent the men of talent disseminated through it from becoming only the expert instruments of absurd projects! If, what is the more likely event, instead of that unusual degree of virtue, they should be actuated by sinister ambition, and a lust of meretricious glory, then the feeble part of the assembly, to whom at first they conform, becomes in its turn the dupe and instrument of their designs. In this political traffic, the leaders will be obliged to bow to the ignorance of their followers, and the followers to become subservient to the worst designs of their leaders.

To secure any degree of sobriety in the propositions made by the leaders in any public assembly, they ought to respect, in some degree perhaps to fear, those whom they conduct. To be led any otherwise than blindly, the followers must be qualified, if not for actors, at least for judges; they must also be judges of natural weight and authority. Nothing can secure a steady and moderate conduct in such assemblies, but that the body of them should be respectably composed, in point of condition in life, of permanent property, of education, and of such habits as enlarge and liberalize the understanding.

In the calling of the states-general of France, the first thing that struck me, was a great departure from the ancient course. I found the representation for the third estate composed of six hundred persons. They were equal in number to the representatives of both the other orders. If the orders were to act separately, the number would not, beyond the consideration of the expense, be of much moment. But when it became apparent that the three orders were to be melted down into one, the policy and necessary effect of this numerous representation became obvious. A very small desertion from either of the other two orders must throw the power of both into the hands of the third. In fact, the whole power of the state was soon resolved into that body. Its due composition became therefore of infinitely the greater importance.

Judge, sir, of my surprise, when I found that a very great proportion of the assembly (a majority, I believe, of the members who attended) was composed of practitioners in the law. It was composed, not of distinguished magistrates, who had given pledges to their country of their science, prudence, and integrity; not of leading advocates, the glory of the bar; not of renowned professors in universities—but for the far greater part, as it must in such a number, of the inferior, unlearned, mechanical, merely instrumental members of the profession. There were distinguished exceptions; but the general composition was of obscure provincial advocates, of stewards of petty local jurisdictions, country attornies, notaries, and the whole train of the ministers of municipal litigation, the fomentors and conductors of the petty war of village vexation. From the moment I read the list, I saw distinctly, and very nearly as it has happened, all that was to follow.

The degree of estimation in which any profession is held becomes the standard of the estimation in which the professors hold themselves. Whatever the personal merits of many individual lawyers might have been, and in many it was undoubtedly very considerable, in that military kingdom no part of the profession had been much regarded, except the highest of all, who often united to their professional offices great family splendour, and were invested with great power and authority. These certainly were highly respected, and even with no small degree of awe. The next rank was not much esteemed; the mechanical part was in a very low degree of repute. Whenever the supreme authority is vested in a body so composed, it must evidently produce the consequences of supreme authority placed in the hands of men not taught habitually to respect themselves; who had no previous fortune in character at stake; who could not be expected to bear with moderation, or to conduct with discretion, a power, which they themselves, more than any others, must be surprised to find in their hands. Who could flatter himself that these men, suddenly, and, as it were, by enchantment, snatched from the humblest rank of subordination, would not be intoxicated with their unprepared greatness? Who could conceive that men, who are habitually meddling, daring, subtle, active, of litigious dispositions and unquiet minds would easily fall back into their old condition of obscure contention, and laborious, low, and unprofitable chicane? Who could doubt but that, at any expense to the state, of which they understood nothing, they must pursue their private interests which they understood but too well? It was not an event depending on chance, or contingency. It was inevitable; it was necessary; it was planted in the nature of things. They must *join* (if their capacity did not permit them to *lead*) in any project which could procure to them a *litigious constitution;* which could lay open to them those innumerable lucrative jobs, which follow in the train of all great convulsions and revolutions in the state, and particularly in all great and violent permutations of property. Was it to be expected that they would attend to the stability of property, whose existence had always depended upon whatever rendered property questionable, ambiguous, and insecure? Their objects would be enlarged with their elevation, but their disposition and habits, and mode of accomplishing their designs, must remain the same.

Well! But these men were to be tempered and restrained by other descriptions, of more sober and more enlarged understandings. Were they then to be awed by the supereminent authority and awful dignity of a handful of country clowns, who have seats in that assembly, some of whom are said not to be able to read and write? and by not a greater number of traders, who, though somewhat more instructed, and more conspicuous in the order of society, had never known anything beyond their counting-house. No! both these descriptions were more formed to be overborne and swayed by the intrigues and artifices of lawyers, than to become their counterpoise. With such a dangerous disproportion, the whole must needs be governed by them. To the faculty of law was joined a pretty considerable proportion of the faculty of medicine. This faculty had not, any more than that of the law, possessed in France its just estimation. Its professors, therefore, must have the qualities of men not habituated to sentiments of dignity. But supposing they had ranked as they ought to do, and as with us they do actually, the sides of sick beds are not the academies for forming statesmen and legislators. Then came the dealers in stocks and funds, who must be eager, at any expense, to change their ideal paper wealth for the more solid substance of land. To these were joined men of other descriptions, from whom as little knowledge of, or attention to, the interests of a great state was to be expected, and as little regard to the stability of any institution; men formed to be instruments, not controls. Such in general was the composition of the *Tiers Etat* in the National Assembly; in which was scarcely to be perceived the slightest traces of what we call the natural landed interest of the country.

We know that the British House of Commons, without shutting its doors to any merit in any class, is, by the sure operation of adequate causes, filled with everything illustrious in rank, in descent, in hereditary and in acquired opulence, in cultivated talents, in military, civil, naval, and politic distinction, that the country can afford. But supposing, what hardly can be supposed as a case, that the House of Commons should be composed in the same manner with the *Tiers Etat* in France, would this dominion of chicane be borne with patience, or even conceived without horror? God forbid I should insinuate anything derogatory to that profession, which is another priesthood, administrating the rights of sacred justice. But whilst I revere men in the functions which belong to them, and would do as much as one man can do to prevent their exclusion from any, I cannot, to flatter them, give the lie to nature. They are good and useful in the composition; they must be mischievous if they preponderate so as virtually to become the whole. Their very excellence in their peculiar functions may be far from a qualification for others. It cannot escape observation, that when men are too much confined to professional and faculty habits, and as it were inveterate in the recurrent employment of that narrow circle, they are rather disabled than qualified for whatever depends on the knowledge of mankind, on experience in mixed affairs, on a comprehensive, connected view of the various, complicated, external and internal interests, which go to the formation of that multifarious thing called a state.

After all, if the House of Commons were to have a wholly professional and faculty composition, what is the power of the House of Commons, circumscribed and shut in by the immoveable barriers of laws, usages, positive rules of doctrine and practice, counterpoised by the House of Lords, and every moment of its existence at the discretion of the crown to continue, prorogue, or dissolve us? The power of the House of Commons, direct or indirect, is indeed great; and long may it be able to preserve its greatness, and the spirit belonging to true greatness, at the full; and it will do so, as long as it can keep the breakers of law in India from becoming the makers of law for England. The power, however, of the House of Commons, when least diminished, is as a drop of water in the ocean, compared to that residing in a settled majority of your National Assembly. That assembly, since the destruction of the orders, has no fundamental law, no strict convention, no respected usage to restrain it. Instead of finding themselves obliged to conform to a fixed constitution, they have a power to make a constitution which shall conform to their designs. Nothing in heaven or upon earth can serve as a control on them. What ought to be the heads, the hearts, the dispositions, that are qualified, or that dare, not only to make laws under a fixed constitution, but at one heat to strike out a totally new constitution for a great kingdom, and in every part of it, from the monarch on the throne to the vestry of a parish? But *"fools rush in where angels fear to tread."* In such a state of unbounded power for undefined and undefinable purposes, the evil of a moral and almost physical inaptitude of the man to the function must be the greatest we can conceive to happen in the management of human affairs.

Having considered the composition of the third estate as it stood in its original frame, I took a view of the representatives of the clergy. There too it appeared, that full as little regard was had to the general security of property, or to the aptitude of the deputies for their public purposes, in the principles of their election. That election was so contrived, as to send a very large proportion of mere country curates to the great and arduous work of new-modelling a state; men who never had seen the state so much as in a picture; men who knew nothing of the world beyond the bounds of an obscure village; who, immersed in hopeless poverty, could regard all property, whether secular or ecclesiastical, with no other eye than that of envy; among whom must be many who, for the smallest hope of the meanest dividend in plunder, would readily join in any attempts upon a body of wealth, in which they could hardly look to have any share, except in a general scramble. Instead of balancing the power of the active chicaners in the other assembly, these curates must necessarily become the active coadjutors, or at best the passive instruments, of those by whom they had been habitually guided in their petty village concerns. They too could hardly be the most conscientious of their kind, who presuming upon their incompetent understanding, could intrigue for a trust which led from their natural relation to their flocks, and their natural spheres of action, to undertake the regeneration of kingdoms. This preponderating weight, being added to the force of the body of chicane in the *Tiers Etat,* completed that momentum of ignorance, rashness, presumption, and lust of plunder, which nothing has been able to resist.

To observing men it must have appeared from the beginning, that the majority of the Third Estate, in conjunction with such a deputation from the clergy as I have described, whilst it pursued the destruction of the nobility, would inevitably become subservient to the worst designs of individuals in that class. In the spoil and humiliation of their own order these individuals would possess a sure fund for the pay of their new followers. To squander away the objects which made the happiness of their fellows, would be to them no sacrifice at all. Turbulent, discontented men of quality, in proportion as they are puffed up with personal pride and arrogance, generally despise their own order. One of the first symptoms they discover of a selfish and mischievous ambition, is a profligate disregard of a dignity which they partake with others. To be attached to the subdivision, to love the little platoon we belong to in society, is the first principle (the germ as it were) of public affections. It is the first link in the series by which we proceed towards a love to our country, and to mankind. The interest of that portion of social arrangement is a trust in the hands of all those who compose it; and as none but bad men would justify it in abuse, none but traitors would barter it away for their own personal advantage.

There were in the time of our civil troubles in England (I do not know whether you have any such in your assembly in France) several persons, like the then Earl of Holland, who by themselves or their families had brought an odium on the throne, by the prodigal dispensation of its bounties towards them, who afterwards joined in the rebellions arising from the discontents of which they were themselves the cause; men who helped to subvert that throne to which they owed, some of them, their existence, others all that power which they employed to ruin their benefactor. If any bounds are set to the rapacious demands of that sort of people, or that others are permitted to partake in the objects they would engross, revenge and envy soon fill up the craving void that is left in their avarice. Confounded by the complication of distempered passions, their reason is disturbed; their views become vast and perplexed; to others inexplicable; to themselves uncertain. They find, on all sides, bounds to their unprincipled ambition in any fixed order of things. But in the fog and haze of confusion all is enlarged, and appears without any limit.

When men of rank sacrifice all ideas of dignity to an ambition without a distinct object, and work with low instruments and for low ends, the whole composition becomes low and base. Does not something like this now appear in France? Does it not produce something ignoble and inglorious? a kind of meanness in all the prevalent policy? a tendency in all that is done to lower along with individuals all the dignity and importance of the state? Other revolutions have been conducted by persons, who, whilst they attempted or affected changes in the commonwealth, sanctified their ambition by advancing the dignity of the people whose peace they troubled. They had long views. They aimed at the rule, not at the destruction, of their country. They were men of great civil and great military talents, and if the terror, the ornament of their age. They were not like Jew brokers, contending with each other who could best remedy with fraudulent circulation and depreciated paper the wretchedness and ruin brought on their country by their degenerate councils. The compliment made to one of the great bad men of the old stamp (Cromwell) by his kinsman, a favourite poet of that time, shows what it was he proposed, and what indeed to a great degree he accomplished, in the success of his ambition:

> Still as *you* rise, the *state* exalted too,
> Finds no distemper whilst 'tis changed by *you;*
> Changed like the world's great scene, when without noise
> The rising sun night's *vulgar* lights destroys.

These disturbers were not so much like men usurping power, as asserting their natural place in society. Their rising was to illuminate and beautify the world. Their conquest over their competitors was by outshining them. The hand that, like a destroying angel, smote the country, communicated to it the force and energy under which it suffered. I do not say (God forbid), I do not say that the virtues of such men were to be taken as a balance to their crimes: but they were some corrective to their effects. Such was, as I said, our Cromwell. Such were your whole race of Guises, Condés, and Colignis. Such the Richelieus, who in more quiet times acted in the spirit of a civil war. Such, as better men, and in a less dubious cause, were your Henry the Fourth and your Sully, though nursed in civil confusions, and not wholly without some of their taint. It is a thing to be wondered at, to see how very soon France, when she had a moment to respire, recovered and emerged from the longest and most dreadful civil war that ever was known in any nation. Why? Because among all their massacres, they had not slain the *mind* in their country. A conscious dignity, a noble pride, a generous sense of glory and emulation, was not extinguished. On the contrary, it was kindled and inflamed. The organs also of the state, however shattered, existed. All the prizes of honour and virtue, all the rewards, all the distinctions remained. But your present confusion, like a palsy, has attacked the fountain of life itself. Every person in your country, in a situation to be actuated by a principle of honour, is disgraced and degraded, and can entertain no sensation of life, except in a mortified and humiliated indignation. But this generation will quickly pass away. The next generation of the nobility will resemble the artificers and clowns, and money-jobbers, usurers, and Jews, who will be always their fellows, sometimes their masters. Believe me, sir, those who attempt to level, never equalise. In all societies, consisting of various descriptions of citizens, some description must be uppermost. The levellers therefore only change and pervert the natural order of things; they load the edifice of society, by setting up in the air what the solidity of the structure requires to be on the ground. The association of tailors and carpenters, of which the republic (of Paris, for instance) is composed, cannot be equal to the situation, into which, by the worst of usurpations, an usurpation on the prerogatives of nature, you attempt to force them.

The Chancellor of France at the opening of the states, said, in a tone of oratorical flourish, that all occupations were honourable. If he meant only, that no honest employment was disgraceful, he would not have gone beyond the truth. But in asserting that anything is honourable, we imply some distinction in its favour. The occupation of a hair-dresser, or of a working tallow-chandler, cannot be a matter of honour to any person—to say nothing of a number of other more servile employments. Such descriptions of men ought not to suffer oppression from the state; but the state suffers oppression, if such as they, either individually or collectively, are permitted to rule. In this you think you are combating prejudice, but you are at war with nature.[10]

I do not, my dear sir, conceive you to be of that sophistical, captious spirit, or of that uncandid dulness, as to require, for every general observation or sentiment, an explicit detail of the correctives and exceptions, which reason will presume to be included in all the general propositions which come from reasonable men. You do not imagine, that I wish to confine power, authority, and distinction to blood, and names, and titles. No, sir. There is no qualification for government but virtue and wisdom, actual or presumptive. Wherever they are actually found, they have, in whatever state, condition, profession, or trade, the passport of Heaven to human place and honour. Woe to the country which would madly and impiously reject the service of the talents and virtues, civil, military, or religious, that are given to grace and to serve it; and would condemn to obscurity everything formed to diffuse lustre and glory around a state! Woe to that country too, that, passing into the opposite extreme, considers a low education, a mean contracted view of things, a sordid, mercenary occupation, as a preferable title to command! Everything ought to be open; but not indifferently to every man. No rotation; no appointment by lot; no mode of election operating in the spirit of sortition, or rotation, can be generally good in a government conversant in extensive objects. Because they have no tendency, direct or indirect, to select the man with a view to the duty, or to accommodate the one to the other. I do not hesitate to say, that the road to eminence and power, from obscure condition, ought not to be made too easy, nor a thing too much of course. If rare merit be the rarest of all rare things, it ought to pass through some sort of probation. The temple of honour ought to be seated on an eminence. If it be opened through virtue, let it be remembered too, that virtue is never tried but by some difficulty and some struggle.

Nothing is a due and adequate representation of a state, that does not represent its ability, as well as its property. But as ability is a vigorous and active principle, and as property is sluggish, inert, and timid, it never can be safe from the invasion of ability, unless it be, out of all proportion, predominant in the representation. It must be represented too in great masses of accumulation, or it is not rightly protected. The characteristic essence of property, formed out of the combined principles of its acquisition and conservation, is to be *unequal.* The great masses therefore which excite envy, and tempt rapacity, must be put out of the possibility of danger. Then they form a natural rampart about the lesser properties in all their gradations. The same quantity of property, which is by the natural course of things divided among many, has not the same operation. Its defensive power is weakened as it is diffused. In this diffusion each man's portion is less than what, in the eagerness of his desires, he may flatter himself to obtain by dissipating the accumulations of others. The plunder of the few would indeed give but a share inconceivably small in the distribution to the many. But the many are not capable of making this calculation; and those who lead them to rapine never intend this distribution.

The power of perpetuating our property in our families is one of the most valuable and interesting circumstances belonging to it, and that which tends the most to the perpetuation of society itself. It makes our weakness subservient to our virtue; it grafts benevolence even upon avarice. The possessors of family wealth, and of the distinction which attends hereditary possession (as most concerned in it), are the natural securities for this transmission. With us the House of Peers is formed upon this principle. It is wholly composed of hereditary property and hereditary distinction; and made therefore the third of the legislature; and, in the last event, the sole judge of all property in all its subdivisions. The House of Commons too, though not necessarily, yet in fact, is always so composed, in the far greater part. Let those large proprietors be what they will, and they have their chance of being amongst the best, they are, at the very worst, the ballast in the vessel of the commonwealth. For though hereditary wealth, and the rank which goes with it, are too much idolized by creeping sycophants, and the blind, abject admirers of power, they are too rashly slighted in shallow speculations of the petulant, assuming, short-sighted coxcombs of philosophy. Some decent, regulated pre-eminence, some preference (not exclusive appropriation) given to birth, is neither unnatural, nor unjust, nor impolitic.

It is said, that twenty-four millions ought to prevail over two hundred thousand. True; if the constitution of a kingdom be a problem of arithmetic. This sort of discourse does well enough with the lamp-post for its second: to men who *may* reason calmly, it is ridiculous. The will of the many, and their interest, must very often differ; and great will be the difference when they make an evil choice. A government of five hundred country attornies and obscure curates is not good for twenty-four millions of men, though it were chosen by eight and forty millions; nor is it the better for being guided by a dozen of persons of quality, who have betrayed their trust in order to obtain that power. At present, you seem in everything to have stayed out of the high road of nature. The property of France does not govern it. Of course property is destroyed, and rational liberty has no existence. All you have got for the present is a paper circulation, and a stock-jobbing constitution: and, as to the future, do you seriously think that the territory of France, upon the republican system of eighty-three independent municipalities (to say nothing of the parts that compose them), can ever be governed as one body, or can ever be set in motion by the impulse of one mind? When the National Assembly has completed its work, it will have accomplished its ruin. These commonwealths will not long bear a state of subjection to the republic of Paris. They will not bear that this one body should monopolize the captivity of the king, and the dominion over the assembly calling itself national. Each will keep its own portion of the spoil of the church to itself; and it will not suffer either that spoil, or the more just fruits of their industry, or the natural produce of their soil, to be sent to swell the insolence, or pamper the luxury, of the mechanics of Paris. In this they will see none of the equality, under the pretence of which they have been tempted to throw off their allegiance to their sovereign, as well as the ancient constitution of their country. There can be no capital city in such a constitution as they have lately made. They have forgot, that when they framed democratic governments, they had virtually dismembered their country. The person, whom they persevere in calling king, has not power left to him by the hundredth part sufficient to hold together this collection of republics. The republic of Paris will endeavour indeed to complete the debauchery of the army, and illegally to perpetuate the assembly, without resort to its constituents, as the means of continuing its despotism. It will make efforts, by becoming the heart of a boundless paper circulation, to draw everything to itself; but in vain. All this policy in the end will appear as feeble as it is now violent.

If this be your actual situation, compared to the situation to which you were called, as it were by the voice of God and man, I cannot find it in my heart to congratulate you on the choice you have made, or the success which has attended your endeavours. I can as little recommend to any other nation a conduct grounded on such principles, and productive of such effects. That I must leave to those who can see farther into your affairs than I am able to do, and who best know how far your actions are favourable to their designs. The gentlemen of the Revolution Society, who were so early in their congratulations, appear to be strongly of opinion that there is some scheme of politics relative to this country, in which your proceedings may, in some way, be useful. For your Dr. Price, who seems to have speculated himself into no small degree of fervour upon this subject, addresses his auditory in the following very remarkable words: "I cannot conclude without recalling *particularly* to your recollection a consideration which I have *more than once alluded to,* and which probably your thoughts have *been all along anticipating;* a consideration with which my *mind is impressed more than I can express.* I mean the consideration of the *favourableness of the present times to all exertions in the cause of liberty.*"

It is plain that the mind of this *political* preacher was at the time big with some extraordinary design; and it is very probable that the thoughts of his audience, who understood him better than I do, did all along run before him in his reflection, and in the whole train of consequences to which it led.

Before I read that sermon, I really thought I had lived in a free country; and it was an error I cherished, because it gave me a greater liking to the country I lived in. I was indeed aware, that a jealous, ever-waking vigilance, to guard the treasure of our liberty, not only from invasion, but from decay and corruption, was our best wisdom, and our first duty. However, I consider that treasure rather as a possession to be secured, than as a prize to be contended for. I did not discern how the present time came to be so very favourable to all *exertions* in the cause of freedom. The present time differs from any other only by the circumstance of what is doing in France. If the example of that nation is to have an influence on this, I can easily conceive why some of their proceedings which have an unpleasant aspect, and are not quite reconcilable to humanity, generosity, good faith, and justice, are palliated with so much milky good-nature towards the actors, and borne with so much heroic fortitude towards the sufferers. It is certainly not prudent to discredit the authority of an example we mean to follow. But allowing this, we are led to a very natural question: What is that cause of liberty, and what are those exertions in its favour, to which the example of France is be done away in favour of a geometrical and arithmetical constitution? Is the House of Lords to be voted useless? Is episcopacy to be abolished? Are the church lands to be sold to Jews and jobbers; or given to bribe new-invented municipal republics into a participation in sacrilege? Are all the taxes to be voted grievances, and the revenue reduced to a patriotic contribution, or patriotic presents? Are silver shoe-buckles to be substituted in the place of the land tax and the malt tax, for the support of the naval strength of this kingdom? Are all orders, ranks, and distinctions to be confounded, that out of universal anarchy, joined to national bankruptcy, three or four thousand democracies should be formed into eighty-three, and that they may all, by some sort of unknown attractive power, be organized into one? For this great end is the army to be seduced from its discipline and its fidelity, first by every kind of debauchery, and then by the terrible precedent of a donative in the increase of pay? Are the curates to be seduced from their bishops, by holding out to them the delusive hope of a dole out of the spoils of their own order? Are the citizens of London to be drawn from their allegiance by feeding them at the expense of their fellow-subjects? Is a compulsory paper currency to be substituted in the place of the legal coin of this kingdom? Is what remains of the plundered stock of public revenue to be employed in the wild project of maintaining two armies to watch over and to fight with each other? If these are the ends and means of the Revolution Society, I admit they are well assorted; and France may furnish them for both with precedents in point.

I see that your example is held out to shame us. I know that we are supposed a dull, sluggish race, rendered passive by finding our situation tolerable, and prevented by a mediocrity of freedom from ever attaining to its full perfection. Your leaders in France began by affecting to admire, almost to adore, the British constitution; but as they advanced, they came to look upon it with a sovereign contempt. The friends of your National Assembly amongst us have full as mean an opinion of what was formerly thought the glory of their country. The Revolution Society has discovered that the English nation is not free. They are convinced that the inequality in our representation is a "defect in our constitution *so gross and palpable,* as to make it excellent chiefly in *form* and *theory*." That a representation in the legislature of a kingdom is not only the basis of all constitutional liberty in it, but of *"all legitimate government;* that without it a *government* is nothing but an *usurpation*"—that "when the representation is *partial,* the kingdom possesses liberty only *partially;* and if extremely partial, it gives only a *semblance;* and if not only extremely partial, but corruptly chosen, it becomes a *nuisance.*"[11] Dr. Price considers this inadequacy of representation as our *fundamental grievance;* and though, as to the corruption of this semblance of representation, he hopes it is not yet arrived to its full perfection of depravity, he fears that "nothing will be done towards gaining for us this *essential blessing,* until some *great abuse of power* again provokes our resentment, or some *great calamity* again alarms our fears, or perhaps till the acquisition of a *pure and equal representation by other countries,* whilst we are *mocked* with the *shadow,* kindles our shame." To this he subjoins a note in these words: "A representation chosen chiefly by the treasury, and a *few* thousands of the *dregs* of the people, who are generally paid for their votes."

You will smile here at the consistency of those democratists, who, when they are not on their guard, treat the humbler part of the community with the greatest contempt, whilst, at the same time, they pretend to make them the depositories of all power. It would require a long discourse to point out to you the many fallacies that lurk in the generality and equivocal nature of the terms "inadequate representation." I shall only say here, in justice to that old-fashioned constitution, under which we have long prospered, that our representation has been found perfectly adequate to all the purposes for which a representation of the people can be desired or devised. I defy the enemies of our constitution to show the contrary. To detail the particulars in which it is found so well to promote its ends, would demand a treatise on our practical constitution. I state here the doctrine of the Revolutionists, only that you and others may see what an opinion these gentlemen entertain of the constitution of their country, and why they seem to think that some great abuse of power, or some great calamity, as giving a chance for the blessing of a constitution according to their ideas, would be much palliated to their feelings; you see *why they* are so much enamoured of your fair and equal representation, which being once obtained, the same effects might follow. You see they consider our House of Commons as only "a semblance," "a form," "a theory," "a shadow," "a mockery," perhaps "a nuisance."

These gentlemen value themselves on being systematic; and not without reason. They must therefore look on this gross and palpable defect of representation, this fundamental grievance (so they call it), as a thing not only vicious in itself, but as rendering our whole government absolutely *illegitimate,* and not at all better than a downright *usurpation.* Another revolution, to get rid of this illegitimate and usurped government, would of course be perfectly justifiable, if not absolutely necessary. Indeed their principle, if you observe it with any attention, goes much further than to an alteration in the election of the House of Commons; for, if popular representation, or choice, is necessary to the *legitimacy* of all government, the House of Lords is, at one stroke, bastardized and corrupted in blood. That House is no representative of the people at all, even in "semblance or in form." The case of the crown is altogether as bad. In vain the crown may endeavour to screen itself against these gentlemen by the authority of the establishment made on the Revolution. The Revolution which is resorted to for a title, on their system, wants a title itself. The Revolution is built, according to their theory, upon a basis not more solid than our present formalities, as it was made by a House of Lords, not representing any one but themselves; and by a House of Commons exactly such as the present, that is, as they term it, by a mere "shadow and mockery" of representation.

Something they must destroy, or they seem to themselves to exist for no purpose. One set is for destroying the civil power through the ecclesiastical; another, for demolishing the ecclesiastic through the civil. They are aware that the worst consequences might happen to the public in accomplishing this double ruin of church and state; but they are so heated with their theories, that they give more than hints, that this ruin, with all the mischiefs that must lead to it and attend it, and which to themselves appear quite certain, would not be unacceptable to them, or very remote from their wishes. A man amongst them of great authority, and certainly of great talents, speaking of a supposed alliance between church and state, says, "perhaps *we must wait for the fall of the civil powers* before this most unnatural alliance be broken. Calamitous no doubt will that time be. But what convulsion in the political world ought to be a subject of lamentation, if it be attended with so desirable an effect?" You see with what a steady eye these gentlemen are prepared to view the greatest calamities which can befall their country.

It is no wonder therefore, that with these ideas of everything in their constitution and government at home, either in church or state, as illegitimate and usurped, or at best as a vain mockery, they look abroad with an eager and passionate enthusiasm. Whilst they are possessed by these notions, it is vain to talk to them of the practice of their ancestors, the fundamental laws of their country, the fixed form of a constitution, whose merits are confirmed by the solid test of long experience, and an increasing public strength and national prosperity. They despise experience as the wisdom of unlettered men; and as for the rest, they have wrought under-ground a mine that will blow up, at one grand explosion, all examples of antiquity, all precedents, charters, and acts of parliament. They have "the rights of men." Against these there can be no prescription; against these no agreement is binding: these admit no temperament, and no compromise: anything withheld from their full demand is so much of fraud and injustice. Against these their rights of men let no government look for security in the length of its continuance, or in the justice and lenity of its administration. The objections of these speculatists, if its forms do not quadrate with their theories, are as valid against such an old and beneficent government, as against the most violent tyranny, or the greenest usurpation. They are always at issue with governments, not on a question of abuse, but a question of competency, and a question of title. I have nothing to say to the clumsy subtilty of their political metaphysics. Let them be their amusement in the schools. "Illa *se jactat in aula*—Æolus, *et clauso ventorum carcere regnet.*" But let them not break prison to burst like a *Levanter,* to sweep the earth with their hurricane, and to break up the fountains of the great deep to overwhelm us.

Far am I from denying in theory, full as far is my heart from withholding in practice (if I were of power to give or to withhold) the *real* rights of men. In denying their false claims of right, I do not mean to injure those which are real, and are such as their pretended rights would totally destroy. If civil society be made for the advantage of man, all the advantages for which it is made become his right. It is an institution of beneficence; and law itself is only beneficence acting by a rule. Men have a right to live by that rule; they have a right to do justice, as between their fellows, whether their fellows are in public function or in ordinary occupation. They have a right to the fruits of their industry; and to the means of making their industry fruitful. They have a right to the acquisitions of their parents; to the nourishment and improvement of their offspring; to instruction in life, and to consolation in death. Whatever each man can separately do, without trespassing upon others, he has a right to do for himself; and he has a right to a fair portion of all which society, with all its combinations of skill and force, can do in his favour. In this partnership all men have equal rights; but not to equal things. He that has but five shillings in the partnership, has as good a right to it, as he that has five hundred pounds has to his larger proportion. But he has not a right to an equal dividend in the product of the joint stock; and as to the share of power, authority, and direction which each individual ought to have in the management of the state, that I must deny to be amongst the direct original rights of man in civil society; for I have in my contemplation the civil social man, and no other. It is a thing to be settled by convention.

If civil society be the offspring of convention, that convention must be its law. That convention must limit and modify all the descriptions of constitution which are formed under it. Every sort of legislative, judicial, or executory power are its creatures. They can have no being in any other state of things; and how can any man claim under the conventions of civil society, rights which do not so much as suppose its existence? rights which are absolutely repugnant to it? One of the first motives to civil society, and which becomes one of its fundamental rules, is, *that no man should be judge in his own cause.* By this each person has at once divested himself of the first fundamental right of uncovenanted man, that is, to judge for himself, and to assert his own cause. He abdicates all rights to be his own governor. He inclusively, in a great measure, abandons the right of self-defence, the first law of nature. Men cannot enjoy the rights of an uncivil and of a civil state together. That he may obtain justice, he gives up his right of determining what it is in points the most essential to him. That he may secure some liberty, he makes a surrender in trust of the whole of it.

Government is not made in virtue of natural rights, which may and do exist in total independence of it; and exist in much greater clearness, and in a much greater degree of abstract perfection: but their abstract perfection is their practical defect. By having a right to everything they want everything. Government is a contrivance of human wisdom to provide for human *wants.* Men have a right that these wants should be provided for by this wisdom. Among these wants is to be reckoned the want, out of civil society, of a sufficient restraint upon their passions. Society requires not only that the passions of individuals should be subjected, but that even in the mass and body, as well as in the individuals, the inclinations of men should frequently be thwarted, their will controlled, and their passions brought into subjection. This can only be done *by a power out of themselves;* and not, in the exercise of its function, subject to that will and to those passions which it is its office to bridle and subdue. In this sense the restraints on men, as well as their liberties, are to be reckoned among their rights. But as the liberties and the restrictions vary with times and circumstances, and admit of infinite modifications, they cannot be settled upon any abstract rule; and nothing is so foolish as to discuss them upon that principle.

The moment you abate anything from the full rights of men, each to govern himself, and suffer any artificial, positive limitation upon those rights, from that moment the whole organization of government becomes a consideration of convenience. This it is which makes the constitution of a state, and the due distribution of its powers, a matter of the most delicate and complicated skill. It requires a deep knowledge of human nature and human necessities, and of the things which facilitate or obstruct the various ends, which are to be pursued by the mechanism of civil institutions. The state is to have recruits to its strength, and remedies to its distempers. What is the use of discussing a man's abstract right to food or medicine? The question is upon the method of procuring and administering them. In that deliberation I shall always advise to call in the aid of the farmer and the physician, rather than the professor of metaphysics.

The science of constructing a commonwealth, or renovating it, or reforming it, is, like every other experimental science, not to be taught à priori. Nor is it a short experience that can instruct us in that practical science; because the real effects of moral causes are not always immediate; but that which in the first instance is prejudicial may be excellent in its remoter operation; and its excellence may arise even from the ill effects it produces in the beginning. The reverse also happens: and very plausible schemes, with very pleasing commencements, have often shameful and lamentable conclusions. In states there are often some obscure and almost latent causes, things winch appear at first view of little moment, on which a very great part of its prosperity or adversity may most essentially depend. The science of government being therefore so practical in itself, and intended for such practical purposes, a matter which requires experience, and even more experience than any person can gain in his whole life, however sagacious and observing he may be, it is with infinite caution that any man ought to venture upon pulling down an edifice, which has answered in any tolerable degree for ages the common purposes of society, or on building it up again, without having models and patterns of approved utility before his eyes.

These metaphysic rights entering into common life, like rays of light which pierce into a dense medium, are, by the laws of nature, refracted from their straight line. Indeed in the gross and complicated mass of human passions and concerns, the primitive rights of men undergo such a variety of refractions and reflections, that it becomes absurd to talk of them as if they continued in the simplicity of their original direction. The nature of man is intricate; the objects of society are of the greatest possible complexity: and therefore no simple disposition or direction of power can be suitable either to man's nature, or to the quality of his affairs. When I hear the simplicity of contrivance aimed at and boasted of in any new political constitutions, I am at no loss to decide that the artificers are grossly ignorant of their trade, or totally negligent of their duty. The simple governments are fundamentally defective, to say no worse of them. If you were to contemplate society in but one point of view, all these simple modes of polity are infinitely captivating. In effect each would answer its single end much more perfectly than the more complex is able to attain all its complex purposes. But it is better that the whole should be imperfectly and anomalously answered, than that, while some parts are provided for with great exactness, others might be totally neglected, or perhaps materially injured, by the over-care of a favourite member.

The pretended rights of these theorists are all extremes: and in proportion as they are metaphysically true, they are morally and politically false. The rights of men are in a sort of *middle*, incapable of definition, but not impossible to be discerned. The rights of men in governments are their advantages; and these are often in balances between differences of good; in compromises sometimes between good and evil, and sometimes between evil and evil. Political reason is a computing principle; adding, subtracting, multiplying, and dividing, morally and not metaphysically, or mathematically, true moral denominations.

By these theorists the right of the people is almost always sophistically confounded with their power. The body of the community, whenever it can come to act, can meet with no effectual resistance; but till power and right are the same, the whole body of them has no right inconsistent with virtue, and the first of all virtues, prudence. Men have no right to what is not reasonable, and to what is not for their benefit; for though a pleasant writer said, *Liceat perire poetis*, when one of them, in cold blood, is said to have leaped into the flames of a volcanic revolution, *Ardentem frigidus* Ætnam *insiluit*, I consider such a frolic rather as an unjustifiable poetic license, than as one of the franchises of Parnassus; and whether he were poet, or divine, or politician, that chose to exercise this kind of right, I think that more wise, because more charitable, thoughts would urge me rather to save the man, than to preserve his brazen slippers as the monuments of his folly.

The kind of anniversary sermons to which a great part of what I write refers, if men are not shamed out of their present course, in commemorating the fact, will cheat many out of the principles, and deprive them of the benefits, of the revolution they commemorate. I confess to you, sir, I never liked this continual talk of resistance, and revolution, or the practice of making the extreme medicine of the constitution its daily bread. It renders the habit of society dangerously valetudinary: it is taking periodical doses of mercury sublimate, and swallowing down repeated provocatives of cantharides to our love of liberty.

This distemper of remedy, grown habitual, relaxes and wears out, by a vulgar and prostituted use, the spring of that spirit which is to be exerted on great occasions. It was in the most patient period of Roman servitude that themes of tyrannicide made the ordinary exercise of boys at school—*cum perimit sævos classis numerosa tyrannos.*

In the ordinary state of things, it produces in a country like ours the worst effects, even on the cause of that liberty which it abuses with the dissoluteness of an extravagant speculation. Almost all the high-bred republicans of my time have, after a short space, become the most decided, thorough-paced courtiers; they soon left the business of a tedious, moderate, but practical resistance, to those of us whom, in the pride and intoxication of their theories, they have slighted as not much better than Tories. Hyprocrisy, of course, delights in the most sublime speculations; for, never intending to go beyond speculation, it costs nothing to have it magnificent. But even in cases where rather levity than fraud was to be suspected in these ranting speculations, the issue has been much the same. These professors, finding their extreme principles not applicable to cases which call only for a qualified, or, as I may say, civil and legal resistance, in such cases employ no resistance at all. It is with them a war or a revolution, or it is nothing. Finding their schemes of politics not adapted to the state of the world in which they live, they often come to think lightly of all public principle; and are ready, on their part, to abandon for a very trivial interest what they find of very trivial value. Some indeed are of more steady and persevering natures; but these are eager politicians out of parliament, who have little to tempt them to abandon their favourite projects. They have some change in the church or state, or both, constantly in their view. When that is the case, they are always bad citizens, and perfectly unsure connexions. For, considering their speculative designs as of infinite value, and the actual arrangement of the state as of no estimation, they are at best indifferent about it. They see no merit in the good, and no fault in the vicious, management of public affairs; they rather rejoice in the latter, as more propitious to revolution. They see no merit or demerit in any man, or any action, or any political principle, any further than as they may forward or retard their design of change: they therefore take up, one day, the most violent and stretched prerogative, and another time the wildest democratic ideas of freedom, and pass from the one to the other without any sort of regard to cause, to person, or to party.

In France you are now in the crisis of a revolution, and in the transit from one form of government to another—you cannot see that character of men exactly in the same situation in which we see it in this country. With us it is militant; with you it is triumphant; and you know how it can act when its power is commensurate to its will. I would not be supposed to confine those observations to any description of men, or to comprehend all men of any description within them No! far from it. I am as incapable of that injustice, as I am of keeping terms with those who profess principles of extremities; and who, under the name of religion, teach little else than wild and dangerous politics. The worst of these politics of revolution is this: they temper and harden the breast, in order to prepare it for the desperate strokes which are sometimes used in extreme occasions. But as these occasions may never arrive, the mind receives a gratuitous taint; and the moral sentiments suffer not a little, when no political purpose is served by the depravation. This sort of people are so taken up with their theories about the rights of man, that they have totally forgotten his nature. Without opening one new avenue to the understanding, they have succeeded in stopping up those that lead to the heart. They have perverted in themselves, and in those that attend to them, all the well-placed sympathies of the human breast.

This famous sermon of the Old Jewry breathes nothing but this spirit through all the political part. Plots, massacres, assassinations, seem to some people a trivial price for obtaining a revolution. A cheap, bloodless reformation, a guiltless liberty, appear flat and vapid to their taste. There must be a great change of scene; there must be a magnificent stage effect; there must be a grand spectacle to rouse the imagination, grown torpid with the lazy enjoyment of sixty years' security, and the still unanimating repose of public prosperity. The preacher found them all in the French Revolution. This inspires a juvenile warmth through his whole frame. His enthusiasm kindles as he advances; and when he arrives at his peroration it is in a full blaze. Then viewing, from the Pisgah of his pulpit, the free, moral, happy, flourishing, and glorious state of France, as in a bird's-eye landscape of a promised land, he breaks out into the following rapture:

"What an eventful period is this! I am *thankful* that I have lived to it; I could almost say, *Lord, now lettest thou thy servant depart in peace, for mine eyes have seen thy salvation.* I have lived to see a *diffusion* of knowledge, which has undermined superstition and error. I have lived to see *the rights of men* better understood than ever; and nations panting for liberty which seemed to have lost the idea of it. I have lived to see *thirty millions of people,* indignant and resolute, spurning at slavery, and demanding liberty with an irresistible voice. *Their king led in triumph, and an arbitrary monarch surrendering himself to his subjects.*"[12]

Before I proceed further, I have to remark, that Dr. Price seems rather to overvalue the great acquisitions of light which he has obtained and diffused in this age. The last century appears to me to have been quite as much enlightened. It had, though in a different place, a triumph as memorable as that of Dr. Price; and some of the great preachers of that period partook of it as eagerly as he has done in the triumph of France. On the trial of the Rev. Hugh Peters for high treason, it was deposed, that when King Charles was brought to London for his trial, the Apostle of Liberty in that day conducted the *triumph.* "I saw," says the witness, "his Majesty in the coach with six horses, and Peters riding before the king, *triumphing.*" Dr. Price, when he talks as if he had made a discovery, only follows a precedent; for, after the commencement of the king's trial, this precursor, the same Dr. Peters, concluding a long prayer at the Royal Chapel at Whitehall (he had very triumphantly chosen his place), said, "I have prayed and preached these twenty years; and now I may say with old Simeon, *Lord, now lettest thou thy servant depart in peace, for mine eyes have seen thy salvation.*"[13] Peters had not the fruits of his prayer;

for he neither departed so soon as he wished, nor in peace. He became (what I heartily hope none of his followers may be in this country) himself a sacrifice to the triumph which he led as pontiff. They dealt at the Restoration, perhaps, too hardly with this poor good man. But we owe it to his memory and his sufferings that he had as much illumination, and as much zeal, and had as effectually undermined all *the superstition and error* which might impede the great business he was engaged in, as any who follow and repeat after him, in this age, which would assume to itself an exclusive title to the knowledge of the rights of men, and all the glorious consequences of that knowledge.

After this sally of the preacher of the Old Jewry, which differs only in place and time, but agrees perfectly with the spirit and letter of the rapture of 1648, the Revolution Society, the fabricators of governments, the heroic band of *cashierers* of *monarchs,* electors of sovereigns, and leaders of kings in triumph, strutting with a proud consciousness of the diffusion of the knowledge they had thus gratuitously received. To make this bountiful communication, they adjourned from the church in the Old Jewry to the London Tavern; where the same Dr. Price, in whom the fumes of his oracular tripod were not entirely evaporated, moved and carried the resolution, or address of congratulation, transmitted by Lord Stanhope to the National Assembly of France.

I find a preacher of the gospel profaning the beautiful and prophetic ejaculation, commonly called *"nunc dimittis"* made on the first presentation of our Saviour in the temple, and applying it, with an inhuman and unnatural rapture, to the most horrid, atrocious, and afflicting spectacle that perhaps ever was exhibited to the pity and indignation of mankind. This *"leading in triumph,"* a thing in its best form unmanly and irreligious, which fills our preacher with such unhallowed transports, must shock, I believe, the moral taste of every well-born mind. Several English were the stupified and indignant spectators of that triumph. It was (unless we have been strangely deceived) a spectacle more resembling a procession of American savages, entering into Onondaga, after some of their murders called victories, and leading into hovels hung round with scalps, their captives, overpowered with the scoffs and buffets of women as ferocious as themselves, much more than it resembled the triumphal pomp of a civilized, martial nation; if a civilized nation, or any men who had a sense of generosity, were capable of a personal triumph over the fallen and afflicted.

This, my dear sir, was not the triumph of France. I must believe that, as a nation, it overwhelmed you with shame and horror. I must believe that the National Assembly find themselves in a state of the greatest humiliation in not being able to punish the authors of this triumph, or the actors in it; and that they are in a situation in which any inquiry they may make upon the subject must be destitute even of the appearance of liberty or impartiality. The apology of that assembly is found in their situation; but when we approve what they *must* bear, it is in us the degenerate choice of a vitiated mind.

With a compelled appearance of deliberation, they vote under the dominion of a stern necessity. They sit in the heart, as it were, of a foreign republic: they have their residence in a city whose constitution has emanated neither from the charter of their king, nor from their legislative power. There they are surrounded by an army not raised either by the authority of their crown, or by their command; and which, if they should order to dissolve itself, would instantly dissolve them. There they sit, after a gang of assassins had driven away some hundreds of the members; whilst those who held the same moderate principles, with more patience or better hope, continued every day exposed to outrageous insults and murderous threats. There a majority, sometimes real, sometimes pretended, captive itself, compels a captive king to issue as royal edicts, at third hand, the polluted nonsense of their most licentious and giddy coffeehouses. It is notorious, that all their measures are decided before they are debated. It is beyond doubt, that under the terror of the bayonet, and the lamp-post, and the torch to their houses, they are obliged to adopt all the crude and desperate measures suggested by clubs composed of a monstrous medley of all conditions, tongues, and nations. Among these are found persons, in comparison of whom Catiline would be thought scrupulous, and Cethegus a man of sobriety and moderation. Nor is it in these clubs alone that the public measures are deformed into monsters. They undergo a previous distortion in academies, intended as so many seminaries for these clubs, which are set up in all the places of public resort. In these meetings of all sorts, every counsel, in proportion as it is daring, and violent, and perfidious, is taken for the mark of superior genius. Humanity and compassion are ridiculed as the fruits of superstition and ignorance. Tenderness to individuals is considered as treason to the public. Liberty is always to be estimated perfect as property is rendered insecure. Amidst assassination, massacre, and confiscation, perpetrated or meditated, they are forming plans for the good order of future society. Embracing in their arms the carcases of base criminals, and promoting their relations on the title of their offences, they drive hundreds of virtuous persons to the same end, by forcing them to subsist by beggery or by crime.

The assembly, their organ, acts before them the farce of deliberation with as little decency as liberty. They act like the comedians of a fair before a riotous audience; they act amidst the tumultuous cries of a mixed mob of ferocious men, and of women lost to shame, who, according to their insolent fancies, direct, control, applaud, explode them; and sometimes mix and take their seats amongst them; domineering over them with a strange mixture of servile petulance and proud, presumptuous authority. As they have inverted order in all things, the gallery is in the place of the house. This assembly, which overthrows kings and kingdoms, has not even the physiognomy and aspect of a grave legislative body—*nec color imperii, nec frons ulla senatus.* They have a power given to them, like that of the evil principle, to subvert and destroy; but none to construct, except such machines as may be fitted for further subversion and further destruction.

Who is it that admires, and from the heart is attached to, national representative assemblies, but must turn with horror and disgust from such a profane burlesque, and abominable perversion of that sacred institute? Lovers of monarchy, lovers of republics, must alike abhor it. The members of your assembly must themselves groan under the tyranny of which they have all the shame, none of the direction, and little of the profit. I am sure many of the members who compose even the majority of that body must feel as I do, notwithstanding the applauses of the Revolution Society. Miserable king! Miserable assembly! How must that assembly be silently scandalized with those of their members, who could call a day which seemed to blot the sun out of heaven, "*un beau jowl.*"[14] How must they be inwardly indignant at hearing others, who thought fit to declare to them, "that the vessel of the state would fly forward in her course towards regeneration with more speed than ever," from the stiff gale of treason and murder, which preceded our preacher's triumph! What must they have felt, whilst, with outward patience, and inward indignation, they heard of the slaughter of innocent gentlemen in their houses, that "the blood spilled was not the most pure!" What must they have felt, when they were besieged by complaints of disorders which shook their country to its foundations, at being compelled coolly to tell the complainants, that they were under the protection of the law, and that they would address the king (the captive king) to cause the laws to be enforced for their protection; when the enslaved ministers of that captive king had formally notified to them, that there were neither law, nor authority, nor power left to protect! What must they have felt at being obliged, as a felicitation on the present new year, to request their captive king to forget the stormy period of the last, on account of the great good which *he* was likely to produce to his people; to the complete attainment of which good they adjourned the practical demonstrations of their loyalty, assuring him of their obedience, when he should no longer possess any authority to command!

This address was made with much good nature and affection, to be sure. But among the revolutions in France must be reckoned a considerable revolution in their ideas of politeness. In England we are said to learn manners at second-hand from your side of the water, and that we dress our behaviour in the frippery of France. If so, we are still in the old cut; and have not so far conformed to the new Parisian mode of good breeding, as to think it quite in the most refined strain of delicate compliment (whether in condolence or congratulation) to say, to the most humiliated creature that crawls upon the earth, that great public benefits are derived from the murder of his servants, the attempted assassination of himself and of his wife, and the mortification, disgrace, and degradation, that he has personally suffered. It is a topic of consolation which our ordinary of Newgate would be too humane to use to a criminal at the foot of the gallows. I should have thought that the hangman of Paris, now that he is liberalized by the vote of the National Assembly, and is allowed his rank and arms in the herald's college of the rights of men, would be too generous, too gallant a man, too full of the sense of his new dignity, to employ that cutting consolation to any of the persons whom the *leze nation* might bring under the administration of his *executive power.*

A man is fallen indeed, when he is thus flattered. The anodyne draught of oblivion, thus drugged, is well calculated to preserve a galling wakefulness, and to feel the living ulcer of a corroding memory. Thus to administer the opiate portion of amnesty, powdered with all the ingredients of scorn and contempt, is to hold to his lips, instead of "the balm of hurt minds," the cup of human misery full to the brim, and to force him to drink it to the dregs.

Yielding to reasons, at least as forcible as those which were so delicately urged in the compliment on the new year, the king of France will probably endeavour to forget these events and that compliment. But history, who keeps a durable record of all our acts, and exercises her awful censure over the proceedings of all sorts of sovereigns, will not forget either those events, or the era of this liberal refinement in the intercourse of mankind. History will record, that on the morning of the 6th of October, 1789, the king and queen of France, after a day of confusion, alarm, dismay, and slaughter, lay down, under the pledged security of public faith, to indulge nature in a few hours of respite, and troubled, melancholy repose. From this sleep the queen was first startled by the voice of the sentinel at her door, who cried out to her to save herself by flight—that this was the last proof of fidelity he could give—that they were upon him, and he was dead. Instantly he was cut down. A band of cruel ruffians and assassins, reeking with his blood, rushed into the chamber of the queen, and pierced with a hundred strokes of bayonets and poniards the bed, from whence this persecuted woman had but just time to fly almost naked, and, through ways unknown to the murderers, had escaped to seek refuge at the feet of a king and husband, not secure of his own life for a moment.

This king, to say no more of him, and this queen, and their infant children (who once would have been the pride and hope of a great and generous people) were then forced to abandon the sanctuary of the most splendid palace in the world, which they left swimming in blood, polluted by massacre, and strewed with scattered limbs and mutilated carcases. Thence they were conducted into the capital of their kingdom. Two had been selected from the unprovoked, unresisted, promiscuous slaughter, which was made of the gentlemen of birth and family who composed the king's body guard. These two gentlemen, with all the parade of an execution of justice, were cruelly and publicly dragged to the block, and beheaded in the great court of the palace. Their heads were stuck upon spears, and led the procession; whilst the royal captives who followed in the train were slowly moved along, amidst the horrid yells, and shrilling screams, and frantic dances, and infamous contumelies, and all the unutterable abominations of the furies of hell, in the abused shape of the vilest of women. After they had been made to taste, drop by drop, more than the bitterness of death, in the slow torture of a journey of twelve miles, protracted to six hours, they were, under a guard, composed of those very soldiers who had thus conducted them through this famous triumph, lodged in one of the old palaces of Paris, now converted into a bastile for kings.

Is this a triumph to be consecrated at altars? to be commemorated with grateful thanksgiving? to be offered to the divine humanity with fervent prayer and enthusiastic ejaculation? These Theban and Thracian orgies, acted in France, and applauded only in the Old Jewry, I assure you, kindle prophetic enthusiasm in the minds but of very few people in this kingdom: although a saint and apostle, who may have revelations of his own, and who has so completely vanquished all the mean superstitions of the heart, may incline to think it pious and decorous to compare it with the entrance into the world of the Prince of Peace, proclaimed in a holy temple by a venerable sage, and not long before not worse announced by the voice of angels to the quiet innocence of shepherds.

At first I was at a loss to account for this fit of unguarded transport. I knew, indeed, that the sufferings of monarchs make a delicious repast to some sort of palates. There were reflections which might serve to keep this appetite within some bounds of temperance. But when I took one circumstance into my consideration, I was obliged to confess, that much allowance ought to be made for the society, and that the temptation was too strong for common discretion; I mean, the circumstance of the Io Pæan of the triumph, the animating cry which called "for *all* the bishops to be hanged on the lamp-posts,"[15] might well have brought forth a burst of enthusiasm on the foreseen consequences of this happy day. I allow to so much enthusiasm some little deviation from prudence. I allow this prophet to break forth into hymns of joy and thanksgiving on an event which appears like the precursor of the Millennium, and the projected fifth monarchy, in the destruction of all church establishments. There was, however (as in all human affairs there is), in the midst of this joy, something to exercise the patience of these worthy gentlemen, and to try the long-suffering of their faith. The actual murder of the king and queen, and their child, was wanting to the other auspicious circumstances of this *"beautiful day."* The actual murder of the bishops, though called for by so many holy ejaculations, was also wanting. A group of regicide and sacrilegious slaughter, was indeed boldly sketched. It unhappily was left unfinished, in this great history-piece of the massacre of innocents. What hardy pencil of a great master, from the school of rights of men, will finish it, is to be seen hereafter. The age has not yet the complete benefit of that diffusion of knowledge that has undermined superstition and error; and the king of France wants another object or two to consign to oblivion, in consideration of all the good which is to arise from his own sufferings, and the patriotic crimes of an enlightened age.[16]

Although this work of our new light and knowledge did not go to the length that in all probability it was intended it should be carried, yet I must think that such treatment of any human creatures must be shocking to any but those who are made for accomplishing revolutions. But I cannot stop here. Influenced by the inborn feelings of my nature, and not being illuminated by a single ray of this new-sprung modern light, I confess to you, sir, that the exalted rank of the persons suffering, and particularly the sex, the beauty, and the amiable qualities of the descendant of so many kings and emperors, with the tender age of royal infants, insensible only through infancy and innocence of the cruel outrages to which their parents were exposed, instead of being a subject of exultation, adds not a little to my sensibility on that most melancholy occasion.

I hear that the august person, who was the principal object of our preacher's triumph, though he supported himself, felt much on that shameful occasion. As a man, it became him to feel for his wife and his children, and the faithful guards of his person, that were massacred in cold blood about him; as a prince, it became him to feel for the strange and frightful transformation of his civilized subjects, and to be more grieved for them than solicitous for himself. It derogates little from his fortitude, while it adds infinitely to the honour of his humanity. I am very sorry to say it, very sorry indeed, that such personages are in a situation in which it is not becoming in us to praise the virtues of the great.

I hear, and I rejoice to hear, that the great lady, the other object of the triumph, has borne that day (one is interested that beings made for suffering should suffer well) and that she bears all the succeeding days, that she bears the imprisonment of her husband, and her own captivity, and the exile of her friends, and the insulting adulation of addresses, and the whole weight of her accumulated wrongs, with a serene patience, in a manner suited to her rank and race, and becoming the offspring of a sovereign distinguished for her piety and her courage: that, like her, she has lofty sentiments; that she feels with the dignity of a Roman matron; that in the last extremity she will save herself from the last disgrace; and that, if she must fall, she will fall by no ignoble hand.

It is now sixteen or seventeen years since I saw the queen of France, then the dauphiness, at Versailles; and surely never lighted on this orb, which she hardly seemed to touch, a more delightful vision. I saw her just above the horizon, decorating and cheering the elevated sphere she just began to move in—glittering like the morning-star, full of life, and splendour, and joy. Oh! What a revolution! And what a heart must I have to contemplate without emotion that elevation and that fall! Little did I dream when she added titles of veneration to those of enthusiastic, distant, respectful love, that she should ever be obliged to carry the sharp antidote against disgrace concealed in that bosom; little did I dream that I should have lived to see such disasters fallen upon her in a nation of gallant men, in a nation of men of honour, and of cavaliers. I thought ten thousand swords must have leaped from their scabbards to avenge even a look that threatened her with insult. But the age of chivalry is gone. That of sophisters, economists, and calculators, has succeeded; and the glory of Europe is extinguished for ever. Never, never more shall we behold that generous loyalty to rank and sex, that proud submission, that dignified obedience, that subordination of the heart, which kept alive, even in servitude itself, the spirit of an exalted freedom. The unbought grace of life, the cheap defence of nations, the nurse of manly sentiment and heroic enterprise, is gone! It is gone, that sensibility of principle, that chastity of honour, which felt a stain like a wound, which inspired courage whilst it mitigated ferocity, which ennobled whatever it touched, and under which vice itself lost half its evil, by losing all its grossness.

This mixed system of opinion and sentiment had its origin in the ancient chivalry; and the principle, though varied in its appearance by the varying state of human affairs, subsisted and influenced through a long succession of generations, even to the time we live in. If it should ever be totally extinguished, the loss I fear will be great. It is this which has given its character to modern Europe. It is this which has distinguished it under all its forms of government, and distinguished it to its advantage, from the states of Asia, and possibly from those states which flourished in the most brilliant periods of the antique world. It was this, which, without confounding ranks, had produced a noble equality, and handed it down through all the gradations of social life. It was this opinion which mitigated kings into companions, and raised private men to be fellows with kings. Without force or opposition, it subdued the fierceness of pride and power; it obliged sovereigns to submit to the soft collar of social esteem, compelled stern authority to submit to elegance, and gave a dominating vanquisher of laws to be subdued by manners.

But now all is to be changed. All the pleasing illusions, which made power gentle and obedience liberal, which harmonized the different shades of life, and which, by a bland assimilation, incorporated into politics the sentiments which beautify and soften private society, are to be dissolved by this new conquering empire of light and reason. All the decent drapery of life is to be rudely torn off. All the superadded ideas, furnished from the wardrobe of a moral imagination, which the heart owns, and the understanding ratifies, as necessary to cover the defects of our naked, shivering nature, and to raise it to dignity in our own estimation, are to be exploded as a ridiculous, absurd, and antiquated fashion.

On this scheme of things, a king is but a man, a queen is but a woman; a woman is but an animal, and an animal not of the highest order. All homage paid to the sex in general as such, and without distinct views, is to be regarded as romance and folly. Regicide, and parricide, and sacrilege, are but fictions of superstition, corrupting jurisprudence by destroying its simplicity. The murder of a king, or a queen, or a bishop, or a father, are only common homicide; and if the people are by any chance, or in any way, gainers by it, a sort of homicide much the most pardonable, and into which we ought not to make too severe a scrutiny.

On the scheme of this barbarous philosophy, which is the offspring of cold hearts and muddy understandings, and which is as void of solid wisdom as it is destitute of all taste and elegance, laws are to be supported only by their own terrors, and by the concern which each individual may find in them from his own private speculations, or can spare to them from his own private interests. In the groves of *their* academy, at the end of every vista, you see nothing but the gallows. Nothing is left which engages the affections on the part of the commonwealth. On the principles of this mechanic philosophy, our institutions can never be embodied, if I may use the expression, in persons; so as to create in us love, veneration, admiration, or attachment. But that sort of reason which banishes the affections is incapable of filling their place. These public affections, combined with manners, are required sometimes as supplements, sometimes as correctives, always as aids to law. The precept given by a wise man, as well as a great critic, for the construction of poems, is equally true as to states: *Non satis est pulchra esse poemata, dulcia sunto.* There ought to be a system of manners in every nation, which a well-formed mind would be disposed to relish. To make us love our country, our country ought to be lovely.

But power, of some kind or other, will survive the shock in which manners and opinions perish; and it will find other and worse means for its support. The usurpation which, in order to subvert ancient institutions, has destroyed ancient principles, will hold power by arts similar to those by which it has acquired it. When the old feudal and chivalrous spirit of *fealty,* which, by freeing kings from fear, freed both kings and subjects from the precautions of tyranny, shall be extinct in the minds of men, plots and assassinations will be anticipated by preventive murder and preventive confiscation, and that long roll of grim and bloody maxims, which form the political code of all power, not standing on its own honour, and the honour of those who are to obey it. Kings will be tyrants from policy, when subjects are rebels from principle.

When ancient opinions and rules of life are taken away, the loss cannot possibly be estimated. From that moment we have no compass to govern us; nor can we know distinctly to what port we steer. Europe, undoubtedly, taken in a mass, was in a flourishing condition the day on which your revolution was completed. How much of that prosperous state was owing to the spirit of our old manners and opinions is not easy to say; but as such causes cannot be indifferent in their operation, we must presume, that, on the whole, their operation was beneficial.

We are but too apt to consider things in the state in which we find them, without sufficiently adverting to the causes by which they have been produced, and possibly may be upheld. Nothing is more certain, than that our manners, our civilization, and all the good things which are connected with manners and with civilization, have, in this European world of ours, depended for ages upon two principles; and were indeed the result of both combined; I mean the spirit of a gentleman, and the spirit of religion. The nobility and the clergy, the one by profession, the other by patronage, kept learning in existence, even in the midst of arms and confusions, and whilst governments were rather in their causes, than formed. Learning paid back what it received to nobility and to priesthood; and paid it with usury, by enlarging their ideas, and by furnishing their minds. Happy if they had all continued to know their indissoluble union, and their proper place! Happy if learning, not debauched by ambition, had been satisfied to continue the instructor, and not aspired to be the master! Along with its natural protectors and guardians, learning will be cast into the mire, and trodden down under the hoofs of a swinish multitude.[17]

If, as I suspect, modern letters owe more than they are always willing to own to ancient manners, so do other interests which we value full as much as they are worth. Even commerce, and trade, and manufacture, the gods of our economical politicians, are themselves perhaps but creatures; are themselves but effects, which, as first causes, we choose to worship. They certainly grew under the same shade in which learning flourished. They too may decay with their natural protecting principles. With you, for the present at least, they all threaten to disappear together. Where trade and manufactures are wanting to a people, and the spirit of nobility and religion remains, sentiment supplies, and not always ill supplies, their place; but if commerce and the arts should be lost in an experiment to try how well a state may stand without these old fundamental principles, what sort of a thing must be a nation of gross, stupid, ferocious, and, at the same time, poor and sordid, barbarians, destitute of religion, honour, or manly pride, possessing nothing at present, and hoping for nothing hereafter?

I wish you may not be going fast, and by the shortest cut, to that horrible and disgustful situation. Already there appears a poverty of conception, a coarseness and vulgarity, in all the proceedings of the Assembly and of all their instructors. Their liberty is not liberal. Their science is presumptuous ignorance. Their humanity is savage and brutal.

It is not clear, whether in England we learned those grand and decorous principles and manners, of which considerable traces yet remain, from you, or whether you took them from us. But to you, I think, we trace them best. You seem to me to be *gentis incunabula nostræ*. France has always more or less influenced manners in England; and when your fountain is choked up and polluted, the stream will not run long, or not run clear, with us, or perhaps with any nation. This gives all Europe, in my opinion, but too close and connected a concern in what is done in France. Excuse me, therefore, if I have dwelt too long on the atrocious spectacle of the 6th of October, 1789, or have given too much scope to the reflections which have arisen in my mind on occasion of the most important of all revolutions, which may be dated from that day, I mean a revolution in sentiments, manners, and moral opinions. As things now stand, with everything respectable destroyed without us, and an attempt to destroy within us every principle of respect, one is almost forced to apologize for harbouring the common feelings of men.

Why do I feel so differently from the Reverend Dr. Price, and those of his lay flock who will choose to adopt the sentiments of his discourse? For this plain reason—because it is *natural* I should; because we are so made, as to be affected at such spectacles with melancholy sentiments upon the unstable condition of mortal prosperity, and the tremendous uncertainty of human greatness; because in those natural feelings we learn great lessons; because in events like these our passions instruct our reason; because when kings are hurled from their thrones by the Supreme Director of this great drama, and become the objects of insult to the base, and of pity to the good, we behold such disasters in the moral, as we should behold a miracle in the physical, order of things. We are alarmed into reflection; our minds (as it has long since been observed) are purified by terror and pity; our weak, unthinking pride is humbled under the dispensations of a mysterious wisdom. Some tears might be drawn from me, if such a spectacle were exhibited on the stage. I should be truly ashamed of finding in myself that superficial, theatric sense of painted distress, whilst I could exult over it in real life. With such a perverted mind, I could never venture to show my face at a tragedy. People would think the tears that Garrick formerly, or that Siddons not long since, have extorted from me, were the tears of hypocrisy; I should know them to be the tears of folly.

Indeed the theatre is a better school of moral sentiments than churches, where the feelings of humanity are thus outraged. Poets who have to deal with an audience not yet graduated in the school of the rights of men, and who must apply themselves to the moral constitution of the heart, would not dare to produce such a triumph as a matter of exultation. There, where men follow their natural impulses, they would not bear the odious maxims of a Machiavelian policy, whether applied to the attainment of monarchial or democratic tyranny. They would reject them on the modern, as they once did on the ancient stage, where they could not bear even the hypothetical proposition of such wickedness in the mouth of a personated tyrant, though suitable to the character he sustained. No theatric audience in Athens would bear what has been borne, in the midst of the real tragedy of this triumphal day; a principal actor weighing, as it were in scales hung in a shop of horrors—so much actual crime against so much contingent advantage—and after putting in and out weights, declaring that the balance was on the side of the advantages. They would not bear to see the crimes of new democracy posted as in a ledger against the crimes of old despotism, and the bookkeepers of politics finding democracy still in debt, but by no means unable or unwilling to pay the balance. In the theatre, the first intuitive glance, without any elaborate process of reasoning, will show, that this method of political computation would justify every extent of crime. They would see, that on these principles, even where the very worst acts were not perpetrated, it was owing rather to the fortune of the conspirators, than to their parsimony in the expenditure of treachery and blood. They would soon see, that criminal means once tolerated are soon preferred. They present a shorter cut to the object than through the highway of the moral virtues. Justifying perfidy and murder for public benefit, public benefit would soon become the pretext, and perfidy and murder the end; until rapacity, malice, revenge, and fear more dreadful than revenge, could satiate their insatiable appetites. Such must be the consequences of losing, in the splendour of these triumphs of the rights of men, all natural sense of wrong and right.

But the reverend pastor exults in this "leading in triumph," because truly Louis the Sixteenth was "an arbitrary monarch;" that is, in other words, neither more nor less than because he was Louis the Sixteenth, and because he had the misfortune to be born king of France, with the prerogatives of which, a long line of ancestors, and a long acquiescence of the people, without any act of his, had put him in possession. A misfortune it has indeed turned out to him, that he was born king of France. But misfortune is not crime, nor is indiscretion always the greatest guilt. I shall never think that a prince, the acts of whose whole reign was a series of concessions to his subjects, who was willing to relax his authority, to remit his prerogatives, to call his people to a share of freedom, not known, perhaps not desired, by their ancestors; such a prince, though he should be subjected to the common frailties attached to men and to princes, though he should have once thought it necessary to provide force against the desperate designs manifestly carrying on against his person, and the remnants of his authority; though all this should be take into consideration, I shall be led with great difficulty to think he deserves the cruel and insulting triumph of Paris, and of Dr. Price. I tremble for the cause of liberty, from such an example to kings. I tremble for the cause of humanity, in the unpunished outrages of the most wicked of mankind. But there are some people of that low and degenerate fashion of mind, that they look up with a sort of complacent awe and admiration to kings, who know how to keep firm in their seat, to hold a strict hand over their subjects, to assert their prerogative, and, by the awakened vigilance of a severe despotism, to guard against the very first approaches of freedom. Against such as these they never elevate their voice. Deserters from principle, listed with fortune, they never see any good in suffering virtue, nor any crime in prosperous usurpation.

If it could have been made clear to me, that the king and queen of France (those I mean who were such before the triumph) were inexorable and cruel tyrants, that they had formed a deliberate scheme for massacring the National Assembly (I think I have seen something like the latter insinuated in certain publications), I should think their captivity just. If this be true, much more ought to have been done, but done, in my opinion, in another manner. The punishment of real tyrants is a noble and awful act of justice; and it has with truth been said to be consolatory to the human mind. But if I were to punish a wicked king, I should regard the dignity in avenging the crime. Justice is grave and decorous, and in its punishments rather seems to submit to a necessity, than to make a choice. Had Nero, or Agrippina, or Louis the Eleventh, or Charles the Ninth, been the subject; if Charles the Twelfth of Sweden, after the murder of Patkul, or his predecessor Christina, after the murder of Monaldeschi, had fallen into your hands, sir, or into mine, I am sure our conduct would have been different.

If the French king, or king of the French (or by whatever name he is known in the new vocabulary of your constitution) has in his own person, and that of his queen, really deserved these unavowed, but unavenged, murderous attempts, and those frequent indignities more cruel than murder, such a person would ill deserve even that subordinate executory trust, which I understand is to be placed in him; nor is he fit to be called chief in a nation which he has outraged and oppressed. A worse choice for such an office in a new commonwealth, than that of a deposed tyrant, could not possibly be made. But to degrade and insult a man as the worst of criminals, and afterwards to trust him in your highest concerns, as a faithful, honest, and zealous servant, is not consistent with reasoning, nor prudent in policy, nor safe in practice. Those who could make such an appointment must be guilty of a more flagrant breach of trust than any they have yet committed against the people. As this is the only crime in which your leading politicians could have acted inconsistently, I conclude that there is no sort of ground for these horrid insinuations. I think no better of all the other calumnies.

In England, we give no credit to them. We are generous enemies: we are faithful allies. We spurn from us with disgust and indignation the slanders of those who bring us their anecdotes with the attestation of the flower-de-luce on their shoulder. We have Lord George Gordon fast in Newgate; and neither his being a public proselyte to Judaism, nor his having, in his zeal against catholic priests and all sorts of ecclesiastics, raised a mob (excuse the term, it is still in use here) which pulled down all our prisons, have preserved to him a liberty, of which he did not render himself worthy by a virtuous use of it. We have rebuilt Newgate, and tenanted the mansion. We have prisons almost as strong as the Bastile, for those who dare to libel the queens of France. In this spiritual retreat, let the noble libeller remain. Let him there meditate on his Thalmud, until he learns a conduct more becoming his birth and parts, and not so disgraceful to the ancient religion to which he has become a proselyte; or until some persons from your side of the water, to please your new Hebrew brethren, shall ransom him. He may then be enabled to purchase, with the old hoards of the synagogue, and a very small poundage on the long compound interest of the thirty pieces of silver (Dr. Price has shown us what miracles compound interest will perform in 1790 years) the lands which are lately discovered to have been usurped by the Gallican church. Send us your Popish archbishop of Paris, and we will send you our Protestant Rabbin. We shall treat the person you send us in exchange like a gentleman and an honest man, as he is; but pray let him bring with him the fund of his hospitality, bounty, and charity; and, depend upon it, we shall never confiscate a shilling of that honourable and pious fund, nor think of enriching the treasury with the spoils of the poor-box.

To tell you the truth, my dear sir, I think the honour of our nation to be somewhat concerned in the disclaimer of the proceedings of this society of the Old Jewry and the London Tavern. I have no man's proxy. I speak only for myself, when I disclaim, as I do with all possible earnestness, all communion with the actors in that triumph, or with the admirers of it. When T assert anything else, as concerning the people of England, I speak from observation, not from authority; but I speak from the experience I have had in a pretty extensive and mixed communication with the inhabitants of this kingdom, of all descriptions and ranks, and after a course of attentive observation, began early in life, and continued for nearly forty years. I have often been astonished, considering that we are divided from you but by a slender dyke of about twenty-four miles, and that the mutual intercourse between the two countries has lately been very great, to find how little you seem to know of us. I suspect that this is owing to your forming a judgment of this nation from certain publications, which do, very erroneously, if they do at all, represent the opinions and dispositions generally prevalent in England. The vanity, restlessness, petulance, and spirit of intrigue, of several petty cabals, who attempt to hide their total want of consequence in bustle and noise, and puffing, and mutual quotation of each other, makes you imagine that our contemptuous neglect of their abilities is a mark of general acquiescence in their opinions. No such thing, I assure you. Because half a dozen grasshoppers under a fern make the field ring with their importunate chink, whilst thousands of great cattle, reposed beneath the shadow of the British oak, chew the cud and are silent, pray do not imagine that those who make the noise are the only inhabitants of the field; that, of course, they are many in number; or that, after all, they are other than the little, shrivelled, meagre, hopping, though loud and troublesome, insects of the hour.

I almost venture to affirm, that not one in a hundred amongst us participates in the "triumph" of the Revolution Society. If the king and queen of France, and their children, were to fall into our hands by the chance of war, in the most acrimonious of all hostilities (I deprecate such an event, I deprecate such hostility), they would be treated with another sort of triumphal entry into London. We formerly have had a king of France in that situation; you have read how he was treated by the victor in the field; and in what manner he was afterwards received in England. Four hundred years have gone over us; but I believe we are not materially changed since that period. Thanks to our sullen resistance to innovation, thanks to the cold sluggishness of our national character, we still bear the stamp of our forefathers. We have not (as I conceive) lost the generosity and dignity of thinking of the fourteenth century; nor as yet have we subtilized ourselves into savages. We are not the converts of Rousseau; we are not the disciples of Voltaire; Helvetius has made no progress amongst us. Atheists are not our preachers; madmen are not our lawgivers. We know that *we* have made no discoveries, and we think that no discoveries are to be made, in morality; nor many in the great principles of government, nor in the ideas of liberty, which were understood long before we were born, altogether as well as they will be after the grave has heaped its mould upon our presumption, and the silent tomb shall have imposed its law on our pert loquacity. In England we have not yet been completely embowelled of our natural entrails; we still feel within us, and we cherish and cultivate, those inbred sentiments which are the faithful guardians, the active monitors of our duty, the true supporters of all liberal and manly morals. We have not been drawn and trussed, in order that we may be filled, like stuffed birds in a museum, with chaff and rags and paltry blurred shreds of paper about the rights of man. We preserve the whole of our feelings still native and entire, unsophisticated by pedantry and infidelity. We have real hearts of flesh and blood beating in our bosoms. We fear God; we look up with awe to kings; with affection to parliaments; with duty to magistrates; with reverence to priests; and with respect to nobility.[18] Why? Because such ideas are brought before our minds, it is *natural* to be so affected; because all other feelings are false and spurious, and tend to corrupt our minds, to vitiate our primary morals, to render us unfit for rational liberty; and by teaching us a servile, licentious, and abandoned insolence, to be our low sport for a few holidays, to make us perfectly fit for, and justly deserving of, slavery, through the whole course of our lives.

You see, sir, that in this enlightened age I am bold enough to confess, that we are generally men of untaught feeling; that instead of casting away all our old prejudices, we cherish them to a very considerable degree, and, to take more shame to ourselves, we cherish them because they are prejudices; and the longer they have lasted, and the more generally they have prevailed, the more we cherish them. We are afraid to put men to live and trade each on his own private stock of reason; because we suspect that this stock in each man is small, and that the individuals would do better to avail themselves of the general bank and capital of nations and of ages. Many of our men of speculation, instead of exploding general prejudices, employ their sagacity to discover the latent wisdom which prevails in them. If they find what they seek, and they seldom fail, they think it more wise to continue the prejudice, with the reason involved, than to cast away the coat of prejudice, and to leave nothing but the naked reason; because prejudice, with its reason, has a motive to give action to that reason, and an affection which will give it permanence. Prejudice is of ready application in the emergency; it previously engages the mind in a steady course of wisdom and virtue, and does not leave the man hesitating in the moment of decision, sceptical, puzzled, and unresolved. Prejudice renders a man's virtue his habit; and not a series of unconnected acts. Through just prejudice, his duty becomes a part of his nature.

Your literary men, and your politicians, and so do the whole clan of the enlightened among us, essentially differ in these points. They have no respect for the wisdom of others; but they pay it off by a very full measure of confidence in their own. With them it is a sufficient motive to destroy an old scheme of things, because it is an old one. As to the new, they are in no sort of fear with regard to the duration of a building run up in haste; because duration is no object to those who think little or nothing has been done before their time, and who place all their hopes in discovery. They conceive, very systematically, that all things which give perpetuity are mischievous, and therefore they are at inexpiable war with all establishments. They think that government may vary like modes of dress, and with as little ill effect: that there needs no principle of attachment, except a sense of present conveniency, to any constitution of the state. They always speak as if they were of opinion that there is a singular species of compact between them and their magistrates, which binds the magistrate, but which has nothing reciprocal in it, but that the majesty of the people has a right to dissolve it without any reason, but its will. Their attachment to their country itself is only so far as it agrees with some of their fleeting projects; it begins and ends with that scheme of polity which falls in with their momentary opinion.

These doctrines, or rather sentiments, seem prevalent with your new statesmen. But they are wholly different from those on which we have always acted in this country.

I hear it is sometimes given out in France, that what is doing among you is after the example of England. I beg leave to affirm, that scarcely anything done with you has originated from the practice or the prevalent opinions of this people, either in the act or in the spirit of the proceeding. Let me add, that we are as unwilling to learn these lessons from France, as we are sure that we never taught them to that nation. The cabals here, who take a sort of share in your transactions, as yet consist of but a handful of people. If unfortunately by their intrigues, their sermons, their publications, and by a confidence derived from an expected union with the counsels and forces of the French nation, they should draw considerable numbers into their faction, and in consequence should seriously attempt anything here in imitation of what has been done with you, the event, I dare venture to prophesy, will be, that, with some trouble to their country, they will soon accomplish their own destruction. This people refused to change their law in remote ages from respect to the infallibility of popes; and they will not now alter it from a pious implicit faith in the dogmatism of philosophers; though the former was armed with the anathema and crusade, and though the latter should act with the libel and the lamp-iron.

Formerly your affairs were your own concern only. We felt for them as men; but we kept aloof from them, because we were not citizens of France. But when we see the model held up to ourselves, we must feel as Englishmen, and feeling, we must provide as Englishmen. Your affairs, in spite of us, are made a part of our interest; so far at least as to keep at a distance your panacea, or your plague. If it be a panacea, we do not want it. We know the consequences of unnecessary physic. If it be a plague, it is such a plague that the precautions of the most severe quarantine ought to be established against it.

I hear on all hands that a cabal, calling itself philosophic, receives the glory of many of the late proceedings; and that their opinions and systems are the true actuating spirit of the whole of them. I have heard of no party in England, literary or political, at any time, known by such a description. It is not with you composed of those men, is it? whom the vulgar, in their blunt, homely style, commonly call atheists and infidels? If it be, I admit that we too have had writers of that description, who made some noise in their day. At present they repose in lasting oblivion. Who, born within the last forty years, has read one word of Collins, and Toland, and Tindal, and Chubb, and Morgan, and that whole race who called themselves Freethinkers? Who now reads Bolingbroke? Who ever read him through? Ask the booksellers of London what is become of all these lights of the world.

In a few years their few successors will go to the family vault of "all the Capulets." But whatever they were, or are, with us, they were and are wholly unconnected individuals. With us they kept the common nature of their kind, and were not gregarious. They never acted in corps, or were known as a faction in the state, nor presumed to influence in that name or character, or for the purposes of such a faction, on any of our public concerns. Whether they ought so to exist, and so be permitted to act, is another question. As such cabals have not existed in England, so neither has the spirit of them had any influence in establishing the original frame of our constitution, or in any one of the several reparations and improvements it has undergone. The whole has been done under the auspices, and is confirmed by the sanctions, of religion and piety. The whole has emanated from the simplicity of our national character, and from a sort of native plainness and directness of understanding, which for a long time characterized those men who have successively obtained authority amongst us. This disposition still remains; at least in the great body of the people.

We know, and what is better, we feel inwardly, that religion is the basis of civil society, and the source of all good and of all comfort.[19] In England we are so convinced of this, that there is no rust of superstition, with which the accumulated absurdity of the human mind might have crusted it over in the course of ages, that ninety-nine in a hundred of the people of England would not prefer to impiety. We shall never be such fools as to call in an enemy to the substance of any system to remove its corruptions, to supply its defects, or to perfect its construction. If our religious tenets should ever want a further elucidation, we shall not call on atheism to explain them. We shall not light up our temple from that unhallowed fire. It will be illuminated with other lights. It will be perfumed with other incense, than the infectious stuff which is imported by the smugglers of adulterated metaphysics. If our ecclesiastical establishment should want a revision, it is not avarice or rapacity, public or private, that we shall employ for the audit, or receipt, or application of its consecrated revenue. Violently condemning neither the Greek nor the Armenian, nor, since heats are subsided, the Roman system of religion, we prefer the Protestant; not because we think it has less of the Christian religion in it, but because, in our judgment it has more. We are Protestants, not from indifference, but from zeal.

We know, and it is our pride to know, that man is by his constitution a religious animal; that atheism is against, not only our reason, but our instincts; and that it cannot prevail long. But if, in the moment of riot, and in a drunken delirium from the hot spirit drawn out of the alembic of hell, which in France is now so furiously boiling, we should uncover our nakedness, by throwing off that Christian religion which has hitherto been our boast and comfort, and one great source of civilization amongst us, and amongst many other nations, we are apprehensive (being well aware that the mind will not endure a void) that some uncouth, pernicious, and degrading superstition might take place of it.

For that reason, before we take from our establishment the natural, human means of estimation, and give it up to contempt, as you have done, and in doing it have incurred the penalties you well deserve to suffer, we desire that some other may be presented to us in the place of it. We shall then form our judgment.

On these ideas, instead of quarrelling with establishments, as some do, who have made a philosophy and a religion of their hostility to such institutions, we cleave closely to them. We are resolved to keep an established church, and established monarchy, an established aristocracy, and an established democracy, each in the degree it exists, and in no greater. I shall show you presently how much each of these we possess.

It has been the misfortune (not, as these gentlemen think it, the glory) of this age, that everything is to be discussed, as if the constitution of our country were to be always a subject rather of altercation, than enjoyment. For this reason, as well as for the satisfaction of those among you (if any such you have among you) who may wish to profit of examples, I venture to trouble you with a few thoughts upon each of these establishments. I do not think they were unwise in ancient Rome, who, when they wished to new-model their laws, set commissioners to examine the best constituted republics within their reach.

First, I beg leave to speak of our church establishment, which is the first of our prejudices, not a prejudice destitute of reason, but involving in it profound and extensive wisdom. I speak of it first. It is first, and last, and midst in our minds. For, taking ground on that religious system, of which we are now in possession, we continue to act on the early received and uniformly continued sense of mankind. That sense not only, like a wise architect, hath built up the august fabric of states, but like a provident proprietor, to preserve the structure from profanation and ruin, as a sacred temple purged from all the impurities of fraud, and violence, and injustice, and tyranny, hath solemnly and for ever consecrated the commonwealth, and all that officiate in it. This consecration is made, that all who administer in the government of men, in which they stand in the person of God himself, should have high and worthy notions of their function and destination; that their hope should be full of immortality; that they should not look to the paltry pelf of the moment, nor to the temporary and transient praise of the vulgar, but to a solid, permanent existence, in the permanent part of their nature, and to a permanent fame and glory, in the example they leave as a rich inheritance to the world.

Such sublime principles ought to be infused into persons of exalted situations; and religious establishments provided, that may continually revive and enforce them. Every sort of moral, every sort of civil, every sort of politic institution, aiding the rational and natural ties that connect the human understanding and affections to the divine, are not more than necessary, in order to build up that wonderful structure, Man; whose prerogative it is, to be in a great degree a creature of his own making; and who, when made as he ought to be made, is destined to hold no trivial place in the creation. But whenever man is put over men, as the better nature ought ever to preside, in that case more particularly, he should as nearly as possible be approximated to his perfection.

The consecration of the state, by a state religious establishment, is necessary also to operate with a wholesome awe upon free citizens; because, in order to secure their freedom, they must enjoy some determinate portion of power. To them therefore a religion connected with the state, and with their duty towards it, becomes even more necessary than in such societies, where the people, by the terms of their subjection, are confined to private sentiments, and the management of their own family concerns. All persons possessing any portion of power ought to be strongly and awfully impressed with an idea that they act in trust: and that they are to account for their conduct in that trust to the one great Master, Author, and Founder of society.

This principle ought even to be more strongly impressed upon the minds of those who compose the collective sovereignty, than upon those of single princes. Without instruments, these princes can do nothing. Whoever uses instruments, in finding helps, finds also impediments. Their power is therefore by no means complete; nor are they safe in extreme abuse. Such persons, however elevated by flattery, arrogance, and self-opinion, must be sensible, that, whether covered or not by positive law, in some way or other they are accountable even here for the abuse of their trust. If they are not cut off by a rebellion of their people, they may be strangled by the very janissaries kept for their security against all other rebellion. Thus we have seen the king of France sold by his soldiers for an increase of pay. But where popular authority is absolute and unrestrained, the people have an infinitely greater, because a far better founded, confidence in their own power. They are themselves, in a great measure, their own instruments. They are nearer to their objects. Besides, they are less under responsibility to one of the greatest controlling powers on earth, the sense of fame and estimation. The share of infamy, that is likely to fall to the lot of each individual in public acts, is small indeed; the operation of opinion being in the inverse ratio to the number of those who abuse power. Their own approbation of their own acts has to them the appearance of a public judgment in their favour. A perfect democracy is therefore the most shameless thing in the world. As it is the most shameless, it is also the most fearless. No man apprehends in his person that he can be made subject to punishment. Certainly the people at large never ought: for as all punishments are for example towards the conservation of the people at large, the people at large can never become the subject of punishment by human hand.[20] It is therefore of infinite importance that they should not be suffered to imagine that their will, any more than that of kings, is the standard of right and wrong. They ought to be persuaded that they are full as little entitled, and far less qualified, with safety to themselves, to use any arbitrary power whatsoever; that therefore they are not, under a false show of liberty, but in truth, to exercise an unnatural, inverted domination, tyrannically to exact, from those who officiate in the state, not an entire devotion to their interest, which is their right, but an abject submission to their occasional will; extinguishing thereby, in all those who serve them, all moral principle, all sense of dignity, all use of judgment, and all consistency of character; whilst by the very same process they give themselves up a proper, a suitable, but a most contemptible prey to the servile ambition of popular sycophants, or courtly flatterers.

When the people have emptied themselves of all the lust of selfish will, which without religion it is utterly impossible they ever should, when they are conscious that they exercise, and exercise perhaps in a higher link of the order of delegation, the power, which to be legitimate must be according to that eternal, immutable law, in which will and reason are the same, they will be more careful how they place power in base and incapable hands. In their nomination to office, they will not appoint to the exercise of authority, as to a pitiful job, but as to a holy function; not according to their sordid, selfish interest, nor to their wanton caprice, nor to their arbitrary will; but they will confer that power (which any man may well tremble to give or to receive) on those only, in whom they may discern that predominant proportion of active virtue and wisdom, taken together and fitted to the charge, such, as in the great and inevitable mixed mass of human imperfections and infirmities, is to be found.

When they are habitually convinced that no evil can be acceptable, either in the act or the permission, to him whose essence is good, they will be better able to extirpate out of the minds of all magistrates, civil, ecclesiastical, or military, anything that bears the least resemblance to a proud and lawless domination.

But one of the first and most leading principles on which the commonwealth and the laws are consecrated, is lest the temporary possessors and life-renters in it, unmindful of what they have received from their ancestors, or of what is due to their posterity, should act as if they were the entire masters; that they should not think it among their rights to cut off the entail, or commit waste on the inheritance, by destroying at their pleasure the whole original fabric of their society; hazarding to leave to those who come after them a ruin instead of an habitation—and teaching these successors as little to respect their contrivances, as they had themselves respected the institutions of their forefathers. By this unprincipled facility of changing the state as often, and as much, and in as many ways, as there are floating fancies or fashions, the whole chain and continuity of the commonwealth would be broken. No one generation could link with the other. Men would become little better than the flies of a summer.

And first of all, the science of jurisprudence, the pride of the human intellect, which, with all its defects, redundancies, and errors, is the collected reason of ages, combining the principles of original justice with the infinite variety of human concerns, as a heap of old exploded errors, would be no longer studied. Personal self-sufficiency and arrogance (the certain attendants upon all those who have never experienced a wisdom greater than their own) would usurp the tribunal. Of course no certain laws, establishing invariable grounds of hope and fear, would keep the actions of men in a certain course, or direct them to a certain end. Nothing stable in the modes of holding property, or exercising function, could form a solid ground on which any parent could speculate in the education of his offspring, or in a choice for their future establishment in the world. No principles would be early worked into the habits. As soon as the most able instructor had completed his laborious course of instruction, instead of sending forth his pupil, accomplished in a virtuous discipline, fitted to procure him attention and respect, in his place in society, he would find everything altered; and that he had turned out a poor creature to the contempt and derision of the world, ignorant of the true grounds of estimation. Who would insure a tender and delicate sense of honour to beat almost with the first pulses of the heart, when no man could know what would be the test of honour in a nation, continually varying the standard of its coin? No part of life would retain its acquisitions. Barbarism with regard to science and literature, unskilfulness with regard to arts and manufactures, would infallibly succeed to the want of a steady education and settled principle; and thus the commonwealth itself would, in a few generations, crumble away, be disconnected into the dust and powder of individuality, and at length dispersed to all the winds of heaven.

To avoid therefore the evils of inconstancy and versatility, ten thousand times worse than those of obstinacy and the blindest prejudice, we have consecrated the state, that no man should approach to look into its defects or corruptions but with due caution; that he should never dream of beginning its reformation by its subversion; that he should approach to the faults of the state as to the wounds of a father, with pious awe and trembling solicitude. By this wise prejudice we are taught to look with horror on those children of their country, who are prompt rashly to hack that aged parent in pieces, and put him into the kettle of magicians, in hopes that by their poisonous weeds, and wild incantations, they may regenerate the paternal constitution, and renovate their father's life.

Society is indeed a contract. Subordinate contracts for objects of mere occasional interest may be dissolved at pleasure—but the state ought to be considered as nothing better than a partnership agreement in a trade of pepper and coffee, calico or tobacco, or some other such low concern, to be taken up for a little temporary interest, and to be dissolved by the fancy of the parties. It is to be looked on with other reverence; because it is not a partnership in things subservient only to the gross animal existence of a temporary and perishable nature. It is a partnership in all science; a partnership in all art; a partnership in every virtue, and in all perfection. As the ends of such a partnership cannot be obtained in many generations, it becomes a partnership not only between those who are living, but between those who are living, those who are dead, and those who are to be born. Each contract of each particular state is but a clause in the great primæval contract of eternal society, linking the lower with the higher natures, connecting the visible and invisible world, according to a fixed compact sanctioned by the inviolable oath which holds all physical and all moral natures, each in their appointed place. This law is not subject to the will of those, who by an obligation above them, and infinitely superior, are bound to submit their will to that law. The municipal corporations of that universal kingdom are not morally at liberty at their pleasure, and on their speculations of a contingent improvement, wholly to separate and tear asunder the bands of their subordinate community, and to dissolve it into an unsocial, uncivil, unconnected chaos of elementary principles. It is the first and supreme necessity only, a necessity that is not chosen, but chooses, a necessity paramount to deliberation, that admits no discussion, and demands no evidence, which alone can justify a resort to anarchy. This necessity is no exception to the rule; because this necessity itself is a part too of that moral and physical disposition of things, to which man must be obedient by consent or force: but if that which is only submission to necessity should be made the object of choice, the law is broken, nature is disobeyed, and the rebellious are outlawed, cast forth, and exiled, from this world of reason, and order, and peace, and virtue, and fruitful penitence, into the antagonist world of madness, discord, vice, confusion, and unavailing sorrow.

These, my dear sir, are, were, and, I think, long will be, the sentiments of not the least learned and reflecting part of this kingdom. They, who are included in this description, form their opinions on such grounds as such persons ought to form them. The less inquiring receive them from an authority, which those whom Providence dooms to live on trust need not be ashamed to rely on. These two sorts of men move in the same direction, though in a different place. They both move with the order of the universe. They all know or feel this great ancient truth: "Quod illi principi et præpotenti Deo qui omnem hunc mundum regit, nihil eorum quæ quidem fiant in terris acceptius quam concilia et cœtus hominum jure sociati quæ civitates appellantur." They take this tenet of the head and heart, not from the great name which it immediately bears, nor from the greater from whence it is derived; but from that which alone can give true weight and sanction to any learned opinion, the common nature and common relation of men. Persuaded that all things ought to be done with reference, and referring all to the point of reference to which all should be directed, they think themselves bound, not only as individuals in the sanctuary of the heart, or as congregated in that personal capacity, to renew the memory of their high origin and cast; but also in their corporate character to perform their national homage to the institutor, and author, and protector of civil society; without which civil society man could not by any possibility arrive at the perfection of which his nature is capable, nor even make a remote and faint approach to it. They conceive that He who gave our nature to be perfected by our virture, willed also the necessary means of its perfection. He willed therefore the state. He willed its connexion with the source and original archetype of all perfection. They who are convinced of this his will, which is the law of laws, and the sovereign of sovereigns, cannot think it reprehensible that this our corporate fealty and homage, that this our recognition of a signiory paramount, I had almost said this oblation of the state itself, as a worthy offering on the high altar of universal praise, should be performed as all public, solemn acts are performed, in buildings, in music, in decoration, in speech, in the dignity of persons, according to the customs of mankind, taught by their nature; this is, with modest splendour and unassuming state, with mild majesty and sober pomp. For those purposes they think some part of the wealth of the country is as usefully employed as it can be in fomenting the luxury of individuals. It is the public ornament. It is the public consolation. It nourishes the public hope. The poorest man finds his own importance and dignity in it, whilst the wealth and pride of individuals at every moment makes the man of humble rank and fortune sensible of his inferiority, and degrades and vilifies his condition. It is for the man in humble life, and to raise his nature, and to put him in mind of a state in which the privileges of opulence will cease, when he will be equal by nature, and may be more than equal by virtue, that this portion of the general wealth of his country is employed and sanctified.

I assure you I do not aim at singularity. I give you opinions which have been accepted amongst us, from very early times to this moment, with a continued and general approbation, and which indeed are so worked into my mind, that I am unable to distinguish what I have learned from others from the results of my own meditation.

It is on some such principles that the majority of the people of England, far from thinking a religious national establishment unlawful, hardly think it lawful to be without one. In France you are wholly mistaken if you do not believe us above all other things attached to it, and beyond all other nations; and when this people has acted unwisely and unjustifiably in its favour (as in some instances they have done most certainly), in their very errors you will at least discover their zeal.

This principle runs through the whole system of their polity. They do not consider their church establishment as convenient, but as essential to their state; not as a thing heterogeneous and separable; something added for accommodation; what they may either keep or lay aside, according to their temporary ideas of convenience. They consider it as the foundation of their whole constitution, with which, and with every part of which, it holds an indissoluble union. Church and state are ideas inseparable in their minds, and scarcely is the one ever mentioned without mentioning the other.

Our education is so formed as to confirm and fix this impression. Our education is in a manner wholly in the hands of ecclesiastics, and in all stages from infancy to manhood. Even when our youth, leaving schools and universities, enter that most important period of life which begins to link experience and study together, and when with that view they visit other countries, instead of old domestics whom we have seen as governors to principal men from other parts, three-fourths of those who go abroad with our young nobility and gentlemen are ecclesiastics; not as austere masters, nor as mere followers; but as friends and companions of a graver character, and not seldom persons as well born as themselves. With them, as relations, they most constantly keep up a close connexion through life. By this connexion we conceive that we attach our gentlemen to the church; and we liberalize the church by an intercourse with the leading characters of the country.

So tenacious are we of the old ecclesiastical modes and fashions of institution, that very little alteration has been made in them since the fourteenth or fifteenth century: adhering in this particular, as in all things else, to our old settled maxim, never entirely nor at once to depart from antiquity. We found these old institutions, on the whole, favourable to morality and discipline; and we thought they were susceptible of amendment, without altering the ground. We thought that they were capable of receiving and meliorating, and above all of preserving, the accessions of science and literature, as the order of Providence should successively produce them. And after all, with this Gothic and monkish education (for such it is in the ground-work) we may put in our claim to as ample and as early a share in all the improvements in science, in arts, and in literature, which have illuminated and adorned the modern world, as any other nation in Europe: we think one main cause of this improvement was our not despising the patrimony of knowledge which was left us by our forefathers.

It is from our attachment to a church establishment, that the English nation did not think it wise to intrust that great, fundamental interest of the whole to what they trust no part of their civil or military public service, that is, to the unsteady and precarious contribution of individuals. They go further. They certainly never have suffered, and never will suffer, the fixed estate of the church to be converted into a pension, to depend on the treasury, and to be delayed, withheld, or perhaps to be extinguished, by fiscal difficulties: which difficulties may sometimes be pretended for political purposes, and are in fact often brought on by the extravagance, negligence, and rapacity of politicians. The people of England think that they have constitutional motives, as well as religious, against any project of turning their independent clergy into ecclesiastical pensioners of state. They tremble for their liberty, from the influence of a clergy dependent on the crown; they tremble for the public tranquillity from the disorders of a factious clergy, if it were made to depend upon any other than the crown. They therefore made their church, like their king and their nobility, independent.

From the united considerations of religion and constitutional policy, from their opinion of a duty to make sure provision for the consolation of the feeble and the instruction of the ignorant, they have incorporated and identified the estate of the church with the mass of *private property*, of which the state is not the proprietor, either for use or dominion, but the guardian only and the regulator. They have ordained that the provision of this establishment might be as stable as the earth on which it stands, and should not fluctuate with the Euripus of funds and actions.

The men of England, the men, I mean, of light and leading in England, whose wisdom (if they have any) is open and direct, would be ashamed, as of a silly, deceitful trick, to profess any religion in name, which, by their proceedings, they appear to contemn. If by their conduct (the only language that rarely lies) they seemed to regard the great ruling principle of the moral and the natural world, as a mere invention to keep the vulgar in obedience, they apprehend that by such a conduct they would defeat the politic purpose they have in view. They would find it difficult to make others believe in a system to which they manifestly give no credit themselves. The Christian statesmen of this land would indeed first provide for the *multitude;* because it is the *multitude;* and is therefore, as such, the first object in the ecclesiastical institution, and in all institutions. They have been taught, that the circumstance of the gospel's being preached to the poor, was one of the great tests of its true mission. They think, therefore, that those do not believe it, who do not take care it should be preached to the poor. But as they know that charity is not confined to any one description, but ought to apply itself to all men who have wants, they are not deprived of a due and anxious sensation of pity to the distresses of the miserable great. They are not repelled through a fastidious delicacy, at the stench of their arrogance and presumption, from a medicinal attention to their mental blotches and running sores. They are sensible, that religious instruction is of more consequence to them than to any others; from the greatness of the temptation to which they are exposed; from the important consequences that attend their faults; from the contagion of their ill example; from the necessity of bowing down the stubborn neck of their pride and ambition to the yoke of moderation and virtue; from a consideration of the fat stupidity and gross ignorance concerning what imports men most to know, which prevails at courts, and at the head of armies, and in senates, as much as at the loom and in the field.

The English people are satisfied, that to the great the consolations of religion are as necessary as its instructions. They too are among the unhappy. They feel personal pain, and domestic sorrow. In these they have no privilege, but are subject to pay their full contingent to the contributions levied on mortality. They want this sovereign balm under their gnawing cares and anxieties, which, being less conversant about the limited wants of animal life, range without limit, and are diversified by infinite combinations, in the wild and unbounded regions of imagination. Some charitable dole is wanting to these, our often very unhappy brethren, to fill the gloomy void that reigns in minds which have nothing on earth to hope or fear; something to relieve in the killing languor and over-laboured lassitude of those who have nothing to do; something to excite an appetite to existence in the palled satiety which attends on all pleasures which may be bought, where nature is not left to her own process, where even desire is anticipated, and therefore fruition defeated by meditated schemes and contrivances of delight; and no interval, no obstacle, is interposed between the wish and the accomplishment.

The people of England know how little influence the teachers of religion are likely to have with the wealthy and powerful of long standing, and how much less with the newly fortunate, if they appear in a manner no way assorted to those with whom they must associate, and over whom they must even exercise, in some cases, something like an authority. What must they think of that body of teachers, if they see it in no part above the establishment of their domestic servants? If the poverty were voluntary, there might be some difference. Strong instances of self-denial operate powerfully on our minds; and a man who has no wants has obtained great freedom, and firmness, and even dignity. But as the mass of any description of men are but men, and their poverty cannot be voluntary, that disrespect, which attends upon all lay poverty, will not depart from the ecclesiastical. Our provident constitution has therefore taken care that those who are to instruct presumptuous ignorance, those who are to be censors over insolent vice, should neither incur their contempt, nor live upon their alms; nor will it tempt the rich to a neglect of the true medicine of their minds. For these reasons, whilst we provide first for the poor, and with a parental solicitude, we have not relegated religion (like something we were ashamed to show) to obscure municipalities, or rustic villages. No! we will have her to exalt her mitred front in courts and parliaments. We will have her mixed throughout the whole mass of life, and blended with all the classes of society. The people of England will show to the haughty potentates of the world, and to their talking sophisters, that a free, a generous, an informed nation honours the high magistrates of its church; that it will not suffer the insolence of wealth and titles, or any other species of proud pretension, to look down with scorn upon what they look up to with reverence; nor presume to trample on that acquired personal nobility, which they intend always to be, and which often is, the fruit, not the reward, (for what can be the reward?) of learning, piety, and virtue. They can see, without pain or grudging, an archbishop precede a duke. They can see a bishop of Durham, or a bishop of Winchester, in possession of ten thousand pounds a year; and cannot conceive why it is in worse hands than estates to the like amount in the hands of this earl, or that squire; although it may be true, that so many dogs and horses are not kept by the former, and fed with the victuals which ought to nourish the children of the people. It is true, the whole church revenue is not always employed, and to every shilling, in charity; nor perhaps ought it; but something is generally so employed. It is better to cherish virtue and humanity, by leaving much to free will, even with some loss to the object, than to attempt to make men mere machines and instruments of a political benevolence. The world on the whole will gain by a liberty, without which virtue cannot exist.

When once the commonwealth has established the estates of the church as property, it can, consistently, hear nothing of the more or the less. Too much and too little are treason against property. What evil can arise from the quantity in any hand, whilst the supreme authority has the full, sovereign superintendence over this, as over all property, to prevent every species of abuse; and, whenever it notably deviates, to give to it a direction agreeable to the purposes of its institution.

In England most of us conceive that it is envy and malignity towards those who are often the beginners of their own fortune, and not a love of the self-denial and mortification of the ancient church, that makes some look askance at the distinctions, and honours, and revenues, which, taken from no person, are set apart for virtue. The ears of the people of England are distinguishing. They hear these men speak broad. Their tongue betrays them. Their language is in the *patois* of fraud; in the cant and gibberish of hyprocrisy. The people of England must think so, when these praters affect to carry back the clergy to that primitive, evangelic poverty, which, in the spirit, ought always to exist in them (and in us too, however we may like it) but in the thing must be varied, when the relation of that body to the state is altered; when manners, when modes of life, when indeed the whole order of human affairs, has undergone a total revolution. We shall believe those reformers then to be honest enthusiasts, not, as now we think them, cheats and deceivers, when we see them throwing their own goods into common, and submitting their own persons to the austere discipline of the early church.

With these ideas rooted in their minds, the Commons of Great Britain, in the national emergencies, will never seek their resource from the confiscation of the estates of the church and poor. Sacrilege and proscription are not among the ways and means of our committee of supply. The Jews in Change Alley have not yet dared to hint their hopes of a mortgage on the revenues belonging to the see of Canterbury. I am not afraid that I shall be disavowed, when I assure you, that there is not *one* public man in this kingdom, whom you would wish to quote, no not one, of any party or description, who does not reprobate the dishonest, perfidious, and cruel confiscation which the National Assembly has been compelled to make of that property, which it was their first duty to protect.

It is with the exultation of a little national pride I tell you, that those amongst us who have wished to pledge the societies of Paris in the cup of their abominations have been disappointed. The robbery of your church has proved a security to the possessions of ours. It has roused the people. They see with horror and alarm that enormous and shameless act of proscription. It has opened, and will more and more open, their eyes upon the selfish enlargement of mind, and the narrow liberality of sentiment, of insidious men, which, commencing in close hypocrisy and fraud, have ended in open violence and rapine. At home we behold similar beginnings. We are on our guard against similar conclusions.

I hope we shall never be so totally lost to all sense of the duties imposed upon us by the law of social union, as, upon any pretext of public service, to confiscate the goods of a single unoffending citizen. Who but a tyrant (a name expressive of everything which can vitiate and degrade human nature) could think of seizing on the property of men, unaccused, unheard, untried, by whole descriptions, by hundreds and thousands together? Who, that had not lost every trace of humanity, could think of casting down men of exalted rank and sacred function, some of them of an age to call at once for reverence and compassion, of casting them down from the highest situation in the commonwealth, wherein they were maintained by their own landed property, to a state of indigence, depression, and contempt?

The confiscators truly have made some allowance to their victims from the scraps and fragments of their own tables, from which they have been so harshly driven, and which have been so bountifully spread for a feast to the harpies of usury. But to drive men from independence to live on alms, is itself great cruelty. That which might be a tolerable condition to men in one state of life, and not habituated to other things, may, when all these circumstances are altered, be a dreadful revolution; and one to which a virtuous mind would feel pain in condemning any guilt, except that which would demand the life of the offender. But to many minds this punishment of *degradation* and *infamy* is worse than death. Undoubtedly it is an infinite aggravation of this cruel suffering, that the persons who were taught a double prejudice in favour of religion, by education, and by the place they held in the administration of its functions, are to receive the remnants of their property as alms from the profane and impious hands of those who had plundered them of all the rest; to receive (if they are at all to receive) not from the charitable contributions of the faithful, but from the insolent tenderness of known and avowed atheism, the maintenance of religion, measured out to them on the standard of the contempt in which it is held; and for the purpose of rendering those who receive the allowance vile, and of no estimation, in the eyes of mankind.

But this act of seizure of property, it seems, is a judgment in law, and not a confiscation. They have, it seems, found out in the academies of the *Palais Royal,* and the *Jacobins,* that certain men had no right to the possessions which they held under law, usage, the decisions of courts, and the accumulated prescription of a thousand years. They say that ecclesiastics are fictitious persons, creatures of the state, whom at pleasure they may destroy, and of course limit and modify in every particular; that the goods they possess are not properly theirs, but belong to the state which created the fiction; and we are therefore not to trouble ourselves with what they may suffer in their natural feelings and natural persons, on account of what is done towards them in this their constructive character. Of what import is it under what names you injure men, and deprive them of the just emoluments of a profession, in which they were not only permitted but encouraged by the state to engage; and upon the supposed certainty of which emoluments they had formed the plan of their lives, contracted debts, and led multitudes to an entire dependence upon them?

You do not imagine, sir, that I am going to compliment this miserable distinction of persons with any long discussion. The arguments of tyranny are as contemptible as its force is dreadful. Had not your confiscators, by their early crimes, obtained a power which secures indemnity to all the crimes of which they have since been guilty, or that they can commit, it is not the syllogism of the logician, but the lash of the executioner, that would have refuted a sophistry which becomes an accomplice of theft and murder. The sophistic tyrants of Paris are loud in their declamations against the departed regal tyrants, who in former ages have vexed the world. They are thus bold, because they are safe from the dungeons and iron cages of their old masters. Shall we be more tender of the tyrants of our own time, when we see them acting worse tragedies under our eyes? shall we not use the same liberty that they do, when we can use it with the same safety? when to speak honest truth only requires a contempt of the opinions of those whose actions we abhor?

This outrage on all the rights of property was at first covered with what, on the system of their conduct, was the most astonishing of all pretexts—a regard to national faith. The enemies to property at first pretended a most tender, delicate, and scrupulous anxiety for keeping the king's engagements with the public creditor. These professors of the rights of men are so busy in teaching others, that they have not leisure to learn anything themselves; otherwise they would have known, that it is to the property of the citizen, and not to the demands of the creditor of the state, that the first and original faith of civil society is pledged. The claim of the citizen is prior in time, paramount in title, superior in equity. The fortunes of individuals, whether possessed by acquisition, or by descent, or in virtue of a participation in the goods of some community, were no part of the creditor's security, expressed or implied. They never so much as entered into his head when he made his bargain. He well knew that the public, whether represented by a monarch or by a senate, can pledge nothing but the public estate; and it can have no public estate, except in what it derives from a just and proportioned imposition upon the citizens at large. This was engaged, and nothing else could be engaged, to the public creditor. No man can mortgage his injustice as a pawn for his fidelity.

It is impossible to avoid some observation on the contradictions caused by the extreme rigour and the extreme laxity of this new public faith, which influenced in this transaction, and which influenced not according to the nature of the obligation, but to the description of the persons to whom it was engaged. No acts of the old government of the kings of France are held valid in the National Assembly, except his pecuniary engagements; acts of all others of the most ambiguous legality. The rest of the acts of that royal government are considered in so odious a light, that to have a claim under its authority is looked on as a sort of crime. A pension, given as a reward for service to the state, is surely as good a ground of property as any security for money advanced to the state. It is better; for money is paid, and well paid, to obtain that service. We have however seen multitudes of people under this description in France, who never had been deprived of their allowances by the most arbitrary ministers, in the most arbitrary times, by this assembly of the rights of men, robbed without mercy. They were told, in answer to their claim to the bread earned with their blood, that their services had not been rendered to the country that now exists.

This laxity of public faith is not confined to those unfortunate persons. The Assembly, with perfect consistency it must be owned, is engaged in a respectable deliberation how far it is bound by the treaties made with other nations under the former government, and their committee is to report which of them they ought to ratify, and which not. By this means they have put the external fidelity of this virgin state on a par with its internal.

It is not easy to conceive upon what rational principle the royal government should not, of the two, rather have possessed the power of rewarding service, and making treaties, in virtue of its prerogative, than that of pledging to creditors the revenue of the state, actual and possible. The treasure of the nation, of all things, has been the least allowed to the prerogative of the king of France, or to the prerogative of any king in Europe. To mortgage the public revenue implies the sovereign dominion, in the fullest sense, over the public purse. It goes far beyond the trust even of a temporary and occasional taxation. The acts however of that dangerous power (the distinctive mark of a boundless despotism) have been alone held sacred. Whence arose this preference given by a democratic assembly to a body of property deriving its title from the most critical and obnoxious of all the exertions of monarchical authority? Reason can furnish nothing to reconcile inconsistency; nor can partial favour be accounted for upon equitable principles. But the contradiction and partiality which admit no justification, are not the less without an adequate cause; and that cause I do not think it difficult to discover.

By the vast debt of France a great monied interest has insensibly grown up, and with it a great power. By the ancient usages which prevailed in that kingdom, the general circulation of property, and in particular the mutual convertibility of land into money, and of money into land, had always been a matter of difficulty. Family settlements, rather more general and more strict than they are in England, the *jus retractus,* the great mass of landed property held by the crown, and, by a maxim of the French law, held unalienably, the vast estates of the ecclesiastic corporations—all these had kept the landed and monied interest more separated in France, less miscible, and the owners of the two distinct species of property not so well disposed to each other as they are in this country.

The monied property was long looked on with rather an evil eye by the people. They saw it connected with their distresses, and aggravating them. It was no less envied by the old landed interests, partly for the same reasons that rendered it obnoxious to the people, but much more so as it eclipsed, by the splendour of an ostentatious luxury, the unendowed pedigrees and naked titles of several among the nobility. Even when the nobility, which represented the more permanent landed interest, united themselves by marriage (which sometimes was the case) with the other description, the wealth which saved the family from ruin, was supposed to contaminate and degrade it. Thus the enmities and heart-burnings of these parties were increased even by the usual means by which discord is made to cease and quarrels are turned into friendship. In the mean time, the pride of the wealthy men, not noble or newly noble, increased with its cause. They felt with resentment an inferiority, the grounds of which they did not acknowledge. There was no measure to which they were not willing to lend themselves, in order to be revenged of the outrages of this rival pride, and to exalt their wealth to what they considered as its natural rank and estimation. They struck at the nobility through the crown and the church. They attacked them particularly on the side on which they thought them the most vulnerable, that is, the possessions of the church, which, through the patronage of the crown, generally devolved upon the nobility. The bishoprics, and the great commendatory abbeys, were, with few exceptions, held by that order.

In this state of real, though not always perceived, warfare between the noble ancient landed interest and the new monied interest, the greatest because the most applicable strength was in the hands of the latter. The monied interest is in its nature more ready for any adventure; and its possessors more disposed to new enterprises of any kind. Being of a recent acquisition, it falls in more naturally with any novelties. It is therefore the kind of wealth which will be resorted to by all who wish for change.

Along with the monied interest, a new description of men had grown up, with whom that interest soon formed a close and marked union; I mean the political men of letters. Men of letters, fond of distinguishing themselves, are rarely averse to innovation. Since the decline of the life and greatness of Louis the Fourteenth, they were not so much cultivated either by him, or by the regent, or the successors to the crown; nor were they engaged to the court by favours and emoluments so systematically as during the splendid period of that ostentatious and not impolitic reign. What they lost in the old court protection, they endeavoured to make up by joining in a sort of incorporation of their own; to which the two academies of France, and afterwards the vast undertaking of the Encyclopædia, carried on by a society of these gentlemen, did not a little contribute.

The literary cabal had some years ago formed something like a regular plant for the destruction of the Christian religion. This object they pursued with a degree of zeal which hitherto had been discovered only in the propagators of some system of piety. They were possessed with a spirit of proselytism in the most fanatical degree; and from thence, by an easy progress, with the spirit of persecution according to their means.[21] What was not to be done towards their great end by any direct or immediate act, might be wrought by a longer process through the medium of opinion. To command that opinion, the first step is to establish a dominion over those who direct it. They contrived to possess themselves, with great method and perseverance, of all the avenues to literary fame. Many of them indeed stood high in the ranks of literature and science. The world had done them justice; and in favour of general talents forgave the evil tendency of their peculiar principles. This was true liberality; which they returned by endeavouring to confine the reputation of sense, learning, and taste to themselves or their followers. I will venture to say that this narrow, exclusive spirit has not been less prejudicial to literature and to taste, than to morals and true philosophy. These atheistical fathers have a bigotry of their own; and they have learnt to talk against monks with the spirit of a monk. But in some things they are men of the world. The resources of intrigue are called in to supply the defects of argument and wit. To this system of literary monopoly was joined an unremitting industry to blacken and discredit in every way, and by every means, all those who did not hold to their faction.

To those who have observed the spirit of their conduct, it has long been clear that nothing was wanted but the power of carrying the intolerance of the tongue and of the pen into a persecution which strike at property, liberty, and life.

The desultory and faint persecution carried on against them, more from compliance with form and decency, than with serious resentment, neither weakened their strength, nor relaxed their efforts. The issue of the whole was, that, what with opposition, and what with success, a violent and malignant zeal, of a kind hitherto unknown in the world, had taken an entire possession of their minds, and rendered their whole conversation, which otherwise would have been pleasing and instructive, perfectly disgusting. A spirit of cabal, intrigue, and proselytism, pervaded all their thoughts, words, and actions. And, as controversial zeal soon turns its thoughts on force, they began to insinuate themselves into a correspondence with foreign princes; in hopes, through their authority, which at first they flattered, they might bring about the changes they had in view. To them it was indifferent whether these changes were to be accomplished by the thunderbolt of despotism, or by the earthquake of popular commotion. The correspondence between this cabal and the late king of Prussia will throw no small light upon the spirit of all their proceedings.[22] For the same purpose for which they intrigued with princes, they cultivated, in a distinguished manner, the monied interest of France; and partly through the means furnished by those whose peculiar offices gave them the most extensive and certain means of communication, they carefully occupied all the avenues to opinion.

Writers, especially when they act in a body, and with one direction, have great influence on the public mind; the alliance, therefore, of these writers with the monied interest[23] had no small effect in removing the popular odium and envy which attended that species of wealth. These writers, like the propagators of all novelties, pretended to a great zeal for the poor, and the lower orders, whilst in their satires they rendered hateful, by every exaggeration, the faults of courts, of nobility, and of priesthood. They became a sort of demagogues. They served as a link to unite, in favour of one object, obnoxious wealth to restless and desperate poverty.

As these two kinds of men appear principal leaders in all the late transactions, their junction and pohtics will serve to account, not upon any principles of law or of policy, but as a *cause,* for the general fury with which all the landed property of ecclesiastical corporations has been attacked; and the great care which, contrary to their pretended principles, has been taken, of a monied interest originating from the authority of the crown. All the envy against wealth and power was artificially directed against other descriptions of riches. On what other principle than that which I have stated can we account for an appearance so extraordinary and unnatural as that of the ecclesiastical possessions, which had stood so many successions of ages and shocks of civil violences, and were girded at once by justice, and by prejudice, being applied to the payment of debts, comparatively recent, invidious, and contracted by a decried and subverted government?

Was the public estate a sufficient stake for the public debts? Assume that it was not, and that a loss *must* be incurred somewhere. When the only estate lawfully possessed, and which the contracting parties had in contemplation at the time in which their bargain was made, happens to fail, who according to the principles of natural and legal equity, ought to be the sufferer? Certainly it ought to be either the party who trusted, or the party who persuaded him to trust; or both; and not third parties who had no concern with the transaction. Upon any insolvency they ought to suffer who are weak enough to lend upon bad security or they who fraudulently held out a security that was not valid. Laws are acquainted with no other rules of decision. But by the new institute of the rights of men, the only persons, who in equity ought to suffer, are the only persons who are to be saved harmless: those are to answer the debt who neither were lenders nor borrowers, mortgagers nor mortgagees.

What had the clergy to do with these transactions? What had they to do with any public engagement further than the extent of their own debt? To that, to be sure, their estates were bound to the last acre. Nothing can lead more to the true spirit of the Assembly, which fits for public confiscation, with its new equity, and its new morality, than an attention to their proceeding with regard to this debt of the clergy. The body of confiscators, true to that monied interest for which they were false to every other, have found the clergy competent to incur a legal debt. Of course they declared them legally entitled to the property which their power of incurring the debt and mortgaging the estate implied; recognising the rights of those persecuted citizens, in the very act in which they were thus grossly violated.

If, as I said, any persons are to make good deficiencies to the public creditor, besides the public at large, they must be those who managed the agreement. Why therefore are not the estates of all the comptrollers-general confiscated?[24] Why not those of the long succession of ministers, financiers, and bankers who have been enriched whilst the nation was impoverished by their dealings and their counsels? Why is not the estate of M. Laborde declared forfeited rather than of the archbishop of Paris, who has had nothing to do in the creation or in the jobbing of the public funds? Or, if you must confiscate old landed estates in favour of the money-jobbers, why is the penalty confined to one description? I do not know whether the expenses of the Duke de Choiseul have left anything of the infinite sums which he had derived from the bounty of his master, during the transactions of a reign which contributed largely by every species of prodigality in war and peace, to the present debt of France. If any such remains, why is not this confiscated? I remember to have been in Paris during the time of the old government. I was there just after the Duke d'Aiguillon had been snatched (as it was generally thought) from the block by the hand of a protecting despotism. He was a minister, and had some concern in the affairs of that prodigal period. Why do I not see his estate delivered up to the municipalities in which it is situated? The noble family of Noailles have long been servants (meritorious servants I admit) to the crown of France, and have had of course some share in its bounties. Why do I hear nothing of the application of their estates to the public debt? Why is the estate of the Duke de Rochefoucault more sacred than that of the Cardinal de Rochefoucault? The former is, I doubt not, a worthy person; and (if it were not a sort of profaneness to talk of the use, as affecting the title to property) he makes a good use of his revenues; but it is no disrespect to him to say, what authentic information well warrants me in saying, that the use made of a property equally valid, by his brother[25] the cardinal archbishop of Rouen, was far more laudable and far more public-spirited. Can one hear of the proscription of such persons, and the confiscation of their effects, without indignation and horror? He is not a man who does not feel such emotions on such occasions. He does not deserve the name of a free-man who will not express them.

Few barbarous conquerors have ever made so terrible a revolution in property. None of the heads of the Roman factions, when they established "*crudelem illam hastam*" in all their auctions of rapine, have ever set up to sale the goods of the conquered citizen to such an enormous amount. It must be allowed in favour of those tyrants of antiquity, that what was done by them could hardly be said to be done in cold blood. Their passions were inflamed, their tempers soured, their understandings confused, with the spirit of revenge, with the innumerable reciprocated and recent inflictions and retaliations of blood and rapine. They were driven beyond all bounds of moderation by the apprehension of the return of power with the return of property, to the families of those they had injured beyond all hope of forgiveness.

These Roman confiscators, who were yet only in the elements of tyranny, and were not instructed in the rights of men to exercise all sorts of cruelties on each other without provocation, thought it necessary to spread a sort of colour over their injustice. They considered the vanquished party as composed of traitors who had borne arms, or otherwise had acted with hostility, against the commonwealth. They regarded them as persons who had forfeited their property by their crimes. With you, in your improved state of the human mind, there was no such formality. You seized upon five millions sterling of annual rent, and turned forty or fifty thousand human creatures out of their houses, because "such was your pleasure." The tyrant Harry the Eighth of England, as he was not better enlightened than the Roman Mariuses and Syllas, and had not studied in your new schools, did not know what an effectual instrument of despotism was to be found in that grand magazine of offensive weapons, the rights of men. When he resolved to rob the abbeys, as the club of the Jacobins have robbed all the ecclesiastics, he began by setting on foot a commission to examine into the crimes and abuses which prevailed in those communities. As it might be expected, his commission reported truths, exaggerations, and falsehoods. But truly or falsely, it reported abuses and offences. However, as abuses might be corrected, as every crime of persons does not infer a forfeiture with regard to communities, and as property, in that dark age, was not discovered to be a creature of prejudice, all those abuses (and there were enow of them) were hardly thought sufficient ground for such a confiscation as it was for his purpose to make. He therefore procured the formal surrender of these estates. All these operose proceedings were adopted by one of the most decided tyrants in the rolls of history, as necessary preliminaries, before he could venture, by bribing the members of his two servile houses with a share of the spoil, and holding out to them an eternal immunity from taxation, to demand a confirmation of his iniquitous proceedings by an act of parliament. Had fate reserved him to our times, four technical terms would have done his business, and saved him all this trouble; he needed nothing more than one short form of incantation—*"Philosophy, Light, Liberality, the Rights of Men."*

I can say nothing in praise of those acts of tyranny, which no voice has hitherto ever commended under any of their false colours; yet in these false colours an homage was paid by despotism to justice. The power which was above all fear and all remorse was not set above all shame. Whilst shame keeps its watch, virtue is not wholly extinguished in the heart; nor will moderation be utterly exiled from the minds of tyrants.

I believe every honest man sympathizes in his reflections with our political poet on that occasion, and will pray to avert the omen whenever these acts of rapacious despotism present themselves to his view or his imagination:

> May no such storm
> Fall on our times, where ruin must reform.
> Tell me (my Muse) what monstrous dire offence,
> What crimes could any Christian king incense
> To such a rage? Was 't luxury, or lust?
> Was *he* so temperate, so chaste, so just?
> Were these their crimes? they were his own much more,
> But wealth is crime enough to him that's poor.[26]

This same wealth, which is at all times treason and *lese nation* to indigent and rapacious despotism, under all modes of polity, was your temptation to violate property, law, and religion, united in one object. But was the state of France so wretched and undone, that no other resource but rapine remained to preserve its existence? On this point I wish to receive some information. When the states met, was the condition of the finances of France such, that, after economizing on principles of justice and mercy through all departments, no fair repartition of burthens upon all the orders could possibly restore them? If such an equal imposition would have been sufficient, you well know it might easily have been made. M. Necker, in the budget which he laid before the orders assembled at

Versailles, made a detailed exposition of the state of the French nation.[27]

If we give credit to him, it was not necessary to have recourse to any new impositions whatsoever, to put the receipts of France on a balance with its expenses. He stated the permanent charges of all descriptions, including the interest of a new loan of four hundred millions, at 531,444,000 livres; the fixed revenue at 475,294,000, making the deficiency 56,150,000, or short of £2,200,000 sterling. But to balance it, he brought forward savings and improvements of revenue (considered as entirely certain) to rather more than the amount of that deficiency; and he concludes with these emphatical words (p. 39), "Quel pays, Messieurs, que celui, où, *sans impôts* et avec de simples objets *inapperçus,* on peut faire disparoître un deficit qui a fait tant de bruit en Europe." As to the reimbursement, the sinking of debt, and the other great objects of public credit and political arrangement indicated in Mons. Necker's speech, no doubt could be entertained, but that a very moderate and proportioned assessment on the citizens without distinction would have provided for all of them to the fullest extent of their demand.

If this representation of Mons. Necker was false, then the Assembly are in the highest degree culpable for having forced the king to accept as his minister, and since the king's deposition, for having employed, as *their* minister, a man who had been capable of abusing so notoriously the confidence of his master and their own; in a matter too of the highest moment, and directly appertaining to his particular office. But if the representation was exact (as having always, along with you, conceived a high degree of respect for M. Necker, I make no doubt it was), then what can be said in favour of those, who, instead of moderate, reasonable, and general contribution, have in cold blood, and impelled by no necessity, had recourse to a partial and cruel confiscation?

Was that contribution refused on a pretext of privilege, either on the part of the clergy, or on that of the nobility? No, certainly. As to the clergy, they even ran before the wishes of the third order. Previous to the meeting of the states, they had in all their instructions expressly directed their deputies to renounce every immunity, which put them upon a footing distinct from the condition of their fellow-subjects. In this renunciation the clergy were even more explicit than the nobility.

But let us suppose that the deficiency had remained at the fifty-six millions (or £.2,200,000 sterling), as at first stated by M. Necker. Let us allow that all the resources he opposed to that deficiency were impudent and groundless fictions; and that the Assembly (or their lords of articles[28] at the Jacobins) were from thence justified in laying the whole burthen of that deficiency on the clergy—yet allowing all this, a necessity of £2,200,000 sterling will not support a confiscation to the amount of five millions. The imposition of £2,200,000 on the clergy, as partial, would have been oppressive and unjust, but it would not have been altogether ruinous to those on whom it was imposed; and therefore it would not have answered the real purpose of the managers.

Perhaps persons unacquainted with the state of France, on hearing the clergy and the noblesse were privileged in point of taxation, may be led to imagine, that, previous to the Revolution, these bodies had contributed nothing to the state. This is a great mistake. They certainly did not contribute equally with each other, nor either of them equally with the commons. They both however contributed largely. Neither nobility nor clergy enjoyed any exemption from the excise on consumable commodities, from duties of custom, or from any of the other numerous *indirect* impositions, which in France, as well as here, make so very large a proportion of all payments to the public. The noblesse paid the capitation. They paid also a land-tax, called the twentieth penny, to the height sometimes of three, sometimes of four, shillings in the pound; both of them *direct* impositions of no light nature, and no trivial produce. The clergy of the provinces annexed by conquest to France (which in extent make about an eighth part of the whole, but in wealth a much larger proportion) paid likewise to the capitation and the twentieth penny, at the rate paid by the nobility. The clergy in the old provinces did not pay the capitation; but they had redeemed themselves at the expense of about 24 millions, or a little more than a million sterling. They were exempted from the twentieths: but then they made free gifts; they contracted debts for the state; and they were subject to some other charges, the whole computed at about a thirteenth part of their clear income. They ought to have paid annually about forty thousand pounds more, to put them on a par with the contribution of the nobility.

When the terrors of this tremendous proscription hung over the clergy, they made an offer of a contribution, through the archbishop of Aix, which, for its extravagance, ought not to have been accepted. But it was evidently and obviously more advantageous to the public creditor, than anything which could rationally be promised by the confiscation. Why was it not accepted? The reason is plain. There was no desire that the church should be brought to serve the state. The service of the state was made a pretext to destroy the church. In their way to the destruction of the church they would not scruple to destroy their country: and they have destroyed it. One great end in the project would have been defeated, if the plan of extortion had been adopted in lieu of the scheme of confiscation. The new landed interest connected with the new republic, and connected with it for its very being, could not have been created. This was among the reasons why that extravagant ransom was not accepted.

The madness of the project of confiscation, on the plan that was first pretended, soon became apparent. To bring this unwieldy mass of landed property, enlarged by the confiscation of all the vast landed domain of the crown, at once into market, was obviously to defeat the profits proposed by the confiscation, by depreciating the value of those lands, and indeed of all the landed estates throughout France. Such a sudden diversion of all its circulating money from trade to land, must be an additional mischief. What step was taken? Did the Assembly, on becoming sensible of the inevitable ill effects of their projected sale, revert to the offers of the clergy? No distress could oblige them to travel in a course which was disgraced by any appearance of justice. Giving over all hopes from a general immediate sale, another project seems to have succeeded. They proposed to take stock in exchange for the church lands. In that project great difficulties arose in equalizing the objects to be exchanged. Other obstacles also presented themselves, which threw them back again upon some project of sale. The municipalities had taken an alarm. They would not hear of transferring the whole plunder of the kingdom to the stockholders in Paris. Many of those municipalities had been (upon system) reduced to the most deplorable indigence. Money was nowhere to be seen. They were therefore led to the point that was so ardently desired. They panted for a currency of any kind which might revive their perishing industry. The municipalities were then to be admitted to a share in the spoil, which evidently rendered the first scheme (if ever it had been seriously entertained) altogether impracticable. Public exigencies pressed upon all sides. The minister of finance reiterated his call for supply with a most urgent, anxious, and boding voice. Thus pressed on all sides, instead of the first plan of converting their bankers into bishops and abbots, instead of paying the old debt, they contracted a new debt, at 3 per cent., creating a new paper currency, founded on an eventual sale of the church lands. They issued this paper currency to satisfy in the first instance chiefly the demands made upon them by the *bank of discount,* the great machine, or paper-mill, of their fictitious wealth.

The spoil of the church was now become the only resource of all their operations in finance, the vital principle of all their politics, the sole security for the existence of their power. It was necessary by all, even the most violent means, to put every individual on the same bottom, and to bind the nation in one guilty interest to uphold this act, and the authority of those by whom it was done. In order to force the most reluctant into a participation of their pillage, they rendered their paper circulation compulsory in all payments. Those who consider the general tendency of their schemes to this one object as a centre, and a centre from which afterwards all their measures radiate, will not think that I dwell too long upon this part of the proceedings of the National Assembly.

To cut off all appearance of connexion between the crown and public justice, and to bring the whole under implicit obedience to the dictators in Paris, the old independent judicature of the parliaments, with all its merits, and all its faults, was wholly abolished. Whilst the parliaments existed, it was evident that the people might some time or other come to resort to them, and rally under the standard of their ancient laws. It became however a matter of consideration, that the magistrates and officers, in the courts now abolished, *had purchased their places* at a very high rate, for which, as well as for the duty they performed, they received but a very low return of interest. Simple confiscation is a boon only for the clergy—to the lawyers some appearances of equity are to be observed; and they are to receive compensation to an immense amount. Their compensation becomes part of the national debt, for the liquidation of which there is the one exhaustless fund. The lawyers are to obtain their compensation in the new church paper, which is to march with the new principles of judicature and legislature. The dismissed magistrates are to take their share of martyrdom with the ecclesiastics, or to receive their own property from such a fund, and in such a manner, as all those, who have been seasoned with the ancient principles of jurisprudence, and had been the sworn guardians of property, must look upon with horror. Even the clergy are to receive their miserable allowance out of the depreciated paper, which is stamped with the indelible character of sacrilege, and with the symbols of their own ruin, or they must starve. So violent an outrage upon credit, property, and liberty, as this compulsory paper currency, has seldom been exhibited by the alliance of bankruptcy and tyranny, at any time, or in any nation.

In the course of all these operations, at length comes out the grand *arcanum;* that in reality, and in a fair sense, the lands of the church (so far as anything certain can be gathered from their proceedings) are not to be sold at all. By the late resolutions of the National Assembly, they are indeed to be delivered to the highest bidder. But it is to be observed, that *a certain portion only of the purchase money is to be laid down.* A period of twelve years is to be given for the payment of the rest. The philosophic purchasers are therefore, on payment of a sort of fine, to be put instantly into possession of the estate. It becomes in some respects a sort of gift to them; to be held on the feudal tenure of zeal to the new establishment. This project is evidently to let in a body of purchasers without money. The consequence will be, that these purchasers, or rather grantees, will pay, not only from the rents as they accrue, which might as well be received by the state, but from the spoil of the materials of buildings, from waste in woods, and from whatever money, by hands habituated to the gripings of usury, they can wring from the miserable peasant. He is to be delivered over to the mercenary and arbitrary discretion of men, who will be stimulated to every species of extortion by the growing demands on the growing profits of an estate held under the precarious settlement of a new political system.

When all the frauds, impostures, violences, rapines, burnings, murders, confiscations, compulsory paper currencies, and every description of tyranny and cruelty employed to bring about and to uphold this Revolution, have their natural effect, that is, to shock the moral sentiments of all virtuous and sober minds, the abettors of this philosophic system immediately strain their throats in a declamation against the old monarchical government of France. When they have rendered that deposed power sufficiently black, they then proceed in argument, as if all those who disapprove of their new abuses must of course be partisans of the old; that those who reprobate their crude and violent schemes of liberty ought to be treated as advocates for servitude. I admit that their necessities do compel them to this base and contemptible fraud. Nothing can reconcile men to their proceedings and projects, but the supposition that there is no third option between them and some tyranny as odious as can be furnished by the records of history, or by the invention of poets. This prattling of theirs hardly deserves the name of sophistry. It is nothing but plain impudence. Have these gentlemen never heard, in the whole circle of the worlds of theory and practice, of anything between the despotism of the monarch and the despotism of the multitude? Have they never heard of a monarchy directed by laws, controlled and balanced by the great hereditary wealth and hereditary dignity of a nation; and both again controlled by a judicious check from the reason and feeling of the people at large, acting by a suitable and permanent organ? Is it then impossible that a man may be found, who, without criminal ill intention, or pitiable absurdity, shall prefer such a mixed and tempered government to either of the extremes; and who may repute that nation to be destitute of all wisdom and of all virtue, which, having in its choice to obtain such a government with ease, *or rather to confirm it when actually possessed,* thought proper to commit a thousand crimes, and to subject their country to a thousand evils, in order to avoid it? Is it then a truth so universally acknowledged, that a pure democracy is the only tolerable form into which human society can be thrown, that a man is not permitted to hesitate about its merits, without the suspicion of being a friend to tyranny, that is, of being a foe to mankind?

I do not know under what description to class the present ruling authority in France. It affects to be a pure democracy, though I think it in a direct train of becoming shortly a mischievous and ignoble oligarchy. But for the present I admit it to be a contrivance of the nature and effect of what it pretends to. I reprobate no form of government merely upon abstract principles. There may be situations in which the purely democratic form will become necessary. There may be some (very few, and very particularly circumstanced) where it would be clearly desirable. This I do not take to be the case of France, or of any other great country. Until now, we have seen no examples of considerable democracies. The ancients were better acquainted with them. Not being wholly unread in the authors, who had seen the most of those constitutions, and who best understood them, I cannot help concurring with their opinion, that an absolute democracy, no more than absolute monarchy, is to be reckoned among the legitimate forms of government. They think it rather the corruption and degeneracy, than the sound constitution of a republic. If I recollect rightly, Aristotle observes, that a democracy has many striking points of resemblance with a tyranny.[29] Of this I am certain, that in a democracy, the majority of the citizens is capable of exercising the most cruel oppressions upon the minority, whenever strong divisions prevail in that kind of polity, as they often must; and that oppression of the minority will extend to far greater numbers, and will be carried on with much greater fury, than can almost ever be apprehended from the dominion of a single sceptre. In such a popular persecution, individual sufferers are in a much more deplorable condition than in any other. Under a cruel prince they have the balmy compassion of mankind to assuage the smart of their wounds; they have the plaudits of the people to animate their generous constancy under their sufferings: but those who are subjected to wrong under multitudes, are deprived of all external consolation. They seem deserted by mankind, overpowered by a conspiracy of their whole species.

But admitting democracy not to have that inevitable tendency to party tyranny, which I suppose it to have, and admitting it to possess as much good in it when unmixed, as I am sure it possesses when compounded with other forms; does monarchy, on its part, contain nothing at all to recommend it? I do not often quote Bolingbroke, nor have his works in general left any permanent impression on my mind. He is a presumptuous and a superficial writer. But he has one observation, which, in my opinion, is not without depth and solidity. He says, that he prefers a monarchy to other governments; because you can better ingraft any description of republic on a monarchy than anything of monarchy upon the republican forms. I think him perfectly in the right. The fact is so historically; and it agrees well with the speculation.

I know how easy a topic it is to dwell on the faults of departed greatness. By a revolution in the state, the fawning sycophant of yesterday is converted into the austere critic of the present hour. But steady, independent minds, when they have an object of so serious a concern to mankind as government under their contemplation, will disdain to assume the part of satirists and declaimers. They will judge of human institutions as they do of human characters. They will sort out the good from the evil, which is mixed in mortal institutions, as it is in mortal men.

Your government in France, though usually, and I think justly, reputed the best of the unqualified or ill-qualified monarchies, was still full of abuses. These abuses accumulated in a length of time, as they must accumulate in every monarchy not under the constant inspection of a popular representative. I am a stranger to the faults and defects of the subverted government of France; and I think I am not inclined by nature or policy to make a panegyric upon anything which is a just and natural object of censure. But the question is not now of the vices of that monarchy, but of its existence. Is it then true, that the French government was such as to be incapable or undeserving of reform; so that it was of absolute necessity that the whole fabric should be at once pulled down, and the area cleared for the erection of a theoretic, experimental edifice in its place? All of France was of a different opinion in the beginning of the year 1789. The instructions to the representatives to the states-general, from every district in that kingdom, were filled with projects for the reformation of that government, without the remotest suggestion of a design to destroy it. Had such a design been then even insinuated, I believe there would have been but one voice, and that voice for rejecting it with scorn and horror. Men have been sometimes led by degrees, sometimes hurried, into things of which, if they could have seen the whole together, they never would have permitted the most remote approach. When those instructions were given, there was no question but that abuses existed, and that they demanded a reform; or is there now. In the interval between the instructions and the Revolution, things changed their shape; and, in consequence of that change, the true question at present is, Whether those who would have reformed, or those who have destroyed, are in the right?

To hear some men speak of the late monarchy of France, you would imagine that they were talking of Persia bleeding under the ferocious sword of Tahmas Kouli Khân; or at least describing the barbarous anarchic despotism of Turkey, where the finest countries in the most genial climates in the world are wasted by peace more than any countries have been worried by war; where arts are unknown, where manufactures languish, where science is extinguished, where agriculture decays, where the human race itself melts away and perishes under the eye of the observer. Was this the case of France? I have no way of determining the question but by a reference to facts. Facts do not support this resemblance. Along with much evil, there is some good in monarchy itself; and some corrective to its evil from religion, from laws, from manners, from opinions, the French monarchy must have received; which rendered it (though by no means a free, and therefore by no means a good, constitution) a despotism rather in appearance than in reality.

Among the standards upon which the effects of government on any country are to be estimated, I must consider the state of its population as not the least certain. No country in which population flourishes, and is in progressive improvement, can be under a *very* mischievous government. About sixty years ago, the Intendants of the generalities of France made, with other matters, a report of the population of their several districts. I have not the books, which are very voluminous, by me, nor do I know where to procure them (I am obliged to speak by memory, and therefore the less positively), but I think the population of France was by them, even at that period, estimated at twenty-two millions of souls. At the end of the last century it had been generally calculated at eighteen. On either of these estimations, France was not ill peopled. M. Necker, who is an authority for his own time at least equal to the Intendants for theirs, reckons, and upon apparently sure principles, the people of France, in the year 1780, at twenty-four millions six hundred and seventy thousand. But was this the probable ultimate term under the old establishment? Dr. Price is of opinion, that the growth of population in France was by no means at its *acmé* in that year. I certainly defer to Dr. Price's authority a good deal more in these speculations, than I do in his general politics. This gentleman, taking ground on M. Necker's data, is very confident that since the period of that minister's calculation, the French population has increased rapidly; so rapidly, that in the year 1789 he will not consent to rate the people of that kingdom at a lower number than thirty millions. After abating much (and much I think ought to be abated) from the sanguine calculation of Dr. Price, I have no doubt that the population of France did increase considerably during this later period: but supposing that it increased to nothing more than will be sufficient to complete the twenty-four millions six hundred and seventy thousand to twenty-five millions, still a population of twenty-five millions, and that in an increasing progress, on a space of about twenty-seven thousand square leagues, is immense. It is, for instance, a good deal more than the proportionable population of this island, or even than that of England, the best peopled part of the united kingdom.

It is not universally true, that France is a fertile country. Considerable tracts of it are barren, and labour under other natural disadvantages. In the portions of that territory where things are more favourable, as far as I am able to discover, the numbers of the people correspond to the indulgence of nature.[30] The Generality of Lisle (this I admit is the strongest example) upon an extent of four hundred and four leagues and a half, about ten years ago, contained seven hundred and thirty-four thousand six hundred souls, which is one thousand seven hundred and seventy-two inhabitants to each square league. The middle term for the rest of France is about nine hundred inhabitants to the same admeasurement.

I do not attribute this population to the deposed government; because I do not like to compliment the contrivances of men with what is due in a great degree to the bounty of Providence. But that decried government could not have obstructed, most probably it favoured, the operation of those causes (whatever they were), whether of nature in the soil, or habits of industry among the people, which has produced so large a number of the species throughout that whole kingdom, and exhibited in some particular places such prodigies of population. I never will suppose that fabric of a state to be the worst of all political institutions, which, by experience, is found to contain a principle favourable (however latent it may be) to the increase of mankind.

The wealth of a country is another, and no contemptible standard, by which we may judge whether, on the whole, a government be protecting or destructive. France far exceeds England in the multitude of her people; but I apprehend that her comparative wealth is much inferior to ours; that it is not so equal in the distribution, nor so ready in the circulation. I believe the difference in the form of the two governments to be amongst the causes of this advantage on the side of England. I speak of England, not of the whole British dominions; which, if compared with those of France, will, in some degree, weaken the comparative rate of wealth upon our side. But that wealth, which will not endure a comparison with the riches of England, may constitute a very respectable degree of opulence. M. Necker's book, published in 1785, contains an accurate and interesting collection of facts relative to public economy and to political arithmetic; and his speculations on the subject are in general wise and liberal. In that work he gives an idea of the state of France, very remote from the portrait of a country whose government was a perfect grievance, an absolute evil, admitting no cure but through the violent and uncertain remedy of a total revolution. He affirms, that from the year 1726 to the year 1784, there was coined at the mint of France, in the species of gold and silver, to the amount of about one hundred millions of pounds sterling.[31]

It is impossible that M. Necker should be mistaken in the amount of bullion which has been coined in the mint. It is a matter of official record. The reasonings of this able financer, concerning the quantity of gold and silver which remained for circulation, when he wrote in 1785, that is, about four years before the deposition and imprisonment of the French king, are not of equal certainty; but they are laid on grounds so apparently solid, that it is not easy to refuse a considerable degree of assent to his calculation. He calculates the *numeraire,* or what we call *specie,* then actually existing in France, at about eighty-eight millions of the same English money. A great accumulation of wealth for one country, large as that country is! M. Necker was so far from considering this influx of wealth as likely to cease, when he wrote in 1785, that he presumes upon a future annual increase of two per cent. upon the money brought into France during the periods from which he computed.

Some adequate cause must have originally introduced all the money coined at its mint into that kingdom; and some cause as operative must have kept at home, or returned into its bosom, such a vast flood of treasure as M. Necker calculates to remain for domestic circulation. Suppose any reasonable deductions from M. Necker's computation, the remainder must still amount to an immense sum. Causes thus powerful to acquire, and to retain, cannot be found in discouraged industry, insecure property, and a positively destructive government. Indeed, when I consider the face of the kingdom of France; the multitude and opulence of her cities; the useful magnificence of her spacious high roads and bridges; the opportunity of her artificial canals and navigations opening the conveniences of maritime communication through a solid continent of so immense an extent; when I turn my eyes to the stupendous works of her ports and harbours, and to her whole naval apparatus, whether for war or trade; when I bring before my view the number of her fortifications, constructed with so bold and masterly a skill, and made and maintained at so prodigious a charge, presenting an armed front and impenetrable barrier to her enemies upon every side; when I recollect how very small a part of that extensive region is without cultivation, and to what complete perfection the culture of many of the best productions of the earth have been brought in France; when I reflect on the excellence of her manufactures and fabrics, second to none but ours, and in some particulars not second; when I contemplate the grand foundations of charity, public and private; when I survey the state of all the arts that beautify and polish life; when I reckon the men she has bred for extending her fame in war, her able statesmen, the multitude of her profound lawyers and theologians, her philosophers, her critics, her historians and antiquaries, her poets and her orators, sacred and profane; I behold in all this something which awes and commands the imagination, which checks the mind on the brink of precipitate and indiscriminate censure, and which demands that we should very seriously examine, what and how great are the latent vices that could authorize us at once to level so spacious a fabric with the ground. I do not recognize in this view of things, the despotism of Turkey. Nor do I discern the character of a government, that has been, on the whole, so oppressive, or so corrupt, or so negligent, as to be utterly unfit *for all reformation.* I must think such a government well deserved to have its excellencies heightened, its faults corrected, and its capacities improved into a British constitution.

Whoever has examined into the proceedings of that deposed government for several years back, cannot fail to have observed, amidst the inconstancy and fluctuation natural to courts, an earnest endeavour towards the prosperity and improvement of the country; he must admit, that it had long been employed, in some instances wholly to remove, in many considerably to correct, the abusive practices and usages that had prevailed in the state; and that even the unlimited power of the sovereign over the persons of his subjects, inconsistent, as undoubtedly it was, with law and liberty, had yet been every day growing more mitigated in the exercise. So far from refusing itself to reformation, that government was open, with a censurable degree of facility, to all sorts of projects and projectors on the subject. Rather too much countenance was given to the spirit of innovation, which soon was turned against those who fostered it, and ended in their ruin. It is but cold, and no very flattering, justice to that fallen monarchy, to say, that, for many years, it trespassed more by levity and want of judgment in several of its schemes, than from any defect in diligence or in public spirit. To compare the government of France for the last fifteen or sixteen years with wise and well-constituted establishments during that, or during any period, is not to act with fairness. But if in point of prodigality in the expenditure of money, or in point of rigour in the exercise of power, it be compared with any of the former reigns, I believe candid judges will give little credit to the good intentions of those who dwell perpetually on the donations to favourites, or on the expenses of the court, or on the horrors of the Bastile, in the reign of Louis the Sixteenth.[32]

Whether the system, if it deserves such a name, now built on the ruins of that ancient monarchy, will be able to give a better account of the population and wealth of the country, which it has taken under its care, is a matter very doubtful. Instead of improving by the change, I apprehend that a long series of years must be told, before it can recover in any degree the effects of this philosophic revolution, and before the nation can be replaced on its former footing. If Dr. Price should think fit, a few years hence, to favour us with an estimate of the population of France, he will hardly be able to make up his tale of thirty millions of souls, as computed in 1789, or the Assembly's computation of twenty-six millions of that year; or even M. Necker's twenty-five millions in 1780. I hear that there are considerable emigrations from France; and that many, quitting that voluptuous climate, and that seductive *Circean* liberty, have taken refuge in the frozen regions, and under the British despotism, of Canada.

In the present disappearance of coin, no person could think it the same country, in which the present minister of the finances has been able to discover fourscore millions sterling in specie. From its general aspect one would conclude that it had been for some time past under the special direction of the learned academicians of Laputa and Balnibarbi.[33] Already the population of Paris has so declined, that M. Necker stated to the National Assembly the provision to be made for its subsistence at a fifth less than what had formerly been found requisite.[34] It is said (and I have never heard it contradicted) that a hundred thousand people are out of employment in that city, though it is become the seat of the imprisoned court and National Assembly. Nothing, I am credibly informed, can exceed the shocking and disgusting spectacle of mendicancy displayed in that capital. Indeed the votes of the National Assembly leave no doubt of the fact. They have lately appointed a standing committee of mendicancy. They are contriving at once a vigorous police on this subject, and, for the first time, the imposition of a tax to maintain the poor, for whose present relief great sums appear on the face of the public accounts of the year.[35] In the mean time the leaders of the legislative clubs and coffeehouses are intoxicated with admiration at their own wisdom and ability. They speak with the most sovereign contempt of the rest of the world. They tell the people, to comfort them in the rags with which they have clothed them, that they are a nation of philosophers; and, sometimes, by all the arts of quackish parade, by show, tumult, and bustle, sometimes by the alarms of plots and invasions, they attempt to drown the cries of indigence, and divert the eyes of the observer from the ruin and wretchedness of the state. A brave people will certainly prefer liberty accompanied with a virtuous poverty to a depraved and wealthy servitude. But before the price of comfort and opulence is paid, one ought to be pretty sure it is real liberty which is purchased, and that she is to be purchased at no other price. I shall always, however, consider that liberty as very equivocal in her appearance, which has not wisdom and justice for her companions; and does not lead prosperity and plenty in her train.

When I sent this book to the press, I entertained some doubt concerning the nature and extent of the last article in the above accounts, which, is only under a general head, without any detail. Since then I have seen M. de Calonne's work. I must think it a great loss to me that I had not that advantage earlier. M. de Calonne thinks this article to be on account of general subsistence; but as he is not able to comprehend how so great a loss as upwards of £1,661,000 sterling could be sustained on the difference between the price and the sale of grain, he seems to attribute this enormous head of charge to secret expenses of the Revolution. I cannot say anything positively on that subject. The reader is capable of judging, by the aggregate of these immense charges, on the state and condition of France; and the system of public economy adopted in that nation. These articles of account produced no inquiry or discussion in the National Assembly.

The advocates for this Revolution, not satisfied with exaggerating the vices of their ancient government, strike at the fame of their country itself, by painting almost all that could have attracted the attention of strangers, I mean their nobility and their clergy, as objects of horror. If this were only a libel, there had not been much in it. But it has practical consequences. Had your nobility and gentry, who formed the great body of your landed men, and the whole of your military officers, resembled those of Germany, at the period when the Hanse-towns were necessitated to confederate against the nobles in defence of their property—had they been like the *Orsini* and *Vitelli* in Italy, who used to sally from their fortified dens to rob the trader and traveller—had they been such as the *Mamelukes* in Egypt, or the *Nayres* on the coast of Malabar, I do admit, that too critical an inquiry might not be advisable into the means of freeing the world from such a nuisance. The statues of Equity and Mercy might be veiled for a moment. The tenderest minds, confounded with the dreadful exigence in which morality submits to the suspension of its own rules in favour of its own principles, might turn aside whilst fraud and violence were accomplishing the destruction of a pretended nobility which disgraced, whilst it persecuted, human nature. The persons most abhorrent from blood, and treason, and arbitrary confiscation, might remain silent spectators of this civil war between the vices.

But did the privileged nobility who met under the king's precept at Versailles, in 1789, or their constituents, deserve to be looked on as the *Nayres* or *Mamelukes* of this age, or as the *Orsini* and *Vitelli* of ancient times? If I had then asked the question I should have passed for a madman. What have they since done that they were to be driven into exile, that their persons should be hunted about, mangled, and tortured, their families dispersed, their houses laid in ashes, and that their order should be abolished, and the memory of it, if possible, extinguished, by ordaining them to change the very names by which they were usually known? Read their instructions to their representatives. They breathe the spirit of liberty as warmly, and they recommend reformation as strongly, as any other order. Their privileges relative to contribution were voluntarily surrendered; as the king, from the beginning, surrendered all pretence to a right of taxation. Upon a free constitution there was but one opinion in France. The absolute monarchy was at an end. It breathed its last, without a groan, without struggle, without convulsion. All the struggle, all the dissension, arose afterwards upon the preference of a despotic democracy to a government of reciprocal control. The triumph of the victorious party was over the principles of a British constitution.

I have observed the affectation, which for many years past, has prevailed in Paris even to a degree perfectly childish, of idolizing the memory of your Henry the Fourth. If anything could put one out of humour with that ornament to the kingly character, it would be this overdone style of insidious panegyric. The persons who have worked this engine the most busily, are those who have ended their panegyrics in dethroning his successor and descendant; a man, as good-natured, at the least, as Henry the Fourth; altogether as fond of his people; and who has done infinitely more to correct the ancient vices of the state than that great monarch did, or we are sure he ever meant to do. Well it is for his panegyrists that they have not him to deal with. For Henry of Navarre was a resolute, active, and politic prince. He possessed indeed great humanity and mildness; but a humanity and mildness that never stood in the way of his interests. He never sought to be loved without putting himself first in a condition to be feared. He used soft language with determined conduct. He asserted and maintained his authority in the gross, and distributed his acts of concession only in the detail. He spent the income of his prerogative nobly; but he took care not to break in upon the capital; never abandoning for a moment any of the claims which he made under the fundamental laws, nor sparing to shed the blood of those who opposed him, often in the field, sometimes upon the scaffold. Because he knew how to make his virtues respected by the ungrateful, he has merited the praises of those, whom, if they had lived in his time, he would have shut up in the Bastile, and brought to punishment along with the regicides whom he hanged after he had famished Paris into a surrender.

If these panegyrists are in earnest in their admiration of Henry the Fourth, they must remember, that they cannot think more highly of him than he did of the noblesse of France; whose virtue, honour, courage, patriotism, and loyalty were his constant theme.

But the nobility of France are degenerated since the days of Henry the Fourth. This is possible. But it is more than I can believe to be true in any great degree. I do not pretend to know France as correctly as some others; but I have endeavoured through my whole life to make myself acquainted with human nature; otherwise I should be unfit to take even my humble part in the service of mankind. In that study I could not pass by a vast portion of our nature, as it appeared modified in a country but twenty-four miles from the shore of this island. On my best observation, compared with my best inquiries, I found your nobility for the greater part composed of men of high spirit, and of a delicate sense of honour, both with regard to themselves individually, and with regard to their whole corps, over whom they kept, beyond what is common in other countries, a censorial eye. They were tolerably well bred; very officious, humane, and hospitable; in their conversation frank and open; with a good military tone; and reasonably tinctured with literature, particularly of the authors in their own language. Many had pretensions far above this description. I speak of those who were generally met with.

As to their behaviour to the inferior classes, they appeared to me to comport themselves towards them with good-nature, and with something more nearly approaching to familiarity, than is generally practised with us in the intercourse between the higher and lower ranks of life. To strike any person, even in the most abject condition, was a thing in a manner unknown, and would be highly disgraceful. Instances of other ill-treatment of the humble part of the community were rare: and as to attacks made upon the property or the personal liberty of the commons, I never heard of any whatsoever from *them;* nor, whilst the laws were in vigour under the ancient government, would such tyranny in subjects have been permitted. As men of landed estates, I had no fault to find with their conduct, though much to reprehend, and much to wish changed, in many of the old tenures. Where the letting of their land was by rent, I could not discover that their agreements with their farmers were oppressive; nor when they were in partnership with the farmer, as often was the case, have I heard that they had taken the lion's share. The proportions seemed not inequitable. They might be exceptions; but certainly they were exceptions only. I have no reason to believe that in these respects landed noblesse of France were worse than the landed gentry of this country; certainly in no respect more vexatious than the landholders, not noble, of their own nation. In cities the nobility had no manner of power; in the country very little. You know, sir, that much of the civil government, and the police in the most essential parts, was not in the hands of that nobility which presents itself first to our consideration. The revenue, the system and collection of which were the most grievous parts of the French government, was not administered by the men of the sword; nor were they answerable for the vices of its principle, or the vexations, where any such existed, in its management.

Denying, as I am well warranted to do, that the nobility had any considerable share in the oppression of the people, in cases in which real oppression existed, I am ready to admit that they were not without considerable faults and errors. A foolish imitation of the worst part of the manners of England, which impaired their natural character, without substituting in its place what perhaps they meant to copy, has certaintly rendered them worse than formerly they were. Habitual dissoluteness of manners continued beyond the pardonable period of life, was more common amongst them than it is with us; and it reigned with the less hope of remedy, though possibly with something of less mischief, by being covered with more exterior decorum. They countenanced too much that licentious philosophy which has helped to bring on their ruin. There was another error amongst them more fatal. Those of the commons, who approached to or exceed many of the nobility in point of wealth, were not fully admitted to the rank and estimation which wealth, in reason and good policy, ought to bestow in every country; though I think not equally with that of other nobility. The two kinds of aristocracy were too punctiliously kept asunder; less so, however, than in Germany and some other nations.

This separation, as I have already taken the liberty of suggesting to you, I conceive to be one principal cause of the destruction of the old nobility. The military, particularly, was too exclusively reserved for men of family. But, after all, this was an error of opinion, which a conflicting opinion would have rectified. A permanent assembly, in which the commons had their share of power, would soon abolish whatever was too invidious and insulting in these distinctions; and even the faults in the morals of the nobility would have been probably corrected, by the greater varieties of occupation and pursuit to which a constitution by orders would have given rise.

All this violent cry against the nobility I take to be a mere work of art. To be honoured and even privileged by the laws, opinions, and inveterate usages of our country, growing out of the prejudice of ages, has nothing to provoke horror and indignation in any man. Even to be too tenacious of those privileges is not absolutely a crime. The strong struggle in every individual to preserve possession of what he has found to belong to him. and to distinguish him, is one of the securities against injustice and despotism implanted in our nature. It operates as an instinct to secure property, and to preserve communities in a settled state. What is there to shock in this? Nobility is a graceful ornament to the civil order. It is the Corinthian capital of polished society. *Omnes boni nobilitati semper favemus,* was the saying of a wise and good man. It is indeed one sign of a liberal and benevolent mind to incline to it with some sort of partial propensity. He feels no ennobling principle in his own heart, who wishes to level all the artificial institutions which have been adopted for giving a body to opinion, and permanence to fugitive esteem. It is a sour, malignant, envious disposition, without taste for the reality, or for any image or representation of virtue, that sees with joy the unmerited fall of what had long flourished in splendour and in honour. I do not like to see anything destroyed; any void produced in society; any ruin on the face of the land. It was therefore with no disappointment or dissatisfaction that my inquiries and observations did not present to me any incorrigible vices in the noblesse of France, or any abuse which could not be removed by a reform very short of abolition. Your noblesse did not deserve punishment: but to degrade is to punish.

It was with the same satisfaction I found that the result of my inquiry concerning your clergy was not dissimilar. It is no soothing news to my ears, that great bodies of men are incurably corrupt. It is not with much credulity I listen to any, when they speak evil of those whom they are going to plunder. I rather suspect that vices are feigned or exaggerated, when profit is looked for in their punishment. An enemy is a bad witness; a robber is a worse. Vices and abuses there were undoubtedly in that order, and must be. It was an old establishment, and not frequently revised. But I saw no crimes in the individuals that merited confiscation of their substance, nor those cruel insults and degradations, and that unnatural persecution, which have been substituted in the place of meliorating regulation.

If there had been any just cause for this new religious persecution, the atheistic libellers, who act as trumpeters to animate the populace to plunder, do not love any body so much as not to dwell with complacence on the vices of the existing clergy. This they have not done. They find themselves obliged to rake into the histories of former ages (which they have ransacked with a malignant and profligate industry) for every instance of oppression and persecution which has been made by that body or in its favour, in order to justify, upon very iniquitous, because very illogical, principles of retaliation, their own persecutions, and their own cruelties. After destroying all other genealogies and family distinctions, they invent a sort of pedigree of crimes. It is not very just to chastise men for the offenses of their natural ancestors: but to take the fiction of ancestry in a corporate succession, as a ground for punishing men who have no relation to guilty acts, except in names and general descriptions, is a sort of refinement in injustice belonging to the philosophy of this enlightened age. The Assembly punishes men, many, if not most, of whom abhor the violent conduct of ecclesiastics in former times as much as their present persecutors can do, and who would be as loud and as strong in the expression of that sense, if they were not well aware of the purposes for which all this declamation is employed.

Corporate bodies are immortal for the good of the members, but not for their punishment. Nations themselves are such corporations.

As well might we in England think of waging inexpiable war upon all Frenchmen for the evils which they have brought upon us in the several periods of our mutual hostilities. You might, on your part, think yourselves justified in falling upon all Englishmen on account of the unparalleled calamities brought on the people of France by the unjust invasions of our Henries and our Edwards. Indeed we should be mutually justified in this exterminatory war upon each other, full as much as you are in the unprovoked persecution of your present countrymen, on account of the conduct of men of the same name in other times.

We do not draw the moral lessons we might from history. On the contrary, without care it may be used to vitiate our minds and to destroy our happiness. In history a great volume is unrolled for our instruction, drawing the materials of future wisdom from the past errors and infirmities of mankind. It may, in the perversion, serve for a magazine, furnishing offensive and defensive weapons for parties in church and state, and supplying the means of keeping alive, or reviving, dissensions and animosities, and adding fuel to civil fury. History consists, for the greater part, of the miseries brought upon the world by pride, ambition, avarice, revenge, lust, sedition, hypocrisy, ungoverned zeal, and all the train of disorderly appetites, which shake the public with the same "troublous storms that toss / The private state, and render life unsweet."

These vices are the *causes* of those storms. Religion, morals, laws, prerogatives, privileges, liberties, rights of men, are the *pretexts*. The pretexts are always found in some specious appearance of a real good. You would not secure men from tyranny and sedition, by rooting out of the mind the principles to which these fraudulent pretexts apply? If you did, you would root out everything that is valuable in the human breast. As these are the pretexts, so the ordinary actors and instruments in great public evils are kings, priests, magistrates, senates, parliaments, national assemblies, judges, and captains. You would not cure the evil by resolving, that there should be no more monarchs, nor ministers of state, nor of the gospel; no interpreters of law; no general officers; no public councils. You might change the names. The things in some shape must remain. A certain *quantum* of power must always exist in the community, in some hands, and under some appellation. Wise men will apply their remedies to vices, not to names; to the causes of evil which are permanent, not to the occasional organs by which they act, and the transitory modes in which they appear. Otherwise you will be wise historically, a fool in practice. Seldom have two ages the same fashion in their pretexts and the same modes of mischief. Wickedness is a little more inventive. Whilst you are discussing fashion, the fashion is gone by. The very same vice assumes a new body. The spirit transmigrates; and far from losing its principle of life by the change of its appearance, it is renovated in its new organs with a fresh vigour of a juvenile activity. It walks abroad, it continues its ravages, whilst you are gibbeting the carcase, or demolishing the tomb. You are terrifying yourselves with ghosts and apparitions, whilst your house is the haunt of robbers. It is thus with all those, who, attending only to the shell and husk of history, think they are waging war with intolerance, pride, and cruelty, whilst, under colour of abhorring the ill principles of antiquated parties, they are authorizing and feeding the same odious vices in different factions, and perhaps in worse.

Your citizens of Paris formerly had lent themselves as the ready instruments to slaughter the followers of Calvin, at the infamous massacre of St. Bartholomew. What should we say to those who could think of retaliating on the Parisians of this day the abominations and horrors of that time? They are indeed brought to abhor *that* massacre. Ferocious as they are, it is not difficult to make them dislike it; because the politicians and fashionable teachers have no interest in giving their passions exactly the same direction. Still however they find it their interest to keep the same savage dispositions alive. It was but the other day that they caused this very massacre to be acted on the stage for the diversion of the descendants of those who committed it. In this tragic farce they produced the cardinal of Lorraine in his robes of function, ordering general slaughter. Was this spectacle intended to make the Parisians abhor persecution, and loathe the effusion of blood? No; it was to teach them to persecute their own pastors; it was to excite them, by raising a disgust and horror of their clergy, to an alacrity in hunting down to destruction an order, which, if it ought to exist at all, ought to exist not only in safety, but in reverence. It was to stimulate their cannibal appetites (which one would think had been gorged sufficiently) by variety and seasoning; and to quicken them to an alertness in new murders and massacres, if it should suit the purpose of the Guises of the day. An assembly, in which sat a multitude of priests and prelates, was obliged to suffer this indignity at its door. The author was not sent to the galleys, nor the players to the house of correction. Not long after this exhibition, those players came forward to the Assembly to claim the rites of that very religion which they had dared to expose, and to show their prostituted faces in the senate, whilst the archbishop of Paris, whose function was known to his people only by his prayers and benedictions, and his wealth only by his alms, is forced to abandon his house, and to fly from his flock (as from ravenous wolves) because, truly, in the sixteenth century, the cardinal of Lorraine was a rebel and a murderer.[36]

Such is the effect of the perversion of history, by those, who, for the same nefarious purposes, have perverted every other part of learning. But those who will stand upon that elevation of reason, which places centuries under our eye, and brings things to the true point of comparison, which obscures little names, and effaces the colours of little parties, and to which nothing can ascend but the spirit and moral quality of human actions, will say to the teachers of the Palais Royal, the cardinal of Lorraine was the murderer of the sixteenth century, you have the glory of being the murderers in the eighteenth; and this is the only difference between you. But history in the nineteenth century, better understood, and better employed, will, I trust, teach a civilized posterity to abhor the misdeeds of both these barbarous ages. It will teach future priests and magistrates not to retaliate upon the speculative and inactive atheists of future times, the enormities committed by the present practical zealots and furious fanatics of that wretched error, which, in its quiescent state, is more than punished, whenever it is embraced. It will teach posterity not to make war upon either religion or philosophy, for the abuse which the hypocrites of both have made of the two most valuable blessings conferred upon us by the bounty of the universal Patron, who in all things eminently favours and protects the race of man.

If your clergy, or any clergy, should show themselves vicious beyond the fair bounds allowed to human infirmity, and to those professional faults which can hardly be separated from professional virtues, though their vices never can countenance the exercise of oppression, I do admit, that they would naturally have the effect of abating very much of our indignation against the tyrants who exceed measure and justice in their punishment. I can allow in clergymen, through all their divisions, some tenaciousness of their own opinion, some overflowings of zeal for its propagation, some predilection to their own state and office, some attachment to the interest of their own corps, some preference to those who listen with docility to their doctrines, beyond those who scorn and deride them. I allow all this, because I am a man who have to deal with men, and who would not, through a violence of toleration, run into the greatest of all intolerance. I must bear with infirmities until they fester into crimes.

Undoubtedly, the natural progress of the passions, from frailty to vice, ought to be prevented by a watchful eye and a firm hand. But is it true that the body of your clergy had passed those limits of a just allowance? From the general style of your late publications of all sorts, one would be led to believe that your clergy in France were a sort of monster an horrible composition of superstition, ignorance, sloth, fraud, avarice, and tyranny. But is this true? Is it true, that the lapse of time, the cessation of conflicting interests, the woeful experience of the evils resulting from party rage, have had no sort of influence gradually to meliorate their minds? Is it true, that they were daily renewing invasions on the civil power, troubling the domestic quiet of their country, and rendering the operations of its government feeble and precarious? Is it true, that the clergy of our times have pressed down the laity with an iron hand, and were, in all places, lighting up the fires of a savage persecution? Did they by every fraud endeavour to increase their estates? Did they use to exceed the due demands on estates that were their own? Or, rigidly screwing up right into wrong, did they convert a legal claim into a vexatious extortion? When not possessed of power, were they filled with the vices of those who envy it? Were they inflamed with a violent, litigious spirit of controversy? Goaded on with the ambition of intellectual sovereignty, were they ready to fly in the face of all magistracy, to fire churches, to massacre the priests of other descriptions, to pull down altars, and to make their way over the ruins of subverted governments to an empire of doctrine, sometimes flattering, sometimes forcing, the consciences of men from the jurisdiction of public institutions into a submission to their personal authority, beginning with a claim of liberty, and ending with an abuse of power?

These, or some of these, were the vices objected, and not wholly without foundation, to several of the churchmen of former times, who belonged to the two great parties, which then divided and distracted Europe.

If there was in France, as in other countries there visibly is, a great abatement, rather than any increase of these vices, instead of loading the present clergy with the crimes of other men, and the odious character of other times, in common equity they ought to be praised, encouraged, and supported, in their departure from a spirit which disgraced their predecessors, and for having assumed a temper of mind and manners more suitable to their sacred function.

When my occasions took me into France, towards the close of the late reign, the clergy, under all their forms, engaged a considerable part of my curiosity. So far from finding (except from one set of men, not then very numerous, though very active) the complaints and discontents against that body, which some publications had given me reason to expect, I perceived little or no public or private uneasiness on their account. On further examination, I found the clergy, in general, persons of moderate minds and decorous manners; I include the seculars, and the regulars of both sexes. I had not the good fortune to know a great many of the parochial clergy: but in general I received a perfectly good account of their morals, and of their attention to their duties. With some of the higher clergy I had a personal acquaintance; and of the rest in that class, a very good means of information. They were, almost all of them, persons of noble birth. They resembled others of their own rank; and where there was any difference, it was in their favour. They were more fully educated than the military noblesse; so as by no means to disgrace their profession by ignorance, or by want of fitness for the exercise of their authority. They seemed to me, beyond the clerical character, liberal and open; with the hearts of gentlemen, and men of honour; neither insolent nor servile in their manners and conduct. They seemed to me rather a superior class; a set of men, amongst whom you would not be surprised to find a *Fenelon.* I saw among the clergy in Paris (many of the description are not to be met with anywhere) men of great learning and candour; and I had reason to believe, that this description was not confined to Paris. What I found in other places, I know was accidental; and therefore to be presumed a fair sample. I spent a few days in a provincial town, where, in the absence of the bishop, I passed my evenings with three clergymen, his vicars-general, persons who would have done honour to any church. They were all well informed; two of them of deep, general, and extensive erudition, ancient and modern, oriental and western; particularly in their own profession. They had a more extensive knowledge of our English divines than I expected; and they entered into the genius of those writers with a critical accuracy. One of these gentlemen is since dead, the Abbé *Morangis.* I pay this tribute, without reluctance, to the memory of that noble, reverend, learned, and excellent person; and I should do the same, with equal cheerfulness, to the merits of the others, who I believe are still living, if I did not fear to hurt those whom I am unable to serve.

Some of these ecclesiastics of rank are, by all titles, persons deserving of general respect. They are deserving of gratitude from me, and from many English. If this letter should ever come into their hands, I hope they will believe there are those of our nation who feel for their unmerited fall, and for the cruel confiscation of their fortunes, with no common sensibility. What I say of them is a testimony, as far as one feeble voice can go, which I owe to truth. Whenever the question of this unnatural persecution is concerned, I will pay it. No one shall prevent me from being just and grateful. The time is fitted for the duty; and it is particularly becoming to show our justice and gratitude, when those, who have deserved well of us and of mankind, are labouring under popular obloquy, and the persecutions of oppressive power.

You had before your Revolution about a hundred and twenty bishops. A few of them were men of eminent sanctity, and charity without limit. When we talk of the heroic, of course we talk of rare virtue. I believe the instances of eminent depravity may be as rare amongst them as those of transcendent goodness. Examples of avarice and of licentiousness may be picked out, I do not question it, by those who delight in the investigation which leads to such discoveries. A man as old as I am will not be astonished that several, in every description, do not lead that perfect life of self-denial, with regard to wealth or to pleasure, which is wished for by all, by some expected, but by none exacted with more rigour, than by those who are the most attentive to their own interests, or the most indulgent to their own passions. When I was in France, I am certain that the number of vicious prelates was not great. Certain individuals among them, not distinguishable for the regularity of their lives, made some amends for their want of the severe virtues, in their possession of the liberal; and were endowed with qualities which made them useful in the church and state. I am told, that, with a few exceptions, Louis the Sixteenth had been more attentive to character, in his promotions to that rank, than his immediate predecessor; and I believe (as some spirit of reform has prevailed through the whole reign) that it may be true. But the present ruling power has shown a disposition only to plunder the church. It has punished *all* prelates; which is to favour the vicious, at least in point of reputation. It has made a degrading pensionary establishment, to which no man of liberal ideas or liberal condition will destine his children. It must settle into the lowest classes of the people. As with you the inferior clergy are not numerous enough for their duties; as these duties are, beyond measure, minute and toilsome, as you have left no middle classes of clergy at their ease, in future nothing of science or erudition can exist in the Gallican church. To complete the project, without the least attention to the rights of patrons, the Assembly has provided in future an elective clergy; an arrangement which will drive out of the clerical profession all men of sobriety; all who can pretend to independence in their function or their conduct; and which will throw the whole direction of the public mind into the hands of a set of licentious, bold, crafty, factious, flattering wretches, of such condition and such habits of life as will make their contemptible pensions (in comparison of which the stipend of an exciseman is lucrative and honourable) an object of low and illiberal intrigue. Those officers, whom they still call bishops, are to be elected to a provision comparatively mean, through the same arts (that is, electioneering arts) by men of all religious tenets that are known or can be invented. The new lawgivers have not ascertained anything whatsoever concerning their qualifications, relative either to doctrine or to morals; no more than they have done with regard to the subordinate clergy: nor does it appear but that both the higher and the lower may, at their discretion, practise or preach any mode of religion or irreligion that they please. I do not yet see what the jurisdiction of bishops over their subordinates is to be, or whether they are to have any jurisdiction at all.

In short, sir, it seems to me, that this new ecclesiastical establishment is intended only to be temporary, and preparatory to the utter abolition, under any of its forms, of the Christian religion, whenever the minds of men are prepared for this last stroke against it, by the accomplishment of the plan for bringing its ministers into universal contempt. They who will not believe, that the philosophical fanatics, who guide in these matters, have long entertained such a design, are utterly ignorant of their character and proceedings. These enthusiasts do not scruple to avow their opinion, that a state can subsist without any religion better than with one; and that they are able to supply the place of any good which may be in it, by a project of their own—namely, by a sort of education they have imagined, founded in a knowledge of the physical wants of men; progressively carried to an enlightened self-interest, which, when well understood, they tell us, will identify with an interest more enlarged and public. The scheme of this education has been long known. Of late they distinguish it (as they have got an entirely new nomenclature of technical terms) by the name of a *Civic Education.*

I hope their partisans in England (to whom I rather attribute very inconsiderate conduct, than the ultimate object in this detestable design) will succeed neither in the pillage of the ecclesiastics, nor in the introduction of a principle of popular election to our bishoprics and parochial cures. This, in the present condition of the world, would be the last corruption of the church; the utter ruin of the clerical character; the most dangerous shock that the state ever received through a misunderstood arrangement of religion. I know well enough that the bishoprics and cures, under kingly and seignoral patronage, as now they are in England, and as they have been lately in France, are sometimes acquired by unworthy methods; but the other mode of ecclesiastical canvass subjects them infinitely more surely and more generally to all the evil arts of low ambition, which, operating on and through greater numbers, will produce mischief in proportion.

Those of you, who have robbed the clergy, think that they shall easily reconcile their conduct to all Protestant nations; because the clergy, whom they have thus plundered, degraded, and given over to mockery and scorn, are of the Roman Catholic, that is, *of their own* pretended persuasion. I have no doubt that some miserable bigots will be found here, as well as elsewhere, who hate sects and parties different from their own, more than they love the substance of religion; and who are more angry with those who differ from them in their particular plans and systems, than displeased with those who attack the foundation of our common hope. These men will write and speak on the subject in the manner that is to be expected from their temper and character. Burnet says, that, when he was in France, in the year 1683, "the method which carried over the men of the finest parts to Popery was this—they brought themselves to doubt of the whole Christian religion. When that was once done, it seemed a more indifferent thing of what side or form they continued outwardly." If this was then the ecclesiastical policy of France, it is what they have since but too much reason to repent of. They preferred atheism to a form of religion not agreeable to their ideas. They succeeded in destroying that form; and atheism has succeeded in destroying them. I can readily give credit to Burnet's story; because I have observed too much of a similar spirit (for a little of it is "much too much") amongst ourselves. The humour, however, is not general.

The teachers who reformed our religion in England bore no sort of resemblance to your present reforming doctors in Paris. Perhaps they were (like those whom they opposed) rather more than could be wished under the influence of a party spirit; but they were more sincere believers; men of the most fervent and exalted piety; ready to die (as some of them did die) like true heroes in defence of their particular ideas of Christianity; as they would with equal fortitude, and more cheerfully, for their stock of general truth, for the branches of which they contended with their blood. These men would have disavowed with horror those wretches who claimed a fellowship with them upon no other titles than those of their having pillaged the persons with whom they maintained controversies, and their having despised the common religion, for the purity of which they exerted themselves with a zeal, which unequivocally bespoke their highest reverence for the substance of that system which they wished to reform. Many of their descendants have retained the same zeal, but (as less engaged in conflict) with more moderation. They do not forget that justice and mercy are substantial parts of religion. Impious men do not recommend themselves to their communion by iniquity and cruelty towards any description of their fellow-creatures.

We hear these new teachers continually boasting of their spirit of toleration. That those persons should tolerate all opinions, who think none to be of estimation, is a matter of small merit. Equal neglect is not impartial kindness. The species of benevolence, which arises from contempt, is no true charity. There are in England an abundance of men who tolerate in the true spirit of toleration. They think the dogmas of religion, though in different degrees, are all of moment: and that amongst them there is, as amongst all things of value, a just ground of preference. They favour, therefore, and they tolerate. They tolerate, not because they despise opinions, but because they respect justice. They would reverently and affectionately protect all religions, because they love and venerate the great principle upon which they all agree, and the great object to which they are all directed. They begin more and more plainly to discern, that we have all a common cause, as against a common enemy. They will not be so misled by the spirit of faction, as not to distinguish what is done in favour of their subdivision, from those acts of hostility, which, through some particular description, are aimed at the whole corps, in which they themselves, under another denomination, are included. It is impossible for me to say what may be the character of every description of men amongst us. But I speak for the greater part; and for them, I must tell you, that sacrilege is no part of their doctrine of good works; that, so far from calling you into their fellowship on such title, if your professors are admitted to their communion, they must carefully conceal their doctrine of the lawfulness of the proscription of innocent men; and that they must make restitution of all stolen goods whatsoever. Till then they are none of ours.

You may suppose that we do not approve your confiscation of the revenues of bishops, and deans, and chapters, and parochial clergy possessing independent estates arising from land, because we have the same sort of establishment in England. That objection, you will say, cannot hold as to the confiscation of the goods of monks and nuns, and the abolition of their order. It is true that this particular part of your general confiscation does not affect England, as a precedent in point: but the reason implies, and it goes a great way. The long parliament confiscated the lands of deans and chapters in England on the same ideas upon which your assembly set to sale the lands of the monastic orders. But it is in the principle of injustice that the danger lies, and not in the description of persons on whom it is first exercised. I see, in a country very near us, a course of policy pursued, which sets justice, the common concern of mankind, at defiance. With the National Assembly of France, possession is nothing, law and usage are nothing. I see the National Assembly openly reprobate the doctrine of prescription, which one of the greatest of their own lawyers[37] tells us, with great truth, is a part of the law of nature. He tells us, that the positive ascertainment of its limits, and its security from invasion, were among the causes for which civil society itself has been instituted. If prescription be once shaken, no species of property is secure, when it once becomes an object large enough to tempt the cupidity of indigent power. I see a practice perfectly correspondent to their contempt of this great fundamental part of natural law. I see the confiscators begin with bishops, and chapters, and monasteries; but I do not see them end there. I see the princes of the blood, who, by the oldest usages of that kingdom, held large landed estates (hardly with the compliment of a debate), deprived of their possessions, and, in lieu of their stable, independent property, reduced to the hope of some precarious, charitable pension, at the pleasure of an assembly, which of course will pay little regard to the rights of pensioners at pleasure, when it despises those of legal proprietors. Flushed with the insolence of their first inglorious victories, and pressed by the distresses caused by their lust of unhallowed lucre, disappointed but not discouraged, they have at length ventured completely to subvert all property of all descriptions throughout the extent of a great kingdom. They have compelled all men, in all transactions of commerce, in the disposal of lands, in civil dealing, and through the whole communion of life, to accept as perfect payment and good and lawful tender, the symbols of their speculations on a projected sale of their plunder. What vestiges of liberty or property have they left? The tenant-right of a cabbage-garden, a year's interest in a hovel, the good-will of an ale-house or a baker's shop, the very shadow of a constructive property, are more ceremoniously treated in our parliament, than with you the oldest and most valuable landed possessions, in the hands of the most respectable personages, or than the whole body of the monied and commercial interest of your country. We entertain a high opinion of the legislative authority; but we have never dreamt that parliaments had any right whatever to violate property, to overrule prescription, or to force a currency of their own fiction in the place of that which is real, and recognised by the law of nations. But you, who began with refusing to submit to the most moderate restraints, have ended by establishing an unheard-of despotism. I find the ground upon which your confiscators go is this; that indeed their proceedings could not be supported in a court of justice; but that the rules of prescription cannot bind a legislative assembly.[38] So that this legislative assembly of a free nation sits, not for the security, but for the destruction, of property, and not of property only, but of every rule and maxim which can give it stability, and of those instruments which can alone give it circulation.

When the Anabaptists of Munster, in the sixteenth century, had filled Germany with confusion, by their system of levelling, and their wild opinions concerning property, to what country in Europe did not the progress of their fury furnish just cause of alarm? Of all things, wisdom is the most terrified with epidemical fanaticism, because of all enemies it is that against which she is the least able to furnish any kind of resource. We cannot be ignorant of the spirit of atheistical fanaticism, that is inspired by a multitude of writings, dispersed with incredible assiduity and expense, and by sermons delivered in all the streets and places of public resort in Paris. These writings and sermons have filled the populace with a black and savage atrocity of mind, which supersedes in them the common feelings of nature, as well as all sentiments of morality and religion; insomuch that these wretches are induced to bear with a sullen patience the intolerable distresses brought upon them by the violent convulsions and permutations that have been made in property.[39] The spirit of proselytism attends this spirit of fanaticism. They have societies to cabal and correspond at home and abroad for the propagation of their tenets. The republic of Berne, one of the happiest, the most prosperous, and the best governed countries upon earth, is one of the great objects, at the destruction of which they aim. I am told they have in some measure succeeded in sowing there the seeds of discontent. They are busy throughout Germany. Spain and Italy have not been untried. England is not left out of the comprehensive scheme of their malignant charity: and in England we find those who stretch out their arms to them, who recommend their example from more than one pulpit, and who choose in more than one periodical meeting, publicly to correspond with them, to applaud them, and to hold them up as objects for imitation; who receive from them tokens of confraternity, and standards consecrated amidst their rights and mysteries;[40] who suggest to them leagues of perpetual amity, at the very time when the power, to which our constitution has exclusively delegated the federative capacity of this kingdom, may find it expedient to make war upon them.

It is not the confiscation of our church property from this example in France that I dread, though I think this would be no trifling evil. The great source of my solicitude is, lest it should ever be considered in England as the policy of a state to seek a resource in confiscations of any kind; or that any one description of citizens should be brought to regard any of the others as their proper prey.[41] Nations are wading deeper and deeper into an ocean of boundless debt. Public debts, which at first were a security to governments, by interesting many in the public tranquillity, are likely in their excess to become the means of their subversion. If governments provide for these debts by heavy impositions, they perish by becoming odious to the people. If they do not provide for them they will be undone by the efforts of the most dangerous of all parties; I mean an extensive, discontented monied interest, injured and not destroyed. The men who compose this interest look for their security, in the first instance, to the fidelity of government; in the second, to its power. If they find the old governments effete, worn out, and with their springs relaxed, so as not to be of sufficient vigour for their purposes, they may seek new ones that shall be possessed of more energy; and this energy will be derived, not from an acquisition of resources, but from a contempt of justice. Revolutions are favourable to confiscation; and it is impossible to know under what obnoxious names the next confiscations will be authorized. I am sure that the principles predominant in France extend to very many persons, and descriptions of persons, in all countries who think their innoxious indolence their security. This kind of innocence in proprietors may be argued into inutility; and inutility into an unfitness for their estates. Many parts of Europe are in open disorder. In many others there is a hollow murmuring under ground; a confused movement is felt, that threatens a general earthquake in the political world. Already confederacies and correspondencies of the most extraordinary nature are forming, in several countries.[42] In such a state of things we ought to hold ourselves upon our guard. In all mutations (if mutations must be) the circumstance which will serve most to blunt the edge of their mischief, and to promote what good may be in them, is, that they should find us with our minds tenacious of justice, and tender of property.

But it will be argued, that this confiscation in France ought not to alarm other nations. They say it is not made from wanton rapacity; that it is a great measure of national policy, adopted to remove an extensive, inveterate, superstitious mischief. It is with the greatest difficulty that I am able to separate policy from justice. Justice itself is the great standing policy of civil society; and any eminent departure from it, under any circumstances, lies under the suspicion of being no policy at all.

When men are encouraged to go into a certain mode of life by the existing laws, and protected in that mode as in a lawful occupation—when they have accommodated all their ideas and all their habits to it—when the law had long made their adherence to its rules a ground of reputation, and their departure from them a ground of disgrace and even of penalty—I am sure it is unjust in legislature, by an arbitrary act, to offer a sudden violence to their minds and their feelings; forcibly to degrade them from their state and condition, and to stigmatize with shame and infamy that character, and those customs, which before had been made the measure of their happiness and honour. If to this be added an expulsion from their habitations, and a confiscation of all their goods, I am not sagacious enough to discover how this despotic sport, made of the feelings, consciences, prejudices, and properties of men, can be discriminated from the rankest tyranny.

If the injustice of the course pursued in France be clear, the policy of the measure, that is, the public benefit to be expected from it, ought to be at least as evident, and at least as important. To a man who acts under the influence of no passion, who has nothing in view in his projects but the public good, a great difference will immediately strike him between what policy would dictate on the original introduction of such institutions, and on a question of their total abolition, where they have cast their roots wide and deep, and where, by long habit, things more valuable than themselves are so adapted to them, and in a manner interwoven with them, that the one cannot be destroyed without notably impairing the other. He might be embarrassed if the case were really such as sophisters represent it in their paltry style of debating. But in this, as in most questions of state, there is a middle. There is something else than the mere alternative of absolute destruction, or un-reformed existence. *Spartam nactus es; hanc exorna.* This is, in my opinion, a rule of profound sense, and ought never to depart from the mind of an honest reformer. I cannot conceive how any man can have brought himself to that pitch of presumption, to consider his country as nothing but *carte blanche,* upon which he may scribble whatever he pleases. A man full of warm, speculative benevolence may wish his society otherwise constituted than he finds it; but a good patriot, and a true politician, always considers how he shall make the most of the existing materials of his country. A disposition to preserve, and an ability to improve, taken together, would be my standard of a statesman. Everything else is vulgar in the conception, perilous in the execution.

There are moments in the fortune of states, when particular men are called to make improvements, by great mental exertion. In those moments, even when they seem to enjoy the confidence of their prince and country, and to be invested with full authority, they have not always apt instruments. A politician, to do great things, looks for a *power,* what our workmen call a *purchase;* and if he finds that power, in politics as in mechanics, he cannot be at a loss to apply it. In the monastic institutions, in my opinion, was found a great *power* for the mechanism of politic benevolence. There were revenues with a public direction; there were men wholly set apart and dedicated to public purposes, without any other than public ties and public principles; men without the possibility of converting the estate of the community into a private fortune; men denied to self-interests, whose avarice is for some community; men to whom personal poverty is honour, and implicit obedience stands in the place of freedom. In vain shall a man look to the possibility of making such things when he wants them. The winds blow as they list. These institutions are the products of enthusiasm; they are the instruments of wisdom. Wisdom cannot create materials; they are the gifts of nature or of chance; her pride is in the use. The perennial existence of bodies corporate and their fortunes are things particularly suited to a man who has long views; who meditates designs that require time in fashioning, and which propose duration when they are accomplished. He is not deserving to rank high, or even to be mentioned in the order of great statesmen, who, having obtained the command and direction of such a power as existed in the wealth, the discipline, and the habits of such corporations, as those which you have rashly destroyed, cannot find any way of converting it to the great and lasting benefit of his country. On the view of this subject, a thousand uses suggest themselves to a contriving mind. To destroy any power, growing wild from the rank productive force of the human mind, is almost tantamount, in the moral world, to the destruction of the apparently active properties of bodies in the material. It would be like the attempt to destroy (if it were in our competence to destroy) the expansive force of fixed air in nitre, or the power of steam, or of electricity, or of magnetism. These energies always existed in nature, and they were always discernible. They seemed, some of them unserviceable, some noxious, some no better than a sport to children; until contemplative ability, combining with practic skill, tamed their wild nature, subdued them to use, and rendered them at once the most powerful and the most tractable agents, in subservience to the great views and designs of men. Did fifty thousand persons, whose mental and whose bodily labour you might direct, and so many hundred thousand a year of a revenue, which was neither lazy nor superstitious, appear too big for your abilities to wield? Had you no way of using the men but by converting monks into pensioners? Had you no way of turning the revenue to account, but through the improvident resource of a spendthrift sale? If you were thus destitute of mental funds, the proceeding is in its natural course. Your politicians do not understand their trade; and therefore they sell their tools.

But the institutions savour of superstition in their very principle; and they nourish it by a permanent and standing influence. This I do not mean to dispute; but this ought not to hinder you from deriving from superstition itself any resources which may thence be furnished for the public advantage. You derive benefits from many dispositions and many passions of the human mind, which are of as doubtful a colour, in the moral eye, as superstition itself. It was your business to correct and mitigate everything which was noxious in this passion, as in all the passions. But is superstition the greatest of all possible vices? In its possible excess I think it becomes a very great evil. It is, however, a moral subject; and of course admits of all degrees and all modifications. Superstition is the religion of feeble minds; and they must be tolerated in an intermixture of it, in some trifling or some enthusiastic shape or other, else you will deprive weak minds of a resource found necessary to the strongest. The body of all true religion consists, to be sure, in obedience to the will of the Sovereign of the world; in a confidence in his declarations; and in imitation of his perfections. The rest is our own. It may be prejudicial to the great end; it may be auxiliary. Wise men, who as such are not *admirers* (not admirers at least of the *Munera Terræ*), are not violently attached to these things, nor do they violently hate them. Wisdom is not the most severe corrector of folly. They are the rival follies, which mutually wage so unrelenting a war; and which make so cruel a use of their advantages, as they can happen to engage the immoderate vulgar, on the one side, or the other, in their quarrels. Prudence would be neuter; but if, in the contention between fond attachment and fierce antipathy concerning things in their nature not made to produce such heats, a prudent man were obliged to make a choice of what errors and excesses of enthusiasm he would condemn or bear, perhaps he would think the superstition which builds, to be more tolerable than that which demolishes—that which adorns a country, than that which deforms it—that which endows, than that which plunders—that which disposes to mistaken beneficence, than that which stimulates to real injustice—that which leads a man to refuse to himself lawful pleasures, than that which snatches from others the scanty subsistence of their self-denial. Such, I think, is very nearly the state of the question between the ancient founders of monkish superstition, and the superstition of the pretended philosophers of the hour.

For the present I postpone all consideration of the supposed public profit of the sale, which however I conceive to be perfectly delusive. I shall here only consider it as a transfer of property. On the policy of that transfer I shall trouble you with a few thoughts.

In every prosperous community something more is produced than goes to the immediate support of the producer. This surplus forms the income of the landed capitalist. It will be spent by a proprietor who does not labour. But this idleness is itself the spring of labour; this repose the spur to industry. The only concern of the state is, that the capital taken in rent from the land, should be returned again to the industry from whence it came; and that its expenditure should be with the least possible detriment to the morals of those who expend it, and to those of the people to whom it is returned.

In all the views of receipt, expenditure, and personal employment, a sober legislator would carefully compare the possessor whom he was recommended to expel, with the stranger who was proposed to fill his place. Before the inconveniences are incurred which *must* attend all violent revolutions in property through extensive confiscation, we ought to have some rational assurance that the purchasers of the confiscated property will be in a considerable degree more laborious, more virtuous, more sober, less disposed to extort an unreasonable proportion of the gains of the labourer, or to consume on themselves a larger share than is fit for the measure of an individual; or that they should be qualified to dispense the surplus in a more steady and equal mode, so as to answer the purposes of a politic expenditure, than the old possessors, call those possessors bishops, or canons, or commendatory abbots, or monks, or what you please. The monks are lazy. Be it so. Suppose them no otherwise employed than by singing in the choir. They are as usefully employed as those who neither sing nor say. As usefully even as those who sing upon the stage. They are as usefully employed as if they worked from dawn to dark in the innumerable servile, degrading, unseemly, unmanly, and often most unwholesome and pestiferous occupations, to which by the social economy so many wretches are inevitably doomed. If it were not generally pernicious to disturb the natural course of things, and to impede, in any degree, the great wheel of circulation which is turned by the strangely-directed labour of these unhappy people, I should be infinitely more inclined forcibly to rescue them from their miserable industry, than violently to disturb the tranquil repose of monastic quietude. Humanity, and perhaps policy, might better justify me in the one than in the other. It is a subject on which I have often reflected, and never reflected without feeling from it. I am sure that no consideration, except the necessity of submitting to the yoke of luxury, and the despotism of fancy, who in their own imperious way will distribute the surplus product of the soil, can justify the toleration of such trades and employments in a well-regulated state. But for this purpose of distribution, it seems to me, that the idle expenses of monks are quite as well directed as the idle expenses of us lay-loiterers.

When the advantages of the possession and of the project are on a par, there is no motive for a change. But in the present case, perhaps, they are not upon a par, and the difference is in favour of the possession. It does not appear to me, that the expenses of those whom you are going to expel, do in fact take a course so directly and so generally leading to vitiate and degrade and render miserable those through whom they pass, as the expenses of those favourites whom you are intruding into their houses. Why should the expenditure of a great landed property, which is a dispersion of the surplus product of the soil, appear intolerable to you or to me, when it takes its course through the accumulation of vast libraries, which are the history of the force and weakness of the human mind; through great collections of ancient records, medals, and coins, which attest and explain laws and customs; through paintings and statues, that, by imitating nature, seem to extend the limits of creation; through grand monuments of the dead, which continue the regards and connexions of life beyond the grave; through collections of the specimens of nature, which become a representative assembly of all the classes and families of the world, that by disposition facilitate, and, by exciting curiosity, open the avenues to science? If by great permanent establishments, all these objects of expense are better secured from the inconstant sport of personal caprice and personal extravagance, are they worse than if the same tastes prevailed in scattered individuals? Does not the sweat of the mason and carpenter, who toil in order to partake the sweat of the peasant, flow as pleasantly and as salubriously, in the construction and repair of the majestic edifices of religion, as in the painted booths and sordid sties of vice and luxury; as honourably and as profitably in repairing those sacred works, which grow hoary with innumerable years, as on the momentary receptacles of transient voluptuousness; in opera-houses, and brothels, and gaming-houses, and club-houses, and obelisks in the Champ de Mars? Is the surplus product of the olive and the vine worse employed in the frugal sustenance of persons, whom the fictions of a pious imagination raise to dignity by construing in the service of God, than in pampering the innumerable multitude of those who are degraded by being made useless domestics, subservient to the pride of man? Are the decorations of temples an expenditure less worthy a wise man, than ribbons, and laces, and national cockades, and petit maisons, and petit soupers, and all the innumerable fopperies and follies, in which opulence sports away the burthen of its superfluity?

We tolerate even these; not from love of them, but for fear of worse. We tolerate them, because property and liberty, to a degree, require that toleration. But why proscribe the other, and surely, in every point of view, the more laudable use of estates? Why, through the violation of all property, through an outrage upon every principle of liberty, forcibly carry them from the better to the worse?

This comparison between the new individuals and the old corps is made upon a supposition that no reform could be made in the latter. But, in a question of reformation, I always consider corporate bodies, whether sole or consisting of many, to be much more susceptible of a public direction by the power of the state, in the use of their property, and in the regulation of modes and habits of life in their members, than private citizens ever can be, or perhaps ought to be: and this seems to be a very material consideration for those who undertake anything which merits the name of a politic enterprise. So far as to the estates of monasteries.

With regard to the estates possessed by bishops and canons, and commendatory abbots, I cannot find out for what reason some landed estates may not be held otherwise than by inheritance. Can any philosophic spoiler undertake to demonstrate the positive or the comparative evil of having a certain, and that too a large, portion of landed property, passing in succession through persons whose title to it is, always in theory, and often in fact, an eminent degree of piety, morals, and learning; a property, which, by its destination, in their turn, and on the score of merit, gives to the noblest families renovation and support, to the lowest the means of dignity and elevation; a property, the tenure of which is the performance of some duty (whatever value you may choose to set upon that duty) and the character of whose proprietors demands, at least, an exterior decorum, and gravity of manners; who are to exercise a generous but temperate hospitality; part of whose income they are to consider as a trust for charity; and who, even when they fail in their trust, when they slide from their character, and degenerate into a mere common secular nobleman or gentleman, are in no respect worse than those who may succeed them in their forfeited possessions? Is it better that estates should be held by those who have no duty, than by those who have one? By those whose character and destination point to virtues, than by those who have no rule and direction in the expenditure of their estates but their own will and appetite? Nor are these estates held altogether in the character or with the evils supposed inherent in mortmain. They pass from hand to hand with a more rapid circulation than any other. No excess is good; and therefore too great a proportion of landed property may be held officially for life: but it does not seem to me of material injury to any commonwealth, that there should exist some estates that have a chance of being acquired by other means than the previous acquisition of money.

This letter is grown to a great length, though it is indeed short with regard to the infinite extent of the subject. Various avocations have from time to time called my mind from the subject. I was not sorry to give myself leisure to observe whether, in the proceedings of the National Assembly, I might not find reasons to change or to qualify some of my first sentiments. Everything has confirmed me more strongly in my first opinions. It was my original purpose to take a view of the principles of the National Assembly with regard to the great and fundamental establishments; and to compare the whole of what you have substituted in the place of what you have destroyed, with the several members of our British constitution. But this plan is of a greater extent than at first I computed, and I find that you have little desire to take the advantage of any examples. At present I must content myself with some remarks upon your establishments; reserving for another time what I proposed to say concerning the spirit of our British monarchy, aristocracy, and democracy, as practically they exist.

I have taken a view of what has been done by the governing power in France. I have certainly spoke of it with freedom. Those whose principle it is to despise the ancient, permanent sense of mankind, and to set up a scheme of society of new principles, must naturally expect that such of us, who think better of the judgment of the human race than of theirs, should consider both them and their devices, as men and schemes upon their trial. They must take it for granted that we attend much to their reason, but not at all to their authority. They have not one of the great influencing prejudices of mankind in their favour. They avow their hostility to opinion. Of course they must expect no support from that influence, which, with every other authority, they have deposed from the seat of its jurisdiction.

I can never consider this Assembly as anything else than a voluntary association of men, who have availed themselves of circumstances to seize upon the power of the state. They have not the sanction and authority of the character under which they first met. They have assumed another of a very different nature; and have completely altered and inverted all the relations in which they originally stood. They do not hold the authority they exercise under any constitutional law of the state. They have departed from the instructions of the people by whom they were sent; which instructions, as the Assembly did not act in virtue of any ancient usage or settled law, were the sole source of their authority. The most considerable of their acts have not been done by great majorities; and in this sort of near divisions, which carry only the constructive authority of the whole, strangers will consider reasons as well as resolutions.

If they had set up this new, experimental government, as a necessary substitute for an expelled tyranny, mankind would anticipate the time of prescription, which, through long usage, mellows into legality governments that were violent in their commencement. All those who have affections which lead them to the conservation of civil order would recognise, even in its cradle, the child as legitimate, which has been produced from those principles of cogent expediency to which all just governments owe their birth, and on which they justify their continuance. But they will be late and reluctant in giving any sort of countenance to the operations of a power, which has derived its birth from no law and no necessity; but which on the contrary has had its origin in those vices and sinister practices by which the social union is often disturbed and sometimes destroyed. This Assembly has hardly a year's prescription. We have their own word for it that they have made a revolution. To make a revolution is a measure which, *prima fronte,* requires an apology. To make a revolution is to subvert the ancient state of our country; and no common reasons are called for to justify so violent a proceeding. The sense of mankind authorizes us to examine into the mode of acquiring new power, and to criticise on the use that is made of it, with less awe and reverence than that which is usually conceded to a settled and recognised authority.

In obtaining and securing their power, the Assembly proceeds upon principles the most opposite to those which appear to direct them in the use of it. An observation on this difference will let us into the true spirit of their conduct. Everything which they have done, or continue to do, in order to obtain and keep their power, is by the most common arts. They proceed exactly as their ancestors of ambition have done before them. Trace them through all their artifices, frauds, and violences, you can find nothing at all that is new. They follow precedents and examples with the punctilious exactness of a pleader. They never depart an iota from the authentic formulas of tyranny and usurpation. But in all the regulations relative to the public good, the spirit has been the very reverse of this. There they commit the whole to the mercy of untried speculations; they abandon the dearest interests of the public to those loose theories, to which none of them would choose to trust the slightest of his private concerns. They make this difference, because in their desire of obtaining and securing power they are thoroughly in earnest; there they travel in the beaten road. The public interests, because about them they have no real solicitude, they abandon wholly to chance: I say to chance, because their schemes have nothing in experience to prove their tendency beneficial.

We must always see with a pity not unmixed with respect, the errors of those who are timid and doubtful of themselves with regard to points wherein the happiness of mankind is concerned. But in these gentlemen there is nothing of the tender, parental solicitude, which fears to cut up the infant for the sake of an experiment. In the vastness of their promises, and the confidence of their predictions, they far outdo all the boasting of empirics. The arrogance of their pretensions, in a manner provokes and challenges us to an inquiry into their foundation.

I am convinced that there are men of considerable parts among the popular leaders in the National Assembly. Some of them display eloquence in their speeches and their writings. This cannot be without powerful and cultivated talents. But eloquence may exist without a proportionable degree of wisdom. When I speak of ability, I am obliged to distinguish. What they have done towards the support of their system bespeaks no ordinary men. In the system itself, taken as the scheme of a republic constructed for procuring the prosperity and security of the citizen, and for promoting the strength and grandeur of the state, I confess myself unable to find out anything which displays, in a single instance, the work of a comprehensive and disposing mind, or even the provisions of a vulgar prudence. Their purpose everywhere seems to have been to evade and slip aside from *difficulty*. This it has been the glory of the great masters in all the arts to confront, and to overcome; and when they had overcome the first difficulty, to turn it into an instrument for new conquests over new difficulties; thus to enable them to extend the empire of their science; and even to push forward, beyond the reach of their original thoughts, the land-marks of the human understanding itself. Difficulty is a severe instructor, set over us by the supreme ordinance of a parental Guardian and Legislator, who knows us better than we know ourselves, as he loves us better too. *Pater ipse colendi haud facilem esse viam voluit.* He that wrestles with us strengthens our nerves, and sharpens our skill. Our antagonist is our helper. This amicable conflict with difficulty obliges us to an intimate acquaintance with our object, and compels us to consider it in all its relations. It will not suffer us to be superficial. It is the want of nerves of understanding for such a task, it is the degenerate fondness for tricking short-cuts, and little fallacious facilities, that has in so many parts of the world created governments with arbitrary powers. They have created the late arbitrary monarchy of France. They have created the arbitrary republic of Paris. With them defects in wisdom are to be supplied by the plentitude of force. They get nothing by it. Commencing their labours on a principle of sloth, they have the common fortune of slothful men. The difficulties, which they rather had eluded than escaped, meet them again in their course; they multiply and thicken on them; they are involved, through a labyrinth of confused detail, in an industry without limit, and without direction; and, in conclusion, the whole of their work becomes feeble, vicious, and insecure.

It is this inability to wrestle with difficulty which has obliged the arbitrary Assembly of France to commence their schemes of reform with abolition and total destruction.[43] But is it in destroying and pulling down that skill is displayed? Your mob can do this as well at least as your assemblies. The shallowest understanding, the rudest hand, is more than equal to that task. Rage and phrensy will pull down more in half an hour, than prudence, deliberation, and foresight can build up in a hundred years. The errors and defects of old establishments are visible and palpable. It calls for little ability to point them out; and where absolute power is given, it requires but a word wholly to abolish the vice and the establishment together. The same lazy but restless disposition, which loves sloth and hates quiet, directs the politicians, when they come to work for supplying the place of what they have destroyed. To make everything the reverse of what they have seen is quite as easy as to destroy. No difficulties occur in what has never been tried. Criticism is almost baffled in discovering the defects of what has not existed; and eager enthusiasm and cheating hope have all the wide field of imagination, in which they may expatiate with little or no opposition.

At once to preserve and to reform is quite another thing. When the useful parts of an old establishment are kept, and what is superadded is to be fitted to what is retained, a vigorous mind, steady, persevering attention, various powers of comparison and combination, and the resources of an understanding fruitful in expedients, are to be exercised; they are to be exercised in a continued conflict with the combined force of opposite vices, with the obstinacy that rejects all improvement, and the levity that is fatigued and disgusted with everything of which it is in possession. But you may object: "A process of this kind is slow. It is not fit for an assembly, which glories in performing in a few months the work of ages. Such a mode of reforming, possibly, might take up many years." Without question it might; and it ought. It is one of the excellencies of a method in which time is amongst the assistants, that its operation is slow, and in some cases almost imperceptible. If circumspection and caution are a part of wisdom, when we work only upon inanimate matter, surely they become a part of duty too, when the subject of our demolition and construction is not brick and timber, but sentient beings, by the sudden alteration of whose state, condition, and habits, multitudes may be rendered miserable. But it seems as if it were the prevalent opinion in Paris, that an unfeeling heart, and an undoubting confidence, are the sole qualifications for a perfect legislator. Far different are my ideas of that high office. The true lawgiver ought to have a heart full of sensibility. He ought to love and respect his kind, and to fear himself. It may be allowed to his temperament to catch his ultimate object with an intuitive glance; but his movements towards it ought to be deliberate. Political arrangement, as it is a work for social ends, is to be only wrought by social means. There mind must conspire with mind. Time is required to produce that union of minds which alone can produce all the good we aim at. Our patience will achieve more than our force. If I might venture to appeal to what is so much out of fashion in Paris, I mean to experience, I should tell you, that in my course I have known, and, according to my measure, have co-operated with great men; and I have never yet seen any plan which has not been mended by the observations of those who were much inferior in understanding to the person who took the lead in the business. By a slow but well-sustained progress, the effect of each step is watched; the good or ill success of the first gives light to us in the second; and so, from light to light, we are conducted with safety through the whole series. We see that the parts or the system do not clash. The evils latent in the most promising contrivances are provided for as they arise. One advantage is as little as possible sacrificed to another. We compensate, we reconcile, we balance. We are enabled to unite into a consistent whole the various anomalies and contending principles that are found in the minds and affairs of men. From hence arises, not an excellence in simplicity, but one far superior, an excellence in composition. Where the great interests of mankind are concerned through a long succession of generations, that succession ought to be admitted into some share in the councils which are so deeply to affect them. If justice requires this, the work itself requires the aid of more minds than one age can furnish. It is from this view of things that the best legislators have been often satisfied with the establishment of some sure, solid, and ruling principle in government; a power like that which some of the philosophers have called a plastic nature; and having fixed the principle, they have left it afterwards to its own operation.

To proceed in this manner, that is, to proceed with a presiding principle, and a prolific energy, is with me the criterion of profound wisdom. What your politicians think the marks of a bold, hardy genius, are only proofs of a deplorable want of ability. By their violent haste and their defiance of the process of nature, they are delivered over blindly to every projector and adventurer, to every alchymist and empiric. They despair of turning to account anything that is common. Diet is nothing in their system of remedy. The worst of it is, that this their despair of curing common distempers by regular methods, arises not only from defect of comprehension, but, I fear, from some malignity of disposition. Your legislators seem to have taken their opinions of all professions, ranks, and offices, from the declamations and buffooneries of satirists; who would themselves be astonished if they were held to the letter of their own descriptions. By listening only to these, your leaders regard all things only on the side of their vices and faults, and view those vices and faults under every colour of exaggeration. It is undoubtedly true, though it may seem paradoxical; but in general, those who are habitually employed in finding and displaying faults, are unqualified for the work of reformation: because their minds are not only unfurnished with patterns of the fair and good, but by habit they come to take no delight in the contemplation of those things. By hating vices too much, they come to love men too little. It is therefore not wonderful, that they should be indisposed and unable to serve them. From hence arises the complexional disposition of some of your guides to pull everything in pieces. At this malicious game they display the whole of their *quadrimanous* activity. As to the rest, the paradoxes of eloquent writers, brought forth purely as a sport of fancy, to try their talents, to rouse attention and excite surprise, are taken up by these gentlemen, not in the spirit of the original authors, as means of cultivating their taste and improving their style. These paradoxes become with them serious grounds of action, upon which they proceed in regulating the most important concerns of the state. Cicero ludicrously describes Cato as endeavouring to act, in the commonwealth, upon the school paradoxes, which exercised the wits of the junior students in the Stoic philosophy. If this was true of Cato, these gentlemen copy after him in the manner of some persons who lived about his time—*pede nudo Catonem.* Mr. Hume told me that he had from Rousseau himself the secret of his principles of composition. That acute though eccentric observer had perceived, that to strike and interest the public, the marvellous must be produced; that the marvellous of the heathen mythology had long since lost its effects; that giants, magicians, fairies, and heroes of romance which succeeded, had exhausted the portion of credulity which belonged to their age; that now nothing was left to the writer but that species of the marvellous which might still be produced, and with as great an effect as ever, though in another way; that is, the marvellous in life, in manners, in characters, and in extraordinary situations, giving rise to new and unlooked-for strokes in politics and morals. I believe, that were Rousseau alive, and in one of his lucid intervals, he would be shocked at the practical phrensy of his scholars, who in their paradoxes are servile imitators, and even in their incredulity discover an implicit faith.

Men who undertake considerable things, even in a regular way, ought to give us ground to presume ability. But the physician of the state, who, not satisfied with the cure of distempers, undertakes to regenerate constitutions, ought to show uncommon powers. Some very unusual appearances of wisdom ought to display themselves on the face of the designs of those, who appeal to no practice, and who copy after no model. Has any such been manifested? I shall take a view (it shall for the subject be a very short one) of what the Assembly has done, with regard, first, to the constitution of the legislature; in the next place, to that of the executive power; then to that of the judicature; afterwards to the model of the army; and conclude with the system of finance; to see whether we can discover in any part of their schemes the portentous ability, which may justify these bold undertakers in the superiority which they assume over mankind.

It is in the model of the sovereign and presiding part of this new republic, that we should expect their grand display. Here they were to prove their title to their proud demands. For the plan itself at large, and for the reasons on which it is grounded, I refer to the journals of the Assembly of the 29th of September, 1789, and to the subsequent proceedings which have made any alterations in the plan. So far as in a matter somewhat confused I can see light, the system remains substantially as it has been originally framed. My few remarks will be such as regard its spirit, its tendency, and its fitness for framing a popular commonwealth, which they profess theirs to be, suited to the ends for which any commonwealth, and particularly such a commonwealth, is made. At the same time, I mean to consider its consistency with itself and its own principles.

Old establishments are tried by their effects. If the people are happy, united, wealthy, and powerful, we presume the rest. We conclude that to be good from whence good is derived. In old establishments various correctives have been found for their aberrations from theory. Indeed they are the results of various necessities and expediences. They are not often constructed after any theory; theories are rather drawn from them. In them we often see the end best obtained, where the means seem not perfectly reconcilable to what we may fancy was the original scheme. The means taught by experience may be better suited to political ends than those contrived in the original project. They again react upon the primitive constitution, and sometimes improve the design itself, from which they seem to have departed. I think all this might be curiously exemplified in the British Constitution. At worst, the errors and deviations of every kind in reckoning are found and computed, and the ship proceeds in her course. This is the case of old establishments; but in a new and merely theoretic system, it is expected that every contrivance shall appear, on the face of it, to answer its ends; specially where the projectors are no way embarrassed with an endeavour to accommodate the new building to an old one, either in the walls or on the foundations.

The French builders, clearing away as mere rubbish whatever they found, and, like their ornamental gardeners, forming everything into an exact level, propose to rest the whole local and general legislature on three bases of three different kinds; one geometrical, one arithmetical, and the third financial; the first of which they call the *basis of territory*; the second, the *basis of population*; and the third, the *basis of contribution*. For the accomplishment of the first of these purposes, they divide the area of their country into eighty-three pieces, regularly square, of eighteen leagues by eighteen. These large divisions are called *Departments.* These they portion, proceeding by square measurement, into seventeen hundred and twenty districts, called *Communes.* These again they subdivide, still proceeding by square measurement, into smaller districts called *Cantons*, making in all 6400.

At first view this geometrical basis of theirs presents not much to admire or to blame. It calls for no great legislative talents. Nothing more than an accurate land surveyor, with his chain, sight, and theodolite, is requisite for such a plan as this. In the old divisions of the country, various accidents at various times, and the ebb and flow of various properties and jurisdictions, settled their bounds. These bounds were not made upon any fixed system undoubtedly. They were subject to some inconveniences: but they were inconveniences for which use had found remedies, and habit had supplied accommodation and patience. In this new pavement of square within square, and this organization, and semi-organization, made on the system of Empedocles and Buffon, and not upon any politic principle, it is impossible that innumerable local inconveniences, to which men are not habituated, must not arise. But these I pass over, because it requires an accurate knowledge of the country, which I do not possess, to specify them.

When these state surveyors came to take a view of their work of measurement, they soon found, that in politics the most fallacious of all things was geometrical demonstration. They had then recourse to another basis (or rather buttress) to support the building, which tottered on that false foundation. It was evident, that the goodness of the soil, the number of the people, their wealth, and the largeness of their contribution, made such infinite variations between square and square, as to render mensuration a ridiculous standard of power in the commonwealth, and equality in geometry the most unequal of all measures in the distribution of men. However, they could not give it up. But dividing their political and civil representation into three parts, they allotted one of those parts to the square measurement, without a single fact or calculation to ascertain whether this territorial proportion of representation was fairly assigned, and ought upon any principle really to be a third. Having however given to geometry this portion (of a third for her dower) out of compliment, I suppose, to that sublime science, they left the other two to be scuffled for between the other parts, population and contribution.

When they came to provide for population, they were not able to proceed quite so smoothly as they had done in the field of their geometry. Here their arithmetic came to bear upon their juridical metaphysics. Had they stuck to their metaphysic principles, the arithmetical process would be simple indeed. Men, with them, are strictly equal, and are entitled to equal rights in their own government. Each head, on this system, would have its vote, and every man would vote directly for the person who was to represent him in the legislature. "But soft—by regular degrees, not yet." This metaphysic principle, to which law, custom, usage, policy, reason, were to yield, is to yield itself to their pleasure. There must be many degrees, and some stages, before the representative can come in contact with his constituent. Indeed, as we shall soon see, these two persons are to have no sort of communion with each other. First, the voters in the *Canton,* who compose what they call *primary assemblies,* are to have a *qualification.* What! a qualification on the indefeasible rights of men? Yes; but it shall be a very small qualification. Our injustice shall be very little oppressive; only the local valuation of three days' labour paid to the public. Why, this is not much, I readily admit, for anything but the utter subversion of your equalising principle. As a qualification it might as well be let alone; for it answers no one purpose for which qualifications are established; and, on your ideas, it excludes from a vote the man of all others whose natural equality stands the most in need of protection and defence: I mean the man who has nothing else but his natural equality to guard him. You order him to buy the right, which you before told him nature had given to him gratuitously at his birth, and of which no authority on earth could lawfully deprive him. With regard to the person who cannot come up to your market, a tyrannous aristocracy, as against him, is established at the very outset, by you who pretend to be its sworn foe.

The gradation proceeds. These primary assemblies of the *Canton* elect deputies to the *Commune*; one for every two hundred qualified inhabitants. Here is the first medium put between the primary elector and the representative legislator; and here a new turnpike is fixed for taxing the rights of men with a second qualification: for none can be elected into the *Commune* who does not pay the amount of ten days' labour. Nor have we yet done. There is still to be another gradation.[44] These *Communes*, chosen by the *Canton*, choose to the *Department*; and the deputies of the *Department* choose their deputies to the *National Assembly*. Here is a third barrier of a senseless qualification. Every deputy to the National Assembly must pay, in direct contribution, to the value of a *mark of silver*. Of all these qualifying barriers we must think alike; that they are impotent to secure independence; strong only to destroy the rights of men.

In all this process, which in its fundamental elements affects to consider only *population* upon a principle of natural right, there is a manifest attention to *property*; which, however just and reasonable on other schemes, is on theirs perfectly unsupportable.

When they come to their third basis, that of *Contribution*, we find that they have more completely lost sight of their rights of men. This last basis rests *entirely* on property. A principle totally different from the equality of men, and utterly irreconcilable to it, is thereby admitted; but no sooner is tills principle admitted, than (as usual) it is subverted; and it is not subverted (as we shall presently see) to approximate the inequality of riches to the level of nature. The additional share in the third portion of representation (a portion reserved exclusively for the higher contribution) is made to regard the *district* only, and not the individuals in it who pay. It is easy to perceive, by the course of their reasonings, how much they were embarrassed by their contradictory ideas of the rights of men and the privileges of riches. The committee of constitution do as good as admit that they are wholly irreconcilable. "The relation with regard to the contributions, is without doubt *null* (say they) when the question is on the balance of the political rights as between individual and individual; without which *personal equality would be destroyed*, and *an aristocracy of the rich* would be established. But this inconvenience entirely disappears when the proportional relation of the contribution is only considered in the *great masses*, and is solely between province and province; it serves in that case only to form a just reciprocal proportion between the cities, without affecting the personal rights of the citizens."

Here the principle of *contribution*, as taken between man and man, is reprobated as *null*, and destructive to equality; and as pernicious too; because it leads to the establishment of an *aristocracy of the rich*. However, it must not be abandoned. And the way of getting rid of the difficulty is to establish the inequality as between department and department, leaving all the individuals in each department upon an exact par. Observe, that this parity between individuals had been before destroyed, when the qualifications within the departments were settled; nor does it seem a matter of great importance whether the equality of men be injured by masses or individually. An individual is not of the same importance in a mass represented by a few, as in a mass represented by many. It would be too much to tell a man jealous of his equality, that the elector has the same franchise who votes for three members as he who votes for ten.

Now take it in the other point of view, and let us suppose their principle of representation according to contribution, that is, according to riches, to be well imagined, and to be a necessary basis for their republic. In this their third basis they assume, that riches ought to be respected, and that justice and policy require that they should entitle men, in some mode or other, to a larger share in the administration of public affairs; it is now to be seen how the Assembly provides for the pre-eminence, or even for the security, of the rich, by conferring, in virtue of their opulence, that larger measure of power to their district which is denied to them personally. I readily admit (indeed I should lay it down as a fundamental principle) that in a republican government, which has a democratic basis, the rich do require an additional security above what is necessary to them in monarchies. They are subject to envy, and through envy to oppression. On the present scheme it is impossible to divine what advantage they derive from the aristocratic preference upon which the unequal representation of the masses is founded. The rich cannot feel it, either as a support to dignity, or as security to fortune: for the aristocratic mass is generated from purely democratic principles; and the preference given to it in the general representation has no sort of reference to, or connexion with, the persons, upon account of whose property this superiority of the mass is established. If the contrivers of this scheme meant any sort of favour to the rich, in consequence of their contribution, they ought to have conferred the privilege either on the individual rich, or on some class formed of rich persons (as historians represent Servius Tullius to have done in the early constitution of Rome); because the contest between the rich and the poor is not a struggle between corporation and corporation, but a contest between men and men; a competition not between districts, but between descriptions. It would answer its purpose better if the scheme were inverted; that the votes of the masses were rendered equal; and that the votes within each mass were proportioned to property.

Let us suppose one man in a district (it is an easy supposition) to contribute as much as a hundred of his neighbours. Against these he has but one vote. If there were but one representative for the mass, his poor neighbours would outvote him by a hundred to one for that single representative. Bad enough. But amends are to be made him. How? The district, in virtue of his wealth, is to choose, say ten members instead of one: that is to say, by paying a very large contribution he has the happiness of being outvoted, a hundred to one, by the poor, for ten representatives, instead of being outvoted exactly in the same proportion for a single member. In truth, instead of benefiting by this superior quantity of representation, the rich man is subjected to an additional hardship. The increase of representation within his province sets up nine persons more, and as many more than nine as there may be democratic candidates, to cabal and intrigue, and to flatter the people at his expense and to his oppression. An interest is by this means held out to multitudes of the inferior sort, in obtaining a salary of eighteen livres a day (to them a vast object), besides the pleasure of a residence in Paris, and their share in the government of the kingdom. The more the objects of ambition are multiplied and become democratic, just in that proportion the rich are endangered.

Thus it must fare between the poor and the rich in the province deemed aristocratic, which in its internal relation is the very reverse of that character. In its external relation, that is, its relation to the other provinces, I cannot see how the unequal representation, which is given to masses on account of wealth, becomes the means of preserving the equipoise and the tranquillity of the commonwealth. For if it be one of the objects to secure the weak from being crushed by the strong (as in all society undoubtedly it is), how are the smaller and poorer of these masses to be saved from the tyranny of the more wealthy? Is it by adding to the wealthy further and more systematical means of oppressing them? When we come to a balance of representation between corporate bodies, provincial interests, emulations, and jealousies are full as likely to arise among them as among individuals; and their divisions are likely to produce a much hotter spirit of dissension, and something leading much more nearly to a war.

I see that these aristocratic masses are made upon what is called the principle of direct contribution. Nothing can be a more unequal standard than this. The indirect contribution, that which arises from duties on consumption, is in truth a better standard, and follows and discovers wealth more naturally than this of direct contribution. It is difficult indeed to fix a standard of local preference on account of the one, or of the other, or of both, because some provinces may pay the more of either or of both, on account of causes not intrinsic, but originating from those very districts over whom they have obtained a preference in consequence of their ostensible contribution. If the masses were independent, sovereign bodies, who were to provide for a federative treasury by distinct contingents, and that the revenue had not (as it has) many impositions running through the whole, which affect men individually, and not corporately, and which, by their nature, confound all territorial limits, something might be said for the basis of contribution as founded on masses. But of all things, this representation, to be measured by contribution, is the most difficult to settle upon principles of equity in a country, which considers its districts as members of a whole. For a great city, such as Bordeaux, or Paris, appears to pay a vast body of duties, almost out of all assignable proportion to other places, and its mass is considered accordingly. But are these cities the true contributors in that proportion? No. The consumers of the commodities imported into Bordeaux, who are scattered through all France, pay the import duties of Bordeaux. The produce of the vintage in Guienne and Languedoc give to that city the means of its contribution growing out of an export commerce. The landholders who spend their estates in Paris, and are thereby the creators of that city, contribute for Paris from the provinces out of which their revenues arise. Very nearly the same arguments will apply to the representative share given on account of *direct* contribution: because the direct contribution must be assessed on wealth real or presumed; and that local wealth will itself arise from causes not local, and which therefore in equity ought not to produce a local preference.

It is very remarkable, that in this fundamental regulation, which settles the representation of the mass upon the direct contribution, they have not yet settled how that direct contribution shall be laid, and how apportioned. Perhaps there is some latent policy towards the continuance of the present Assembly in this strange procedure. However, until they do this, they can have no certain constitution. It must depend at last upon the system of taxation, and must vary with every variation in that system. As they have contrived matters, their taxation does not so much depend on their constitution, as their constitution on their taxation. This must introduce great confusion among the masses; as the variable qualification for votes within the district must, if ever real contested elections take place, cause infinite internal controversies.

To compare together the three bases, not on their political reason, but on the ideas on which the Assembly works, and to try its consistency with itself, we cannot avoid observing, that the principle which the committee call the basis of *population,* does not begin to operate from the same point with the two other principles called the bases of *territory* and of *contribution,* which are both of an aristocratic nature. The consequence is, that, where all three begin to operate together, there is the most absurd inequality produced by the operation of the former on the two latter principles. Every canton contains four square leagues, and is estimated to contain, on the average, 4000 inhabitants, or 680 voters in the *primary assemblies,* which vary in numbers with the population of the canton, and send *one deputy* to the *commune* for every 200 voters. *Nine cantons* make a *commune.*

Now let us take a *canton* containing *a sea-port town of trade,* or *a great manufacturing town.* Let us suppose the population of this canton to be 12,700 inhabitants, or 2193 voters, forming *three primary assemblies,* and *sending ten deputies* to the *commune.*

Oppose to this *one* canton *two* others of the remaining eight in the same commune. These we may suppose to have their fair population of 4000 inhabitants and 680 voters each, or 8000 inhabitants and 1360 voters, both together. These will form only *two primary assemblies,* and send only *six* deputies to the *commune.*

When the assembly of the *commune* comes to vote on the *basis of territory,* which principle is first admitted to operate in that assembly, the *single canton,* which has *half* the territory of the *other two,* will have *ten* voices to *six* in the election of *three deputies* to the assembly of the department, chosen on the express ground of a representation of territory. This inequality, striking as it is, will be yet highly aggravated, if we suppose, as we fairly may, the *several* other cantons of the *commune* to fall proportion ably short of the average population, as much as the *principal canton* exceeds it.

Now as to *the basis of contribution,* which also is a principle admitted first to operate in the assembly of the *commune.* Let us again take one *canton,* such as is stated above. If the whole of the direct contributions paid by a great trading or manufacturing town be divided equally among the inhabitants, each individual will be found to pay much more than an individual living in the country according to the same average. The whole paid by the inhabitants of the former will be more than the whole paid by the inhabitants of the latter—we may fairly assume one-third more. Then the 12,700 inhabitants, or 2193 voters of the canton, will pay as much as 19,050 inhabitants, or 3289 voters of the *other cantons,* which are nearly the estimated proportion of inhabitants and voters of *five* other cantons. Now the 2193 voters will, as I before said, send only *ten* deputies to the assembly; the 3289 voters will send *sixteen.* Thus, for an *equal* share in the contribution of the whole *commune,* there will be a difference of *sixteen* voices to *ten* in voting for deputies to be chosen on the principle of representing the general contribution of the whole *commune.*

By the same mode of computation we shall find 15,875 inhabitants, or 2741 voters of the *other* cantons, who pay *one-sixth* LESS to the contribution of the whole *commune,* will have *three* voices MORE than the 12,700 inhabitants, or 2193 voters of the *one* canton.

Such is the fantastical and unjust inequality between mass and mass, in this curious repartition of the rights of representation arising out of *territory* and *contribution.* The qualifications which these confer are in truth negative qualifications, that give a right in an inverse proportion to the possession of them.

In this whole contrivance of the three bases, consider it in any light you please, I do not see a variety of objects reconciled in one consistent whole, but several contradictory principles reluctantly and irreconcilably brought and held together by your philosophers, like wild beasts shut up in a cage, to claw and bite each other to their mutual destruction.

I am afraid I have gone too far into their way of considering the formation of a constitution. They have much, but bad, metaphysics; much, but bad, geometry; much, but false, proportionate arithmetic; but if it were all as exact as metaphysics, geometry, and arithmetic ought to be, and if their schemes were perfectly consistent in all their parts, it would make only a more fair and sightly vision. It is remarkable, that, in a great arrangement of mankind, not one reference whatsoever is to be found to anything moral or anything politic; nothing that relates to the concerns, the actions, the passions, the interests of men. *Hominem non sapiunt.*

You see I only consider this constitution as electoral, and leading by steps to the National Assembly. I do not enter into the internal government of the departments, and their genealogy through the communes and cantons. These local governments are, in the original plan, to be as nearly as possible composed in the same manner and on the same principles with the elective assemblies. They are each of them bodies perfectly compact and rounded in themselves.

You cannot but perceive in this scheme, that it has a direct and immediate tendency to sever France into a variety of republics, and to render them totally independent of each other, without any direct constitutional means of coherence, connexion, or subordination, except what may be derived from their acquiescence in the determinations of the general congress of the ambassadors from each independent republic. Such in reality is the National Assembly, and such governments I admit do exist in the world, though in forms infinitely more suitable to the local and habitual circumstances of their people. But such associations, rather than bodies politic, have generally been the effect of necessity, not choice; and I believe the present French power is the very first body of citizens, who having obtained full authority to do with their country what they pleased, have chosen to dissever it in this barbarous manner.

It is impossible not to observe, that, in the spirit of this geometrical distribution, and arithmetical arrangement, these pretended citizens treat France exactly like a country of conquest. Acting as conquerors, they have imitated the policy of the harshest of that harsh race. The policy of such barbarous victors, who contemn a subdued people, and insult their feelings, has ever been, as much as in them lay, to destroy all vestiges of the ancient country, in religion, in polity, in laws, and in manners; to confound all territorial limits; to produce a general poverty; to put up their properties to auction; to crush their princes, nobles, and pontiffs; to lay low everything which had lifted its head above the level, or which could serve to combine or rally, in their distresses, the disbanded people, under the standard of old opinion. They have made France free in the manner in which those sincere friends to the rights of mankind, the Romans, freed Greece, Macedon, and other nations. They destroyed the bonds of their union, under colour of providing for the independence of each of their cities.

When the members who compose these new bodies of cantons, communes, and departments, arrangements purposely produced through the medium of confusion, begin to act, they will find themselves in a great measure strangers to one another. The electors and elected throughout, especially in the rural *cantons,* will be frequently without any civil habitudes or connexions, or any of that natural discipline which is the soul of a true republic. Magistrates and collectors of revenue are now no longer acquainted with their districts, bishops with their dioceses, or curates with their parishes. These new colonies of the rights of men bear a strong resemblance to that sort of military colonies which Tacitus has observed upon in the declining policy of Rome. In better and wiser days (whatever course they took with foreign nations) they were careful to make the elements of methodical subordination and settlement to be coeval; and even to lay the foundations of civil discipline in the military.[45] But, when all the good arts had fallen into ruin, they proceeded, as your Assembly does, upon the equality of men, and with as little judgment, and as little care for those things which make a republic tolerable or durable. But in this, as well as almost every instance, your new commonwealth is born, and bred, and fed, in those corruptions which mark degenerated and worn-out republics. Your child comes into the world with the symptoms of death; the *facies Hippocratica* forms the character of its physiognomy, and the prognostic of its fate.

The legislators who framed the ancient republics knew that their business was too arduous to be accomplished with no better apparatus than the metaphysics of an under-graduate, and the mathematics and arithmetic of an exciseman. They had to do with men, and they were obliged to study human nature. They had to do with citizens, and they were obliged to study the effects of those habits which are communicated by the circumstances of civil life. They were sensible that the operation of this second nature on the first produced a new combination; and thence arose many diversities amongst men, according to their birth, their education, their professions, the periods of their lives, their residence in towns or in the country, their several ways of acquiring and of fixing property, and according to the quality of the property itself, all which rendered them as it were so many different species of animals. From hence they thought themselves obliged to dispose their citizens into such classes, and to place them in such situations in the state, as their peculiar habits might qualify them to fill, and to allot to them such appropriated privileges as might secure to them what their specific occasions required, and which might furnish to each description such force as might protect it in the conflict caused by the diversity of interests, that must exist, and must contend, in all complex society: for the legislator would have been ashamed, that the coarse husbandman should well know how to assort and to use his sheep, horses, and oxen, and should have enough of common sense, not to abstract and equalize them all into animals, without providing for each kind an appropriate food, care, and employment; whilst he, the economist, disposer, and shepherd of his own kindred, subliming himself into an airy metaphysician, was resolved to know nothing of his flocks but as men in general. It is for this reason that Montesquieu observed very justly, that in their classification of the citizens, the great legislators of antiquity made the greatest display of their powers, and even soared above themselves. It is here that your modern legislators have gone deep into the negative series, and sunk even below their own nothing. As the first sort of legislators attended to the different kinds of citizens, and combined them into one commonwealth, the others, the metaphysical and alchemistical legislators, have taken the direct contrary course. They have attempted to confound all sorts of citizens, as well as they could, into one homogeneous mass; and then they divided this their amalgama into a number of incoherent republics. They reduce men to loose counters, merely for the sake of simple telling, and not to figures whose power is to arise from their place in the table. The elements of their own metaphysics might have taught them better lessons. The troll of their categorical table might have informed them that there was something else in the intellectual world besides *substance* and *quantity.* They might learn from the catechism of metaphysics that there were eight heads more,[46] in every complex deliberation, which they have never thought of; though these, of all the ten, are the subjects on which the skill of man can operate anything at all.

So far from this able disposition of some of the old republican legislators, which follows with a solicitous accuracy the moral conditions and propensities of men, they have levelled and crushed together all the orders which they found, even under the coarse unartificial arrangement of the monarchy, in which mode of government the classing of the citizens is not of so much importance as in a republic. It is true, however, that every such classification, if properly ordered, is good in all forms of government; and composes a strong barrier against the excesses of despotism, as well as it is the necessary means of giving effects and permanence to a republic. For want of something of this kind, if the present project of a republic should fail, all securities to a moderated freedom fail along with it; all the indirect restraints which mitigate despotism are removed; insomuch that if monarchy should ever again obtain an entire ascendency in France, under this or under any other dynasty, it will probably be, if not voluntarily tempered, at setting out, by the wise and virtuous counsels of the prince, the most completely arbitrary power that has ever appeared on earth. This is to play a most desperate game.

The confusion which attends on all such proceedings, they even declare to be one of their objects, and they hope to secure their constitution by a terror of a return of those evils which attended their making it. "By this," say they, "its destruction will become difficult to authority, which cannot break it up without the entire disorganization of the whole state." They presume, that if this authority should ever come to the same degree of power that they have acquired, it would make a more moderate and chastised use of it, and would piously tremble entirely to disorganize the state in the savage manner that they have done. They expect, from the virtues of returning despotism, the security which is to be enjoyed by the offspring of their popular vices.

I wish, sir, that you and my readers would give an attentive perusal to the work of M. de Calonne, on this subject. It is indeed not only an eloquent, but an able and instructive, performance. I confine myself to what he says relative to the constitution of the new state, and to the condition of the revenue. As to the disputes of this minister with his rivals, I do not wish to pronounce upon them. As little do I mean to hazard any opinion concerning his ways and means, financial or political, for taking his country out of its present disgraceful and deplorable situation of servitude, anarchy, bankruptcy, and beggary. I cannot speculate quite so sanguinely as he does: but he is a

Frenchman, and has a closer duty relative to those objects, and better means of judging of them, than I can have. I wish that the formal avowal which he refers to, made by one of the principal leaders in the Assembly, concerning the tendency of their scheme to bring France not only from a monarchy to a republic, but from a republic to a mere confederacy, may be very particularly attended to. It adds new force to my observations: and indeed M. de Calonne's work supplies my deficiencies by many new and striking arguments on most of the subjects of this letter.[47]

It is this resolution, to break their country into separate republics, which has driven them into the greatest number of their difficulties and contradictions. If it were not for this, all the questions of exact equality, and these balances, never to be settled, of individual rights, population, and contribution, would be wholly useless. The representation, though derived from parts, would be a duty which equally regarded the whole. Each deputy to the Assembly would be the representative of France, and of all its descriptions, of the many and of the few, of the rich and of the poor, of the great districts and of the small. All these districts would themselves be subordinate to some standing authority, existing independently of them, an authority in which their representation, and everything that belongs to it, originated, and to which it was pointed. This standing, unalterable, fundamental government would make, and it is the only thing which could make, that territory truly and properly a whole. With us, when we elect popular representatives, we send them to a council, in which each man individually is a subject, and submitted to a government complete in all its ordinary functions. With you the elective Assembly is the sovereign, and the sole sovereign; all the members are therefore integral parts of this sole sovereignty. But with us it is totally different. With us the representative, separated from the other parts, can have no action and no existence. The government is the point of reference of the several members and districts of our representation. This is the centre of our unity. This government of reference is a trustee for the *whole,* and not for the parts. So is the other branch of our public council, I mean the House of Lords. With us the king and the lords are several and joint securities for the equality of each district, each province, each city. When did you hear in Great Britain of any province suffering from the inequality of its representation; what district from having no representation at all? Not only our monarchy and our peerage secure the equality on which our unity depends, but it is the spirit of the House of Commons itself. The very inequality of representation, which is so foolishly complained of, is perhaps the very thing which prevents us from thinking or acting as members for districts. Cornwall elects as many members as all Scotland. But is Cornwall better taken care of than Scotland? Few trouble their heads about any of your bases, out of some giddy clubs. Most of those who wish for any change, upon any plausible grounds, desire it on different ideas.

Your new constitution is the very reverse of ours in its principle; and I am astonished how any persons could dream of holding out anything done in it, as an example for Great Britain. With you there is little, or rather no, connexion between the last representative and the first constituent. The member who goes to the National Assembly is not chosen by the people, nor accountable to them. There are three elections before he is chosen: two sets of magistracy intervene between him and the primary assembly, so as to render him, as I have said, an ambassador of a state, and not the representative of the people within a state. By this the whole spirit of the election is changed; nor can any corrective, which your constitution-mongers have devised, render him anything else than what he is. The very attempt to do it would inevitably introduce a confusion, if possible, more horrid than the present. There is no way to make a connexion between the original constituent and the representative, but by the circuitous means which may lead the candidate to apply in the first instance to the primary electors, in order that by their authoritative instructions (and something more perhaps) these primary electors may force the two succeeding bodies of electors to make a choice agreeable to their wishes. But this would plainly subvert the whole scheme. It would be to plunge them back into that tumult and confusion of popular election, which, by their interposed gradation of elections, they mean to avoid, and at length to risk the whole fortune of the state with those who have the least knowledge of it, and the least interest in it. This is a perpetual dilemma, into which they are thrown by the vicious, weak, and contradictory principles they have chosen. Unless the people break up and level this gradation, it is plain that they do not at all substantially elect to the Assembly; indeed they elect as little in appearance as reality.

What is it we all seek for in an election? To answer its real purposes, you must first possess the means of knowing the fitness of your man; and then you must retain some hold upon him by personal obligation or dependence. For what end are these primary electors complimented, or rather mocked, with a choice? They can never know anything of the qualities of him that is to serve them, nor has he any obligation whatsoever to them. Of all the powers unfit to be delegated by those who have any real means of judging, that most peculiarly unfit is what relates to a *personal* choice. In case of abuse, that body of primary electors never can call the representative to an account for his conduct. He is too far removed from them in the chain of representation. If he acts improperly at the end of his two years' lease, it does not concern him for two years more. By the new French constitution the best and the wisest representatives go equally with the worst into this *Limbus Patrum*. Their bottoms are supposed foul, and they must go into dock to be refitted. Every man who has served in an assembly is ineligible for two years after. Just as these magistrates begin to learn their trade, like chimney-sweepers, they are disqualified for exercising it. Superficial, new, petulant acquisition, and interrupted, dronish, broken, ill recollection, is to be the destined character of all your future governors. Your constitution has too much of jealousy to have much of sense in it. You consider the breach of trust in the representative so principally, that you do not at all regard the question of his fitness to execute it.

This purgatory interval is not unfavourable to a faithless representative, who may be as good a canvasser as he was a bad governor. In this time he may cabal himself into a superiority over the wisest and most virtuous. As, in the end, all the members of this elective constitution are equally fugitive, and exist only for the election, they may be no longer the same persons who had chosen him, to whom he is to be responsible when he solicits for a renewal of his trust. To call all the secondary electors of the *Commune* to account, is ridiculous, impracticable, and unjust; they may themselves have been deceived in their choice, as the third set of electors, those of the *Department,* may be in theirs. In your elections responsibility cannot exist.

Finding no sort of principle of coherence with each other in the nature and constitution of the several new republics of France, I considered what cement the legislators had provided for them from any extraneous materials. Their confederations, their *spectacles,* their civic feasts, and their enthusiasm, I take no notice of; they are nothing but mere tricks; but tracing their policy through their actions, I think I can distinguish the arrangements by which they propose to hold these republics together. The first, is the *confiscation,* with the compulsory paper currency annexed to it; the second, is the supreme power of the city of Paris; the third, is the general army of the state. Of this last I shall reserve what I have to say, until I come to consider the army as a head by itself.

As to the operation of the first (the confiscation and paper currency) merely as a cement, I cannot deny that these, the one depending on the other, may for some time compose some sort of cement if their madness and folly in the management, and in the tempering of the parts together, does not produce a repulsion in the very outset. But allowing to the scheme some coherence and some duration, it appears to me, that if, after a while, the confiscation should not be found sufficient to support the paper coinage (as I am morally certain it will not), then, instead of cementing, it will add infinitely to the dissociation, distraction, and confusion of these confederate republics, both with relation to each other, and to the several parts within themselves. But if the confiscation should so far succeed as to sink the paper currency, the cement is gone with the circulation. In the mean time its binding force will be very uncertain, and it will straiten or relax with every variation in the credit of the paper.

One thing only is certain in this scheme, which is an effect seemingly collateral, but direct, I have no doubt, in the minds of those who conduct this business, that is, its effect in producing an *Oligarchy* in every one of the republics. A paper circulation, not founded on any real money deposited or engaged for, amounting already to four-and-forty millions of English money, and this currency by force substituted in the place of the coin of the kingdom, becoming thereby the substance of its revenue, as well as the medium of all its commercial and civil intercourse, must put the whole of what power, authority, and influence is left, in any form whatsoever it may assume, into the hands of the managers and conductors of this circulation.

In England we feel the influence of the bank; though it is only the centre of a voluntary dealing. He knows little indeed of the influence of money upon mankind, who does not see the force of the management of a monied concern, which is so much more extensive, and in its nature so much more depending on the managers, than any of ours. But this is not merely a money concern. There is another member in the system inseparably connected with this money management. It consists in the means of drawing out at discretion portions of the confiscated lands for sale; and carrying on a process of continual transmutation of paper into land, and land into paper. When we follow this process in its effects, we may conceive something of the intensity of the force with which this system must operate. By this means the spirit of money-jobbing and speculation goes into the mass of land itself, and incorporates with it. By this kind of operation, that species of property becomes (as it were) volatilized; it assumes an unnatural and monstrous activity, and thereby throws into the hands of the several managers, principal and subordinate, Parisian and provincial, all the representative of money, and perhaps a full tenth part of all the land in France, which has now acquired the worst and most pernicious part of the evil of a paper circulation, the greatest possible uncertainty in its value. They have reversed the Latonian kindness to the landed property of Delos. They have sent theirs to be blown about, like the light fragments of a wreck, *oras et littora circum.*

The new dealers, being all habitually adventurers, and without any fixed habits or local predilections, will purchase to job out again, as the market of paper, or of money, or of land, shall present an advantage. For though a holy bishop thinks that agriculture will derive great advantages from the *"enlightened"* usurers who are to purchase the church confiscations, I, who am not a good, but an old farmer, with great humility beg leave to tell his late lordship, that usury is not a tutor of agriculture; and if the word "enlightened" be understood according to the new dictionary, as it always is in your new schools, I cannot conceive how a man's not believing in God can teach him to cultivate the earth with the least of any additional skill or encouragement. "Diis immortalibus sero," said an old Roman, when he held one handle of the plough, whilst Death held the other. Though you were to join in the commission all the directors of the two academies to the directors of the *Caisse d'Escompte,* one old, experienced peasant is worth them all. I have got more information upon a curious and interesting branch of husbandry, in one short conversation with an old Carthusian monk, than I have derived from all the Bank directors that I have ever conversed with. However, there is no cause for apprehension from the meddling of money-dealers with rural economy. These gentlemen are too wise in their generation. At first, perhaps, their tender and susceptible imaginations may be captivated with the innocent and unprofitable delights of a pastoral life; but in a little time they will find that agriculture is a trade much more laborious, and much less lucrative, than that which they had left. After making its panegyric, they will turn their backs on it like their great precursor and prototype. They may, like him, begin by singing *"Beatus illepo."* But what will be the end?

Hœe ubi locutus fœnerator Alphius,
Jam jam futurus rusticus
Omnem relegit idibus pecuniam;
Quœrit calendis ponere.

They will cultivate the *Caisse d'Eglise,* under the sacred auspices of this prelate, with much more profit than its vineyards and its corn-fields. They will employ their talents according to their habits and their interests. They will not follow the plough whilst they can direct treasuries, and govern provinces.

Your legislators, in everything new, are the very first who have founded a commonwealth upon gaming, and infused this spirit into it as its vital breath. The great object in these politics is to metamorphose France from a great kingdom into one great play-table; to turn its inhabitants into a nation of gamesters; to make speculation as extensive as life; to mix it with all its concerns; and to divert the whole of the hopes and fears of the people from their usual channels into the impulses, passions, and superstitions of those who live on chances. They loudly proclaim their opinion, that this their present system of a republic cannot possibly exist without this kind of gaming fund; and that the very thread of its life is spun out of the staple of these speculations. The old gaming in funds was mischievous enough undoubtedly; but it was so only to individuals. Even when it had its greatest extent, in the Mississippi and South Sea, it affected but few, comparatively; where it extends further, as in lotteries, the spirit has but a single object. But where the law, which in most circumstances forbids, and in none countenances, gaming, is itself debauched, so as to reverse its nature and policy, and expressly to force the subject to this destructive table, by bringing the spirit and symbols of gaming into the minutest matters, and engaging everybody in it, and in everything, a more dreadful epidemic distemper of that kind is spread than yet has appeared in the world. With you a man can neither earn nor buy his dinner without a speculation. What he receives in the morning will not have the same value at night. What he is compelled to take as pay for an old debt will not be received as the same when he comes to pay a debt contracted by himself; nor will it be the same when by prompt payment he would avoid contracting any debt at all. Industry must wither away. Economy must be driven from your country. Careful provision will have no existence. Who will labour without knowing the amount of his pay? Who will study to increase what none can estimate? Who will accumulate, when he does not know the value of what he saves? If you abstract it from its uses in gaming, to accumulate your paper wealth, would be not the providence of a man, but the distempered instinct of a jackdaw.

The truly melancholy part of the policy of systematically making a nation of gamesters is this, that though all are forced to play, few can understand the game; and fewer still are in a condition to avail themselves of the knowledge. The many must be the dupes of the few who conduct the machine of these speculations. What effect it must have on the country people is visible. The townsman can calculate from day to day; not so the inhabitant of the country. When the peasant first brings his corn to market, the magistrate in the towns obliges him to take the assignat at par; when he goes to the shop with his money, he finds it seven per cent the worse for crossing the way. This market he will not readily resort to again. The towns-people will be inflamed; they will force the country people to bring their corn. Resistance will begin, and the murders of Paris and St. Denis may be renewed through all France.

What signifies the empty compliment paid to the country, by giving it, perhaps, more than its share in the theory of your representation? Where have you placed the real power over monied and landed circulation? Where have you placed the means of raising and falling the value of every man's freehold? Those, whose operations can take from, or add ten per cent, to, the possessions of every man in France, must be the masters of every man in France. The whole of the power obtained by this revolution will settle in the towns among the burghers, and the monied directors who lead them. The landed gentleman, the yeoman, and the peasant, have, none of them, habits, or inclinations, or experience, which can lead them to any share in this the sole source of power and influence now left in France. The very nature of a country life, the very nature of landed property, in all the occupations, and all the pleasures they afford, render combination and arrangement (the sole way of procuring and exerting influence) in a manner impossible amongst country people. Combine them by all the art you can, and all the industry, they are always dissolving into individuality. Anything in the nature of incorporation is almost impracticable amongst them. Hope, fear, alarm, jealousy, the ephemerous tale that does its business and dies in a day, all these things, which are the reins and spurs by which leaders check or urge the minds of followers, are not easily employed, or hardly at all, amongst scattered people. They assemble, they arm, they act, with the utmost difficulty, and at the greatest charge. Their efforts, if ever they can be commenced, cannot be sustained. They cannot proceed systematically. If the country gentlemen attempt an influence through the mere income of their property, what is it to that of those who have ten times their income to sell, and who can ruin their property by bringing their plunder to meet it at market? If the landed man wishes to mortgage, he falls the value of his land, and raises the value of assignats. He augments the power of his enemy by the very means he must take to contend with him. The country gentleman therefore, the officer by sea and land, the man of liberal views and habits, attached to no profession, will be as completely excluded from the government of his country as if he were legislatively proscribed. It is obvious, that in the towns, all the things which conspire against the country gentleman combine in favour of the money manager and director. In towns combination is natural. The habits of burghers, their occupations, their diversion, their business, their idleness, continually bring them into mutual contact. Their virtues and their vices are sociable; they are always in garrison; and they come embodied and half disciplined into the hands of those who mean to form them for civil or military action.

All these considerations leave no doubt on my mind, that, if this monster of a constitution can continue, France will be wholly governed by the agitators in corporations, by societies in the towns formed of directors of assignats, and trustees for the sale of church lands, attornies, agents, money-jobbers, speculators, and adventurers, composing an ignoble oligarchy, founded on the destruction of the crown, the church, the nobility, and the people. Here end all the deceitful dreams and visions of the equality and rights of men. In "the Serbonian bog" of this base oligarchy they are all absorbed, sunk, and lost for ever.

Though human eyes cannot trace them, one would be tempted to think some great offences in France must cry to heaven, which has thought fit to punish it with a subjection to a vile and inglorious domination, in which no comfort or compensation is to be found in any even of those false splendours, which, playing about other tyrannies, prevent mankind from feeling themselves dishonoured even whilst they are oppressed. I must confess I am touched with a sorrow, mixed with some indignation, at the conduct of a few men, once of great rank, and still of great character, who, deluded with specious names, have engaged in a business too deep for the line of their understanding to fathom; who have lent their fair reputation, and the authority of their high-sounding names, to the designs of men with whom they could not be acquainted; and have thereby made their very virtues operate to the ruin of their country.

So far as to the first cementing principle.

The second material of cement for their new republic is the superiority of the city of Paris: and this I admit is strongly connected with the other cementing principle of paper circulation and confiscation. It is in this part of the project we must look for the cause of the destruction of all the old bounds of provinces and jurisdictions, ecclesiastical and secular, and the dissolution of all ancient combinations of things, as well as the formation of so many small unconnected republics. The power of the city of Paris is evidently one great spring of all their politics. It is through the power of Paris, now become the centre and focus of jobbing, that the leaders of this faction direct, or rather command, the whole legislative and the whole executive government. Everything therefore must be done which can confirm the authority of the city over the other republics. Paris is compact; she has an enormous strength, wholly disproportioned to the force of any of the square republics; and this strength is collected and condensed within a narrow compass. Paris has a natural and easy connexion of its parts, which will not be affected by any scheme of a geometrical constitution, nor does it much signify whether its proportion of representation be more or less, since it has the whole draft of fishes in its drag-net. The other divisions of the kingdom being hackled and torn to pieces, and separated from all their habitual means, and even principles of union, cannot, for some time at least, confederate against her. Nothing was to be left in all the subordinate members, but weakness, disconnexion, and confusion. To confirm this part of the plan, the Assembly has lately come to a resolution, that no two of their republics shall have the same commander-in-chief.

To a person who takes a view of the whole, the strength of Paris, thus formed, will appear a system of general weakness. It is boasted that the geometrical policy has been adopted, that all local ideas should be sunk, and that the people should no longer be Gascons, Picards, Bretons, Normans; but Frenchmen, with one country, one heart, and one Assembly. But instead of being all Frenchmen, the greater likelihood is, that the inhabitants of that region will shortly have no country. No man ever was attached by a sense of pride, partiality, or real affection, to a description of square measurement. He never will glory in belonging to the Chequer No. 71, or to any other badge-ticket. We begin our public affections in our families. No cold relation is a zealous citizen. We pass on to our neighbourhoods, and our habitual provincial connexions. These are inns and resting places. Such divisions of our country as have been formed by habit, and not by a sudden jerk of authority, were so many little images of the great country in which the heart found something which it could fill. The love to the whole is not extinguished by this subordinate partiality. Perhaps it is a sort of elemental training to those higher and more large regards, by which alone men come to be affected, as with their own concern, in the prosperity of a kingdom so extensive as that of France. In that general territory itself, as in the old name of provinces, the citizens are interested from old prejudices and unreasoned habits, and not on account of the geometric properties of its figure. The power and pre-eminence of Paris does certainly press down and hold these republics together as long as it lasts. But, for the reasons I have already given you, I think it cannot last very long.

Passing from the civil creating and the civil cementing principles of this constitution, to the National Assembly, which is to appear and act as sovereign, we see a body in its constitution with every possible power, and no possible external control. We see a body without fundamental laws, without established maxims, without respected rules of proceeding, which nothing can keep firm to any system whatsoever. Their idea of their powers is always taken at the utmost stretch of legislative competency, and their examples for common cases from the exceptions of the most urgent necessity. The future is to be in most respect like the present Assembly; but by the mode of the new elections and the tendency of the new circulations, it will be purged of the small degree of internal control existing in a minority chosen originally from various interests, and preserving something of their spirit. If possible, the next Assembly must be worse than the present. The present, by destroying and altering everything, will leave to their successors apparently nothing popular to do. They will be roused by emulation and example to enterprises the boldest and the most absurd. To suppose such an assembly sitting in perfect quietude is ridiculous.

Your all-sufficient legislators, in their hurry to do everything at once, have forgot one thing that seems essential, and which I believe never has been before, in the theory or the practice, omitted by any projector of a republic. They have forgot to constitute a *senate,* or something of that nature and character. Never, before this time, was heard of a body politic composed of one legislative and active assembly, and its executive officers, without such a council; without something to which foreign states might connect themselves; something to which, in the ordinary detail of government, the people could look up; something which might give a bias, and steadiness, and preserve something like consistency in the proceedings of state. Such a body kings generally have as a council. A monarchy may exist without it; but it seems to be in the very essence of a republican government. It holds a sort of middle place between the supreme power exercised by the people, or immediately delegated from them, and the mere executive. Of this there are no traces in your constitution; and, in providing nothing of this kind, your Solons and Numas have, as much as in anything else, discovered a sovereign incapacity.

Let us now turn our eyes to what they have done towards the formation of an executive power. For this they have chosen a degraded king. This their first executive officer is to be a machine, without any sort of deliberative discretion in any one act of his function. At best he is but a channel to convey to the National Assembly such matter as it may import that body to know. If he had been made the exclusive channel, the power would not have been without its importance; though infinitely perilous to those who would choose to exercise it. But public intelligence and statement of facts may pass to the Assembly with equal authenticity, through any other conveyance. As to the means, therefore, of giving a direction to measures by the statement of an authorized reporter, this office of intelligence is as nothing.

To consider the French scheme of an executive officer, in its two natural divisions of civil and political. In the first it must be observed, that, according to the new constitution, the higher parts of judicature, in either of its lines, are not in the king. The king of France is not the fountain of justice. The judges, neither the original nor the appellate, are of his nomination. He neither proposes the candidates, nor has a negative on the choice. He is not even the public prosecutor. He serves only as a notary to authenticate the choice made of the judges in the several districts. By his officers he is to execute their sentence. When we look into the true nature of his authority, he appears to be nothing more than a chief of bumbailiffs, serjeants at mace, catchpoles, jailers, and hangmen. It is impossible to place anything called royalty in a more degrading point of view. A thousand times better had it been for the dignity of this unhappy prince, that he had nothing at all to do with the administration of justice, deprived as he is of all that is venerable, and all that is consolatory, in that function, without power of originating any process; without a power of suspension, mitigation, or pardon. Everything in justice that is vile and odious is thrown upon him. It was not for nothing that the Assembly has been at such pains to remove the stigma from certain offices, when they are resolved to place the person who had lately been their king in a situation but one degree above the executioner, and in an office nearly of the same quality. It is not in nature, that, situated as the king of the French now is, he can respect himself, or can be respected by others.

View this new executive officer on the side of his political capacity, as he acts under the orders of the National Assembly. To execute laws is a royal office; to execute orders is not to be a king. However, a political executive magistracy, though merely such, is a great trust. It is a trust indeed that has much depending upon its faithful and diligent performance, both in the person presiding in it and in all its subordinates. Means of performing this duty ought to be given by regulation; and dispositions towards it ought to be infused by the circumstances attendant on the trust. It ought to be environed with dignity, authority, and consideration, and it ought to lead to glory. The office of execution is an office of exertion. It is not from impotence we are to expect the tasks of power. What sort of person is a king to command executory service, who has no means whatsoever to reward it? Not in a permanent office; not in a grant of land; no, not in a pension of fifty pounds a year; not in the vainest and most trivial title. In France the king is no more the fountain of honour than he is the fountain of justice. All rewards, all distinctions, are in other hands. Those who serve the king can be actuated by no natural motive but fear; by a fear of everything except their master. His functions of internal coercion are as odious as those which he exercises in the department of justice. If relief is to be given to any municipality, the Assembly gives it. If troops are to be sent to reduce them to obedience to the Assembly, the king is to execute the order; and upon every occasion he is to be spattered over with the blood of his people. He has no negative; yet his name and authority is used to enforce every harsh decree. Nay, he must concur in the butchery of those who shall attempt to free him from his imprisonment, or show the slightest attachment to his person or to his ancient authority.

Executive magistracy ought to be constituted in such a manner, that those who compose it should be disposed to love and to venerate those whom they are bound to obey. A purposed neglect, or, what is worse, a literal but perverse and malignant obedience, must be the ruin of the wisest counsels. In vain will the law attempt to anticipate or to follow such studied neglects and fraudulent attentions. To make them act zealously is not in the competence of law. Kings, even such as are truly kings, may and ought to bear the freedom of subjects that are obnoxious to them. They may too, without derogating from themselves, bear even the authority of such persons if it promotes their service. Louis the Thirteenth mortally hated the Cardinal de Richelieu; but his support of that minister against his rivals was the source of all the glory of his reign, and the solid foundation of his throne itself. Louis the Fourteenth, when come to the throne, did not love the Cardinal Mazarin; but for his interests he preserved him in power. When old, he detested Louvois; but for years, whilst he faithfully served his greatness, he endured his person. When George the Second took Mr. Pitt, who certainly was not agreeable to him, into his councils, he did nothing which could humble a wise sovereign. But these ministers, who were chosen by affairs, not by affections, acted in the name of, and in trust for, kings; and not as their avowed, constitutional, and ostensible masters. I think it impossible that any king, when he has recovered his first terrors, can cordially infuse vivacity and vigour into measures which he knows to be dictated by those, who, he must be persuaded, are in the highest degree ill affected to his person. Will any ministers, who serve such a king (or whatever he may be called) with but a decent appearance of respect, cordially obey the orders of those whom but the other day in his name they had committed to the Bastille? Will they obey the orders of those whom, whilst they were exercising despotic justice upon them, they conceived they were treating with lenity; and from whom, in a prison, they thought they had provided an asylum? If you expect such obedience, amongst your other innovations and regenerations, you ought to make a revolution in nature, and provide a new constitution for the human mind. Otherwise, your supreme government cannot harmonize with its executory system. There are cases in which we cannot take up with names and abstractions. You may call half a dozen leading individuals, whom we have reason to fear and hate, the nation. It makes no other difference, than to make us fear and hate them the more. If it had been thought justifiable and expedient to make such a revolution by such means, and through such persons, as you have made yours, it would have been more wise to have completed the business of the fifth and sixth of October. The new executive officer would then owe his situation to those who are his creators as well as his masters; and he might be bound in interest, in the society of crime, and (if in crimes there could be virtues) in gratitude, to serve those who had promoted him to a place of great lucre and great sensual indulgence; and of something more: for more he must have received from those who certainly would not have limited an aggrandized creature, as they have done a submitting antagonist.

A king circumstanced as the present, if he is totally stupified by his misfortunes, so as to think it not the necessity, but the premium and privilege, of life, to eat and sleep, without any regard to glory, can never be fit for the office. If he feels as men commonly feel, he must be sensible, that an office so circumstanced is one in which he can obtain no fame or reputation. He has no generous interest that can excite him to action. At best, his conduct will be passive and defensive. To inferior people such an office might be matter of honour. But to be raised to it, and to descend to it, are different things, and suggest different sentiments. Does he *really* name the ministers? They will have a sympathy with him. Are they forced upon him? The whole business between them and the nominal king will be mutual counteraction. In all other countries, the office of ministers of state is of the highest dignity. In France it is full of peril, and incapable of glory. Rivals however they will have in their nothingness, whilst shallow ambition exists in the world, or the desire of a miserable salary is an incentive to short-sighted avarice. Those competitors of the ministers are enabled by your constitution to attack them in their vital parts, whilst they have not the means of repelling their charges in any other than the degrading character of culprits. The ministers of state in France are the only persons in that country who are incapable of a share in the national councils. What ministers! What councils! What a nation! But they are responsible. It is a poor service that is to be had from responsibility. The elevation of mind to be derived from fear will never make a nation glorious. Responsibility prevents crimes. It makes all attempts against the laws dangerous. But for a principle of active and zealous service, none but idiots could think of it. Is the conduct of a war to be trusted to a man who may abhor its principle; who, in every step he may take to render it successful, confirms the power of those by whom he is oppressed? Will foreign states seriously treat with him who has no prerogative of peace or war; no, not so much as in a single vote by himself or his ministers, or by any one whom he can possibly influence? A state of contempt is not a state for a prince: better get rid of him at once.

I know it will be said that these humours in the court and executive government will continue only through this generation; and that the king has been brought to declare the dauphin shall be educated in a conformity to his situation. If he is made to conform to his situation, he will have no education at all. His training must be worse even than that of an arbitrary monarch. If he reads—whether he reads or not, some good or evil genius will tell him his ancestors were kings. Thenceforward his object must be to assert himself, and to avenge his parents. This you will say is not his duty. That may be; but it is nature; and whilst you pique nature against you, you do unwisely to trust to duty. In this futile scheme of polity, the state nurses in its bosom, for the present, a source of weakness, perplexity, counteraction, inefficiency, and decay; and it prepares the means of its final ruin. In short, I see nothing in the executive force (I cannot call it authority) that has even an appearance of vigour, or that has the smallest degree of just correspondence or symmetry, or amicable relation with the supreme power, either as it now exists, or as it is planned for the future government.

You have settled, by an economy as perverted as the policy, two[48] establishments of government; one real, one fictitious. Both maintained at a vast expense; but the fictitious at, I think, the greatest. Such a machine as the latter is not worth the grease of its wheels. The expense is exorbitant; and neither the show nor the use deserve the tenth part of the charge. Oh! but I don't do justice to the talents of the legislators: I don't allow, as I ought to do, for necessity. Their scheme of executive force was not their choice. This pageant must be kept. The people would not consent to part with it. Right; I understand you. You do, in spite of your grand theories, to which you would have heaven and earth to bend, you do know how to conform yourselves to the nature and circumstances of things. But when you were obliged to conform thus far to circumstances, you ought to have carried your submission farther, and to have made, what you were obliged to take, a proper instrument, and useful to its end. That was in your power. For instance, among many others, it was in your power to leave to your king the right of peace and war. What! to leave to the executive magistrate the most dangerous of all prerogatives? I know none more dangerous; nor any one more necessary to be so trusted. I do not say that this prerogative ought to be trusted to your king, unless he enjoyed other auxiliary trusts along with it, which he does not now hold. But, if he did possess them, hazardous as they are undoubtedly, advantages would arise from such a constitution, more than compensating the risk. There is no other way of keeping the several potentates of Europe from intriguing distinctly and personally with the members of your Assembly, from intermeddling in all your concerns, and fomenting, in the heart of your country, the most pernicious of all factions; factions in the interest and under the direction of foreign powers. From that worst of evils, thank God, we are still free. Your skill, if you had any, would be well employed to find out indirect correctives and controls upon this perilous trust. If you did not like those which in England we have chosen, your leaders might have exerted their abilities in contriving better. If it were necessary to exemplify the consequences of such an executive government as yours, in the management of great affairs, I should refer you to the late reports of M. de Montmorin to the National Assembly, and all the other proceedings relative to the differences between Great Britain and

Spain. It would be treating your understanding with disrespect to point them out to you.

I hear that the persons who are called ministers have signified an intention of resigning their places. I am rather astonished that they have not resigned long since. For the universe I would not have stood in the situation in which they have been for this last twelvemonth. They wished well, I take it for granted, to the Revolution. Let this fact be as it may, they could not, placed as they were upon an eminence, though an eminence of humiliation, but be the first to see collectively, and to feel each in his own department, the evils which have been produced by that revolution. In every step which they took, or forbore to take, they must have felt the degraded situation of their country, and their utter incapacity of serving it. They are in a species of subordinate servitude, in which no men before them were ever seen. Without confidence from their sovereign, on whom they were forced, or from the Assembly who forced them upon him, all the noble functions of their office are executed by committees of the Assembly, without any regard whatsoever to their personal or their official authority. They are to execute, without power; they are to be responsible, without discretion; they are to deliberate, without choice. In their puzzled situation, under two sovereigns, over neither of whom they have any influence, they must act in such a manner as (in effect, whatever they may intend) sometimes to betray the one, sometimes the other, and always to betray themselves. Such has been their situation; such must be the situation of those who succeed them. I have much respect, and many good wishes, for M. Necker. I am obliged to him for attentions. I thought when his enemies had driven him from Versailles, that his exile was a subject of most serious congratulation—*sed multœ urbes et publica vota vicerunt.* He is now sitting on the ruins of the finances, and of the monarchy of France.

A great deal more might be observed on the strange constitution of the executory part of the new government; but fatigue must give bounds to the discussion of subjects, which in themselves have hardly any limits.

As little genius and talent am I able to perceive in the plan of judicature formed by the National Assembly. According to their invariable course, the framers of your constitution have begun with the utter abolition of the parliaments. These venerable bodies, like the rest of the old government, stood in need of reform, even though there should be no change made in the monarchy. They required several more alterations to adopt them to the system of a free constitution. But they had particulars in their constitution, and those not a few, which deserved approbation from the wise. They possessed one fundamental excellence; they were independent. The most doubtful circumstance attendant on their office, that of its being vendible, contributed however to this independency of character. They held for life. Indeed they may be said to have held by inheritance. Appointed by the monarch, they were considered as nearly out of his power. The most determined exertions of that authority against them only showed their radical independence. They composed permanent bodies politic, constituted to resist arbitrary innovation; and from that corporate constitution, and from most of their forms, they were well calculated to afford both certainty and stability to the laws. They had been a safe asylum to secure these laws, in all the revolutions of humour and opinion. They had saved that sacred deposit of the country during the reigns of arbitrary princes, and the struggles of arbitrary factions. They kept alive the memory and record of the constitution. They were the great security to private property; which might be said (when personal liberty had no existence) to be, in fact, as well guarded in France as in any other country. Whatever is supreme in a state, ought to have, as much as possible, its judicial authority so constituted as not only not to depend upon it, but in some sort to balance it. It ought to give a security to its justice against its power. It ought to make its judicature, as it were, something exterior to the state.

These parliaments had furnished, not the best certainly, but some considerable corrective to the excesses and vices of the monarchy. Such an independent judicature was ten times more necessary when a democracy became the absolute power of the country. In that constitution, elective, temporary, local judges, such as you have contrived, exercising their dependent functions in a narrow society, must be the worst of all tribunals. In them it will be vain to look for any appearance of justice towards strangers, towards the obnoxious rich, towards the minority of routed parties, towards all those who in the election have supported unsuccessful candidates. It will be impossible to keep the new tribunals clear of the worst spirit of faction. All contrivances by ballot we know experimentally to be vain and childish to prevent a discovery of inclinations. Where they may the best answer the purposes of concealment, they answer to produce suspicion, and this is a still more mischievous cause of partiality.

If the parliaments had been preserved, instead of being dissolved at so ruinous a change to the nation, they might have served in this new commonwealth, perhaps not precisely the same (I do not mean an exact parallel), but nearly the same, purposes as the court and senate of Areopagus did in Athens; that is, as one of the balances and correctives to the evils of a light and unjust democracy. Every one knows that this tribunal was the great stay of that state; every one knows with what care it was upheld, and with what a religious awe it was consecrated. The parliaments were not wholly free from faction, I admit; but this evil was exterior and accidental, and not so much the vice of their constitution itself, as it must be in your new contrivance of sexennial elective judicatories. Several English commend the abolition of the old tribunals, as supposing that they determined everything by bribery and corruption. But they have stood the test of monarchic and republican scrutiny. The court was well disposed to prove corruption on those bodies when they were dissolved in 1771. Those who have again dissolved them would have done the same if they could—but both inquisitions having failed, I conclude, that gross pecuniary corruption must have been rather rare amongst them.

It would have been prudent, along with the parliaments, to preserve their ancient power of registering, and of remonstrating at least, upon all the decrees of the National Assembly, as they did upon those which passed in the time of the monarchy. It would be a means of squaring the occasional decrees of a democracy to some principles of general jurisprudence. The vice of the ancient democracies, and one cause of their ruin, was, that they ruled, as you do, by occasional decrees, *psephismata*. This practice soon broke in upon the tenour and consistency of the laws; it abated the respect of the people towards them; and totally destroyed them in the end.

Your vesting the power of remonstrance, which, in the time of the monarchy, existed in the parliament of Paris, in your principal executive officer, whom, in spite of common sense, you persevere in calling king, is the height of absurdity. You ought never to suffer remonstrance from him who is to execute. This is to understand neither council nor execution; neither authority nor obedience. The person whom you call king, ought not to have this power, or he ought to have more.

Your present arrangement is strictly judicial. Instead of imitating your monarchy, and seating your judges on a bench of independence, your object is to reduce them to the most blind obedience. As you have changed all things, you have invented new principles of order. You first appoint judges, who, I suppose, are to determine according to law, and then you let them know, that, at some time or other, you intend to give them some law by which they are to determine. Any studies which they have made (if any they have made) are to be useless to them. But to supply these studies, they are to be sworn to obey all the rules, orders, and instructions which from time to time they are to receive from the National Assembly. These if they submit to, they leave no ground of law to the subject. They become complete and most dangerous instruments in the hands of the governing power, which, in the midst of a cause, or on the prospect of it, may wholly change the rule of decision. If these orders of the National Assembly come to be contrary to the will of the people, who locally choose those judges, such confusion must happen as is terrible to think of. For the judges owe their places to the local authority; and the commands they are sworn to obey come from those who have no share in their appointment. In the mean time they have the example of the court of *Chatelet* to encourage and guide them in the exercise of their functions. That court is to try criminals sent to it by the National Assembly, or brought before it by other courses of delation. They sit under a guard to save their own lives. They know not by what law they judge, nor under what authority they act, nor by what tenure they hold. It is thought that they are sometimes obliged to condemn at peril of their lives. This is not perhaps certain, nor can it be ascertained; but when they acquit, we know they have seen the persons whom they discharge, with perfect impunity to the actors, hanged at the door of their court.

The Assembly indeed promises that they will form a body of law, which shall be short, simple, clear, and so forth. That is, by their short laws, they will leave much to the discretion of the judge; whilst they have exploded the authority of all the learning which could make judicial discretion (a thing perilous at best) deserving the appellation of a *sound* discretion.

It is curious to observe, that the administrative bodies are carefully exempted from the jurisdiction of these new tribunals. That is, those persons are exempted from the power of the laws, who ought to be the most entirely submitted to them. Those who execute public pecuniary trusts, ought of all men to be the most strictly held to their duty. One would have thought that it must have been among your earliest cares, if you did not mean that those administrative bodies should be real, sovereign, independent states, to form an awful tribunal, like your late parliaments, or like our king's bench, where all corporate officers might obtain protection in the legal exercise of their functions, and would find coercion if they trespassed against their legal duty. But the cause of the exemption is plain. These administrative bodies are the great instruments of the present leaders in their progress through democracy to oligarchy. They must therefore be put above the law. It will be said, that the legal tribunals which you have made are unfit to coerce them. They are undoubtedly. They are unfit for any rational purpose. It will be said too, that the administrative bodies will be accountable to the general assembly. This I fear is talking without much consideration of the nature of that assembly, or of these corporations. However, to be subject to the pleasure of that assembly, is not to be subject to law either for protection or for constraint.

This establishment of judges as yet wants something to its completion. It is to be crowned by a new tribunal. This is to be a grand state judicature; and it is to judge of crimes committed against the nation, that is, against the power of the Assembly. It seems as if they had something in their view of the nature of the high court of justice erected in England during the time of the great usurpation. As they have not yet finished this part of the scheme, it is impossible to form a right judgment upon it. However, if great care is not taken to form it in a spirit very different from that which has guided them in their proceedings relative to state offenses, this tribunal, subservient to their inquisition, *the committee of research,* will extinguish the last sparks of liberty in France, and settle the most dreadful and arbitrary tyranny ever known in any nation. If they wish to give to this tribunal any appearance of liberty and justice, they must not evoke from or send to it the causes relative to their own members, at their pleasure. They must also remove the seat of that tribunal out of the republic of Paris.[49]

Has more wisdom been displayed in the constitution of your army than what is discoverable in your plan of judicature? The able arrangement of this part is the more difficult, and requires the greater skill and attention, not only as a great concern in itself, but as it is the third cementing principle in the new body of republics, which you call the French nation. Truly it is not easy to divine what that army may become at last. You have voted a very large one, and on good appointments, at least fully equal to your apparent means of payment. But what is the principle of its discipline? or whom is it to obey? You have got the wolf by the ears, and I wish you joy of the happy position in which you have chosen to place yourselves, and in which you are well circumstanced for a free deliberation, relatively to that army, or to anything else.

The minister and secretary of state for the war department is M. de la Tour du Pin. This gentleman, like his colleagues in administration, is a most zealous assertor of the Revolution, and a sanguine admirer of the new constitution, which originated in that event. His statement of facts, relative to the military of France, is important, not only from his official and personal authority, but because it displays very clearly the actual condition of the army in France, and because it throws light on the principles upon which the Assembly proceeds, in the administration of this critical object. It may enable us to form some judgment, how far it may be expedient in this country to imitate the martial policy of France.

M. de la Tour du Pin, on the fourth of last June, comes to give an account of the state of his department, as it exists under the auspices of the National Assembly. No man knows it so well; no man can express it better. Addressing himself to the National Assembly, he says, "His Majesty has *this day* sent me to apprize you of the multiplied disorders of which *every day* he receives the most distressing intelligence. The army (le corps militaire) threatens to fall into the most turbulent anarchy. Entire regiments have dared to violate at once the respect due to the laws, to the king, to the order established by your decrees, and to the oaths which they have taken with the most awful solemnity. Compelled by my duty to give you information of these excesses, my heart bleeds when I consider who they are that have committed them. Those, against whom it is not in my power to withhold the most grievous complaints, are a part of that very soldiery which to this day have been so full of honour and loyalty, and with whom, for fifty years, I have lived the comrade and the friend.

"What incomprehensible spirit of delirium and delusion has all at once led them astray? Whilst you are indefatigable in establishing uniformity in the empire, and moulding the whole into one coherent and consistent body; whilst the French are taught by you, at once the respect which the laws owe to the rights of man, and that which the citizens owe to the laws, the administration of the army presents nothing but disturbance and confusion. I see in more than one corps the bonds of discipline relaxed or broken; the most unheard-of pretensions avowed directly and without any disguise; the ordinances without force; the chiefs without authority; the military chest and the colours carried off; the authority of the king himself [*risum teneatis?*] proudly defied; the officers despised, degraded, threatened, driven away, and some of them prisoners in the midst of their corps, dragging on a precarious life in the bosom of disgust and humiliation. To fill up the measure of all these horrors, the commandants of places have had their throats cut, under the eyes, and almost in the arms, of their own soldiers.

"These evils are great; but they are not the worst consequences which may be produced by such military insurrections. Sooner or later they may menace the nation itself. *The nature of things requires* that the army should never act but as *an instrument*. The moment that, erecting itself into a deliberative body, it shall act according to its own resolutions, the *government, be it what it may, will immediately degenerate into a military democracy;* a species of political monster, which has always ended by devouring those who have produced it.

"After all this, who must not be alarmed at the irregular consultations, and turbulent committees, formed in some regiments by the common soldiers and non-commissioned officers, without the knowledge, or even in contempt of the authority, of their superiors;

although the presence and concurrence of those superiors could give no authority to such monstrous democratic assemblies [comics]."

It is not necessary to add much to this finished picture: finished as far as its canvas admits; but as I apprehend, not taking in the whole of the nature and complexity of the disorders of this military democracy, which, the minister at war truly and wisely observes, wherever it exists, must be the true constitution of the state, by whatever formal appellation it may pass. For, though he informs the Assembly that the more considerable part of the army have not cast off their obedience, but are still attached to their duty, yet those travellers, who have seen the corps whose conduct is the best, rather observe in them the absence of mutiny, than the existence of discipline.

I cannot help pausing here for a moment, to reflect upon the expressions of surprise which this minister has let fall, relative to the excesses he relates. To him the departure of the troops from their ancient principles of loyalty and honour seems quite inconceivable. Surely those to whom he addresses himself know the causes of it but too well. They know the doctrines which they have preached, the degrees which they have passed, the practices which they have countenanced. The soldiers remember the 6th of October. They recollect the French guards. They have not forgotten the taking of the king's castles in Paris and Marseilles. That the governors in both places were murdered with impunity, is a fact that has not passed out of their minds. They do not abandon the principles laid down so ostentatiously and laboriously of the quality of men. They cannot shut their eyes to the degradation of the whole noblesse of France, and the suppression of the very idea of a gentleman. The total abolition of titles and distinctions is not lost upon them. But M. de la Tour du Pin is astonished at their disloyalty, when the doctors of the Assembly have taught them at the same time the respect due to laws. It is easy to judge which of the two sorts of lessons men with arms in their hands are likely to learn. As to the authority of the king, we may collect from the minister himself (if any argument on that head were not quite superfluous) that it is not of more consideration with these troops, than it is with everybody else. "The king," says he, "has over and over again repeated his orders to put a stop to these excesses: but, in so terrible a crisis, *your* [the Assembly's] concurrence is become indispensably necessary to prevent the evils which menace the state. *You* unite to the force of the legislative power, *that of opinion* still more important." To be sure the army can have no opinion of the power or authority of the king. Perhaps the soldier has by this time learned, that the Assembly itself does not enjoy a much greater degree of liberty than that royal figure.

It is now to be seen what has been proposed in this exigency, one of the greatest that can happen in a state. The minister requests the Assembly to array itself in all its terrors, and to call forth all its majesty. He desires that the grave and severe principles announced by them may give vigour to the king's proclamation. After this we should have looked for courts civil and martial; breaking of some corps, decimating of others, and all the terrible means which necessity has employed in such cases to arrest the progress of the most terrible of all evils; particularly, one might expect, that a serious inquiry would be made into the murder of commandants in the view of their soldiers. Not one word of all this, or of anything like it. After they had been told that the soldiery trampled upon the decrees of the Assembly promulgated by the king, the Assembly pass new decrees; and they authorize the king to make new proclamations. After the secretary at war had stated that the regiments had paid no regard to oaths *prêtés avec la plus imposante solemnité*, they propose—what? More oaths. They renew decrees and proclamations as they experience their insufficiency, and they multiply oaths in proportion as they weaken, in the minds of men, the sanctions of religion. I hope that handy abridgments of the excellent sermons of Voltaire, d'Alembert, Diderot, and Helvetius, on the Immortality of the Soul, on a particular superintending Providence, and on a Future State of Rewards and Punishments, are sent down to the soldiers along with their civic oaths. Of this I have no doubt; as I understand that a certain description of reading makes no inconsiderable part of their military exercises, and that they are full as well supplied with the ammunition of pamphlets as of cartridges.

To prevent the mischiefs arising from conspiracies, irregular consultations, seditious committees, and monstrous democratic assemblies ["comitia, cornices"] of the soldiers, and all the disorders arising from idleness, luxury, dissipation, and insubordination, I believe the most astonishing means have been used that ever occurred to men, even in all the inventions of this prolific age. It is no less than this: the king has promulgated in circular letters to all the regiments his direct authority and encouragement, that the several corps should join themselves with the clubs and confederations in the several municipalities, and mix with them in their feasts and civic entertainments! This jolly discipline, it seems, is to soften the ferocity of their minds; to reconcile them to their bottle companions of other descriptions; and to merge particular conspiracies in more general associations.[50] That this remedy would be pleasing to the soldiers, as they are described by M. de la Tour du Pin, I can readily believe; and that, however mutinous otherwise, they will dutifully submit themselves to *these* royal proclamations. But I should question whether all this civic swearing, clubbing, and feasting, would dispose them, more than at present they are disposed, to an obedience to their officers; or teach them better to submit to the austere rules of military discipline. It will make them admirable citizens after the French mode, but not quite so good soldiers after any mode. A doubt might well arise, whether the conversations at these good tables would fit them a great deal the better for the character of *mere instruments*, which this veteran officer and statesman justly observes the nature of things always required an army to be.

Concerning the likelihood of this improvement in discipline, by the free conversation of the soldiers with municipal festive societies, which is thus officially encouraged by royal authority and sanction, we may judge by the state of the municipalities themselves, furnished to us by the war minister in this very speech. He conceives good hopes of the success of his endeavours towards restoring order *for the present* from the good disposition of certain regiments; but he finds something cloudy with regard to the future. As to preventing the return of confusion, "for this, the administration (says he) cannot be answerable to you, as long as they see the municipalities arrogate to themselves an authority over the troops, which your institutions have reserved wholly to the monarch. You have fixed the limits of the military authority and the municipal authority. You have bounded the action, which you have permitted to the latter over the former, to the right of requisition; but never did the letter or the spirit of your decrees authorize the commons in these municipalities to break the officers, to try them, to give orders to the soldiers, to drive them from the posts committed to their guard, to stop them in their marches ordered by the king, or, in a word, to enslave the troops to the caprice of each of the cities, or even market towns, through which they are to pass."

Such is the character and disposition of the municipal society which is to reclaim the soldiery, to bring them back to the true principles of military subordination, and to render them machines in the hands of the supreme power of the country! Such are the distempers of the French troops! Such is their cure! As the army is, so is the navy. The municipalities supersede the orders of the Assembly, and the seamen in their turn supersede the orders of the municipalities. From my heart I pity the condition of a respectable servant of the public, like this war minister, obliged in his old age to pledge the Assembly in their civic cups, and to enter with a hoary head into all the fantastic vagaries of these juvenile politicians. Such schemes are not like propositions coming from a man of fifty years' wear and tear amongst mankind. They seem rather such as ought to be expected from those grand compounders in politics, who shorten the road to their degrees in the state; and have a certain inward fanatical assurance and illumination upon all subjects; upon the credit of which one of their doctors has thought fit, with great applause, and greater success, to caution the Assembly not to attend to old men, or to any persons who valued themselves upon their experience. I suppose all the ministers of state must qualify, and take this test; wholly abjuring the errors and heresies of experience and observation. Every man has his own relish. But I think if I could not attain to the wisdom, I would at least preserve something of the stiff and peremptory dignity of age. These gentlemen deal in regeneration: but at any price I should hardly yield my rigid fibres to be regenerated by them; nor begin, in my grand climacteric, to squall in their new accents, or to stammer, in my second cradle, the elemental sounds of their barbarous metaphysics.[51] *Si isti mihi largiantur ut repueriscam, et in eorum cunis vagiam, valde recusem!*

The imbecility of any part of the puerile and pedantic system, which they call a constitution, cannot be laid open without discovering the utter insufficiency and mischief of every other part with which it comes in contact, or that bears any the remotest relation to it. You cannot propose a remedy for the incompetence of the crown, without displaying the debility of the Assembly. You cannot deliberate on the confusion of the army of the state, without disclosing the worse disorders of the armed municipalities. The military lays open the civil, and the civil betrays the military, anarchy. I wish everybody carefully to peruse the eloquent speech (such it is) of Mons. de la Tour du Pin. He attributes the salvation of the municipalities to the good behaviour of some of the troops. These troops are to preserve the well-disposed part of those municipalities, which is confessed to be the weakest, from the pillage of the worst disposed, which is the strongest. But the municipalities affect a sovereignty, and will command those troops which are necessary for their protection. Indeed they must command them or court them. The municipalities, by the necessity of their situation, and by the republican powers they have obtained, must, with relation to the military, be the masters, or the servants, or the confederates, or each successively; or they must make a jumble of all together, according to circumstances. What government is there to coerce the army but the municipality, or the municipality but the army? To preserve concord where authority is extinguished, at the hazard of all consequences, the Assembly attempts to cure the distempers by the distempers themselves; and they hope to preserve themselves from a purely military democracy, by giving it a debauched interest in the municipal.

If the soldiers once come to mix for any time in the municipal clubs, cabals, and confederacies, an elective attraction will draw them to the lowest and most desperate part. With them will be their habits, affections, and sympathies. The military conspiracies, which are to be remedied by civic confederacies; the rebellious municipalities, which are to be rendered obedient by furnishing them with the means of seducing the very armies of the state that are to keep them in order; all these chimeras of a monstrous and portentous policy must aggravate the confusion from which they have arisen. There must be blood. The want of common judgment manifested in the construction of all their descriptions of forces, and in all their kinds of civil and judicial authorities, will make it flow. Disorders may be quieted in one time and in one part. They will break out in others; because the evil is radical and intrinsic. All these schemes of mixing mutinous soldiers with seditious citizens must weaken still more and more the military connexion of soldiers with their officers, as well as add military and mutinous audacity to turbulent artificers and peasants. To secure a real army, the officer should be first and last in the eye of the soldier; first and last in his attention, observance, and esteem. Officers it seems there are to be, whose chief qualification must be temper and patience. They are to manage their troops by electioneering arts. They must bear themselves as candidates, not as commanders. But as by such means power may be occasionally in their hands, the authority by which they are to be nominated becomes of high importance.

What you may do finally does not appear; nor is it of much moment, whilst the strange and contradictory relation between your army and all the parts of your republic, as well as the puzzled relation of those parts to each other and to the whole, remain as they are. You seem to have given the provisional nomination of the officers, in the first instance, to the king, with a reserve of approbation by the National Assembly. Men who have an interest to pursue are extremely sagacious in discovering the true seat of power. They must soon perceive that those, who can negative indefinitely, in reality appoint. The officers must therefore look to their intrigues in that Assembly, as the sole, certain road to promotion. Still, however, by your new constitution they must begin their solicitation at court. This double negotiation for military rank seems to me a contrivance as well adapted, as if it were studied for no other end, to promote faction in the Assembly itself, relative to this vast military patronage; and then to poison the corps of officers with factions of a nature still more dangerous to the safety of government, upon any bottom on which it can be placed, and destructive in the end to the efficiency of the army itself. Those officers, who lose the promotions intended for them by the crown, must become of a faction opposite to that of the Assembly which has rejected their claims, and must nourish discontents in the heart of the army against the ruling powers. Those officers, on the other hand, who, by carrying their point through an interest in the Assembly, feel themselves to be at best only second in the goodwill of the crown, though first in that of the Assembly, must slight an authority which would not advance and could not retard their promotion. If to avoid these evils you will have no other rule for command or promotion than seniority, you will have an army of formality; at the same time it will become more independent, and more of a military republic. Not they, but the king is the machine. A king is not to be deposed by halves. If he is not everything in the command of an army, he is nothing. What is the effect of a power placed nominally at the head of the army, who to that army is no object of gratitude, or of fear? Such a cipher is not fit for the administration of an object, of all things the most delicate, the supreme command of military men. They must be constrained (and their inclinations lead them to what their necessities require) by a real, vigorous, effective, decided, personal authority. The authority of the Assembly itself suffers by passing through such a debilitating channel as they have chosen. The army will not long look to an assembly acting through the organ of false show, and palpable imposition. They will not seriously yield obedience to a prisoner. They will either despise a pageant, or they will pity a captive king. This relation of your army to the crown will, if I am not greatly mistaken, become a serious dilemma in your politics.

It is besides to be considered, whether an assembly like yours, even supposing that it was in possession of another sort of organ through which its orders were to pass, is fit for promoting the obedience and discipline of an army. It is known, that armies have hitherto yielded a very precarious and uncertain obedience to any senate, or popular authority; and they will least of all yield it to an assembly which is only to have a continuance of two years. The officers must totally lose the characteristic disposition of military men, if they see with perfect submission and due admiration, the dominion of pleaders; especially when they find that they have a new court to pay to an endless succession of those pleaders; whose military policy, and the genius of whose command (if they should have any) must be as uncertain as their duration is transient. In the weakness of one kind of authority, and in the fluctuation of all, the officers of an army will remain for some time mutinous and full of faction, until some popular general, who understands the art of conciliating the soldiery, and who possesses the true spirit of command, shall draw the eyes of all men upon himself. Armies will obey him on his personal account. There is no other way of securing military obedience in this state of things. But the moment in which that event shall happen, the person who really commands the army is your master; the master (that is little) of your king, the master of your Assembly, the master of your whole republic.

How came the Assembly by their present power over the army? Chiefly, to be sure, by debauching the soldiers from their officers. They have begun by a most terrible operation. They have touched the central point, about which the particles that compose armies are at repose. They have destroyed the principle of obedience in the great, essential, critical link between the officer and the soldier, just where the chain of military subordination commences and on which the whole of that system depends. The soldier is told he is a citizen, and has the rights of man and citizen. The right of a man, he is told, is to be his own governor, and to be ruled only by those to whom he delegates that self-government. It is very natural he should think that he ought most of all to have his choice where he is to yield the greatest degree of obedience. He will therefore, in all probability, systematically do, what he does at present occasionally; that is, he will exercise at least a negative in the choice of his officers. At present the officers are known at best to be only permissive, and on their good behaviour. In fact, there have been many instances in which they have been cashiered by their corps. Here is a second negative on the choice of the king; a negative as effectual at least as the other of the Assembly. The soldiers know already that it has been a question, not ill received in the National Assembly, whether they ought not to have the direct choice of their officers, or some proportion of them? When such matters are in deliberation it is no extravagant supposition that they will incline to the opinion most favourable to their pretensions. They will not bear to be deemed the army of an imprisoned king, whilst another army in the same country, with whom too they are to feast and confederate, is to be considered as the free army of a free constitution. They will cast their eyes on the other and more permanent army; I mean the municipal. That corps, they well know, does actually elect its own officers. They may not be able to discern the grounds of distinction on which they are not to elect a Marquis de la Fayette (or what is his new name?) of their own. If this election of a commander-in-chief be a part of the rights of men, why not of theirs? They see elective justices of peace, elective judges, elective curates, elective bishops, elective municipalities, and elective commanders of the Parisian army. Why should they alone be excluded? Are the brave troops of France the only men in that nation who are not the fit judges of military merit, and of the qualifications necessary for a commander-in-chief? Are they paid by the state, and do they therefore lose the rights of men? They are a part of that nation themselves, and contribute to that pay. And is not the king, is not the National Assembly, and are not all who elect the National Assembly, likewise paid? Instead of seeing all these forfeit their rights by their receiving a salary, they perceive that in all these cases a salary is given for the exercise of those rights. All your resolutions, all your proceedings, all your debates, all the works of your doctors in religion and politics, have industriously been put into their hands; and you expect that they will apply to their own case just as much of your doctrines and examples as suits your pleasure.

Everything depends upon the army in such a government as yours; for you have industriously destroyed all the opinions, and prejudices, and, as far as in you lay, all the instincts which support government. Therefore the moment any differences arises between your National Assembly and any part of the nation, you must have recourse to force. Nothing else is left to you; or rather you have left nothing else to yourselves. You see, by the report of your war minister, that the distribution of the army is in a great measure made with a view of internal coercion.[52] You must rule by an army; and you have infused into that army by which you rule, as well as into the whole body of the nation, principles which after a time must disable you in the use you resolve to make of it. The king is to call out troops to act against his people, when the world has been told, and the assertion is still ringing in our ears, that troops ought not to be fire on citizens. The colonies assert to themselves an independent constitution and a free trade. They must be constrained by troops. In what chapter of your code of the rights of men are they able to read, that it is a part of the rights of men to have their commerce monopolized and restrained for the benefit of others? As the colonists rise on you, the negroes rise on them. Troops again—massacre, torture, hanging! These are your rights of men! These are the fruits of metaphysic declarations wantonly made, and shamefully retracted! It was but the other day, that the farmers of land in one of your provinces refused to pay some sorts of rents to the lord of the soil. In consequence of this, you decree, that the country people shall pay all rents and dues, except those which as grievances you have abolished; and if they refuse, then you order the king to march troops against them. You lay down metaphysic propositions which infer universal consequences, and then you attempt to limit logic by despotism. The leaders of the present system tell them of their rights, as men, to take fortresses, to murder guards, to seize on kings without the least appearance of authority even from the Assembly, whilst, as the sovereign legislative body, that Assembly was sitting in the name of the nation—and yet these leaders presume to order out the troops which have acted in these very disorders, to coerce those who shall judge on the principles, and follow the examples, which have been guaranteed by their own approbation.

The leaders teach the people to abhor and reject all feudality as the barbarism of tyranny, and they tell them afterwards how much of that barbarous tyranny they are to bear with patience. As they are prodigal of light with regard to grievances, so the people find them sparing in the extreme with regard to redress. They know that not only certain quitrents and personal duties, which you have permitted them to redeem (but have furnished no money for the redemption), are as nothing to those burthens for which you have made no provision at all. They know, that almost the whole system of landed property in its origin is feudal; that it is the distribution of the possessions of the original proprietors, made by a barbarous conqueror to his barbarous instruments; and that the most grievous effects of the conquest are the land rents of every kind, as without question they are.

The peasants, in all probability, are the descendants of these ancient proprietors, Romans or Gauls. But if they fail, in any degree, in the titles which they make on the principles of antiquaries and lawyers, they retreat into the citadel of the rights of men. There they find that men are equal; and the earth, the kind and equal mother of all, ought not to be monopolized to foster the pride and luxury of any men, who by nature are no better than themselves, and who, if they do not labour for their bread, are worse. They find, that by the laws of nature the occupant and subduer of the soil is the true proprietor; that there is no prescription against nature; and that the agreements (where any there are) which have been made with the landlords, during the time of slavery, are only the effect of duresse and force; and that when the people re-entered into the rights of men, those agreements were made as void, as everything else which had been settled under the prevalence of the old feudal and aristocratic tyranny. They will tell you that they see no difference between an idler with a hat and a national cockade, and an idler in a cowl, or in a rochet. If you ground the title to rents on succession and prescription, they tell you from the speech of M. *Camus,* published by the National Assembly for their information, that things ill begun cannot avail themselves of prescription; that the title of these lords was vicious in its origin; and that force is at least as bad as fraud. As to the title by succession, they will tell you, that the succession of those who have cultivated the soil is the true pedigree of property, and not rotten parchments and silly substitutions; that the lords have enjoyed their usurpation too long; and that if they allow to these lay monks any charitable pension, they ought to be thankful to the bounty of the true proprietor, who is so generous towards a false claimant to his goods.

When the peasants give you back that coin of sophistic reason, on which you have set your image and superscription, you cry it down as base money, and tell them you will pay for the future with French guards, and dragoons, and hussars. You hold up, to chastise them, the second-hand authority of a king, who is only the instrument of destroying without any power of protecting either the people or his own person. Through him it seems you will make yourselves obeyed. They answer, You have taught us that there are no gentlemen; and which of your principles teach us to bow to kings whom we have not elected? We know, without your teaching, that lands were given for the support of feudal dignities, feudal titles, and feudal offices. When you took down the cause as a grievance, why should the more grievous effect remain? As there are now no hereditary honours, and no distinguished families, why are we taxed to maintain what you tell us ought not to exist? You have sent down our old aristocratic landlords in no other character, and with no other title, but that of exactors under your authority. Have you endeavoured to make these your rent-gatherers respectable to us? No. You have sent them to us with their arms reversed, their shields broken, their impresses defaced; and so displumed, degraded, and metamorphosed, such unfeathered two-legged things, that we no longer know them. They are strangers to us. They do not even go by the names of our ancient lords. Physically they may be the same men; though we are not quite sure of that, on your new philosophic doctrines of personal identity. In all other respects they are totally changed. We do not see why we have not as good a right to refuse them their rents, as you have to abrogate all their honours, titles, and distinctions. This we have never commissioned you to do; and it is one instance, among many indeed, of your assumption of undelegated power. We see the burghers of Paris, through their clubs, their mobs, and their national guards, directing you at their pleasure, and giving that as law to you, which, under your authority, is transmitted as law to us. Through you, these burghers dispose of the lives and fortunes of us all. Why should not you attend as much to the desires of the laborious husbandman with regard to our rent, by which we are affected in the most serious manner, as you do to the demands of these insolent burghers, relative to distinctions and titles of honour, by which neither they nor we are affected at all? But we find you pay more regard to their fancies than to our necessities. Is it among the rights of man to pay tribute to his equals? Before this measure of yours, we might have thought we were not perfectly equal. We might have entertained some old, habitual, unmeaning prepossession in favour of those landlords; but we cannot conceive with what other view than that of destroying all respect to them, you could have made the law that degrades them. You have forbidden us to treat them with any of the old formalities of respect, and now you send troops to sabre and to bayonet us into a submission to fear and force, which you did not suffer us to yield to the mild authority of opinion.

The ground of some of these arguments is horrid and ridiculous to all rational ears; but to the politicians of metaphysics who have opened schools for sophistry, and made establishments for anarchy, it is solid and conclusive. It is obvious, that on a mere consideration of the right, the leaders in the Assembly would not in the least have scrupled to abrogate the rents along with the titles and family ensigns. It would be only to follow up the principle of their reasoning, and to complete the analogy of their conduct. But they had newly possessed themselves of a great body of landed property by confiscation. They had this commodity at market; and the market would have been wholly destroyed, if they were to permit the husbandmen to riot in the speculations with which they so freely intoxicated themselves. The only security which property enjoys in any one of its descriptions, is from the interests of their rapacity with regard to some other. They have left nothing but their own arbitrary pleasure to determine what property is to be protected and what subverted.

Neither have they left any principle by which any of their municipalities can be bound to obedience; or even conscientiously obliged not to separate from the whole to become independent, or to connect itself with some other state. The people of Lyons, it seems, have refused lately to pay taxes. Why should they not? What lawful authority is there left to exact them? The king imposed some of them. The old states, methodized by orders, settled the more ancient. They may say to the Assembly, who are you, that are not our kings, nor the states we have elected, nor sit on the principles on which we have elected you? And who are we, that when we see the gabelles, which you have ordered to be paid, wholly shaken off, when we see the act of disobedience afterwards ratified by yourselves, who are we, that we are not to judge what taxes we ought or ought not to pay, and who are not to avail ourselves of the same powers, the validity of which you have approved in others? To this the answer is, we will send troops. The last reason of kings is always the first with your Assembly. This military aid may serve for a time, whilst the impression of the increase of pay remains, and the vanity of being umpires in all disputes is flattered. But this weapon will snap short, unfaithful to the hand that employs it. The Assembly keep a school, where, systematically, and with unremitting perseverance, they teach principles, and form regulations, destructive to all spirit of subordination, civil and military—and then they expect that they shall hold in obedience an anarchic people by an anarchic army.

The municipal army which, according to their new policy, is to balance this national army, if considered in itself only, is of a constitution much more simple, and in every respect less exceptionable. It is a mere democratic body, unconnected with the crown or the kingdom; armed, and trained, and officered at the pleasure of the districts to which the corps severally belong; and the personal service of the individuals, who compose, or the fine in lieu of personal service, are directed by the same authority.[53] Nothing is more uniform. If, however, considered in any relation to the crown, to the National Assembly, to the public tribunals, or to the other army, or considered in a view to any coherence or connexion between its parts, it seems a monster, and can hardly fail to terminate its perplexed movements in some great national calamity. It is a worse preservative of a general constitution, than the systasis of Crete, or the confederation of Poland, or any other ill-devised corrective which has yet been imagined, in the necessities produced by an ill-constructed system of government.

Having concluded my few remarks on the constitution of the supreme power, the executive, the judicature, the military, and on the reciprocal relation of all these establishments, I shall say something of the ability showed by your legislators with regard to the revenue.

In their proceedings relative to this object, if possible, still fewer traces appear of political judgment or financial resource. When the states met, it seemed to be the great objects to improve the system of revenue, to enlarge its collection, to cleanse it of oppression and vexation, and to establish it on the most solid footing. Great were the expectations entertained on that head throughout Europe. It was by this grand arrangement that France was to stand or fall; and this became, in my opinion, very properly, the test by which the skill and patriotism of those who ruled in that Assembly would be tried. The revenue of the state is the state. In effect all depends upon it, whether for support or for reformation. The dignity of every occupation wholly depends upon the quantity and the kind of virtue that may be exerted in it. As all great qualities of the mind which operate in public, and are not merely suffering and passive, require force for their display, I had almost said for their unequivocal existence, the revenue, which is the spring of all power, becomes in its administration the sphere of every active virtue. Public virtue, being of a nature magnificent and splendid, instituted for great things, and conversant about great concerns, requires abundant scope and room, and cannot spread and grow under confinement, and in circumstances straitened, narrow, and sordid. Through the revenue alone the body politic can act in its true genius and character, and therefore it will display just as much of its collective virtue, and as much of that virtue which may characterize those who move it, and are, as it were, its life and guiding principle, as it is possessed of a just revenue. For from hence not only magnanimity, and liberality, and beneficence, and fortitude, and providence, and the tutelary protection of all good arts, derive their food, and the growth of their organs, but continence, and self-denial, and labour, and vigilance, and frugality, and whatever else there is in which the mind shows itself above the appetite, are nowhere more in their proper element than in the provision and distribution of the public wealth. It is therefore not without reason that the science of speculative and practical finance, which must take to its aid so many auxiliary branches of knowledge, stands high in the estimation not only of the ordinary sort, but of the wisest and best men; and as this science has grown with the progress of its object, the prosperity and improvement of nations has generally increased with the increase of their revenues; and they will both continue to grow and flourish, as long as the balance between what is left to strengthen the efforts of individuals, and what is collected for the common efforts of the state, bear to each other a due reciprocal proportion, and are kept in a close correspondence and communication. And perhaps it may be owing to the greatness of revenues, and to the urgency of state necessities, that old abuses in the constitution of finances are discovered, and their true nature a rational theory comes to be more perfectly understood; insomuch, that a smaller revenue might have been more distressing in one period than a far greater is found to be in another; the proportionate wealth even remaining the same. In this state of things, the French Assembly found something in their revenues to preserve, to secure, and wisely to administer, as well as to abrogate and alter. Though their proud assumption might justify the severest tests, yet in trying their abilities on their financial proceedings, I would only consider what is the plain, obvious duty of a common finance minister, and try them up that, and not upon models of ideal perfection.

The objects of a financier are, then, to secure an ample revenue; to impose it with judgment and equality; to employ it economically;

and, when necessity obliges him to make use of credit, to secure its foundations in that instance, and for ever, by the clearness and candour of his proceedings, the exactness of his calculations, and the solidity of his funds. On these heads we may take a short and distinct view of the merits and abilities of those in the National Assembly, who have taken to themselves the management of this arduous concern. Far from any increase of revenue in their hands, I find, by a report of M. Vernier, from the committee of finances, of the second of August last, that the amount of the national revenue, as compared with its produce before the Revolution, was diminished by the sum two hundred millions, or *eight millions sterling* of the annual income, considerably more than one-third the whole.

If this be the result of great ability, never surely was ability displayed in a more distinguished manner, or with so powerful an effect. No common folly, no vulgar incapacity, no ordinary official negligence, even no official crime, no corruption, no peculation, hardly any direct hostility which we have seen in the modern world, could in so short a time have made so complete an overthrow of the finances, and with them, of the strength of a great kingdom. *Cedò quî vestram rempublicam tantam amisistis tam cito?*

The sophisters and declaimers, as soon as the Assembly met, began with decrying the ancient constitution of the revenue in many of its most essential branches, such as the public monopoly of salt. They charged it, as truly as unwisely, with being ill-contrived, oppressive, and partial. This representation they were not satisfied to make use of in speeches preliminary to some plan of reform; they declared it in a solemn resolution or public sentence, as it were judicially, passed upon it; and this they dispersed throughout the nation. At the time they passed the decree, with the same gravity they ordered the same absurd, oppressive, and partial tax to be paid, until they could find a revenue to replace it. The consequence was inevitable. The provinces which had been always exempted from this salt monopoly, some of whom were charged with other contributions, perhaps equivalent, were totally disinclined to bear any part of the burthen, which by an equal distribution was to redeem the others. As to the Assembly, occupied as it was with the declaration and violation of the rights of men, and with their arrangements for general confusion, it had neither leisure nor capacity to contrive, nor authority to enforce, any plan of any kind relative to the replacing the tax or equalizing it, or compensating the provinces, or for conducting their minds to any scheme of accommodation with the other districts which were to be relieved.

The people of the salt provinces, impatient under taxes, damned by the authority which had directed their payment, very soon found their patience exhausted. They thought themselves as skilful in demolishing as the Assembly could be. They relieved themselves by throwing off the whole burthen. Animated by this example, each district, or part of a district, judging of its own grievance by its own feeling, and of its remedy by its own opinion, did as it pleased with other taxes.

We are next to see how they have conducted themselves in contriving equal impositions, proportioned to the means of the citizens, and the least likely to lean heavy on the active capital employed in the generation of that private wealth, from whence the public fortune must be derived. By suffering the several districts, and several of the individuals in each district, to judge of what part of the old revenue they might withhold, instead of better principles of equality, a new inequality was introduced of the most oppressive kind. Payments were regulated by dispositions. The parts of the kingdom which were the most submissive, the most orderly, or the most affectionate to the commonwealth, bore the whole burthen of the state. Nothing turns out to be so oppressive and unjust as a feeble government. To fill up all the deficiencies in the old impositions, and the new deficiencies of every kind which were to be expected, what remained to a state without authority? The National Assembly called for a voluntary benevolence; for a fourth part of the income of all the citizens, to be estimated on the honour of those who were to pay. They obtained something more than could be rationally calculated, but what was far indeed from answerable to their real necessities, and much less to their fond expectations. Rational people could have hoped for little from this their tax in the disguise of a benevolence; a tax weak, ineffective, and unequal; a tax by which luxury, avarice, and selfishness were screened, and the load thrown upon productive capital, upon integrity, generosity, and public spirit—a tax of regulation upon virtue. At length the mask is thrown off, and they are now trying means (with little success) of exacting their benevolence by force.

This benevolence, the ricketty offspring of weakness, was to be supported by another resource, the twin brother of the same prolific imbecility. The patriotic donations were to make good the failure of the patriotic contribution. John Doe was to become security for Richard Roe. By this scheme they took things of much price from the giver, comparatively of small value to the receiver; they ruined several trades; they pillaged the crown of its ornaments, the churches of their plate, and the people of their personal decorations. The invention of these juvenile pretenders to liberty was in reality nothing more than a servile imitation of one of the poorest resources of doting despotism. They took an old huge full-bottomed periwig out of the wardrobe of the antiquated frippery of Louis the Fourteenth, to cover the premature baldness of the National Assembly. They produced this old-fashioned formal folly, though it had been so abundantly exposed in the memoirs of the Duke de St. Simon, if to reasonable men it had wanted any arguments to display its mischief and insufficiency. A device of the same kind was tried in my memory by Louis the Fifteenth, but it answered at no time. However, the necessities of ruinous wars were some excuse for desperate projects. The deliberations of calamity are rarely wise. But here was a season for disposition and providence. It was in a time of profound peace, then enjoyed for five years, and promising a much longer continuance, that they had recourse to this desperate trifling. They were sure to lose more reputation by sporting, in their serious situation, with these toys and playthings of finance, which have filled half their journals, than could possibly be compensated by the poor temporary supply which they afforded. It seemed as if those who adopted such projects were wholly ignorant of their circumstances, or wholly unequal to their necessities. Whatever virtue may be in these devices, it is obvious that neither the patriotic gifts, nor the patriotic contribution, can ever be resorted to again. The resources of public folly are soon exhausted. The whole indeed of their scheme of revenue is to make, by any artifice, an appearance of a full reservoir for the hour, whilst at the same time they cut off the springs and living fountains of perennial supply. The account not long since furnished by M. Necker was meant, without question, to be favourable. He gives a flattering view of the means of getting through the year; but he expresses, as it is natural he should, some apprehension for that which was to succeed. On this last prognostic, instead of entering into the grounds of this apprehension, in order, by a proper foresight, to prevent the prognosticated evil, M. Necker receives a sort of friendly reprimand from the president of the Assembly.

As to their other schemes of taxation, it is impossible to say anything of them with certainty; because they have not yet had their operation: but nobody is so sanguine as to imagine they will fill up any perceptible part of the wide gaping breach which their incapacity has made in their revenues. At present the state of their treasury sinks every day more and more in cash, and swells more and more in fictitious representation. When so little within or without is now found but paper, the representative not of opulence but of want, the creature not of credit but of power, they imagine that our flourishing state in England is owing to that bank-paper, and not the bank-paper to the flourishing condition of our commerce, to the solidity of our credit, and to the total exclusion of all idea of power from any part of the transaction. They forget that, in England, not one shilling of paper-money of any description is received but of choice; that the whole has had its origin in cash actually deposited; and that it is convertible at pleasure, in an instant, and without the smallest loss, into cash again. Our paper is of value in commerce, because in law it is of none. It is powerful on 'Change, because in Westminster Hall it is impotent. In payment of a debt of twenty shillings, a creditor may refuse all the paper of the bank of England. Nor is there amongst us a single public security, of any quality or nature whatsoever, that is enforced by authority. In fact it might be easily shown, that our paper wealth, instead of lessening the real coin, has a tendency to increase it; instead of being a substitute for money, it only facilitates its entry, its exit, and its circulation; that it is the symbol of prosperity, and not the badge of distress. Never was a scarcity of cash, and an exuberance of paper, a subject of complaint in this nation.

Well! but a lessening of prodigal expenses, and the economy which has been introduced by the virtuous and sapient Assembly, make amends for the losses sustained in the receipt of revenue. In this at least they have fulfilled the duty of a financier. Have those, who say so, looked at the expenses of the National Assembly itself? Of the municipalities? Of the city of Paris? Of the increased pay of the two armies? of the new police? Of the new judicatures? Have they even carefully compared the present pension list with the former? These politicians have been cruel, not economical. Comparing the expenses of the former prodigal government and its relation to the then revenues with the expenses of this new system as opposed to the state of its new treasury, I believe the present will be found beyond all comparison more chargeable.[54]

It remains only to consider the proofs of financial ability, furnished by the present French managers when they are to raise supplies on credit. Here I am a little at a stand; for credit, properly speaking, they have none. The credit of the ancient government was not indeed the best; but they could always, on some terms, command money, not only at home, but from most of the countries of Europe where a surplus capital was accumulated; and the credit of that government was improving daily. The establishment of a system of liberty would of course be supposed to give it new strength: and so it would actually have done, if a system of liberty had been established. What offers has their government of pretended liberty had from Holland, from Hamburgh, from Switzerland, from Genoa, from England, for a dealing in their paper? Why should these nations of commerce and economy enter into any pecuniary dealings with a people, who attempt to reverse the very nature of things; amongst whom they see the debtor prescribing at the point of the bayonet, the medium of his solvency to the creditor; discharging one of his engagements with another; turning his very penury into his resource; and paying his interest with his rags?

Their fanatical confidence in the omnipotence of church plunder has induced these philosophers to overlook all care of the public estate, just as the dream of the philosopher's stone induces dupes, under the more plausible delusion of the hermetic art, to neglect all rational means of improving their fortunes. With these philosophic financiers, this universal medicine made of church mummy is to cure all the evils of the state. These gentlemen perhaps do not believe a great deal in the miracles of piety; but it cannot be questioned, that they have an undoubting faith in the prodigies of sacrilege. Is there a debt which presses them? Issue *assignats.* Are compensations to be made, or a maintenance decreed to those whom they have robbed of their freehold in their office, or expelled from their profession? *Assignats.* Is a fleet to be fitted out? *Assignats.* If sixteen millions sterling of these *assignats,* forced on the people, leave the wants of the state as urgent as ever—issue, says one, thirty millions sterling of *assignats*—says another, issue fourscore millions more of *assignats.* The only difference among their financial factions is on the greater or the lesser quantity of *assignats* to be imposed on the public sufferance. They are all professors of *assignats.* Even those, whose natural good sense and knowledge of commerce, not obliterated by philosophy, furnish decisive arguments against this delusion, conclude their arguments, by proposing the emission of *assignats.* I suppose they must talk of *assignats,* as no other language would be understood. All experience of their inefficacy does not in the least discourage them. Are the old *assignats* depreciated at market? What is the remedy? Issue new *assignats. Mais si maladia, opiniatria, non vult se garire, quid illi facere? Assignare—postea assignare; ensuita assignare.* The word is a trifle altered. The Latin of your present doctors may be better than that of your old comedy; their wisdom and the variety of their resources are the same. They have not more notes in their song than the cuckoo; though, far from the softness of that harbinger of summer and plenty, their voice is as harsh and as ominous as that of the raven.

Who but the most desperate adventurers in philosophy and finance could at all have thought of destroying the settled revenue of the state, the sole security for the public credit, in the hope of rebuilding it with the materials of confiscated property? If, however, an excessive zeal for the state should have led a pious and venerable prelate (by anticipation a father of the church)[55] to pillage his own order, and, for the good of the church and people, to take upon himself the place of grand financier of confiscation, and comptroller-general of sacrilege, he and his coadjutors were, in my opinion, bound to show, by their subsequent conduct, that they knew something of the office they assumed. When they had resolved to appropriate to the *Fisc,* a certain portion of the landed property of their conquered country, it was their business to render their bank a real fund of credit, as far as such a bank was capable of becoming so.

To establish a current circulating credit upon any *Land-bank,* under any circumstances whatsoever, has hitherto proved difficult at the very least. The attempt has commonly ended in bankruptcy. But when the Assembly were led, through a contempt of moral, to a defiance of economical, principles, it might at least have been expected, that nothing would be omitted on their part to lessen this difficulty, to prevent any aggravation of this bankruptcy. It might be expected, that, to render your *Land-bank* tolerable, every means would be adopted that could display openness and candour in the statement of the security; everything which could aid the recovery of the demand. To take things in their most favourable point of view, your condition was that of a man of a large landed estate, which he wished to dispose of for the discharge of a debt, and the supply of certain services. Not being able instantly to sell, you wished to mortgage. What would a man of fair intentions, and a commonly clear understanding, do in such circumstances? Ought he not first to ascertain the gross value of the estate; the charges of its management and disposition; the encumbrances perpetual and temporary of all kinds that affect it; then, striking a net surplus, to calculate the just value of the security? When that surplus (the only security to the creditor) had been clearly ascertained, and properly vested in the hands of trustees; then he would indicate the parcels to be sold, and the time and conditions of sale; after this, he would admit the public creditor, if he chose it, to subscribe his stock into this new fund; or he might receive proposals for an *assignat* from those who would advance money to purchase this species of security.

This would be to proceed like men of business, methodically and rationally; and on the only principles of public and private credit that have an existence. The dealer would then know exactly what he purchased; and the only doubt which could hang upon his mind would be, the dread of the resumption of the spoil, which one day might be made (perhaps with an addition of punishment) from the sacrilegious gripe of those execrable wretches who could become purchasers at the auction of their innocent fellow-citizens.

An open and exact statement of the clear value of the property, and of the time, the circumstances, and the place of sale, were all necessary, to efface as much as possible the stigma that has hitherto been branded on every kind of Land-bank. It became necessary on another principle, that is, on account of a pledge of faith previously given on that subject, that their future fidelity in a slippery concern might be established by their adherence to their first engagement. When they had finally determined on a state resource from church booty, they came, on the 14th of April, 1790, to a solemn resolution on the subject; and pledged themselves to their country, "that in the statement of the public charges for each year, there should be brought to account a sum sufficient for defraying the expenses of the R. C. A. religion, the support of the ministers at the altars, the relief of the poor, the pensions to the ecclesiastics, secular as well as regular, of the one and of the other sex, *in order that the estates and goods which are at the disposal of the nation may be disengaged of all charges, and employed by the representatives, or the legislative body, to the great and most pressing exigences of the state.*" They further engaged, on the same day, that the sum necessary for the year 1791 should be forthwith determined.

In this resolution they admit it their duty to show distinctly the expense of the above objects, which, by other resolutions, they had before engaged should be first in the order of provision. They admit that they ought to show the estate clear and disengaged of all charges, and that they should show it immediately. Have they done this immediately, or at any time? Have they ever furnished a rent-roll of the immovable estates, or given in an inventory of the movable effects, which they confiscate to their assignats? In what manner they can fulfil their engagements of holding out to public service, "an estate disengaged of all charges," without authenticating the value of the estate, or the quantum of the charges, I leave it to their English admirers to explain. Instantly upon this assurance, and previously to any one step towards making it good, they issue, on the credit of so handsome a declaration, sixteen millions sterling of their paper. This was manly. Who, after this masterly stroke, can doubt of their abilities in finance? But then, before any other emission of these financial *indulgences,* they took care at least to make good their original promise! If such estimate, either of the value of the estate or the amount of the encumbrances, has been made, it has escaped me. I never heard of it.

At length they have spoken out, and they have made a full discovery of their abominable fraud, in holding out the church lands as a security for any debts, or any service whatsoever. They rob only to enable them to cheat; but in a very short time they defeat the ends both of the robbery and the fraud, by making out accounts for other purposes, which blow up their whole apparatus of force and of deception. I am obliged to M. de Calonne for his reference to the document which proves this extraordinary fact; it had by some means escaped me. Indeed it was not necessary to make out my assertion as to the breach of faith on the declaration of the 14th of April, 1790. By a report of their committee it now appears, that the charge of keeping up the reduced ecclesiastical establishments, and other expenses attendant on religion, and maintaining the religious of both sexes, retained or pensioned, and the other concomitant expenses of the same nature, which they have brought upon themselves by this convulsion in property, exceeds the income of the estates acquired by it in the enormous sum of two millions sterling annually; besides a debt of seven millions and upwards. These are the calculating powers of imposture! This is the finance of philosophy! This is the result of all the delusions held out to engage a miserable people in rebellion, murder, and sacrilege, and to make them prompt and zealous instruments in the ruin of their country! Never did a state, in any case, enrich itself by the confiscations of the citizens. This new experiment has succeeded like all the rest. Every honest mind, every true lover of liberty and humanity, must rejoice to find that injustice is not always good policy, nor rapine the high road to riches. I subjoin with pleasure, in a note, the able and spirited observations of M. de Calonne on this subject.[56]

In order to persuade the world of the bottomless resource of ecclesiastical confiscation, the Assembly have proceeded to other confiscations of estates in offices, which could not be done with any common colour without being compensated out of this grand confiscation of landed property. They have thrown upon this fund, which was to show a surplus, disengaged of all charges, a new charge; namely, the compensation to the whole body of the disbanded judicature; and of all suppressed offices and estates; a charge which I cannot ascertain, but which unquestionably amounts to many French millions. Another of the new charges is an annuity of four hundred and eighty thousand pounds sterling, to be paid (if they choose to keep faith) by daily payments, for the interest of the first assignats. Have they ever given themselves the trouble to state fairly the expense of the management of the church lands in the hands of the municipalities, to whose care, skill, and diligence, and that of their legion of unknown under-agents, they have chosen to commit the charge of the forfeited estates, and the consequence of which had been so ably pointed out by the bishop of Nancy?

But it is unnecessary to dwell on these obvious heads of encumbrance. Have they made out any clear state of the grand encumbrance of all, I mean the whole of the general and municipal establishments of all sorts, and compared it with the regular income by revenue? Every deficiency in these becomes a charge on the confiscated estate, before the creditor can plant his cabbages on an acre of church property. There is no other prop than this confiscation to keep the whole state from tumbling to the ground. In this situation they have purposely covered all that they ought industriously to have cleared, with a thick fog; and then, blindfold themselves, like bulls that shut their eyes when they push, they drive, by the point of the bayonets, their slaves, blindfolded indeed no worse than their lords, to take their fictions for currencies, and to swallow down paper pills by thirty-four millions sterling at a dose. Then they proudly lay in their claim to a future credit, on failure of all their past engagements, and at a time when (if in such a matter anything can be clear) it is clear that the surplus estates will never answer even the first of their mortgages, I mean that of the four hundred millions (or sixteen millions sterling) of *assignats.* In all this procedure I can discern neither the solid sense of plain dealing, nor the subtle dexterity of ingenious fraud. The objections within the Assembly to pulling up the flood-gates for this inundation of fraud are unanswered; but they are thoroughly refuted by a hundred thousand financiers in the street. These are the numbers by which the metaphysic arithmeticians compute. These are the grand calculations on which a philosophical public credit is founded in France. They cannot raise supplies; but they can raise mobs. Let them rejoice in the applauses of the club at Dundee, for their wisdom and patriotism in having thus applied the plunder of the citizens to the service of the state. I hear of no address upon this subject from the directors of the bank of England; though their approbation would be of a *little* more weight in the scale of credit than that of the club at Dundee. But, to do justice to the club, I believe the gentlemen who compose it to be wiser than they appear; that they will be less liberal of their money than of their addresses; and that they would not give a dog's-ear of their most rumpled and ragged Scotch paper for twenty of your fairest assignats.

Early in this year the Assembly issued paper to the amount of sixteen millions sterling: what must have been the state into which the Assembly has brought your affairs, that the relief afforded by so vast a supply has been hardly perceptable? This paper also felt an almost immediate depreciation of five per cent., which in a little time came to about seven. The effect of these assignats on the receipt of the revenue is remarkable. M. Necker found that the collectors of the revenue, who received in coin, paid the treasury in *assignats*. The collectors made seven per cent. by thus receiving in money, and accounting in depreciated paper. It was not very difficult to foresee, that this must be inevitable. It was, however, not the less embarrassing. M. Necker was obliged (I believe, for a considerable part, in the market of London) to buy gold and silver for the mint, which amounted to about twelve thousand pounds above the value of the commodity gained. That minister was of opinion, that, whatever their secret nutritive virtue might be, the state could not live upon *assignats* alone; that some real silver was necessary, particularly for the satisfaction of those who, having iron in their hands, were not likely to distinguish themselves for patience, when they should perceive that, whilst an increase of pay was held out to them in real money, it was again to be fraudulently drawn back by depreciated paper. The minister, in this very natural distress, applied to the Assembly, that they should order the collectors to pay in specie what in specie they had received. It could not escape him, that if the treasury paid three per cent. for the use of a currency, which should be returned seven per cent. worse than the minister issued it, such a dealing could not very greatly tend to enrich the public. The Assembly took no notice of his recommendation. They were in this dilemma: If they continued to receive the assignats, cash must become an alien to their treasury. If the treasury should refuse those paper *amulets,* or should discountenance them in any degree, they must destroy the credit of their sole resource. They seem then to have made their option; and to have given some sort of credit to their paper by taking it themselves; at the same time in their speeches they made a sort of swaggering declaration, something, I rather think, above legislative competence; that is, that there is no difference in value between metallic money and their assignats. This was a good, stout, proof article of faith, pronounced under an anathema, by the venerable fathers of this philosophic synod. *Credat* who will—certainly not *Judœus Apella.*

A noble indignation rises in the minds of your popular leaders on hearing the magic lantern in their show of finance compared to the fraudulent exhibitions of Mr. Law. They cannot bear to hear the sands of his Mississippi compared with the rock of the church, on which they build their system. Pray let them suppress this glorious spirit, until they show to the world what piece of solid ground there is for their assignats, which they have not pre-occupied by other charges. They do injustice to that great, mother fraud, to compare it with their degenerate imitation. It is not true that Law built solely on a speculation concerning the Mississippi. He added the East India trade; he added the African trade; he added the farms of all the farmed revenue of France. All these together unquestionably could not support the structure which the public enthusiasm, not he, chose to build upon these bases. But these were, however, in comparison, generous delusions. They supposed, and they aimed at, an increase of the commerce of France. They opened to it the whole range of the two hemispheres. They did not think of feeding France from its own substance. A grand imagination found in this flight of commerce something to captivate. It was wherewithal to dazzle the eye of an eagle. It was not made to entice the smell of a mole, nuzzling and burying himself in his mother earth, as yours is. Men were not then quite shrunk from their natural dimensions by a degrading and sordid philosophy, and fitted for low and vulgar deceptions. Above all, remember, that, in imposing on the imagination, the then managers of the system made a compliment to the freedom of men. In their fraud there was no mixture of force. This was reserved to our time, to quench the little glimmerings of reason which might break in upon the solid darkness of this enlightened age.

On recollection, I have said nothing of a scheme of finance which may be urged in favour of the abilities of these gentlemen, and which has been introduced with great pomp, though not yet finally adopted, in the National Assembly. It comes with something solid in aid of the credit of the paper circulation; and much has been said of its utility and its elegance. I mean the project for coining into money the bells of the suppressed churches. This is their alchymy. There are some follies which baffle argument; which go beyond ridicule; and which excite no feeling in us but disgust; and therefore I say no more upon it.

It is as little worth remarking any further upon all their drawing and re-drawing, on their circulation for putting off the evil day, on the play between the treasury and the *Caisse d'Escompte,* and on all these old, exploded contrivances of mercantile fraud, now exalted into policy of state. The revenue will not be trifled with. The prattling about the rights of men will not be accepted in payment for a biscuit or a pound of gunpowder. Here then the metaphysicians descend from their airy speculations, and faithfully follow examples. What examples? The examples of bankrupts. But defeated, baffled, disgraced, when their breath, their strength, their inventions, their fancies desert them, their confidence still maintains its ground. In the manifest failure of their abilities, they take credit for their benevolence. When the revenue disappears in their hands, they have the presumption, in some of their late proceedings, to value *themselves* on the relief given to the people. They did not relieve the people. If they entertained such intentions, why did they order the obnoxious taxes to be paid? The people relieved themselves in spite of the Assembly.

But waving all discussion on the parties who may claim the merit of this fallacious relief, has there been, in effect, any relief to the people in any form? Mr. Bailly, one of the grand agents of paper circulation, lets you into the nature of this relief. His speech to the National Assembly contained a high and laboured panegyric on the inhabitants of Paris, for the constancy and unbroken resolution with which they have borne their distress and misery. A fine picture of public felicity! What! great courage and unconquerable firmness of mind to endure benefits, and sustain redress? One would think from the speech of this learned lord mayor, that the Parisians, for this twelvemonth past, had been suffering the straits of some dreadful blockade; that Henry the Fourth had been stopping up the avenues to their supply, and Sully thundering with his ordnance at the gates of Paris; when in reality they are besieged by no other enemies than their own madness and folly, their own credulity and perverseness. But Mr. Bailly will sooner thaw the eternal ice of his Atlantic regions, than restore the central heat to Paris, whilst it remains "smitten with the cold, dry, petrific mace" of a false and unfeeling philosophy. Some time after this speech, that is, on the thirteenth of last August, the same magistrate, giving an account of his government at the bar of the same Assembly, expresses himself as follows: "In the month of July, 1789," [the period of everlasting commemoration,] "the finances of the city of Paris were *yet* in good order; the expenditure was counterbalanced by the receipt, and she had at that time a million" [forty thousand pounds sterling] "in bank. The expenses which she has been constrained to incur, *subsequent to the Revolution,* amount to 2,500,000 livres. From these expenses, and the great falling off in the product of *the free gifts,* not only a momentary, but a *total,* want of money has taken place." This is the Paris, upon whose nourishment, in the course of the last year, such immense sums, drawn from the vitals of all France, have been expended. As long as Paris stands in the place of ancient Rome, so long she will be maintained by the subject provinces. It is an evil inevitably attendant on the dominion of sovereign democratic republics. As it happened in Rome, it may survive that republican domination which gave rise to it. In that case despotism itself must submit to the vices of popularity. Rome, under her emporers, united the evils of both systems; and this unnatural combination was one great cause of her ruin.

To tell the people that they are relieved by the dilapidation of their public estate, is a cruel and insolent imposition. Statesmen, before they valued themselves on the relief given to the people by the destruction of their revenue, ought first to have carefully attended to the solution of this problem: Whether it be more advantageous to the people to pay considerably, and to gain in proportion; or to gain little or nothing, and to be disburthened of all contribution? My mind is made up to decide in favour of the first proposition. Experience is with me, and, I believe, the best opinions also. To keep a balance between the power of acquisition on the part of the subject, and the demands he is to answer on the part of the state, is the fundamental part of the skill of a true politician. The means of acquisition are prior in time and in arrangement. Good order is the foundation of all good things. To be enabled to acquire, the people, without being servile, must be tractable and obedient. The magistrate must have his reverence, the laws their authority. The body of the people must not find the principles of natural subordination by art rooted out of their minds. They must respect that property of which they cannot partake. They must labour to obtain what by labour can be obtained; and when they find, as they commonly do, the success disproportioned to the endeavour, they must be taught their consolation in the final proportions of eternal justice. Of this consolation whoever deprives them, deadens their industry, and strikes at the root of all acquisition as of all conservation. He that does this is the cruel oppressor, the merciless enemy of the poor and wretched; at the same time that by his wicked speculations he exposes the fruits of successful industry, and the accumulations of fortune, to the plunder of the negligent, the disappointed, and the unprosperous.

Too many of the financiers by profession are apt to see nothing in revenue but banks, and circulations, and annuities on lives, and tontines, and perpetual rents, and all the small wares of the shop. In a settled order of the state, these things are not to be slighted, nor is the skill in them to be held of trivial estimation. They are good, but then only good, when they assume the effects of that settled order, and are built upon it. But when men think that these beggarly contrivances may supply a resource for the evils which result from breaking up the foundations of public order, and from causing or suffering the principles of property to be subverted, they will, in the ruin of their country, leave a melancholy and lasting monument of the effect of preposterous politics, and presumptuous, short-sighted, narrow-minded wisdom.

The effects of the incapacity shown by the popular leaders in all the great members of the commonwealth are to be covered with the "all-atoning name" of liberty. In some people I see great liberty indeed; in many, if not in the most, an oppressive, degrading servitude. But what is liberty without wisdom, and without virtue? It is the greatest of all possible evils; for it is folly, vice, and madness, without tuition or restraint. Those who know what virtuous liberty is, cannot bear to see it disgraced by incapable heads, on account of their having high-sounding words in their mouths. Grand, swelling sentiments of liberty I am sure I do not despise. They warm the heart; they enlarge and liberalize our minds; they animate our courage in a time of conflict. Old as I am, I read the fine raptures of Lucan and Corneille with pleasure. Neither do I wholly condemn the little arts and devices of popularity. They facilitate the carrying of many points of moment; they keep the people together; they refresh the mind in its exertions; and they diffuse occasional gaiety over the severe brow of moral freedom. Every politician ought to sacrifice to the graces; and to join compliance with reason. But in such an undertaking as that in France, all these subsidiary sentiments and artifices are of little avail. To make a government requires no great prudence. Settle the seat of power; teach obedience: and the work is done. To give freedom is still more easy. It is not necessary to guide; it only requires to let go the rein. But to form a *free government;* that is, to temper together these opposite elements of liberty and restraint in one consistent work, requires much thought, deep reflection, a sagacious, powerful, and combining mind. This I do not find in those who take the lead in the National Assembly. Perhaps they are not so miserably deficient as they appear. I rather believe it. It would put them below the common level of human understanding. But when the leaders choose to make themselves bidders at an auction of popularity, their talents, in the construction of the state, will be of no service. They will become flatterers instead of legislators; the instruments, not the guides, of the people. If any of them should happen to propose a scheme of liberty, soberly limited, and defined with proper qualifications, he will be immediately outbid by his competitors, who will produce something more splendidly popular. Suspicions will be raised of his fidelity to his cause. Moderation will be stigmatized as the virtue of cowards; and compromise as the prudence of traitors: until, in hopes of preserving the credit which may enable him to temper, and moderate, on some occasions, the popular leader is obliged to become active in propagating doctrines, and establishing powers, that will afterwards defeat any sober purpose at which he ultimately might have aimed.

But am I so unreasonable as to see nothing at all that deserves commendation in the indefatigable labours of this Assembly? I do not deny that, among an infinite number of acts of violence and folly, some good may have been done. They who destroy everything certainly will remove some grievance. They who make everything new, have a chance that they may establish something beneficial. To give them credit for what they have done in virtue of the authority they have usurped, or which can excuse them in the crimes by which that authority has been acquired, it must appear, that the same things could not have been accomplished without producing such a revolution. Most assuredly they might; because almost every one of the regulations made by them, which is not very equivocal, was either in the cession of the king, voluntarily made at the meeting of the states, or in the concurrent instructions to the orders. Some usages have been abolished on just grounds; but they were such, that if they had stood as they were to all eternity, they would little detract from the happiness and prosperity of any state. The improvements of the National Assembly are superficial, their errors fundamental.

Whatever they are, I wish my countrymen rather to recommend to our neighbours the example of the British constitution, than to take models from them for the improvement of our own. In the former they have got an invaluable treasure. They are not, I think, without some causes of apprehension and complaint; but these they do not owe to their constitution, but to their own conduct. I think our happy situation owing to our constitution; but owing to the whole of it, and not any part singly; owing in a great measure to what we have left standing in our several reviews and reformations, as well as to what we have altered or superadded. Our people will find employment enough for a truly patriotic, free, and independent spirit, in guarding what they possess from violation. I would not exclude alteration neither; but even when I changed, it should be to preserve.

I should be led to my remedy by a great grievance. In what I did, I should follow the example of our ancestors. I would make the reparation as nearly as possible in the style of the building. A politic caution, a guarded circumspection, a moral rather than a complexional timidity, were among the ruling principles of our forefathers in their most decided conduct. Not being illuminated with the light of which the gentlemen of France tell us they have got so abundant a share, they acted under a strong impression of the ignorance and fallibility of mankind. He that had made them thus fallible, rewarded them for having in their conduct attended to their nature. Let us imitate their caution, if we wish to deserve their fortune, or to retain their bequests. Let us add, if we please, but let us preserve what they have left; and standing on the firm ground of the British constitution, let us be satisfied to admire, rather than attempt to follow in their desperate flights, the aëronauts of France.

I have told you candidly my sentiments. I think they are not likely to alter yours. I do not know that they ought. You are young; you cannot guide, but must follow the fortune of your country. But hereafter they may be of some use to you, in some future form which your commonwealth may take. In the present it can hardly remain; but before its final settlement it may be obliged to pass, as one of our poets says, "through great varieties of untried beings," and in all its transmigrations to be purified by fire and blood.

I have little to recommend my opinions but long observation and much impartiality. They come from one who has been no tool of power, no flatterer of greatness; and who in his last acts does not wish to belie the tenour of his life. They come from one, almost the whole of whose public exertion has been a struggle for the liberty of others; from one in whose breast no anger durable or vehement has ever been kindled, but by what he considered as tyranny; and who snatches from his share in the endeavours which are used by good men to discredit opulent oppression, the hours he has employed on your affairs; and who in so doing persuades himself he has not departed from his usual office: they come from one who desires honours, distinctions, and emoluments, but little; and who expects them not at all; who has no contempt for fame, and no fear of obloquy; who shuns contention, though he will hazard an opinion: from one who wishes to preserve consistency, but who would preserve consistency by varying his means to secure the unity of his end; and, when the equipoise of the vessel in which he sails may be endangered by overloading it upon one side, is desirous of carrying the small weight of his reasons to that which may preserve its equipoise.

The Origin and Principles of the American Revolution, Compared with the Origin and Principles of the French Revolution

Friedrich Gentz

Translated by John Quincy Adams

Introduction

by Russell Kirk

In the first year of the nineteenth century, John Quincy Adams, only thirty-three years old, was Minister Plenipotentiary of the United States to Prussia. Adams educated himself the whole of his life; and, perfecting his German during his residence in Berlin, he translated from the Berlin *Historisches Journal* (April and May, 1800) a long article on the French and American Revolutions by Friedrich Gentz, a rising Prussian man of letters, three years older than the precocious Adams. Gentz was the founder, editor, and sole contributor to this remarkable magazine of ideas. These were men of mark: Adams would become President of the United States, and Gentz, with Metternich, the architect of European conservatism. "It cannot but afford a gratification to every American attached to his country," Adams wrote to Gentz that June, "to see its revolution so ably vindicated from the imputation of having originated, or been conducted upon the same principles, as that of France."

Gentz had studied under Kant; but Burke's *Reflections* had converted the young man to conservative principles, and, abhorring the theories and consequences of the French Revolution, he had translated the *Reflections* into German, thus exerting his first influence upon European politics and making his reputation. Like Gentz, the younger Adams had been profoundly influenced by Burke; and though he tried to act the role of arbiter between Burke and Paine, Adams really was persuaded by all Burke's principal arguments. His *Letters of Publicola*, published in 1791, had demolished Paine's *Rights of Man* and had cudgelled the French revolutionaries, enraging Jefferson. The Americans, young Adams had written, had not fallen into the pit of radical abstract doctrine:

"Happy, thrice happy the people of America! Whose gentleness of manners and habits of virtue are still sufficient to reconcile the enjoyment of their natural rights, with the peace and tranquillity of their country; whose principles of religious liberty did not result from an indiscriminate contempt of all religion whatever, and whose equal representation in their legislative councils was founded upon an equality really existing among them, and not upon the metaphysical speculations of fanciful politicians, vainly contending against the unalterable course of events, and the established order of nature."

Thus Adams was of one mind with Gentz, and saw in Gentz's essay the most succinct and forceful contrast between the moderate polity of the American colonies, founded upon a respect for prescriptive rights and custom, and the levelling theories of French radicalism. Only the word "Republic" was common to the two new dominations, Adams perceived; and the French Republic already had ceased to contain any element of true representative government. Adams' translation of Gentz was published anonymously at Philadelphia in the same year, and has not been reprinted until 1955.

This little book has Adams' style strongly imprinted upon it in translation; but in thought and structure Gentz's writing bears the mark of Burke's *Reflections* and Schiller's *Thirty Years' War*—books which, by a curious coincidence, incalculably influenced both Gentz and the present editor in their early years. The folly of true and thoroughgoing revolution—which the American War of Independence was not—was the great theme of Gentz's thought and action from 1791 until the end of his life. In 1827, defending his career against the strictures of a woman he loved, he summarized with a high sincerity the principles that had moved him:

"I made my choice in my twenty-fifth year. Fascinated before that by the new German philosophy and also, no doubt, by some supposedly new disclosures in the field of political science, which in those days, however, was still very unfamiliar to me, I recognized my mission clearly and distinctly with the outbreak of the French Revolution. At first I felt, and later knew, that by virtue of the talents and abilities that nature had reposed in me I had been called as a champion of the established, and a foe to innovations. Neither my station in life, my circumstances and expectations at the time, my manner of living, nor any sort of inborn or acquired prejudice, nor any worldly interest, determined this choice. All my earlier political articles were written at a time when, wholly confined to reading and study, I had not the slightest connection with any important political figure, either within or without the country where I lived. That some of these articles should have made my name familiar in higher circles was only natural."

By the power of his pen, indeed, the obscure Gentz rose to be the associate of kings and the designer of the concert of Europe. In the end, he did not prevail against the titanic powers of revolution; but he chose, like Cato at Utica, to defy destiny for the sake of truth. "I have always been conscious that despite the majesty and power of my superiors, despite all the lonely victories that we achieved, the spirit of the age would prove mightier in the end than we; that thoroughly as I have despised the press for its extravagances, it would not lose its dread ascendancy over all our wisdom; and that guile, no more than force, would be able to stay the great wheel of time, as you have written with equal truth and beauty. But that was no reason for me not to carry out the task faithfully and persistently, once it had fallen to me; only an unworthy soldier deserts his flag when fate seems inimical, and I have enough pride to say to myself in darker moments, *Victrix causa diis placuit, sed victa Catoni.*"

Yet the battle is not always to the strong; and as the dead Cato in some sense conquered Caesar, so Gentz's ideas have had their vindication in the twentieth century. The dominant liberal school of the nineteenth-century historians embraced the view that the French Revolution had been a noble and irrevocable stride forward toward a universal domination of peace and enlightenment and brotherhood; and they confounded the American and French revolutions as virtually identical manifestations of the same progressive movement. Even Gladstone, who read Burke through and through, concluded that Burke and his school had been utterly mistaken about the nature of the French Revolution. The Napoleonic interlude, the liberals maintained, had been only a passing reaction against the forces of charity and light which found their expression in French Revolutionary doctrines. It required the catastrophes of the twentieth century, and the grim recurrence of what Professor Talmon calls "totalitarian democracy" and Lord Percy of Newcastle calls "totalist democracy," to convince the liberal mind that possibly something was wrong with the first principles of the French innovators.

With Burke, and with the Adams presidents, Gentz perceived that disaster would come inevitably from the fallacies of Turgot and Condorcet and Rousseau and Paine. This little tract contains the essence of Gentz's whole lifelong argument. The American Revolution, he contends, was—as Burke had said of the Glorious Revolution of 1688—"a revolution not made, but prevented." The American colonists stood up for their prescriptive rights; their claims and expectations were moderate, and founded upon a true apprehension of human nature and natural rights; their constitutions were conservative. But the French revolutionaries hoping to make human nature and society afresh, broke with the past, defied history, embraced theoretic dogma, and so fell under the cruel domination of Giant Ideology. Prudence and prescription guided the steps of the Americans, who simply preserved and continued the English tradition of representative government and private rights; fanaticism and vain expectations led the French to their own destruction. Burke, at the beginning of the American Revolution, had declared that the colonists were trying to conserve, not to destroy; they sought to keep liberties gained through historical experience, not to claim fanciful liberties conjured up by closet-philosophers; they were "not only devoted to liberty, but to liberty according to English ideas, and English principles. Abstract liberty like other mere abstractions is not to be found. Liberty inheres in some sensible object."

Again and again, Gentz touches upon the profound differences between American and French principles which the course of history, since 1776, has now made clear to the scholars of the twentieth century. He contrasts, for instance, the Americans' sound understanding of natural rights with the French illusion of the abstract "right of man," "a sort of magic spell, with which all the ties of nations and of humanity were insensibly dissolved." This is the French heresy of *vox populi, vox Dei,* recently analyzed by Lord Percy of Newcastle in his *Heresy of Democracy.* The pretended right of the "people" to do whatever they liked, Gentz insisted, would swallow up all the ancient and precious and hard-earned rights of groups and individuals. And so it came to pass. The Americans sought security; the French, through their armed doctrine, irresponsible power. "As the American revolution was a defensive revolution, it was of course finished, at the moment, when it had overcome the attack, by which it had been occasioned. The French revolution, true to the character of a most violent offensive revolution, could not but proceed so long as there remained objects for it to attack, and it retained strength for the assault."

The verdict of the historians, liberal or conservative in their assumptions, now veers round to Gentz's position. "The Americans of 1776," Mr. Clinton Rossiter writes, "were among the first men in modern history to defend rather than to seek an open society and constitutional liberty; their political faith, like the appeal to arms it supported, was therefore surprisingly sober. . . . Perhaps the most remarkable characteristic of this political theory was its deep-seated conservatism. However radical the principles of the Revolution may have seemed to the rest of the world, in the minds of the colonists they were thoroughly preservative and respectful of the past. . . . The political theory of the American Revolution, in contrast to that of the French Revolution, was not a theory designed to make the world over." Mr. Louis Hartz, though differing from Professor Rossiter in much, concurs here: "Symbols of a world revolution, the Americans were not in truth world revolutionaries. . . . The past had been good to the Americans, and they knew it. Instead of inspiring them to the fury of Bentham and Voltaire, it often produced a mystical sense of Providential guidance akin to that of Maistre."

With the French, the whole attitude toward history, continuity, and the contract of eternal society was ruinously different. "So France, exhausted by fasting under the monarchy," Taine puts it, "made drunk by the bad drug of the *Social Contract,* and countless other adulterated or fiery beverages, is suddenly struck with paralysis of the brain; at once she is convulsed in every limb through the incoherent play and contradictory twitchings of her discordant organs. At this time she has traversed the period of joyous madness, and is about to enter upon the period of sombre delirium; behold her capable of daring, suffering, and doing all, capable of incredible exploits and abominable barbarities, the moment her guides, as erratic as herself, indicate an enemy or an obstacle to her fury."

A penetrating modern critic of history and politics, Mr. Daniel Boorstin, in *The Genius of American Politics,* comes to a conclusion identical with Gentz's: "The American Revolution was in a very special way conceived as both a vindication of the British past and an affirmation of an American future. The British past was contained in ancient and living institutions rather than in doctrines; and the American future was never to be contained in a theory. The Revolution was thus a prudential decision taken by men of principle rather than the affirmation of a theory."

But the French, as Toqueville wrote, halfway down the stairs, threw themselves out of the window in order to reach the ground more quickly. "By seeming to tend rather to the regeneration of the human race than to the reform of France alone, it roused passions such as the most violent political revolutions had been incapable of awakening. It inspired proselytism, and gave birth to propagandism; and hence assumed that quasi-religious character which so terrified those who saw it, or, rather, became a sort of new religion, imperfect, it is true, without God, worship, or future life, but still able, like Islamism, to cover the earth with its soldiers, its apostles, and its martyrs."

It is the contrast between principle and ideology that Gentz gives us; between prudence and fanaticism; between prescriptive rights and extravagant ambitions; between historical wisdom and utopianism; between free government and democratic despotism. Those conflicting forces are at war in the world still, and the prescriptive wisdom of American politics confronts the levelling frenzy of ideology and the ferocity of the enraptured Jacobin.

Preface

by John Quincy Adams

The Essay, of which a translation is here given, was published in the *Historic Journal,* a monthly print which appears at Berlin; and was written by Mr. Gentz, one of the most distinguished political writers in Germany. It is for two reasons highly interesting to Americans: First, because it contains the clearest account of the rise and progress of the revolution which established their independence, that has ever appeared within so small a compass; and secondly, because it rescues that revolution from the disgraceful imputation of having proceeded from the same principles as that of France. This error has no where been more frequently repeated, no where of more pernicious tendency than in America itself. It has been, here not simply a common-place argument, as Mr. Gentz represents it to have been in Europe, but has been sanctioned by the authority of men, revered for their talents, and who at least ought to have known better.

The essential difference between these two great events, in their *rise,* their *progress,* and their *termination,* is here shewn in various lights, one of which alone is sufficient for an honest man. A modem philosopher may contend that the sheriff, who executes a criminal, and the highwayman, who murders a traveller, act upon the same principles; the plain sense of mankind will still see the same difference between them, that is here proved between the American and French Revolutions—the difference between *right* and *wrong.*

We presume it will afford a pure and honest gratification to the mind of every truly patriotic American reader, to see the honourable testimony borne by an ingenious, well-informed, and impartial foreigner to the principles and conduct of our country's revolution. The judgment of a native American will naturally be biassed by those partialities in favour of his country, from which it is so difficult for the citizen to divest himself as an historian. The causes of hatred and affection must be more remote from the mind of a foreigner, and his decisions must therefore have a greater intrinsic value. The historian of his own country must always in some sort be considered as its advocate; but an impartial foreigner is its judge.

The approbation of such a writer as Mr. Gentz is the more precious too, for not being unqualified. The mild censure, which he passes upon certain parts of our proceedings is the strongest proof of his real impartiality; and though our sentiments as Americans may differ from his, upon various points of political speculation, we shall find very few, if any instances, that have incurred his censure, which our own candour will not equally disapprove.

The Origin and Principles of the American Revolution, Compared with the Origin and Principles of the French Revolution

The Revolution of North America, had, in the course of events, been the nearest neighbour to that of France. A very considerable part of those, who were contemporaries and witnesses of the latter had likewise survived the former. Some of the most important personages, who made a figure in the French revolution, scarce ten years before, had been active on the theatre of that in America. The example of this undertaking, crowned with the most complete success, must have had a more immediate and powerful influence upon those, who destroyed the old government of France, than the example of any earlier European revolution: the circumstances, in which France was, at the breaking out of her revolution, had been, if not wholly, yet for the greatest part brought on by the part she had taken in that of America. In the conduct and language of most of the founders of the French revolution, it was impossible not to perceive an endeavour to imitate the course, the plans, the measures, the forms, and, in part, the language of those, who had conducted that of America; and to consider this, upon all occasions, as at once the model, and the justification of their own.

From all these causes, but especially because the recollection of the American revolution was yet fresh in every mind; because the principles to which it had given currency still sounded in every ear; because the preparatory temper of mind, which it had every where in Europe excited and left behind, favoured every similar, or only seemingly similar undertaking, it became so easy for those, who felt an evident interest in seeing the French revolution superficially compared, and thereby placed on the same ground, and confounded with that of America, to draw the great majority of the public into this fundamentally false point of view. At the period of great commotions, and of animated, vehement, widely grasping discussions, a very small number of men are able, and, perhaps, a still smaller number willing, with vigorous native energy, to penetrate into the essence of events, and take upon themselves the painful task of forming a judgment founded upon long meditation and persevering study. The similarity of the two revolutions was taken upon trust, and as many persons of respectable understanding and discernment had loudly and decisively declared themselves in favour of the American, it became a sort of accredited common-place, "that what had been just in America, could not be unjust in Europe." As, further, the last result of the American revolution had been in the highest degree splendid and glorious; as its issue had been undoubtedly advantageous for America, undoubtedly advantageous for most other states, was undoubtedly advantageous for England herself; as this most important circumstance, and the greater moderation and impartiality which time and tranquillity always bring to the judgments of men, had at last reconciled with this revolution its most violent opponents; an irresistable analogy seemed to justify a similar expectation in respect to that of France; and a second common-place, far more dangerous than the first, because it seized its materials, in the empty space of distant futurity, gathered a great portion of the human race under the spell of the delusive hope, that "what in America, had conduced to the public benefit, will, and must, sooner or later, in France and throughout Europe conduce in like manner to the public benefit."

The melancholy experience of ten disasterous years, has indeed considerably cooled down this belief; but it is not yet altogether extinguished; and even those who, have begun to totter in the faith, without, however, renouncing the principles, by which they justify the French revolution, extricate themselves from their perplexity, by recurring to external and accidental circumstances, which have hindered all the good that might have ensued, to the pretence that the revolution is not yet wholly completed, and to other equally nugatory subterfuges. The justice of the origin of both revolutions, they suppose to be taken for granted; and if one of them has produced more salutary consequences than the other, they impute this to Fortune, which here favours, and there abandons the undertakings of men. An equality of wisdom in the founders of the two revolutions, upon the whole, is as much taken for granted, as an equality of integrity.

Hence, it will certainly be no ungrateful task to compare the two revolutions in their essential features, in their originating causes, and in their first principles with each other. But in order to prepare the way for such a comparison, it will not be superfluous to exhibit in a small compass, the principal features of the origin of the American revolution. It may justly be taken for granted, that since the last ten years have almost exhausted all the powers of attention and of memory, the characteristic features of the origin and first progress of that revolution are no longer distinctly present in the minds even of many of its cotemporaries: there are, besides, some points in the picture of this great event, which, at the time when it happened, escaped almost every observer; and which, not until a later period, discovered themselves in all their vivid colours to the piercing eyes of meditation and experience.[1]

The English colonies in North-America, far from being a designed regular institution of European wisdom, calculated for futurity, had been much more the pure production of European short-sightedness and injustice. Political and religious intolerance, political and religious convulsions, had driven the first settlers from their country:

the single favour indulged them was to leave them to themselves. That their establishments were, in less than two hundred years, to form a great nation, and to give the world a new form, was concealed no less to their own eyes, than to the eyes of those who had ejected them from their bosom.

In the apparent insignificance of those settlements, and in the false measure, by which the profound ignorance of the Europeans estimated the value of such distant possessions, lay the first ground of the extraordinary progress which the North American colonies had already made under the second and third generations of their new inhabitants. Gold and silver alone could then attract the attention of European governments. A distant land, where neither of these was to be found, was, without hesitation, abandoned to its fortunes. From such a country was expected no *revenue;* and what increases not immediately the revenues of the state, could make no pretensions to its support, or to its particular care.

Nevertheless, by the peculiar, creative energy of a rapidly growing mass of enterprising and indefatigably active men, favoured by an extensive, fruitful, and happily situated territory; by simple forms of government, well adapted to their ends, and by profound peace, these colonies, thus neglected, and well nigh forgotten by the mother country, sprang up, after a short infancy, with giant strides, to the fulness and consistency of a brilliant youth. The phenomenon of their unexpected greatness, roused the Europeans, with sudden violence, from the slumber of a thoughtless indifference, and, at length, displayed to them a real new world, fully prepared to rivalize with the old; for which, however, at the same time, it was an inexhaustible source of wealth and enjoyment. Even before the middle of this century, every maritime power of Europe, but England more than all the rest, because the foundation of her colonies had accidentally departed the least from good principles, had discovered, that the peculiar, and only worth of all external European possessions, consisted in the extended market they opened to the industry of the mother country;

that it was not the empty sovereignty over enormous territories; not the barren right of property to gold and silver mines; but solely the encreased facility of sale for European productions, and an advantageous exchange of them for the productions of the most distant regions, which gave to the discovery of America the first rank among all the events beneficial to the world.

No sooner had this great truth begun to be so much as obscurely perceived, than necessarily all the exertions of the mother country concentrated themselves, in giving to their trade with the colonies the greatest extent, and the most advantageous direction; and for this end, even in times so little remote from the present, as those of which I speak, no other means were devised, than a *Monopoly,* In compelling the inhabitants of the colonies to receive exclusively from the mother country, all the necessary European articles they required, and to sell exclusively to her all the productions, by the circulation of which the merchants of the mother country might hope a certain profit, it was supposed that vast market, whose importance became more evident from year to year, would be improved in its whole extent, and under the most profitable conditions.

The error, which lay at the bottom of this system was pardonable. The genuine principles of the nature and sources of wealth, and of the true interests of commercial nations had scarcely yet germed in a few distinguished heads, and were not even developed, much less acknowledged. Nay, if at that early period, a single state could have soared to the elevation of these principles; on one side, had renounced all prejudices, on the other, every paltry jealousy, and felt a lively conviction, that liberty and general competition must be the basis of all true commercial policy, and the wisest principle of trade with the colonies, yet could she not, without sacrificing herself, have listened to this principle. For in leaving her colonies free, she would have run the risque of seeing them fall into the hands of another, who would exclude her from their market. She was not privileged to be wise alone, and to have expected a general concert among the commercial powers would have been folly. As therefore a colonial trade, grounded upon monopoly, was yet better than none, there remained for a state, in the situation of England, even had she most fortunately anticipated the result of a long experience, and of profound meditation, no other system than that of *monopoly*.

To secure to herself the exclusive trade of the colonies was under these circumstances necessarily the highest aim of England's policy. The establishment of this exclusive trade, which naturally arose from the original relations between the colonies and the mother country, had not been difficult to the state; for the emigrants had never received the smallest support. By so much the more expensive had it been to keep them. The possession of the colonies was the occasion of wars. The war of eight years between France and England, which concluded in the year 1763, by the peace of Fontainebleau, and which encreased the English national debt nearly a hundred millions sterling, had the colonial interest for its sole object. The conquest of Canada would not in itself have been worth a tenth part of the sums, which that war cost; the firm establishment of the commercial monopoly was properly the final purpose, for which they were expended.

It is a great question, whether even independent of the unhappy differences, which broke out immediately after the close of that war, its consequences would not have been rather pernicious than salutary to England. The annihilation of the French power in North-America completed the political existence of the English colonies, and supported by the still accelerating progress of their wealth, and of their vigour, gave them a consciousness of security and of stability, which must have become sooner or later dangerous to their connection with the mother country. It is more than improbable that this connection would have been perpetual. It is difficult to believe that under the most favourable circumstances it would have lasted another century. No nation governed its colonies upon more liberal and equitable principles than England; but the unnatural system, which chained the growth of a great people to the exclusive commercial interest of a country, distant from them a thousand leagues, even with the most liberal organization of which it was capable, could not have lasted forever.[2] Yet it would certainly have maintained itself for the next fifty years, and might perhaps have been dissolved in a milder and happier way than has now happened, had not England, under the most wretched of fascinations, fallen upon the idea of procuring in addition to the benefit of an exclusive trade, another immediate benefit, by an American public revenue.

It is hard to decide, which of the secret motives, which on either side were imputed to the ministry of that time first gave existence to this pernicious project. The most pardonable of all, the wish of alleviating the burthen of taxes upon the people of Great Britain, and especially upon the land-holders; a burthen, which the war had so much aggravated, is unluckily at the same time the most improbable. Specie was exactly that in which North America least abounded; to have levied in that country a tax of any real importance could scarcely have occurred to any Englishman with the least smattering of information; and that, amidst the thousand obstacles which must necessarily have opposed the collection of such a tax, its net produce for the treasury would always have melted to nothing, could scarcely escape the sagacity of any person versed in the subject. If we consider it attentively on all sides; if we carefully remark certain expressions of the ministers of that day, and what were afterwards known to be their favourite ideas, as well as the whole course of transactions upon American affairs, we can hardly avoid the belief, that what is generally considered as the *consequence* of the first treasury plan, the jealousy of the parliament's unlimited supremacy was rather the proper motive for this plan; and the secret apprehension that America might grow weary of her fetters, misled them to the dangerous experiment of fastening still narrower chains upon her.

The first step in this untrodden career was taken immediately after the peace of 1763, and under the most unfavourable auspices. The minister of finance, George Grenville, else in every respect an estimable and excellent statesman, but whose mind was either not great or not flexible enough to consider the new system in all its points of view, thought he could force down its execution, just at the period when, by various severe acts of parliament, he had brought back the commercial relations between England and the colonies as close as possible to the principles of monopoly; had pursued the American contraband trade, with the most oppressive regulations, and thereby had excited a great discontent in all minds. The tax with which he proposed to make his first essay, was a stamp-tax upon judicial records, newspapers, &c. to which the parliament, at the commencement of the year 1765, gave its assent.

The colonies had hitherto paid no other taxes, than those, which were necessary for the internal administration; and these proportionately insignificant charges had been prescribed and assessed by the several representative assemblies of each colony. In cases of urgency, for instance, in the course of the late war, these assemblies had raised, and presented to the government, extraordinary and voluntary contributions; but of a public tax, raised by act of parliament, there had been in North America no example. If the parliament, in the law regulating trade, had sometimes introduced a trifling entrance, or clearance duty, the most distant trace had never appeared in any public transaction, of a design to make America contribute immediately to the general exigencies of the British empire.

A long and venerable *observance* had sanctioned this colonial immunity; a thousand equitable considerations, and this above all, that the British commercial monopoly was of itself equivalent to a heavy and invaluable tax, justified this observance; and what was most important of all, even the authority of the parliament to violate this immunity, was controvertible with weapons furnished by the spirit of the English constitution itself. It had always been a favourite maxim of this constitution, that no Briton could be compelled to pay taxes, not imposed by his own representatives, and upon this maxim rested the whole constitutional power of the lower house in parliament. That the inhabitants of the colonies, in every sense of the word, were Britons, no man questioned; and the parliament, which thought itself authorized to tax them, even in that, recognized them as fellow citizens. Yet had they no representatives in parliament, and, owing to their distance, could properly make no pretensions to it. If, therefore, in respect to them, the constitutional principle retained its force, their contributions could only be prescribed by their colonial assemblies, and the British parliament was no more entitled to exercise the right of taxation over them, than over the people of Ireland.

But had this right been only questionable, it was at all events a false and hazardous step to bring it into discussion. To raise a controversy, concerning the bounds of the supreme power in the state, without the most urgent necessity, is in every case contrary to the simplest rules of state policy. Doubly dangerous must such a controversy here be, where it concerned a constitution, whose nature and boundaries had never yet been defined, and were, perhaps, not susceptible of definition. The relation between a colony and the mother country is one of those, which will not bear a strong elucidation; rights of sovereignty, of so peculiar and extraordinary a nature often vanish under the hands of those, who would dissect them. Now, when the mother country has a constitution like that of Britain, it becomes infinitely difficult to introduce into that relation a harmony, which satisfies the understanding, and at the same time the idea of right. It had never been examined how far the legislative authority of parliament, in respect to the colonies, extended; thus much, however, the colonies admitted, and would have continued long to admit, that the parliament was fully authorized to direct and to restrain their trade, in the widest extent of the word. This alone was clear; but this alone was essential to England. An attempt to go further was manifestly to set all at stake.

The appearance of the stamp-act in America was the signal for an universal commotion. The new laws against contraband trade had already irritated the minds of the people, because they plainly manifested the purpose of maintaining the British commercial monopoly in its greatest vigour; but these laws were received in silence, because there was no pretention to the right of complaining against them. Now, a new, and hitherto unexampled system, that of raising in North-America a tax for the treasury of England, was to be introduced, and in a form necessarily odious to the colonies; for a stamp-tax, from various local causes, had always been in North-America an oppressive tax. The opposition spread in a few days among all classes of people; in the lower, it burst forth in excesses of every kind; in the higher, by a stubborn and deliberate resistance, especially by a general agreement to import no merchandize from Great-Britain, until the stamp-act should be repealed. With the temper, which prevailed from one end of the colonies to the other, and with the well known perseverance, bordering upon obstinacy, of the author of the project, perhaps this first struggle might have ended in the total separation, had not just at that time the administration in England fallen into other hands.

The ministry, which in the summer of 1765, took the affairs of the nation in hand, rejected the new system of immediate taxation in America entirely. The mild principles, and the popular maxims of the marquis of Rockingham, made him averse to a path, in which violence alone could lead to the goal; and the secretary of state, general Conway, had been, when the business was first transacted in parliament, Grenville's most powerful and ardent opposer. The stamp-act, in the first session of the year 1766, was repealed; but to preserve the honour of parliament from sinking altogether, with this repeal was connected a declaratory act, intituled, "An Act for securing the Dependence of the Colonies;" in which the right of Great-Britain to legislate for the colonies in all cases whatsoever, was solemnly maintained.

This last step could not, in itself, be indifferent to the Americans; yet the joy at the repeal of the stamp-act was so great, that no regard was paid to the possible consequences of the act, which was attached as a counterbalancing weight of this appeal; and probably peace and concord would have been for a long time restored and secured, had not the English ministry, in a luckless hour, brought again to light the fatal project of raising a revenue from America. The marquis of Rockingham's administration had been dissolved, soon after the repeal of the stamp-act, and had been succeeded by another, at the head of which was indeed the name, but no longer the genius of the earl of Chatham. Charles Townsend, chancellor of the exchequer, a man of splendid talents, but of a frivolous and unsafe character, who was aiming to attain the highest summit of influence in the state, when an early death snatched him away from the career, proposed, in the year 1767, a tax upon the importation of glass, paper, painters' colours and tea into the colonies, and this proposal, although several of the ministers, and among the rest the duke of Grafton, who was at the head of the treasury department had silently contended against it, was by parliament adopted as a law. The defenders of this new plan entrenched themselves behind the feeble argument, that although parliament, by repealing the stamp-act, had renounced a direct taxation of the colonies, yet no renunciation could thence be inferred of indirect taxation, which was intimately connected with the right of regulating trade.

Had this reasoning even silenced the opposition in parliament, it was by no means calculated to satisfy the colonies. The hostile object of the new statute could not escape the shortest sight. The taxes prescribed, being announced merely as impost duties, were indeed reconcileable with the letter of that immunity, which lays so near the heart of the colonists, but their secret object could scarcely be any other, than to wrest by artifice, what was not ventured to be maintained by force. The insignificance of the benefit England could derive from these taxes, which would have produced only about £20,000, but too strongly confirmed this suspicion; and the peculiar character of the new regulations, the iniquity of exacting from a people, compelled to receive all the articles they needed, exclusively from the mother country, a tax upon the importation of such articles, rendered the undertaking completely odious. The imposts of 1767 operated in exactly the same manner as the stamp-act; the general nonimportation agreement was renewed in all the colonies; bitter controversies between the colonial assemblies and the royal governors, violent scenes between the citizens of divers towns and the military, resistance on the one part, menaces on the other foreboded the stroke, which was soon to shake the British empire to its foundations.

The ministry seemed however to make one more stand, upon the very border of the precipice. In the year 1769, by a circular letter of the minister for the colonies, the pleasing prospect of a speedy relief from the odious impost duties was opened to the colonial assemblies, and the decided aversion of the duke of Grafton to the taxation of America, seemed to encourage the hopes which this letter had raised. But no sooner had he, in the beginning of 1770, resigned his office, than the affair took another turn. His successor, lord North, did indeed in the first days of his administration formally propose the repeal of the American imposts, but with the unfortunate exception, that the tax upon tea should be continued as a proof of the legitimate authority of parliament; nor could the most vehement opposition of the united Rockingham and Grenville parties, who painted in the strongest colours the folly of continuing the contest, after the benefit was abandoned, avail anything against this wretched plan.[3] From that hour it was clear that the ministry had no other object than to make the colonies feel their chains. The first steps in this slippery career had their grounds in false representations and partial judgments; instead of these *errors* dangerous *passions* were now introduced, and the peace and welfare of the nation were to be sacrificed to a mistaken ambition, and a destructive jealousy.

Meanwhile, the disposition to resistance had struck deep roots in all the colonies; and the wider the mother country's undertakings departed from their first object, the more the resistance of the Americans departed from its original character. They had at first only denied the right of parliament to tax them; by degrees, the sphere of their opposition extended, and they began to call in question the authority of parliament altogether. When they had once taken this ground, it was in vain to hope to drive them from it. The consciousness of their stability, and their distance from England, their lawful pride in the rights, derived from their British descent, the recollection of the circumstances which had led their forefathers to America, the sight of the flourishing state into which in a period of 150 years they had turned an uninhabitable desert, the injustice, and the harshness of those, who instead of alleviating their dependence by gentle treatment, were daily seeking to render it more oppressive; all this encouraged the new impulse, which their ideas and their wishes had taken. The folly of Great-Britain in abandoning, for the useless discussion of a problematic right, the undisturbed enjoyment of a connection, which though never analysed and dissected with theoretic accuracy, was even in its undefined state so advantageous, became continually more visible; but far from endeavouring with tender caution to heal the dangerous wound, measure upon measure was taken to inflame it. Almost every step taken by the government during this unhappy period, in respect to the internal administration of the colonies, to the courts of justice, to the provincial assemblies, to the relations between the civil and military authorities, seemed expressly calculated at once to embitter and to embolden discontent; and the spirit of insurrection had long been in full possession of every mind, when a new attempt of the ministry, made it suddenly burst forth with the utmost violence.

The persevering refusal of the Americans to import tea into the colonies, so long as the tax upon it, prescribed in the year 1767, and purposely retained in 1770, should not be repealed, had occasioned a considerable loss to the East-India company, in whose magazines, great quantities of this article perished unconsumed. They had offered the minister to pay upon the exportation double the trifling tax of three pence upon the pound, which was yet so odious to the colonies; but this proposal, advantageous as it was, and which opened so honourable an issue from the crisis, was disapproved and rejected, as not according with the system of reducing America to unconditional submission. But as the embarrassment of the company was continually growing greater, they sought to help themselves by another project, and concluded to ship the tea for America upon their own account, there to pay the impost by their own agents and then make their sales. As at the same time, by act of parliament, the exportation was made duty free, whereby the tea, notwithstanding the impost in America, would be at a cheaper market than it had before been, it was hoped that the Americans would abandon all their scruples, and not feeling immediately the tax lurking in the price of the article, would give up all resistance.

The event soon discovered how vain this hope had been. Time had been allowed the colonies to reflect upon their situation, and to judge of the ministerial proceeding in the point of view which was alone essential. The merchants, who during the American agreement against the importation of British tea, had enriched themselves by the contraband trade of foreign teas, might, perhaps, only from mercantile considerations, abhor the undertaking of the East India company, sanctioned by the government; but the great mass of the people, and the most enlightened patriots in America, saw and condemned, in this undertaking, nothing but the evident purpose of carrying through the taxing right of the British parliament. The remarkable circumstance, that England had refused the larger revenue, which the taxes upon exportation from the British ports would have produced, to secure the levying of the much smaller entrance duty in America, betrayed a bitter passionate obstinacy, which together with so many other symptoms of hostility threatened the colonies with a gloomy futurity.

When the first report of these tea-ships having been sent arrived in America, from Newhampshire to Georgia, universal preparations for the most animated resistance were made. The agents of the company no where dared to receive the goods; in New-York, Philadelphia, and many other towns, such strong protestations against unlading the ships were made, that they were compelled to return untouched. In Boston, where the spirit of resistance had been from the beginning the most violent, Governor Hutchinson adopted measures to make the return of the ships impossible before the object should be attained; but his rigor only served to increase the evil. A small number of decided opponents, went on board the ship, and, without doing any other damage, broke open 342 chests of tea, and threw it into the sea.

The account of these tumultuous proceedings, soon after the opening of parliament, in the year 1774, reached England, where, immediately, the thirst for revenge silenced every other feeling; the zeal to maintain the honour and the rights of government, every other council, not only in the minds of the ministers, but likewise in the general opinion of the nation. In this critical moment it was forgotten, that it was not until after the colonies for ten years long, had been driven by a series of vicious and hazardous measures, by attacks continually repeated, and by studied systematic vexations to the utmost extremity, that their just indignation had burst forth in illegal acts.

The necessity for severe measures was indeed now evident, even to the moderate. But unfortunately, resentment overstepped the bounds of equity, and provoked pride the bounds of policy. The immediate authors of the excesses in Boston, might justly have been punished; the East-India company might justly claim to be indemnified by the colonies; the Americans, by their acts of violence, had evidently placed themselves at a disadvantage; and their faults gave the most favourable opportunity to bring them, with wisdom, back within their bounds. But England seemed herself to spurn all the advantages of her present situation, and to have commenced a war, rather against her own welfare and security, than against the opposition in the colonies. The first measure, proposed by lord North, was a law, to close as long as the king should think necessary, the port of Boston, and to transfer the custom-house of that flourishing and important commercial town to another place. Immediately after, appeared a second law, which struck still deeper at the vital principle of the colonies, which scarcely could be justified by the most exaggerated ideas of the parliament's authority, and which could not but unavoidably drive to despair, men, who had already been almost impelled to insurrection by an impost tax. This harsh law declared the province of Massachusetts Bay's charter void, and subjected this province, which by its wealth, its constitution hitherto, and the sentiments of its inhabitants, seemed to be more dangerous to the government, than all the rest, to a new organization, grounded on an absolute dependence upon the crown. At the same time, another act of parliament ordained, that persons, who during the tumults in America, had committed offenses against public officers, in every case, where the governor should have reason to apprehend that they could have no impartial trial there, should be sent to England for trial; a statute, which according to British ideas, deserved the epithet of tyrannical. Finally, the minister brought into parliament a law, giving to the province of Canada, which had been until then under a merely temporary administration, a constitution entirely different from the forms of the other colonial governments; and however the most recent experience might seem to justify the government in this step, it could not but produce the most unfavourable operation in the colonies, who believed to read their own future destiny in the treatment of that neighbouring country.

As soon as these measures were known in America, the general indignation, irritated yet further by the reinforcement of the royal troops in Boston, and by various unpleasant circumstances and oppressions, inseparable from this event, was raised to the highest and most dangerous pitch. Instantaneously, through all the colonies but one voice was heard; that the contest with England could be decided only by the sword. Preparations for the most resolute defence were every where the great occupation; exercises of arms became the sole employment of the citizens. A congress of fifty-one deputies from all the provinces assembled on the 4th of September, 1774, at Philadelphia, to consult upon the common grievances, and upon the means of averting the common danger. The first measures of this assembly consisted in a solemn declaration, that the unjust and oppressive proceedings of parliament against the town of Boston, and the province of Massachusetts-Bay, was to be considered as the cause of all the colonies; and in a recommendation to the inhabitants of North-America to suspend all commercial intercourse with Great-Britain, until the just grievances of the colonies should be redressed. Hereupon, the congress resolved upon an address to the British nation, and another to the king of England, in which the distressed situation of North America was delineated with boldness and energy, but at the same time with evident moderation, and in a language which still deprecated a separation from the mother country, as a very great evil.

It could no longer be concealed to the dullest eye, that the contest with the colonies had assumed a new and formidable character, and had spread to such an extent, as threatened the whole British empire. Yet, nothing is more certain, than that at this decisive moment, it still depended upon the parliament to finish it happily. No resolution, less than that of a total repeal of all the laws, promulgated since 1766, was commensurate with the greatness of the danger; but the thought that the immediate loss of America was at stake, should have reconciled every mind to this only remaining mean of salvation. Unfortunately, the deep exasperation, the inflexible pride, the false ambition, all the angry passions, which this cruel system had introduced and nourished, maintained now likewise their predominance; and a fatal error, the opinion that the victory over the colonies would be infallible and easy, entered into an unholy league with all those passions. The parliament, at the beginning of the year 1775, in a remarkable address to the king, declared, that both houses, convinced that a formal rebellion had broken out in the province of Massachusetts-Bay, would faithfully support him in every measure against rebellious subjects. Immediately afterwards, several laws of unmerciful severity, by which the colonies were deprived of all foreign commerce, and, what was yet harder, even of that fishery upon the coasts of Newfoundland so highly essential to their subsistence, passed by great majorities. Some of the wisest and most venerable statesmen, lord Chatham,[4] lord Camden, lord Shelburne, in the upper house, Edmund Burke, colonel Barré, in others in the house of commons, exerted in vain against these desperate resolutions, all the powers of an astonishing eloquence; such as perhaps had never been surpassed. The several plans of conciliation, which they proposed, were rejected, always with displeasure, sometimes with contempt; the only step towards peace that ever was attempted, rested upon a project of lord North, evidently incompetent to the end; which would scarcely have satisfied the colonies at the outset of the dispute, and certainly could not content them in the year 1775.

The congress assembled, for the second time, in May, 1775, and declared, "that by the violation of the charter of Massachusetts-Bay, the connection between that colony and the crown was dissolved." The conciliatory bills of lord North were rejected; a *continental army* and a *paper currency* were created; colonel Washington was appointed commander in chief of the American troops, &c. The war at this period had, in fact, broken out; it had been opened by the battle of Lexington, on the 19th of April, and while the congress were adopting these resolutions, a second and much bloodier action took place at Bunker's hill, where the loss suffered by the English army gave a severe, though unfortunately, a fruitless lesson to those, who had treated with so much contempt the resistance, and the military talents of the Americans.

Although every hope of peace had now well nigh vanished, the Congress were not however so far discouraged, as to decline venturing, even at this period, a last attempt at conciliation. They resolved a second address to the king, in which the colonies under the most forcible assurances of their submission, and of their unabated wish to remain united with Great Britain, intreated in the most urgent manner, that his majesty would give his assent to any plan whatsoever, calculated to pacify this wretched contest. The address was presented on the 1st. of September 1775, by Mr. Penn, of Pennsylvania, one of the most respectable citizens of North America, who was informed "that no answer would be given to it." Soon after the minister brought into parliament the law, which prohibited all intercourse with the colonies, and declared their ships to be lawful prize; a law, which was justly considered as a declaration of war against America, and by some as a formal abdication of the right of government over the colonies. At the same time, the king concluded alliances with several German princes, who engaged their troops for a great undertaking; and preparations of every kind announced that force alone was to decide the destiny of the British empire. At the close of the session of parliament in February 1776, the bitterness had attained its highest pitch. Even the evident danger, that foreign powers, and France in particular, might take a part in the disturbances in America, and take advantage of England's embarrassment, made no impression upon the ministers and the parliament. When some members of the opposition at the beginning of the year 1776, asserted that according to very authentic accounts, a negociation between the Congress at Philadelphia, and the French court, was already commenced, not only the truth, but even the possibility of this but too well grounded fact was denied. It was maintained "that, such an unexampled fascination," could not be supposed in any nation, "holding colonies itself, in any government wishing to retain the obedience of their own subjects." A reasoning, which in itself rested upon very just principles, but which lost all its conclusive *weight* in the mouth of those, who, by a fascination entirely similar, had come to the point of setting at stake, from mere stupid obstinancy, one of their most precious possessions, and half the existence of their empire.

Since the last months of the year 1775, the war was raging in the bowels of the colonies. The language and the resolves of Parliament in the winter of 1775–1776, taught the Americans that it would be a war for life and death. Every bond of union was broken. Against the return of the old happy days the iron hand of inexorable destiny had barred every gate. On the 4th of July 1776, the Congress declared the Independence of the Thirteen United States.

It belongs not to the purpose of the present essay to continue further this cursory historical recapitulation, since I am here speaking only of the *origin* of the American revolution. It is however sufficiently known, that the *progress* and the *issue* of the war, completely justified the anticipations of those, who would have avoided it *at any price.* It is equally well known, how much the *consequences* of this war, have put to shame the expectations of all parties. The supporters of the war, went upon the principle, that every thing must be hazarded to maintain the possession of the colonies, its opponents, upon the principle that every thing must be *sacrificed* not to lose them; both concurred therefore in the opinion that this loss would give a deep, and perhaps incurable wound to the British empire. Experience has decided. In a few years after the loss of the colonies, England has again become as powerful and flourishing, nay more powerful and flourishing than ever. And whatever of a hurtful nature, that lay in the influence of this event upon the affairs of Europe, has fallen upon *France* alone; upon France, who, according to the general opinion, was to derive the greatest advantages from the American revolution.

If we duly meditate upon the series of facts, which have been here summarily exhibited, and upon some others equally certain and authentic, which will be touched upon in the sequel, the following points of comparison will arise, to show in its clearest light the *essential* difference between the American and French revolutions.

1. The American revolution was grounded partly upon principles, of which the right *was evident,* partly upon such, as it was at least

very questionable, whether they were not right, and from beginning to end upon no one that was clearly and decidedly wrong; the French revolution was an uninterrupted series of steps, the wrong of which could not, upon rigorous principles, for a moment be doubted.

The question, concerning the *right* of a revolution, has, by the frivolous way of thinking, by the shallow sophistry, and even by the immense devastations, and the stupid indifference arisen from them, of this revolutionary age, been in a manner discarded among the idle amusements of scholastic pedants; many who hold themselves for statesmen, think it no longer *worth while so much as* to start the question; yet in the eyes of the thinking, of the wise and the good, will it ever remain, the first and the last.

The relation between the inhabitants of a distant colony, and the government of the mother country, is never to be compared in all respects with the relation between the government and their immediate subjects. In the former, there lies always something strained, something equivocal, something unnatural; for it cannot be denied, the firmest foundation of all sovereignty is in the wants of the governed, and those wants are weaker, are more questionable, withdraw themselves, to express myself so, from the eyes and the feeling, when the government is a thousand leagues distant from the country, which must obey their laws. Besides, all the European states, which founded, or encouraged the foundation of colonies in the other quarters of the globe, considered these colonies, more or less, as mere instruments to *enrich* and strengthen the seat of their own power, and treated the people, who inhabited them, merely as the means of an happier, or more agreeable existence for their own. A maxim, which could not easily be reconciled with the general purposes of society, for which the colonies must have as keen a sense as the mother country, and with the consciousness of independent stability, to which they must sooner or later attain. Hence, the right of an European nation over their colonies must necessarily always be a wavering, insecure, undefined, and often undefinable right. If, however, the form of government in the mother country be simple, and the conditions, upon which the colony was founded, were in themselves clear and definite, then that unavoidable misrelation will be less perceptible. The difficulties on the other hand must be much greater, the collisions more frequent and momentous, when the mother country has a complicated constitution, and when the conditions under which the colonies are connected with her, the rights, which they enjoy by virtue of her particular constitution, the place which they are to hold in that constitution, are not in the precisest manner defined at their very origin.

This was in both points the case with the English colonies, in North America. How far the rights and liberties of a new state, founded by Britons, under the British constitution, should extend, and in what particular relation the inhabitants of such a state should stand, with the several component parts of that mixed constitution? this was a question, which at their origin should have been considered with the utmost attention. This question was never once thought of. The colonies originated at a time, when the British constitution itself had not yet attained its last perfection and consistence.[5] Their charters all proceeded from the *crown.* The parliament had never taken any part in their settlement.

The internal forms of government of these colonies were as various, as the circumstances, under which they had been founded, or formed. Some of the most important had been granted as hereditary property to private persons, so that these, and their heirs, might govern them entirely as they pleased, and were scarcely more than under a nominal dependence upon the crown. In this manner had Maryland been granted to lord Baltimore; North and South-Carolina to lord Clarendon; in this manner Pennsylvania and Delaware belonged to the family of the celebrated Penn. Others, as New-Hampshire, New-York, New-Jersey, and Virginia, were called royal provinces, and in these the king was considered as the immediate sovereign. Lastly, there was a third class of colonies, which were called privileged, and in which the power of the monarch was limited by the original charters. Such was the constitution of Massachusetts, of Rhode Island, and of Connecticut.

The relations between the royal governors, and the provincial assemblies, were in every colony differently defined and modified; but the provincial assemblies were accustomed every where, whether the province was originally privileged, royal, or hereditary, more or less, to exercise the right of enacting laws for the internal police of the province, of levying taxes for meeting the public exigences of the state, and of taking an essential part in every thing belonging to the administration of the country. In no single colony, however its constitution, in respect to its dependance upon the crown, was organized, was there a trace of a constitutional and legal authority, vested in the British parliament. The charters contained none; no definite law, not so much as a partial statute, enacted in Great-Britain, had ever proclaimed, or even made mention of such an authority.

In the beginning, the parliament considered this their absolute exclusion from the sovereignty over the colonies with great indifference; in the preceding century, the bounds of their power in general were so little defined, that not the smallest doubt has been started against the authority of the king, at his pleasure to give, to grant, to constitute, to privilege, to govern, by himself, or allow to be governed, by others, an immense continent in America; this distant and uncultivated land, was besides far too much despised for them to concern themselves about its constitution. But when, on the one side, after the revolution of 1688, the influence of parliament upon all the affairs of government had become greater, firmer, and more general; and when, on the other side, the extraordinary importance of the colonies, in their rapidly growing population, in their constantly improving culture, in their unexpected and splendid flourishing state, was daily more evident, the idea by degrees crept into every mind, that so great and essential a part of the British empire could not possibly be altogether withdrawn from the superintendency of parliament, even though nothing should have been said of it hitherto in the public transactions.

In one single, though truly important point, the parliament had always exercised the legislative power over the colonies, in every thing which concerned trade, whether of export, or of import. Although this was precisely the seat of that mighty monopoly, which seemed to give the colonies their whole value, and which, on the other side, could never be so favourable to their progress as liberty would have been, yet they willingly submitted to the regulations and restraints of all kinds, with which the parliament in ample measure provided them. It appeared natural and equitable to themselves, that the supreme legislative power in the empire, should regulate and direct a concern, which interested not exclusively America, but England too, in a much higher degree. The right of the parliament, therefore, to prescribe laws to the colonies relating to commerce, and to every thing connected with it, was never called in question.

But, as soon as the parliament determined to overstep this right, and to levy taxes in America, without the consent of the local representatives, the most vehement resistance could not fail to break out, and this resistance could as little fail to increase, when, in the progress of the contest, the pretention to bind America by act of parliament, in all cases whatsoever, was advanced, and formally derived from what was called the legal supremacy of parliament. The *omnipotence* of parliament, so often, and so loudly, then resounded by the antagonists of the colonies, was a very just principle for England, but a very invalid one for America. With the parliament, bating the trade laws, to which the colonists submitted from reason and necessity, America had not the least to do. America sent no representatives to parliament, nor did it ever occur to parliament to offer her that power, which would indeed not have been without great difficulties carried into effect. The colonies, nevertheless, possessed all the benefits of the British constitution, and even the greatest part of their forms. Almost in every one of them, there was a *representative assembly*, which supplied the place of a lower house, and a senate, which answered to the house of peers. These assemblies transacted, under the sanction of the monarch, all the affairs, which in England and Ireland were done by the parliaments. They enacted laws, levied taxes, deliberated upon the exigencies, and upon the administration of their provinces. They formed, in concurrence with the king and his governors, a complete government, organized altogether in the spirit of the English constitution, and needed no co-operation of the British parliament. The constitutions of the several provinces, knew only the king, and the provincial representative bodies, and had no more reference to the parliament of Great-Britain, than to the parliaments of France. They had existed more than a century, without knowing any thing of the English parliament, otherwise than by its commercial regulations, which had not always been to them the most agreeable. The pretended right of parliament to prescribe laws and taxes for them, was an arbitrary assumption, against which the colonies, according to all legal principles, might proceed exactly as Great-Britain would have done, had any of the provincial assemblies undertaken, with the concurrence of the king, to levy taxes in England or Scotland, or to overthrow the municipal constitution of London or Westminster, as the parliament had overthrown the charter of Massachusetts-Bay.

The resistance of the colonies, and the unavoidable insurrection, which was finally produced by the continuance of the attack, were, therefore, inasmuch as they respected the parliament, perfectly *right*. The parliament was, in regard to the colonies, to be considered as a *foreign power*. So long as this power had remained within the bounds of its silently acknowledged sphere of operation, the colonies had submitted to it. To give laws beyond those bounds, it was as little authorised, as would have been the legislative power of any other nation. The Americans could resist it with the same right, as they might have resisted the States-General of Holland, or the council of the Indies in Madrid, had these undertaken to impose upon them their manufacturing regulations, or stamp taxes.

The question seems to be more difficult, with what right the colonies could likewise resist the king, who, at any rate, was their legal and acknowledged sovereign? But, if in this respect the lawfulness of their conduct be doubtful, it would at least remain a great point, that its unlawfulness could not be clearly proved, and a closer examination will lead us to a result yet far more favourable to the justification of this conduct.

For there is a very evident distinction between an insurrection in a *simple,* and one in a *complicated,* or *mixed constitution.* In a simple government, every resistance against the supreme power, is absolutely illegal, and requires no further examination to be condemned. In a mixed government, cases may be imagined, in which the matter is very intricate, and therefore problematic and dubious.

In a mixed government, the supreme power, or the proper sovereign, consists always of several component parts connected together and regulated by the constitution. Each of these parts has its constitutional rights and prerogatives; and those of any one part, though in themselves more important, cannot be more sacred than those of any other. When either of them exceeds its legal bounds, and oppresses, or endeavours to destroy another, this latter, unless the constitution be an empty name, must have the right of resisting; and, unless the war, arising from this resistance, be not averted by some fortunate expedient; if the old balance cannot again be restored, the contest must necessarily, and *legally* end with the dissolution of the constitution. For between two independent component parts of the supreme power in a state, there can no more be a judge, than between two independent states. That this is a most unfortunate situation for the whole nation, interested in it, is self evident. The most dreadful circumstance it brings with it, is unquestionably this, that the people in such a controversy never know whom to obey, and whom to resist; for whom to declare, and against whom to act; that all rights and duties are thrown into confusion, and involved in obscurity, and that it becomes a problem, who is within, and who is without the line of insurrection. This evil is inseparable from mixed forms of government;[6] and however great it may be, its possibility can never be excluded from such constitutions. If, for example, the two houses of the British parliament should make the attempt to enact laws, without the sanction of the king, or the king, without the concurrence of parliament, the injured party would beyond all doubt resist, and resist with energy; nor could any one deny that this resistance, even though it should end in civil war and the ruin of the constitution, was perfectly lawful.

The American colonies were precisely in this, or at least in an extremely similar situation. Their constitution before the revolution was evidently a monarchy, more or less limited by the influence of their provincial assemblies. The legislative and executive powers were divided between the king and the provincial assemblies, as in England, between the king and the two houses of parliament. The king and his governor had only a negative upon acts of legislation, and the provincial assemblies in most of the colonies had a considerable share in the government. In all the provinces (Pennsylvania since 1700 excepted) these assemblies were divided into two houses, closely corresponding in their functions, with the two branches of the British parliament. The lower house, or the representative assembly possessed every where the exclusive right of prescribing taxes. In some colonies, for instance, in Maryland, the king, by the charter, *had expressly* renounced all right of taxation. In several others he had, in the literal sense of the word, only reserved the empty title of sovereignty. Connecticut and Rhode-Island were perfect democracies. The colonial assemblies of these provinces chose their governors without the confirmation of the king, and dismissed them at pleasure; they allowed no appeals from their courts of justice; their laws required no royal assent; nay, what is more remarkable, and a proof of their absolute independence, their charters granted them even the right of peace and war.

The king's power was, therefore, in all the colonies, more or less limited; in some, to such a degree that it could not be compared with his legitimate power in Great-Britain; and the colonial assemblies had a constitutional right to resist him, when he violated their constitutional powers. Now, the measures of the ministry, from 1764, were evident attacks, upon those powers. Whether the parliament had advised, or confirmed those attacks, was, as we have before shewn, nothing to the colonies; they had to do only with the king, and the king, according to their constitutions, could levy no taxes, but such as the provincial assemblies proposed. The stamp-act of 1764, was, therefore, a violation of their rights; the impost act of 1767, was a violation of their rights; the act of 1770, which maintained the tea-tax to support the supremacy of parliament, was a gross, and what was worst of all, an insulting violation of their rights. To punish them for their constitutional resistance against these unconstitutional resolves, was a revolting injustice; the mode of punishment (the Boston port-bill, the bill to abolish the Massachusetts charter, &c.) was not merely a violation, it was an entire dissolution of their rights. It was nothing more, than the proclamation of a *fact,* when the congress, in 1775, declared, "that by the abolition of the Massachusetts charter, *the connection between that province and the crown was dissolved.*" No resource was left but that of repelling force by force. The convocation of their first congress, was in itself not an illegal measure. This congress exercised originally only the same rights, which were unquestionably within the powers of every provincial assembly. It represented a legal resistance, and sought the means of preserving to America the constitution she had hitherto possessed. It was not until after the ministry had spurned at peace, rejected every proposal of conciliation, and finally required unconditional submission, that is, had *dissolved the constitution,* that the congress proceeded to the declaration, which substituted a new government, in the stead of that which was destroyed.

Had the colonies had the design (and it cannot be denied that they manifested it clearly enough) in this whole contest to separate the king completely from the parliament, all the means were taken away from them of regulating their conduct, according to a system founded upon such a separation. The most intimate union subsisted between the ministry and the parliament; nor was it possible to resist the one, without quarrelling with the other. The king confirmed the hostile acts of parliament; he ceased to be the constitutional monarch of the colonies, and entered into an alliance with those, whom they considered as usurpers in a legal point of view. Had the king of England allied himself with a foreign power (and in a constitutional sense the parliament was no other to the colonies) against the parliament of Great-Britain, how would it be possible for the parliament to arm against this foreign power, and yet spare the king of England? Or rather, would not the mere undertaking of such an alliance include within itself an immediate justification of every defensive measure taken by the injured party, and an absolute renunciation of the constitution.

I think I have here sufficiently developed the first point in the comparison I proposed, that which relates to the conduct of North-America; there now remains only the easy task of exhibiting the second, which relates to the conduct of France.

The single period of the disturbances in France, when mention was made of militating *rights,* was that in which the parliaments took part, in 1787 and 1788. If the prerogatives of these parliaments were not so great and so unquestionable, as they would have represented them, yet their appeal to them gave at least a colour of lawfulness to their undertakings. That period, however, is to be considered only as preparatory to the real revolution.

From the breaking out of this revolution, the question as to the *lawfulness* of what the popular leaders did, was never (an extraordinary, yet an indubitable fact!) started. The word *right* would have vanished from the French language, had not an imaginary right of the *nation,* to do whatever they, or their representatives should please, appeared as a sort of substitute for all other rights.

This is not the place to analyse this *right of the nation,* sometimes likewise called *right of man,* a sort of magic spell, with which all the ties of nations and of humanity were insensibly dissolved. Those, who were serious in advancing it, grounded it upon the chimerical principle of the sovereignty of the people, which I have endeavoured upon another occasion to elucidate. Thus much is certain, that the leaders of the revolution, under the shelter of this talisman, spared themselves and others the trouble of enquiring into the lawfulness of their proceedings; for in their system, all was right, which they resolved upon in the name of the *people,* or in the name of mankind.

In order to judge of their actions, according to their deserts, they must be snatched away from the tribunal they have erected for themselves, and placed at another bar, whose laws accord better with the dictates of uncorrupted reason, and the eternal prescriptions of *real right.*

When the deputies of the states assembled together in the year 1789, they had beyond all doubt the *right* to undertake great reforms in the government, and even in the constitution of the French monarchy. This right, however, they could exercise only under the three following conditions. First, that they should observe the general forms of an assembly of the states in France, until these forms should in a *lawful* manner be abolished, or changed. Secondly, that their laws should not have the force of laws, until assented to by the monarch. And, thirdly, that they should follow the instructions, given them by their constituents.

In less than six weeks, they had broken through these three fundamental conditions. The deputies of the third state, without the least authority, and with a shameful violation of the rights of the other states, declared that themselves alone constituted the national assembly.

When the king endeavoured to bring them back from this monstrous usurpation to their proper limits, they declared to him that they persisted in it, formally renounced obedience to him, and reduced him finally to the necessity of commanding the two other estates to acknowledge the usurpation.

That in the immeasurable career, which these two first successful acts of violence, had opened, they might no longer meet resistance from any quarter, they declared that the instructions of their constituents were not binding upon them.

They had proceeded thus far, when, partly by their influence and example, partly by faults of the court, which need not be considered here, where the question only relates to *right,* the general rebellion broke out in Paris, and in all the provinces. Far from *disapproving* this rebellion, which, in perfect contrast with the rising of the people in America, had not the most distant connection with the lawful objects of the national assembly, they cherished and fostered it, gave it legislative force and consistence, conferred civic crowns upon its authors, called it an holy and virtuous insurrection, and took care to have it maintained in a continual flame, during the whole period of their government.

Under the shadow of this insurrection, they, who had placed themselves at its head, and taken upon themselves all responsibility, in a period of two years ran through the most remarkable circle of violation of all rights, public and private, that the world ever beheld. They drew up, without ever so much as *asking the free assent of the king,* a constitution so called, the incompetency, the impracticability, the ridiculous absurdity of which was so great, that, even among its authors (another unexampled yet indubitable fact), not a single man would ever have seriously defended it. This constitution they compelled the king, upon pain of being immediately dethroned, to subscribe and swear to.

Scarcely had this happened, when their successors, who by virtue of this constitution alone, had a sort of legal existence, and held something resembling an authority to shew, instead of governing and quieting the state according to this constitution, directed all their secret, and what was still more revolting, all their public measures to its destruction. In less than a year they succeeded in effecting this new usurpation. Without so much as having a *legal pretext,* they suspended the constitution, dethroned the king, assumed to themselves, still forsooth *in the name of the people,* the power of calling a *national convention,* and proclaimed the republic, with fewer formalities, than a man would use to change his dress. By long habit dead to every sentiment of *right,* tormented by all the furies, plunged by their frantic measures, by crimes, and calamities of every kind into the lowest depth of criminal fool-hardiness, they now proclaimed against humanity and all its rights, a formal, irreconcileable war; and to shut behind them every door for return, and to snap the last thread by which they still held together with a lawful existence, they finally murdered justice herself, in the person of the most conscientious and upright monarch, who had ever adorned a throne.

The French revolution, therefore, began by a violation of rights, every step of its progress was a violation of rights, and it was never easy, until it had succeeded to establish absolute wrong, as the supreme and acknowledged maxim of a state completely dissolved, and yet existing only in bloody ruins.

2. The American revolution was from beginning to end, on the part of the Americans, merely a *defensive revolution;* the French was from beginning to end, in the highest sense of the word, *an offensive revolution.*

This difference of itself is essential and decisive; upon it rests, perhaps more than upon any other, the peculiar character, which has distinguished these two revolutions.

The British government began the revolution in America by resolves, for which they could shew no right; the colonies endeavoured by all means in their power to repel them. The colonies wished to maintain their old constitution; the government destroyed it. The resistance, which the colonies opposed against the mother country, was, in every period of this unhappy contest, exactly commensurate with the attack; the total separation was not resolved, until the utter impossibility of preserving the ancient condition was proved.

The stamp-act threw America into the most violent commotion; tumultuous scenes, though attended with no acts of bloody violence, broke out in all the provinces.[7] But they were no where formally sanctioned by the approbation of the legislative authorities. The little congress of 28 deputies of several colonies, who in the year 1765 assembled at New-York, and served as the model for the subsequent larger assembly, passed no other resolution than that "the colonies could only be taxed by their representatives," and expressed this perfectly lawful resolve, in *petitions* to the king. The single general measure, which was then offered, the non-importation agreement, was a voluntary engagement, sanctioned by no public authority.

The *declaratory act,* which appeared in the year 1766, together with the repeal of the stamp-tax, could not possibly be agreeable to the colonies since it expressly and solemnly maintained the right of the British parliament to bind them by law in all cases whatsoever. Yet was this act received with great and remarkable tranquillity; and had the British government, from that time forward, given up forever their unhappy innovations; had they continued to govern the colonies, according to the old constitutional principles, there never would have been uttered a complaint against the declaratory act. It was long afterwards, and when the colonies had been provoked by repeated attacks of every kind, to the utmost extremity, that the provincial assembly of Massachusetts-Bay, declared that statute, an oppression.

The resistance against the impost taxes of 1767, was of the same nature, as that which the stamp-tax had experienced. This new grievance of the colonies, was accompanied with circumstances of the most odious kind: the augmentation of the troops, the conduct of a part of them, the harshness of some governors, the frequent adjournments and violent dissolution of the provincial assemblies, all was calculated to put the patience of the Americans to dangerous proof.

And yet they never overstepped the boundaries, which the constitution and the laws prescribed to them; and in their numerous addresses and protestations, adhered rigorously to what was allowed by law. When in the year 1770, a violent quarrel arose between some of the royal soldiers, and certain citizens of Boston, which ended in the first bloody scene the colonies had in their contest with England yet witnessed, the courts of law, with a glorious impartiality, acquitted the greatest part of the accused and indicted soldiers.

The continuation of the tax upon tea in the year 1770, had no other consequence than to strengthen the voluntary agreement against the importation of English tea; the resolve in the year 1773, which authorised the East-India company to the exportation of their stores of tea, free from duty, and the actual execution of this resolve, could not, indeed but produce a still more unfavourable operation. This measure was altogether calculated to provoke the colonies to a general insurrection. Yet did they keep themselves rigorously within the limits of a necessary defence. The destruction of the tea at Boston was, in fact, no other than a defensive operation. The sale of this tea, or only a part of it, would have involved the compulsive levy of a tax, by the payment of which the constitution of the colonies and all their rights would have been lost. Yet, even then, they proceeded not beyond what was unavoidable, and measured the resistance as exactly as possible by the attack. The tea was thrown into the sea, and not a single hostile step followed upon this undertaking. Nay, although the public authorities of Boston, and of the whole province, held it for necessary, as much as every single citizen, yet they always undeniably discovered themselves ready to grant the fullest indemnity to the East-India company.

Had the ministry, at this period, been contented with an equitable satisfaction; had they, if they must punish, been content to inflict tolerable and proportionable punishments, there is no doubt but America would have remained with her old constitution. Although a great part of the inhabitants of the colonies, in expectation of a distressing and stormy futurity, urged for energy and for arming, yet was this temper still far from being common. It is, for example, a certain fact, that in the important province of Pennsylvania, the majority of the citizens would have voted against taking a part in the measures at Boston, had not the excessive and unwise harshness of the parliament, in a short time, inflamed and united all minds.

The appearance of the act, which closed the port of Boston, of that which, immediately after, took away the Massachusetts charter, the account of all what had passed in parliament upon that occasion, the visible impossibility of eradicating peaceably such deep rooted bitterness—all these circumstances concurred to render a sudden explosion probable; many of the resolves of parliament were indisputably of a nature to furnish sufficient motive for such an explosion. But the provincial assemblies contented themselves with sending deputies to a general congress. Not one over hasty step disturbed the pacific and lawful character of their conduct in this hard and trying period.

The congress, which assembled at Philadelphia, spoke with energetic freedom of the constitutional rights of the colonies, and of the oppressive measures of parliament; but their first resolves were more moderate, than perhaps England herself had expected. An invitation to a general agreement against all trade with Great-Britain was the only active step they allowed themselves; and after all what the parliament had done, this step was of little importance. How far they were remote, even then, from a total separation, and how much the conduct of the colonies deserved the name of a lawful defence, may be learned from the following conclusion of the remarkable address, which this congress immediately before separating, sent to the king.

> We ask only for peace, libery and security. We wish no diminution of royal prerogatives, we demand *no new rights.* From the magnanimity and justice of your majesty, and the parliament, we promise ourselves the redress of our grievances;

> firmly convinced, that when once the causes of our present complaints are removed, our future conduct will not be undeserving of the milder treatment, to which we were in better days accustomed. We call that Being, who tries the inmost heart, to witness, that no other motive, than the fear of the destruction, which threatens us, has had any influence upon our resolutions. We therefore intreat your majesty as the loving father of all people, bound to you by the ties of blood, by laws, affection, and fidelity, not to permit, in the uncertain expectation of a result, which never can compensate for the wretchedness by which it must be attained, any further violation of those sacred ties. So may your majesty in a long and glorious reign, enjoy every earthly bliss, and this bliss, and your undiminished authority descend upon your heirs and their heirs, till time shall be no more.

The American agents in London, Bollan, Franklin and Lee, petitioned to be heard in support of this address, at the bar of the parliament. Their request was rejected.

Soon after, this cruel act, which deprived the colonies of all navigation, and even of the fishery, obtained the force of law; and the very moment, when this harsh law was past, was chosen to make the only proposal of conciliation, which the parliament had ever offered. According to this proposal, which is known by the name of lord North's Conciliatory Plan, every colony, whose representatives would engage to deliver their proportional contribution to the exigencies of the empire, and raise besides the costs of their internal administration, *provided* their offers should be approved by the king and parliament, was to be secured in the exemption from all further taxation. Not to mention that the only object of this plan notoriously was to divide the colonies, that it was offered them by an armed hand, that the *suspicious proviso* made the favourable consequences of its acceptance extremely doubtful, it properly decided the true point of contest, in a manner wholly contradictory to the principles of the Americans. The parliament renounced a right which notoriously did not belong to them. But they renounced it, only to exercise, once for all, what they had wished to exercise by piece-meal. The injustice and inconsistency of this proposal could not for a moment escape the notice of the colonies. The second general congress, which assembled on the 10th of May, 1775, rejected it upon grounds, the force of which must be felt by every impartial mind. "Should we accede," say they, in their answer to this proposal,

> we should expressly declare a wish to purchase the favour of parliament, without knowing at what price it would be set. We hold it superfluous to extort from us, by violence or threats a proportional contribution, to meet the general exigencies of the state, since all the world knows, and the parliament must themselves acknowledge, that whenever thereto required, in a constitutional manner, we have always richly contributed. It is unjust to require permanent contributions of the colonies, so long as Great-Britain possesses the monopoly of their trade; this monopoly is, in itself, the heaviest of all contributions. It is unjust to wish to tax us doubly. If we must contribute in like proportion with the other parts of the empire, al low us, like them too, a free trade with all the world.

These unanswerable arguments were at an immeasurable distance from the language of insolent rebellion.

When, finally, the congress resolved upon the general arming of the country, *defence* was still their single, and exclusive object. The constitution had been long since, without their fault, torn to pieces; they might have proclaimed immediately a new one upon its ruins; but they appealed to arms, to maintain the same constitution, of which the colonies had been, with so much violence, deprived.

The surest proof of this glorious moderation was, that they themselves, after the actual breaking out of hostilities, and when a great part of the inhabitants of America, urged for more energetic measures, did not omit another attempt by petitions and remonstrances, to attain the end of their wishes. In the midst of the most vigorous preparations for a desperate defence, they resolved, in the month of July, 1775,[8] another address to the king, to which was given the inviting and significant name of the *olive branch.* Even in this last address, we read with astonishment, among other things, as follows:

> Devoted to the person, the family, and the government of your majesty, with all the attachment, which only principle and feeling can inspire, connected with Great-Britain, by the strongest ties that can unite human societies together, deeply afflicted at every event that may weaken this connection, we most solemnly assure your majesty, *that we wish nothing more ardently than the restoration of the former harmony* between England and the colonies, and a new union, founded upon a lasting basis, capable of propagating that blessed harmony to the latest generations, and transmit to a grateful posterity your majesty's name, surrounded with that immortal glory which was in every age bestowed upon the saviours of the people. We protest to your majesty, that notwithstanding all our sufferings in this unhappy contest, the hearts of your faithful colonists are far from wishing a reconciliation upon conditions, which could be inconsistent with the dignity, or the welfare of the state from which they sprung, and which they love with filial tenderness. If the grievances, which now bow us down with inexpressible pain to the ground, could in any manner be removed, your majesty will at all times find your faithful subjects in America, willing and ready, with their lives and fortunes, to maintain,

> preserve, and defend the rights and interests of their sovereign, and of their mother country.

This was the address, which Mr. Penn, on the 1st of September, 1775, delivered to the earl of Dartmouth, upon which, some days after, he was informed, *that no answer could be given.* It was not until after this last attempt had proved fruitless, after an unmerciful statute had outlawed American ships, and the levying of foreign troops left them only the choice between the dissolution of their constitution, with unconditional submission, and the same dissolution with the free choice of a new one, that the congress passed the resolve, which reason and necessity prescribed, and declared the colonies independent, because independence was a smaller evil than dependence upon arbitrary will; and their painfully maintained, and painfully defended dependence upon the old laws, was lost forever.

The revolution of America was, therefore, in every sense of the word, a revolution of necessity: England, alone, had by violence effected it: America had contended ten years long, not against England, but against the revolution: America sought not a revolution; she yielded to it, compelled by necessity, not because she wished to extort a better condition than she had before enjoyed, but because she wished to avert a worse one, prepared for her.

Exactly the contrary of all this, was the case in France. The French revolution was *offensive* in its origin, offensive in its progress, offensive in its whole compass, and in every single characteristic moment of its existence. As the American revolution had exhibited a model of moderation in defence, so the French one displayed an unparalleled example of violence and inexorable fury in attack. As the former had always kept the vigour of its defensive measures in rigorous proportion to the exigency, so the latter, from the weakness of the resistance made against it, became more and more violent and terrible, the more cause it had to grow milder.

Could the destroyers of a throne, could the teachers and heroes of a revolutionary age, themselves have formed the character of a prince, under whom they would begin their dreadful experiment, they never could have succeeded better, than in that, which a cruel destiny delivered into their hands. Lewis the 16th promoted the revolution by all the good, and by all the weak sides of his character. He was certainly not equal to the circumstances, under which he had to act, and to the dangers, which he was to overcome; but what rendered his want of energy truly fatal, were his virtues. Had he been less honourable, less benevolent, less humane, less conscientious, perhaps he might yet have saved the monarchy. The unhappy certainty that it was impossible for him, so much as for a moment, to be a tyrant, made him and the state the victims of the most shameful and most revolting tyranny that the world had ever seen. His noble readiness to encourage every thing, which assumed the name of reform, drew him into the first false steps, which shook his throne. His horror of violence tore the sceptre from his benevolent hands. His integrity was the best ally of those, who plunged France and him into the precipice.

He looked with satisfaction towards that assembly of the states, whose effects had in the council of the wicked been long prepared. They rewarded him by the decrees, which excluded him from the government of the kingdom. He would not suffer his troops to use force against the first insurgents. They rewarded him by the general insurrection of the capital and of all the provinces. He endeavoured, even after having lost all his power, and tasted the bitterest afflictions, such as a dethroned monarch only can know, still to turn the evil to good. They improved this insurmountable royal temper, this pure and real civism, to be guilty with less interruption, while he continued to hope; and to crush him with the load of their present crimes, while he looked forward to a better futurity.

It may boldly be maintained almost every thing that has been said of the resistance of the court and of the great, of their conspiracies, of their cabals against the revolution, was merely a wretched fable. That the injured, the oppressed, the plundered could be no friends to their oppressors and plunderers is self-evident; as far as mere hatred is resistance, there was an enormous mass of resistance against the revolution; the leaders had themselves created these internal, these secret hostilities, of which they so often complained. They must have extirpated human nature herself to secure to themselves forgiveness, or a disposition to favour their cruel operations. But, throughout their whole career, they met with no active resistance, and the only circumstance, which could spread a varnish of credibility over their incessant fictions of plots, counter-revolutions, &c. was, that they *deserved* all, that they pretended to suffer.

If we follow this revolution through all its periods, we shall find that the strongest motive for effecting any greater usurpation, for maintaining any greater injustice, for committing any greater crime, constantly was, that a smaller one had immediately before succeeded. The single motive for using persecutions, was, that the victims had already suffered others. This was the character of the French revolution, in wholesale and in retail. The sufferers were punishable, merely because they had suffered; in this bitterest of all offensive wars, they seemed so cautiously to shun every thing that made a shew of resistance, that they sooner forgave a struggling, than a defenceless, enemy.

The relics of the old constitution were not so much boundaries to the omnipotent desolating power of the revolution, as land-marks, designating its victorious progress. The constitution, of 1791, was only a short and voluntary pause; a sort of resting point, at which nobody meant long to wait. The second national assembly did not make a pass, no, not one, which was not an attack upon some ruin or other of the monarchy. The establishment of the republic did not satisfy its authors. The execution of the king scarcely appeased the ravenousness of his butchers, for a single instant. In the year 1793 the thirst for destruction had gone so far, that it was at a loss for an object. The well known saying, that Robespierre meant to reduce the population of France by one half, had its foundation in the lively sense of the impossibility of satisfying the hitherto insatiate revolution, with any thing less, than such a hecatomb.

When there was nothing more left in the country to attack, the offensive frenzy turned itself against the neighbouring states, and finally declared war in solemn decrees against all civil society. It was certainly not the want of will in those, who then conducted this war, if Europe preserved any thing, besides "bread and iron." Fortunately, no strength was great enough long to support such a will. The unavoidable exhaustion of the assailants, and not the power or the merit of the resistance made, saved society; and, finally, brought the work shops themselves, where the weapons for its destruction were forged, within its beneficent bonds again.

As the American revolution was a defensive revolution, it was of course finished, at the moment, when it had overcome the attack, by which it had been occasioned. The French revolution, true to the character of a most violent offensive revolution, could not but proceed so long as there remained objects for it to attack, and it retained strength for the assault.

3. The American revolution, at every stage of its duration, had a fixed and definite object, and moved within definite limits, and by a definite direction towards this object. The French revolution never had a definite object; and in a thousand various directions, continually crossing each other, ran through the unbounded space of a fantastic arbitrary will, and of a bottomless anarchy.

It lay in the very nature of a defensive revolution, like that of America, to proceed from definite objects, and to pursue definite ends. The peculiar situation, and the peculiar character of the North-Americans confirmed and secured this moderate and beneficent quality to the progress of their revolution.

In the course of it, two principal periods may be observed; *that,* from the first breaking out of the contests in 1765, until the declaration of independence in 1776, and *that,* from this declaration, until the peace with England.

In the first period, the single towns and provinces, and afterwards the members of the general congress, had for their declared and sole object the salvation of their constitution, and of their rights and liberties, as they then stood, from the oppressive usurpations of the British parliament. And I think I have clearly shown, in the former sections of this essay, that every step they took, during that critical period was calculated for preservation, not for conquest, for resistance against innovations, not for ardour after them; for defence, not for attack.

In the second period, indeed, a new object came in the place of that, which they had until then pursued: the British parliament had compelled the congress to proclaim the independence of the colonies; but, even this decisive measure by no means threw America into the precipice of lawlessness, into the horrible gulph of an unmeasurable interregnum, or into the slippery career of wild and chimerical theories. The machine of government was, and remained, completely organized: the revolution had taken from the king his negative upon legislative acts, almost the only essential prerogative, which as sovereign of the colonies he immediately exercised: but every province took care that this important function should be performed by another authority, distinct from the legislature, and Georgia and Pennsylvania, were the only ones, which entrusted the legislative powers to an undivided senate. The royal governors, who till then had stood at the head of the executive power, were replaced by others, chosen by the provinces themselves; and as the former governors, owing to their great distance from the mother country, had always held powers in the highest degree discretionary and independent, this alteration could not be much felt. The great and immediate exigences of social life, the local administration, the police, and course of judicial proceeding were continued as before. Nothing but the loose tie, which had connected America with England, was broken; none of the internal relations were discomposed; all the laws remained in force; the condition of persons and of property suffered no other revolution, than that which was necessarily brought with it! "The people," says that very well informed American historian Dr. Ramsay, "scarcely perceived that an alteration in their political constitution had taken place."

As the founders and conducters of the American revolution, from the beginning, knew exactly how far they were to go, and where they must stop; as the new existence of their country, the constitutions of the several provinces, and even the organization of the federal government, at least in its principles was definitely prescribed to them; as their purpose was in no sort to create, but only to preserve, not to erect a new building, but to free the old one from an external, burdensome, straitening scaffolding, and as it never occurred to them, in the rigorous sense of the word, to *reform,* even their own country, much less the whole world, they escaped the most dangerous of all the rocks, which in our times threaten the founders of any great revolution, the deadly passion for making political experiments with abstract theories, and untried systems. It is of the utmost importance, in judging the American revolution, never to lose sight of this point, and by so much the more important, as certain expressions in the early resolves of congress, the maxims of single writers, but especially the frequent appeals of the first leaders of the French revolution to the example of their predecessors in America, have encouraged, and spread abroad the opinion that these, in truth, opened the wide field of revolutionary speculations, and of systematic anarchy. True it is, that the declaration of independence published by the congress, in the name of the colonies, is proceeded by an introduction, in which the *natural* and *unalienable* rights of mankind are considered as the foundation of all government; that after this assertion, so indefinite, and so exposed to the greatest misconstructions, follow certain principles, no less indefinite, no less liable to be abused, from which an inference might be drawn of the unlimited right of the people to change their form of government, and what in the new revolutionary language, is called their *sovereignty.* It is likewise true, that most of the constitutions of the United States, are preceded by those idle *declaration of rights,* so dangerous in their application, from which so much misery has at a later period been derived upon France, and the whole civilized world. Much, however, as it were to be wished, that the legislators of America had disdained this empty pomp of words, that they had exclusively confined themselves within the clear and lawful motives of their resistance; a resistance at first constitutional, and afterwards necessary, and within the limits of their uncontrovertible rights, yet it cannot escape the observation of those, who attentively study the history of their revolution, that they allowed to these speculative ideas, no visible influence upon their practical measures and resolves. They erroneously believed them necessary to justify their first steps;[9] but here the dominion of empty speculation, was forever abandoned. Never, in the whole course of the American revolution, were the *rights of man,* appealed to, for the destruction of the *rights of a citizen;* never was the sovereignty of the people used as a pretext to undermine the respect, due to the laws, or the foundations of social security; no example was ever seen of an individual, or a whole class of individuals, or even the representatives of this, or that single state, who recurred to the declaration of rights, to escape from positive obligation, or to renounce obedience to the common sovereign; finally, never did it enter the head of any legislator, or statesman in America, to combat the lawfulness of foreign constitutions, and to set up the American revolution, as a new epocha in the general relations of civil society.

What was here and there occasionally said by single writers, must carefully be distinguished from the principles and way of thinking of those Americans, who were acknowledged and revered as examples and authorities, but especially from those, who took an active part in the new government. There certainly was in America, a Thomas Paine; and I will not deny but that his celebrated work had influence among certain classes of people, and so far contributed to promote the revolution.[10] But to judge of the spirit and principles of the American revolution by this work, would be as unjust, as to confound the efficaciously active heads in the English revolution, of 1688, with the authors of some popular lampoon against the house of Stewart; or the opposition of lord Chatham, with that of Mr. Wilkes. When Paine's work appeared, in the year 1776, the American revolution had long since assumed its whole form and consistence, and the principles, which will forever characterize it stood firm. In no public resolve, in no public debate, in no state paper of congress, is the most distant expression to be found, which discovers either a formal, or a tacit approbation of a systematical revolutionary policy. And what a contrast between the wild, extravagant, rhapsodical declamation of a Paine, and the mild, moderate, and considerate tone in the speeches and letters of a Washington.

The preciseness of objects, the uniformity of means, and the moderation of principles, which distinguished the American revolution through all its periods, gave likewise to the war, which was carried on for its establishment and completion, a precise and definite, and, therefore, a less formidable character. With this war indeed, the whole train of evils, which usually attend upon war in general, and especially upon civil war, were connected. But as it had only one object, and that was clearly known, and confined within narrow bounds, its possible results, its possible consequences, and its possible duration, could in every case be calculated. America had either to maintain or to give up her independence; in this single alternative was included the whole fate of the contest; and whatever consequence either event might operate upon a distant futurity, neither the victory of the British parliament, nor that (which very early became more probable) of the American congress, could discompose the balance of Europe, or threaten its peace. The governments of our hemisphere could, with all the tranquillity of a perfect neutrality, look forward to the issue of a remote contest, which, without further danger to their external and internal political relations, opened an advantageous prospect to the European commerce. The congress might even form an alliance with one of the greatest European monarchies; for as they only wished to maintain clear and definite rights, as they owed their existence to a revolution, which was forced upon the colonies by external violence, as they had at no time, and in no way, so much as called in question, much less attacked, the lawfulness of other constitutions, and as they had declared war, not against monarchical principles, but only against the oppressive measures of the British ministry, there was, *in itself,* nothing unnatural, nothing revolting, nothing plainly irreconcileable with the maxims of the law of nations, and the laws of self-preservation, in the alliance, which France contracted with them.[11]

The peace, which concluded the American war, secured that existence independent of England, to the new federal republic, for which she had alone and exclusively contended, and immediately after, this republic entered into those peaceable and beneficent relations with all other states, and even with England herself, which the common wants, and the common laws of nations have founded between civilized states. It is true; the American revolution had in latter times a decisive influence upon the great devastations under which Europe groans to this hour; but it would be the highest injustice not to acknowledge that this influence was only accidental. In the origin of that revolution there was nothing that could justify another, or even revolutions in general; no state, other than one, in which all the extraordinary circumstances concurring in the case of the colonies, should again concur, could consider the conduct observed by these, as legitimating a similar conduct, and adopt the principles upon which they proceeded. The precision and lawfulness of their object refused every application of these principles to revolutions, which could not exhibit an object equally definite, and a right equally clear, to the pursuit of that object. The wise moderation, which the leaders of the American revolution introduced into all their declarations, and into every step they took, their glorious abhorrence of every extravagance, even of those proceeding from the most pardonable enthusiasm, the constant distance at which they kept from every thing that may be called proselyting and propagandism—all these happy characteristics of their undertaking must in a legal point of view forever secure humanity against all evil consequences of this revolution; whose only traces remaining, should be in the growing prosperity of a great people, spread over extensive and fertile regions, and above all in the wholesome lesson it gave to the powers of the earth against every attack upon the rights and constitutions of states, from ambition, or a spirit of innovation. The harshest injustice alone could impute to the Americans, what the ill-understood and misused example of their revolution has produced of evil in latter times; it was the work of an hostile demon, who seems to have condemned the close of the eighteenth century, to see the buds of destruction shoot from the most beneficent events, and the most poisonous fruits from the blossoms of its fairest hopes.

The contrast between the French and American revolutions, when you compare them with each other in respect to their *objects* is no less striking than that which has resulted from the comparison of their *origin* and *progress.* As the utmost precision of object, and consequently of principles and of means, distinguished the American revolution through its whole duration, so the utmost want of precision in the object, and consequently a perpetual mutability in the choice of the means and in the modification of principles has been one of the most stubborn, one of the most essential, and certainly one of the most terrible characteristics of the French revolution. Its history was nothing but a long series of uninterrupted developments of this extraordinary phenomenon; single and unexampled in its whole compass as this circumstance may be, it will not much astonish the man, who shall reflect upon its origin, and its nature. For so soon as in a great undertaking, a step is taken wholly out of the boundaries of definite rights, and every thing is declared lawful, which imaginary necessity, or unbridled passion inspires, so soon is the immeasurable field of arbitrary will entered upon; and a revolution, which has no other principle than to attack the existing constitution, must necessarily proceed to the last extremities of imagination and of criminal guilt.

When, by the impotence and the faults of the government, and by the success which crowned the hardiness of its first antagonists, the old constitution of France was dissolved, all those who took an interest in favour of the revolution (and their number was infinitely great, precisely because no one knew exactly what he meant by a revolution) concurred, that an essential and wide spreading alteration must be effected in the whole political constitution of the state. But how far this alteration should extend, how far the old order of things should be preserved, and how the new one should be organized, with regard to all this, no two persons of the legions, who thought themselves called to public activity, were agreed. If we confine ourselves merely to the opinions of those, who in this interval of unbounded anarchy, publicly wrote, or spoke, we shall soon be convinced, that there were then in France, not three, or four, or ten, but thousands of political sects and parties. The impossibility of taking notice of so many individual variations, distinctions, sub-distinctions, and shades of every kind, compelled the contemporaries, and especially those immediately interested in the great spectacle, to class the infinite mass of opinions under certain known principal titles, and thus erase the names of *pure royalists,* of whole and half *monarchists,* of *feuillants,* of *jacobins,* of every degree, &c. Each of these parties, however, could have exhibited almost as many subordinate parties as it contained members.

In this number of political systems, some were built upon a limited monarchy, in the British sense of the word, others upon a thousand-fold new modification of a constitution, monarchical only in name; some wished from the beginning, to treat the revolution merely as a passage to the utter abolition of the monarchy. These pronounced sentence of death upon all the privileges of the higher orders; others wished to leave them the prerogatives of rank. One was for reforming the constitution of the churches; another for extirpating religion: one would have shewn mercy in this general overthrow, at least to the rights of property; another was for passing all positive right, under the sickle of equality. The constitution of 1791, was a desperate and impotent attempt to reconcile together, by a sort of general capitulation, all these contending theories, and the infinitely multiplied motives of interest, of ambition, and of vanity, connected with them; this attempt of course failed, for in the absolute and total indefiniteness, and I might add, the impossibility of ascertaining the last object of the revolution, every individual in France felt but too well, that he had as much right to maintain his private opinion, and to carry through his private purposes, as the members of a committee had to establish theirs; it was, besides, more than doubtful, whether, even the immediate authors of this impracticable constitution, seriously considered it as a last result.

Under the shelter of the inexpressible confusion, in which the storm of these first debates involved the whole country, arose, at first, more timid, but from the last months of the year 1791, growing constantly bolder, and more powerful, the only consistent party; that which had always been of opinion, that it was folly to prescribe to the French revolution, any bounds whatsoever. This party had, indeed, like all the rest, a multitude of subdivisions, and of systems peculiarly modified, and often at violent strife with each other; but all who declared themselves for it, concurred in the great and decisive point of view, that the revolution was to be considered, not as a local transaction, but as one of those, which give a new form to civil society, and which must draw all mankind within its vortex. For the ambition, or for the enthusiasm of this insatiable party, the theatre, which France offered to their thirst for destruction, was too small; they wished to tear up the world from its poles, and commence a new æra for the whole human race. That this was their purpose, from the very breaking out, and even before the breaking out of the French revolution, we need not learn from proselyting tales and imaginary cabals of the illuminati; the writings in which they have unfolded their principles in plain terms, have proved it beyond all contradiction.

To draw near the execution of so gigantic a plan, they had first of all to destroy the last trace of a monarchical form of government in France. It would be hard to maintain, that, after all what had happened since 1789, they had not nearly about the same right to found a republic, as the monarchists, so called, had to introduce a royal democracy. The only thing which seemed against them, in point of right, was the oath which, in common with all the rest, they had taken, to support the constitution of 1791. But, after so many bands had been torn, none but weak heads could flatter themselves, that an empty form would arrest the torrent in its course. At the very time, while, with the cry of "The constitution or death!" they hushed a few credulous souls to repose, they were working with restless activity the mine, which in one instant was to blow up the whole fabric.

But, precisely at this great and important moment, the absolute indefinitude of object, that inextinguishable character of the French revolution, discovered itself in a new and terrible light. The republic had been proclaimed; but this republic was a word without definite meaning, which every one believed he might explain, according to his inclinations, and according to the fantastic whims, which he called his principles. There were just as many republican systems contending for the mastery, as there had been monarchical parties. France was drenched in blood, to decide the great question, whether Brissot, or Marat, the federalists, or the unitists, the Girondists, or the mountaineers, the Dantonians, or the Hebertists, should prescribe a republican constitution. Force alone could determine the issue of this horrible contest; and the victory must necessarily remain to the most resolute. After having torn, for nearly a year, the inmost bowels of their country, without being able to agree upon the form of their republic, a daring faction, at length, fell upon the strange expedient of settling and organizing the revolutionary state itself, as a provisional government, and, under the name of a revolutionary government, brought into play what was called the system of terror; a monstrous and unexampled monument of human error and human frenzy, which in the eyes of posterity will almost degrade the history of our times to a fable. A less cruel faction overthrew and murdered the inventors of this gigantic wickedness; not long afterwards, another devised a new code of anarchy, which was called the constitution of the third year. It is well known, by what an uninterrupted series of revolutions, and counter-revolutions, this constitution was likewise conducted to the unavoidable catastrophe of its destruction.

Just at the period, when the republican party obtained possession of the supreme power, the bloody contest broke out between them and the greatest part of the European states. They had denounced the destruction of all governments; they had declared, that between their revolution and those who rejected it, no further intercourse could exist; they had solemnly absolved all subjects from obedience to their governments. The revolution prepared against Europe, and Europe against the revolution, a war, with which only the most dreadful religious wars, that ever scourged the world, can be compared. On the side of the coalesced powers, the proper object of this war could not be doubtful; and if, unfortunately, it often was, at least it ought never to have been so. But, on the side of France, it was always as indefinite as the object of the revolution itself. Some, as for instance, Robespiere, wished for the present, only to maintain the right of turning their own country into a butchery, with impunity, and to reduce by one half the number of its inhabitants; others had projected extensive plans of conquest, and wished to realize for the French republic, all the dreams, which the ambition of Lewis the XIVth, had formerly inspired; others yet had sworn never to lay down their arms, until they should have led the principles of the revolution in triumph over the whole civilized world, or *have planted, at least,* the tree of liberty, from Lisbon to the frozen sea, and to the Dardanelles.

This war has now, with short and local intervals of insecure and treacherous peace, already desolated the earth eight years long; it has, undoubtedly, for some time past, lost much of its extent, and very much of its original character, and has now nearly declined to a common war; yet when and how it will end, is still a problem, which puts all human penetration to the blush. The fate of the French revolution is, in a great measure, connected with the fate of this war; but its last result depends, besides, upon an infinity of other combinations. There has, perhaps, never yet been a man, who could even imagine, with any clearness, what this result will be. When one of the great masses of the physical world is suddenly started from its quiet centre of gravitation, and hurled with a prodigious impetus into the empty space of air, the point at which it will stop is much harder to conceive, than the continuance of its motion. And, in truth, after the serious question, Who could have a right to begin such a revolution? has remained unanswered, nothing is more difficult than to answer that, which is equally serious: to whom belongs the right of ending it?

4. The American revolution had a mass of resistance, comparatively much smaller to combat, and, therefore, could form and consolidate itself in a manner comparatively much easier, and more simple: the French revolution challenged almost every human feeling, and every human passion, to the most vehement resistance, and could therefore only force its way by violence and crimes.

The American colonies had already, before their revolution, attained a high degree of stability; and the supremacy of the British government in America, was the relation, not so much of an immediate sovereign, as of a superior protector. Hence, the American revolution had more the appearance of a foreign, than of a civil war.

A common feeling of the uprightness of their cause, and a common interest in its issue must necessarily have animated a great and overpowering majority of the inhabitants of North America. The royal governors, the persons more immediately connected with them, and the inconsiderable number of royal troops constituted the only permanent and great opposition party. If a certain number of independent citizens, from principle, or from inclination took the side of the ministry, they were however much too weak to become dangerous to the rest; and their impotence itself protected them against the hatred and intolerance of their countrymen.

There were in the interior of the colonies no sort of zeal or personal prerogatives, and no other distinction of ranks, than what proceeded from the exercise of public functions. Property owing to the novelty of civil society in the country, was much more equally distributed than can be the case in old countries, and the relations between the wealthy and the labouring classes were more simple and therefore more beneficent. As the revolution altered little in the internal organization of the colonies, as it only dissolved an external connection, which the Americans must always have considered rather as a burden, than an advantage; there was nobody, except the few, who took a share in the administration at the head of the country, who was immediately and essentially interested in the preservation of the ancient form. What this form contained of good and useful remained untouched; the revolution only removed that in which it had been oppressive.

How infinitely different was in this point of view the situation of France! If the French revolution had been content merely to destroy with violent hands the old Constitution, without making any attack upon the rights and possessions of private persons, it would, however, have been contrary to the interest of a numerous, and in every respect important class of people, who by the sudden dissolution of the old form of Government, having lost their offices, their incomes, their estimation and their whole civil existence, would of themselves have formed a powerful opposition. But, when in its further progress, it no longer spared any private right whatsoever, when it declared all political prerogatives to be usurpations, deprived the nobility not only of their real privileges, but likewise of their rank and title, robbed the clergy of their possessions, of their influence, and even of their external dignity; by arbitrary laws took from the holders of estates half their revenues; by incessant breaches of the rights of property, converted property itself into an uncertain, equivocal, narrowly straitened enjoyment, by recognizing publicly principles of the most dangerous tendency, held the sword hovering over the head of every one, who had any thing to lose, and aggravated the essential wretchedness, which it every where spread by the ridicule and contempt it shed over every thing that bore the name of possessions, or privileges—then truly it could not fail to accumulate against itself a mass of resistance, which was not to be subdued by ordinary means.

Should the friends of the French revolution declare this important circumstance to be merely accidental; should they impute solely to the good fortune of the American nation, that they found no domestic impediments in the way to their new constitution; and to the ill fortune of the French, that they had to struggle with so many obstinate antagonists; should they consider the former case only as enviable, and the latter only as deserving compassion, yet will the impartial observer, never forget how much merit there was involved in that good, and how much guilt in this ill fortune. The Americans were wise enough to circumscribe themselves within the bounds, which right, on one side, and the nature of things, on the other, had drawn round them. The French in their giddiness no longer acknowledged the prescriptions of the clearest right, nor the prescriptions of nature. They were so proud as to think they could bend impossibility itself, under the arm of their violence, and so daring that they thought the clearest right must yield to the maxims of their arbitrary will. The resistance of which they complained, was with perfect certainty to be forseen; it lay in the unalterable laws of human feelings, and human passions; it was just, it was necessary; it was impossible to believe that it would not take place. Those, who had called it forth by the most cruel injuries, did not fail to be sure to declare it punishable, and did punish thousands, whose only crime consisted in refusing to rejoice at their own ruin. But this double injustice prepared a new resistance, which could be overcome only by new acts of violence. Thus at last, in the barbarous law book of the revolution, suffering itself was made an unpardonable offence; the fear of a just reaction drove the authors of these oppressions to measures of still deepening cruelty against the victims of their first crimes; and the presumption of the natural and inevitable hatred, which these crimes must every where rouse against them, was a sufficient ground to them to treat as an offender deserving death, every man, who did not immediately and actively associate with them.

Although the American revolution never involved itself in this horrible labyrinth, where voluntary iniquities can only be covered by necessary misdeeds, and where every earlier crime became the only justification of a hundred later ones; yet did it not altogether escape the misfortune, which seems inseparable from all sudden and violent changes in the civil and political relations of society. The smallness of the resistance it met with, and the moderation of those who conducted it, preserved it from a multitude of cruel, desperate, and dishonorable measures, which have sullied other revolutions; but its warmest friends will not venture to maintain that it was wholly exempt from injustice and violence. The bitterness against the English government, often degenerated into a spirit of persecution, and involved those, who were suspected of a punishable indifference, or of secret connivance, in the sentence of proscription pronounced against tyranny. The hatred between the friends of independence, and the partizans of the ministry, the whigs and the tories, as they were distinguished by names taken from old English parties, broke out, especially amidst the dangers of the war, sometimes in violent scenes, which tore to pieces the internal harmony of neighbourhoods, and sometimes even of families. The reciprocal cruelties, which from time to time were practised upon prisoners, called to mind the peculiar character, which had never wholly abandoned a civil war. The rights of property likewise were often violated by single communities and single states, and, in some few instances, with the co-operation of the supreme authority. The history of the descendents, of the great and benevolent Penn, driven from the paradise, which he had created, and compelled, like other loyalists, to take refuge in the generosity and magnanimity of England, is no honorable page in the annals of North-America.

But what are all these single instances of injustice and oppression, compared with the universal flood of misery and ruin, which the French revolution let loose upon France, and all the neighbouring countries. If, even in America, private hatred, or local circumstances threatened property or personal security; if here and there even the public authorities became the instruments of injustice, of revenge, and of a persecuting spirit, yet did the poison never flow into every vein of the social body; never, as in France, was the contempt of all rights, and of the very simplest precepts of humanity, made the general maxim of legislation, and the unqualified prescription of systematic tyranny. If in America, the confusion of the moment, the impulse of necessity, or the eruption of the passions, sometimes inflicted misfortune upon innocence, never at least, never as in France, did reason herself, abused, desecrated reason, ascend the theatre of misery, solemnly to justify, by cold blooded, criminal appeals to principles and duties, these revolutionary confusions; and if in America, single families and districts, felt the heavy hand of the revolution and of war, never at least, as in France, were confiscations, banishments, imprisonments, and death, decreed in a mass.

When the American revolution was concluded, the country proceeded with rapid steps to a new, a happy, and a flourishing constitution. Not but that the revolution had left behind it many great and essential ravages: the ties of public order, had, in a long and bloody contest, been on all sides more or less relaxed; peaceful industry had suffered many a violent interruption; the relations of property, the culture of the soil, the internal and foreign trade, the public and private credit, had all considerably suffered by the revolutionary storms, by the insecurity of the external relations, and especially by the devastations of paper money.[12] Even the morals and the character of the people, had been essentially, and not in every respect advantageously affected by the revolution. Although we can draw no conclusion from this circumstance with regard to futurity, yet history must remark with attention, and preserve with care, the confession, which comes from the pen of a calm and impartial witness, the best of all the writers upon the American revolution hitherto (Ramsay): "That by this revolution, the *political, military,* and *literary* talents of the people of the United States, were improved, but their *moral* qualities were deteriorated."

A picture of the condition in which the revolution has left France, is by far too great, too complicated, and too formidable a subject to be touched upon even transiently here. The idea itself of a final result from such a revolution as this, must still be in some sort an indefinite, and perhaps a hazarded idea. Thus much, however, may be asserted with confidence, that between the results of the American and those of the French revolution, no sort of comparison can so much as be conceived.

I might have continued the above parallel through many other respects, and perhaps into single points of detail. I believe, however, that the four principal points of view in which I have treated it, with regard to the *lawfulness of the origin, character of the conduct, quality of the object,* and *compass of resistance,* sufficiently answer the purpose, I proposed to myself, and it appears, at least to me, evident enough, that every parallel between these two revolutions, will serve much more to display the *contrast,* than the *resemblance* between them.

Bibliographical Note

Adams, John Quincy. *Letters of Publicola* (in Volume I, *Writings of John Quincy Adams,* New York, 1913).

Bemis, Samuel Flagg. *John Quincy Adams and the Foundations of American Foreign Policy* (New York, 1950).

Boorstin, Daniel J. *The Genius of American Politics* (Chicago, 1953).

Brogan, D. W. *The Price of Revolution* (London, 1951).

Dakin, Douglas. *Turgot and the Ancien Régime in France* (London, 1939).

Dauer, Manning J. *The Adams Federalists* (Baltimore, 1953).

Hartz, Louis. *The Liberal Tradition hi America* (New York, 1955).

Hoffman, Ross J. S., and Levack, Paul. *Burke's Politics* (New York, 1949).

Kirk, Russell. *The Conservative Mind* (Chicago, 1953).

Mann, Golo. *Secretary of Europe: the Life of Friedrich Gentz* (New Haven, 1946).

Rossiter, Clinton. *Seedtime of the Republic* (New York, 1953).

Taine, Hippolyte. *The French Revolution.* Translated by John Duxand. (3 vols., New York, 1897).

Tocqueville, Alexis de. *Democracy in America.* Edited by Phillips Bradley. (2 vols., New York, 1948).

Tocqueville, Alexis de. *The Old Regime.* Translated by John Bonner. (New York, 1856).

Essay on the Generative Principle of Political Constitutions and Other Human Institutions

Joseph de Maistre

Translated by Elisha Greifer with the assistance of Laurence M. Porter

Introduction

by Elisha Greifer

I

The French Revolution and its principles inspired the first explicit and systematic counter-statements of modern conservatism. Conservatism's leading spokesman, Edmund Burke, attacked those Englishmen who sympathized with French revolutionary principles in his *Reflections on the Revolution in France,* a work that continues to be British conservatism's primary textbook. Less well known to American readers are Burke's admirers and counterparts among conservatives on the Continent. The Austrian Chancellor Metternich was such a political theorist. His secretary, Friedrich von Gentz, earlier a publicist in Berlin, was of the same conservative persuasion. Gentz argued that the American War of Independence should not be confused with the French *social* revolution, an argument that is still of great interest.

The best-known exponents of the anti-revolutionary critique writing in French were the Viscount de Bonald and the Count de Maistre. One has to say "writing in French" because Maistre was a Savoyard, although of French origin, and although French-speaking Savoy was later to be annexed permanently to France, it was then part of the independent kingdom of Sardinia. The Maistre family had for generations been among the patrician families of this enlightened state, which they served as almost hereditary magistrates. When the Savoy was invaded, Maistre left his possessions and his family and took refuge in Switzerland and Italy. He might have returned to recover his estates but chose, out of loyalty, to endure lonely and rather impecunious years as his sovereign's representative to the Russian court. Maistre's years in Russia, waiting out the defeat of Napoleon, have resulted in some thirteen volumes of collected works, letters and diplomatic correspondence, all evidence of a hardly imaginable zeal to confound the revolutionists and to restore the world they had shattered.

Maistre's first major work, *Considerations on France,* written in 1796, antedates his years in Russia. It was clearly inspired by Burke's similarly entitled *Reflections on the Revolution in France,* which had appeared in 1790. Maistre, like Gentz, had a genuine enthusiasm for Burke, and the references to Burke treat him like a master. "Have you read the admirable Burke?" he wrote to a friend the year after Burke's *Reflections* appeared. "I have been completely taken and don't know how to tell you how much he has reinforced my ideas."

Maistre is not a Burke, although he had much to learn from the father of conservatism. Burke was defending from attack a parliamentary England, a nation whose parliament was, to be sure, unreformed and undemocratic but a nation which was, nevertheless, the freest and most tolerant of the great powers. France had been a country of absolutism, whether enlightened or corrupt, of censorship, inequitable taxation, of privilege, of lesser tolerance. Burke did not exempt the old France from criticism so much as argue that would-be revolutionary reform was inevitably worse. But the issue was sharper for a Continental, particularly after the revolutionary excesses had ebbed and when *émigrés* might return to make their peace with the new régime. It was up to a thoroughgoing anti-revolutionary to defend the superiority of the old régime. In his refutation of the Revolution, then, the negative half, Maistre follows Burke; in defending the superiority of the old régime, the positive half, Maistre has new ground to break.

Let us first look at the negative half, the refutation of revolutionary theories. Burke had put succinctly the revolutionary view which was to be refuted. The people of England had a right, his opponents had argued,

1. "to choose our own governors"
2. "to cashier them for misconduct"
3. "to frame a government for ourselves.

This claim, Burke asserted, was both false and pernicious. The historically given Constitution of England, and not metaphysical abstraction, provided Englishmen with their rights.

"You will observe that from Magna Carta to the Declaration of Right it has been the uniform policy of our constitution to claim and assert our liberties, as an *entailed inheritance* derived to us from our forefathers, and to be transmitted to our posterity."

Such a structure is not the product of a transient agreement, and it cannot be fundamentally altered without both violation of fundamental law and reversion to anarchy, in which our inherited and *actual* rights as Englishmen disappear. Hence there is no "right of revolution." All past revolutions in England have *restored* the rightful constitutional heritage from usurpation.[1] The liberties of Englishmen, then, are inextricable from their constitution. But the constitution also provides (here's the rub) an hereditary crown and an hereditary peerage as part of a system of balanced government not to be subjected to fundamental democratic reforms.

This much Maistre follows closely, substituting French whipping posts for the English reformers. His favorite is Rousseau, the French philosopher of social contract, the logical result of which, says Maistre, is the French Revolution. No people, Maistre argues, has ever and can ever give itself a constitution or rights by fiat. A constitution is shrouded in the dim past of the youth of the nation. But this much is clear from history: nations are not founded on social contract. Scraps of paper with words written on them cannot create societies. When we look at the youth of nations, we do not find social contracts as the source of nations or of popular rights. We see sovereigns, aristocracies, rights granted by the *concession* of sovereigns. We see great legislators who do not innovate but only make explicit what was contained in pre-existing elements, and who *always act in the name of the Divinity.* Burke bases social order on prescription and history; Maistre further roots history in Providence. It is the Church which civilizes men to their social duties. And so, after Rousseau, the other great instigator of the Revolution is that most insidious enemy of the Church, Voltaire. *C'est la faute de Voltaire . . . c'est la faute de Rousseau.*

II

The *Essay on the Generative Principle of Political Constitutions* contains most of Maistre's views in brief. It was written in 1808–1809, after his *Considerations on France* and before his *On the Pope* and *Les Soirées de Saint Pétersbourg,* his three longer major works. Yet it conveniently contains elements of all, his critique of the Revolution, his views on Providence, his ultramontane position within the Church. It also gives us a sampling of his charm, his wit, and the taste for paradox that makes him the most readable defender of the older Europe, as sparkling (all critics have observed) as Bonald is dull. The dominant liberal view of history has consequently catalogued Maistre as a bright apologist for a "horrible system" that should be forgotten.

This is only to treat Maistre as a partisan of a certain political faction and not as a political philosopher. He is a partisan, to be sure, and as such, an early proponent of the post-revolutionary alignment of monarchical authority, aristocracy, and the Church. Indeed, on one score, his ultramontane position, he was prophetic. The moral restraint of the modern state by Rome is today much more appealing to liberalism, now that the totalitarian state has appeared. His specific ultramontane views on the Papacy might be said to have been later vindicated, too. In Maistre's day, the Pope could not accept the dedication of his book *On the Pope*, but in 1870, a Vatican Council did enunciate the dogma of papal infallibility, which Maistre had urged. As a partisan of Continental traditionalism, then, Maistre can make comprehensible a constellation of forces, unknown to American history and politics, which is yet a reality in Europe.

A political philosopher ought not to be viewed primarily, and certainly not solely, as a partisan. Plato was a partisan during his day and so was Locke. Yet Plato's philosophy does not ultimately stand or fall on his aristocratic leanings, nor is Locke's analysis of social contract refuted by pointing to his Whig partisanship. Properly, Maistre ought to be treated as a latter-day figure in the grand tradition of political philosophy and judged by the truth of what he says, not by what he did. And we would do well to take him seriously, for he claims to refute the social-contract theory, which we usually consider the basis of our own Declaration of Independence and our written Constitution.

Contract, Maistre says, cannot make authority legitimate. Consequently, it cannot provide the social organism which is necessary if anarchy is to be avoided and if liberties are to have a continuing basis for existence. Only Providence can establish legitimacy. It achieves this by producing nations, each ready made with its fundamental institutions, including, above all, its sovereign. The sovereign may be a republican assembly, as in Geneva, or a balance of monarchy, aristocracy, and democracy, as in the English mixed constitution. (The United States was too young for Maistre to treat at length.) The France produced by Providence, insists Maistre, is a monarchy, and to seek to change what Providence has wrought will not merely lead to disaster; it is impious.

The theological derivation of political authority, it should be observed, is neither original with Maistre (although his analysis contains new features), nor is it specifically Catholic. Catholic and Protestant clergymen alike had preached sermons on that familiar biblical passage which begins:

"Let every soul be subject unto the higher powers. For there is no power but of God: the powers that be are ordained of God."[2]

Calvin wrote a commentary on this passage, and the duties of Lutheran choirmaster Bach led him to write a cantata entitled *Authority Is the Gift of God.* Consequently, the theological treatment of politics is both of ancient lineage and more than sectarian interest in the European tradition, so that Maistre needs no special justification for continuing in this tradition. What Maistre has to say, one concludes, is interesting on two accounts: his general critique of authority[3] and his ultimately theological treatment of sovereignty.

III

Maistre has made a telling argument, it seems to me, against those who would believe that social consent can make any act of a society just. The will of the people is not necessarily the will of God. He further throws doubt on whether a society can even exist without a belief in something beyond the will of its members, *myth,* to integrate it. This critique deserves to be taken seriously, and if liberalism is to survive his onslaught, it must provide acceptable answers.

I would suggest that non-revolutionary liberalism can absorb some of the criticism by *accepting* it and that the American *conservative* brand of liberalism has always done so. Let us examine the argument that social agreement does not make the agreement right or just. The point is that this is not quite what was said by Locke, the social contract theorist who found his way into the Declaration of Independence via the pen of Jefferson. (I have tried to footnote this in the appropriate place in Maistre's text.) Might, it is true, does not make right. But while this is true, it is equally true that *what is,* is not necessarily right. The fact of historical precedent does not create in and of itself final proof of the justice of what is, either. On the score of justice, tradition deserves only respect, not servile obeisance. There is, of course, a religious tradition of obedience to proper authority, but there is also a tradition of religious resistance to tyranny and religious neutrality on purely secular questions, including the form of government.

The crucial argument thus becomes the question of the cohesiveness of society. Maistre is saying that to reform is to destroy. But is it not equally true that to resist reform is to invite decay and destruction? No one welcomes the circumstances in which great change is necessary. But does not *intransigeance* invite it? For historians, Alfred Cobban has said, the problem of the French Revolution is "not why the monarchy fell but why it was not revived." Natural preference for old ways and the excesses of reformers should have ended in voluntary restoration sooner and not in Napoleon. Much of the answer lies in the *intransigeance* of the *émigrés.*

Maistre is the philosopher of *intransigeance,* and it is ironic that his arguments lived to embarrass him during the Restoration, when Louis XVIII, a Bourbon, who *did* wish to forget some things and who *had* learned something from his exile, wanted compromise. Maistre's essay in 1809, was to be published anonymously in 1814. However, his instructions to Bonald were somehow misunderstood, and Bonald allowed it to appear under Maistre's name just after Louis had published the constitutional charter by which he granted a parliamentary monarchy like the British. Is it not ironic that Maistre's attack on innovation and the defense of the *ancien régime* thus seemed to be meant as an attack on Louis' spirit of compromise? It caused Maistre considerable chagrin.[4]

There is still the question of the need for a system of belief which integrates society. Cannot social contract, or democracy today, be part of such a myth? Maistre, by his *intransigeance,* helped cause the old Europe to reject the new aspirations of men rather than to come to terms with it. If the conscience of Europe is still partially split between those who would uphold authority and those who would further freedom, is it not partly the fault of thinkers like Maistre?

Perhaps a final word about the United States. Maistre would not have the United States accepted as a model for Europe, if only, as we have already mentioned, because we should wait for the "babe in arms" to grow up. He was, however, willing to allow that the American colonial growth, the natural constitution, was not monarchical. The ruling king was a distant external power. Almost all of the first colonists were republicans who left England during the time of religious and political troubles. Consequently, the colonists built on these elements and on the English mixed constitution. They did not try to wipe the slate clean, as did the French revolutionaries. There is something to ponder here before we urge our institutions on others.

At the same time, however, we *do* subscribe to the abstractions Maistre deplores. The Rights of Man indeed have a *double* existence for us—as abstract principles (as in the Declaration of Independence) and as common-law tradition (as embodied in the Bill of Rights of our Constitution). Among nations, it is perhaps our unique good fortune—not our wisdom—that both our tradition and our abstractions enjoin us to liberty. We are all liberals; we are all conservatives. God is good, the European maxim now has it, to fools, children, and Americans.

IV

Practically nothing of Maistre's has ever been translated into English, nothing at all in the last hundred years. Consequently, my collaborator in the translation, Mr. Laurence M. Porter, and I have been hard pressed to produce an edition that would be useful to both the general reader and the student. We have modernized punctuation and have tried to use current idiomatic expressions where they are not anachronistic. In addition, I have tried to point up the traditional terms of political thought that Maistre employs and have footnoted briefly the variety of references which Maistre made to events, persons, and literary works which are more obscure now. Maistre makes unidentified and sometimes playful references, not merely to classical authors, but also to his contemporaries. (A few of the worst obscurities have been identified by friends and colleagues,) I have left out only a few Greek citations upon which Maistre puns untranslatably. All of Maistre's citations have been checked for accuracy, since he wrote before the days of painstaking documentation, and I have tried to put the citations in accurate and usable form. Where there are familiar translations, such as the King James Version of the Bible, I have used them. Maistre's footnotes are indicated by arabic numbers, my own by a totally different system. Brackets enclose our occasional insertions into the text. As a stylist, Maistre stands in the front rank of French letters. In preparing this edition for those interested in what he had to say, Mr. Porter and I hope that we have left intact the spirit in which Maistre said it.

Thanks are due Vassar College for assistance in preparing the manuscript. Mrs. Ruth Ashman and Mrs. Mildred Tubby have done an admirable job of deciphering and then typing it.

Essay on the Generative Principle of Political Constitutions and Other Human Institutions

Preface

Politics is perhaps the thorniest of the sciences, due to the ever recurring difficulty in discerning what in it is stable and what changeable. It presents a very strange phenomenon, well calculated to make every prudent man called to the administration of states tremble. Whatever common sense first perceives in this science as an evident truth is almost always found, once tested by experience, not only false but disastrous.

Let us begin at the foundation. If we had never heard governments spoken of and men were called upon to deliberate, for example, on hereditary or elective monarchy, we should justly regard one who should decide for the former as a madman. The arguments against it appear so naturally to reason that it is useless to repeat them. History, however, which is experimental politics, demonstrates that an hereditary monarchy is the government most stable, appropriate, and natural to man, while an elective monarchy, on the contrary, is the worst form of government known.

With respect to population, commerce, prohibitory legislation, and a thousand other important subjects, the most plausible theory is almost always found contradicted and brought to nothing by experience. Let us cite a few examples.

What method must be used to make a state strong? "It is necessary first to encourage population by every possible means." On the contrary, every law tending directly to favor population without regard to other considerations is bad. It is even necessary to endeavor to establish in the state a certain moral force which tends to diminish the number of marriages and to make them less hasty. A gain of births over deaths as shown by tables usually shows only the number of the destitute, etc., etc. French economists outlined the demonstration of these truths, and the excellent work of Malthus has completed it.

How shall food shortages and famine be prevented? "Nothing is more simple. It is necessary to prohibit the export of grains." On the contrary, a premium must be granted those who export them. The authoritative example of England has forced us to swallow this paradox.

How shall the rate of exchange be maintained in favor of a certain country? "It is unquestionably necessary to curtail the export of specie, and, consequently, to ensure by strong legal prohibitions that the state buy no more than it sells." On the contrary, these means have never been employed without worsening the rate of exchange, or what amounts to the same thing, without increasing the indebtedness of a nation. Nor can the opposite course be taken without improving the rate of exchange, that is, without making it evident that the nation has achieved a favorable balance of payments with its neighbors etc., etc.

But the phenomenon we have observed appears most often in the most fundamental and substantial part of politics: the constitution of empires. It is said that the German philosophers have invented the word metapolitics to be to politics what metaphysics is to physics. This new term seems very aptly invented to express the metaphysics of politics, for there is such a thing, and this science deserves profound attention.

An anonymous writer who was much occupied with such speculations and who has strived to fathom the hidden foundations of the social edifice believed himself in the right when, nearly twenty years ago, he advanced the following propositions as so many incontestable axioms diametrically opposed to the theories of that time.[5]

1. No constitution arises from deliberation. The rights of the people are never written, except as simple restatements of previous, unwritten rights.
2. [In the formation of constitutions] human action is so far circumscribed that the men who act become only circumstances. [It is even very common that in pursuing a certain end they attain another.][6]
3. The rights of the PEOPLE, properly so called, proceed almost always from the concessions of sovereigns and thus may be definitely fixed in history, but no one can ascertain the date or the authors of the rights of the monarch and the aristocracy.
4. These concessions themselves have always been preceded by a state of things which rendered them necessary and for which the sovereign was not responsible.
5. Although written laws [*lois*] are merely the declarations of pre-existing laws [*droits*], it is far from true that all these laws can be written.
6. The more of it one puts into writing, the weaker the institution becomes.
7. No nation can give itself liberty if it is not already free,[7] for human influence extends only as far as existing rights have developed.
8. Legislators, strictly defined, are extraordinary men, belonging perhaps only to the world of antiquity and to the youth of nations.

9. Even these legislators, notwithstanding their marvelous power, have only combined parts of what already existed.
10. In a sense, liberty is the gift of kings, for nearly all free nations were established by kings.[8]
11. There never existed a free nation which did not have seeds of liberty as old as itself in its natural constitution. Nor has any nation ever successfully attempted to develop, by its fundamental written laws, rights other than those which existed in its natural constitution.
12. No assembly of men whatsoever can form a nation. Indeed, such an enterprise should be ranked among the most memorable follies.[9]

Since 1796, the date of the first edition of the work we quote,[10] it does not appear that anything has happened in the world which might have induced the author to abandon his theory. On the contrary, we believe it may be worthwhile to develop fully the theory at this time and to trace out all its implications. One of the most important, no doubt, is announced in Chapter X of the same work in these words: Man cannot create a sovereign. "At most, he may be the instrument in dethroning the sovereign and delivering his kingdom to another ruler already royal. . . . *Moreover, there has never been a royal family which could be assigned a plebeian origin. If such a phenomenon appeared, it would mark the beginning of a new world era.*"[11]

We may recall that divine judgment has only recently sanctioned this proposition in sufficiently solemn fashion. But who knows whether the ignorant levity of our age will not say in all seriousness: *If he had wanted it, he would still have his place!*[12] just as some persist in repeating, after two centuries, *If Richard Cromwell had possessed his father's genius, he would have settled the Protectorate in his family,* which is precisely the same as saying that if this family had not ceased to reign, it would reign still.

It is written, "By me princes rule."[13] This is not a church phrase, a metaphor of the preacher. It is a literal truth, simple and palpable. It is a law of the political world. God literally makes kings. He prepares royal races, maturing them under a cloud which conceals their origin. At length they appear, crowned with glory and honor; they take their places; and this is the most certain sign of their legitimacy.

Royal families arise of themselves, as it were, unattended either by violence or marked deliberation but with a certain magnificent tranquillity which is difficult to express. "Legitimate usurpation" would seem the correct phrase (if not too bold) to characterize such origins, which time hastens to consecrate.

Let no one allow the most splendid human appearances to dazzle him.[14] Who has ever concentrated in himself more of them than the extraordinary personage whose fall still resounds throughout Europe? Has there ever been a sovereignty outwardly so well fortified? A greater consolidation of capabilities? A man more powerful, more active, more formidable? For a long time we saw him trample underfoot twenty nations silenced and frozen with terror. Finally, his power had grown firm enough to make hope itself despair. Yet he has fallen, and so low, that Pity, contemplating him, recoils for fear of being touched. Furthermore, we may remark that for a somewhat different reason it has become equally difficult to speak of this man and of the august rival who has rid the world of him. One is beneath insult and the other beyond praise.[15] But I digress.

In a work known only to a few persons at St. Petersburg, the author wrote in 1810: "If when two factions engage in revolutionary conflict we see precious victims[16] fall on one side, we may be sure that it will win at last, despite all appearances to the contrary."

The truth of this assertion also has just been borne out in the most remarkable and startling manner. The moral order has its laws, as does the physical, and their investigation is quite worthy of occupying a true philosopher's meditations. After an entire age of criminal trifling, it is high time to recall what we arc and to trace all knowledge back to its source. This consideration has induced the author to release his little work from the timid portfolio which held it these last five years. He allows the original date to stand and presents it word for word as written at that time. Benevolent intent has called forth this publication, which perhaps is so much the worse for the author, since that sentiment is sometimes quite as blind as love.[17] Be this as it may, he enjoys a well-known privilege. He may doubtless be mistaken at times on unimportant points; he may exaggerate, or speak too confidently; the properties of taste or grammar may be offended, and if so, all the better for the malicious, if such there be. But always the well-founded hope remains to him of displeasing no one, since he loves all the world. Moreover, he is certain of interesting a large and estimable class of men without the possibility of injuring a single one, a confidence altogether reassuring.

Essay on the Generative Principle of Political Constitutions and Other Human Institutions

I

One of the greatest errors of a century which professed them all was to believe that a political constitution could be created and written *a priori,* whereas reason and experience unite in proving that a constitution is a divine work and that precisely the most fundamental and essentially constitutional of a nation's laws could not possibly be written.

II

Certain people have thought to perpetrate an excellent witticism at the expense of Frenchmen by asking, "*In what book was Salic law written?*" But Jérôme Bignon[18] answered quite appropriately, very likely without knowing how right he was, "*that it is written in the hearts of Frenchmen.*" Indeed, let us suppose that such an important law existed only because it was written. Surely whatsoever authority had written it would have the right to annul it, and the law would not have that quality of divine immutability which characterizes truly constitutional laws. The essence of a fundamental law is that no one has the right to abolish it. For how could it stand above *all men,* if *some men* had made it? Popular agreement is not possible. And even if it were, an agreement is still not a *law* at all and obligates no one unless a higher power guarantees its enforcement. Locke sought the nature of law in the expression of aggregate wills [*volontés réunies*]. He must have been favored by chance thus to hit upon the very quality which excludes all idea of *law.* Indeed, aggregate wills form ordinances and not law.[19] The latter inevitably presupposes a higher will which enforces obedience.[20] "In Hobbes' system" (the same which has attracted so much attention in our day through Locke's writings), "the strength of civil law rests only on convention. But what good are these if no natural law exists to decree their enforcement? Promises, contracts, and oaths are mere words. It is as easy to break this trifling bond as to make it. Without the doctrine of a Divine Legislator, all moral obligation becomes illusory. Power on one side, weakness on the other: this constitutes all the bonds of human societies."[21]

That is what a wise, profound theologian has said of moral obligation. It is equally true of political and civil obligations. Law is only truly sanctioned, and properly *law,* when assumed to emanate from a higher will, so that its essential quality is to be *not the will of all* [*la volonté de tons*]. Otherwise, laws would be *mere ordinances.* As the author just quoted states, "those who were free to make these conventions have not deprived themselves of the power of revocation, and their descendants, with no share in making these regulations, are bound even less to observe them."[22] This is the reason that primitive common sense, which, fortunately, is anterior to sophism, has always sought the sanction of laws in a superhuman power, whether recognizing that sovereignty comes from God or in worshiping certain unwritten laws as given by Him.

III

The codifiers of Roman law unpretentiously inserted a remarkable fragment of Greek jurisprudence in the first chapter of their collection. *Among the laws which govern us,* it says, *some are written and others are not.* Nothing could be more simple and yet more profound.

Do we know any Turkish law which explicitly allows the Sultan to condemn a man to death immediately without the intervening decision of a tribunal? Do we know of any *written* law, even a religious one, which forbids this to the sovereigns of Christian Europe?[23] However, the Turk is no more surprised to see his master summarily order a man's execution than to see him go to the mosque. Together with all of Asia, in fact with all antiquity, he believes that the direct power of life and death is legitimate and inherent in royalty. Our princes, however, would shudder at the very idea of condemning a man to death, for in our eyes this condemnation would constitute an atrocious murder. Yet I doubt whether it be possible to forbid our kings this power by a fundamental written law without producing greater evils than those one would have wished to forestall.

IV

Question Roman history about the exact powers of the Senate. It will reveal nothing, at least of the precise limits of this power. In general, it is clear that the people and the Senate mutually balanced each other in an endless struggle. We know that patriotism or exhaustion, weakness or violence ended these perilous battles, but we know no more.[24] Observing these great moments in history, it is sometimes tempting to believe that things would have gone much more smoothly had there been precise laws defining these powers. But this would be a great mistake. Such laws, always compromised by unforeseen events and necessary exceptions, either would not have lasted six months or would have caused the republic to collapse.

V

The English Constitution is an example closer to us, hence more striking. Examine it carefully; you will see that *it only moves* [i.e., works] *while standing still* (if this play on words may be allowed). It maintains itself through exceptions. The writ of *habeas corpus,* for example, has been suspended so often and for such extended periods that one might have suspected the exception had become the rule. Suppose for a moment that the authors of this famous act had undertaken to determine the circumstances in which it could be suspended. They would have obliterated it by so doing.

VI

At the sitting of the House of Commons on June 26, 1807, a Lord cited the authority of a great statesman to prove that the King had no right to dissolve Parliament during its session, but this opinion was contradicted. Where is the law? Try to establish it and to determine entirely *in writing* the instances where the King has this right—you would cause a revolution. One member said that the King has this right in a critical situation. But what is a *critical* situation? Again, try to decide this by writing.

VII

Here is an even stranger example. Everyone remembers the great question so fervently debated in England in 1806. It was whether the holding of a judicial appointment together with membership in the Privy Council accorded with the principles of the English Constitution. At the sitting of that same House of Commons on March 3, a member remarked: *This country is governed by a body not known by the Legislature. It is only,* he added, *connived at.*[25]

In this wise and justly famous England, then, there is a body which governs, and in truth does everything, but *which the Constitution does not recognize.* Delolme[26] has overlooked this feature, which I could corroborate with several others.

After this, can anyone talk to us about written constitutions and constitutional laws made *a priori?* It is inconceivable that a sane person could imagine the possibility of such a chimera. If anyone should attempt to make a law in England giving a constitutional existence to the Privy Council, and subsequently to regulate and limit rigorously its privileges and functions, with the precautions necessary to limit its influence and to prevent its misuse, he would overturn the State.

The true *English Constitution* is that admirable, unique, and infallible public spirit which transcends all praise. It guides everything, conserves everything, and restores everything. What is written is nothing.[27]

VIII

Towards the end of the last century, a great outcry was made against a minister[28] who entertained the project of introducing that same English Constitution (or what was called by that name) into a realm in turmoil which clamored wildly for one of any sort. He was wrong, if you will, at least as much as one who acts in good faith can be wrong. One may fairly assume this, and I believe it with all my heart. But who at that time had the right to condemn him? *Vel duo vel nemo.*[29] He did not say that he wanted to destroy anything of his own accord. He only wished, he claimed, to substitute one thing which seemed reasonable to him for another which was no longer wanted and which for that very reason no longer existed. Besides, if the principle is granted (and indeed it was) *that man can create a constitution,* this minister (who was certainly human) had as much right as anyone, and more, to make his own. Were these doctrines doubted? Was it not a common belief everywhere that a constitution was the work of the intellect, like an ode or a tragedy? Had not Thomas Paine declared, with a profundity that charmed the universities, that a constitution does not exist as long as one cannot put it in his pocket?[30] The unsuspecting, overweening self-confidence of the eighteenth century balked at nothing, and I do not believe that it produced a single stripling of any talent who did not make three things when he left school: an educational system, a constitution, and a world. Therefore, if a mature man at the peak of his ability, deeply learned in the science of economics and in the current philosophy, had attempted only the second of these things, I should have considered him exceedingly moderate. But I confess he appears to me a true prodigy of wisdom and modesty when I see him, substituting (at least, in his opinion) experience for foolish theories, respectfully ask a constitution of England instead of making one himself. You say, *even this was impossible.* But he did not, and how could he have known it? There was no one to tell him so.

IX

The more one examines the role of human agency in forming political constitutions, the more one becomes convinced that it enters only in an infinitely subordinate manner, or as a simple instrument, and I do not believe that the slightest doubt remains as to the unquestionable truth of the following propositions:

1. The fundamental principles of political constitutions exist prior to all written law.
2. Constitutional law [*loi*] is and can only be the development or sanction of a pre-existing and unwritten law [*droit*].
3. What is most essential, most inherently constitutional and truly fundamental law is never written, and could not be, without endangering the State.
4. The weakness and fragility of a constitution are actually in direct proportion to the number of written constitutional articles.[31]

X

On this point, we are often deceived by a sophism so natural that it escapes our notice entirely. Because man acts, he thinks he acts alone. Because he is aware of his freedom, he forgets his dependence. He is more reasonable about the physical world, for although he can, for example, plant an acorn, water it, etc., he is convinced that he does not make oaks, since he has witnessed them growing and perfecting themselves without the aid of human power. Besides, he has not made the acorn. But in the social order, where he is always present and active, he comes to believe that he is the sole author of all that is done through his agency. In a sense, it is as if the trowel thought itself an architect. Doubtless, man is a free, intelligent, and noble creature; *nevertheless, he is an instrument of God.* As Plutarch says in this fine passage "we must not wonder if the greatest and most beautiful things in the world are done by God's will and providence, seeing that in all the principal parts of the world there is a soul. For the body is the organ and tool of the soul and the soul is the instrument of God. And as the body makes many movements by itself, but the more noble are derived from the soul, even so is it with the soul. Some of its operations are self-directed, while in others it is led, disciplined and guided by God, as it pleases Him, being itself the most beautiful and ingenious instrument possible. For it would be strange that the wind, the water, the clouds, and the rains should be instruments of God, with which He nourishes and supports many creatures and also destroys many others, and that He should never make use of living beings to perform His works. For it is far more reasonable that they, depending entirely on God's power, should obey His direction, and accomplish all His will, than that the bow should obey the Scythians, the lyre and flute the Greeks."[32]

No one could write better, and I do not believe that these sublime reflections could be more appropriately applied than to the formation of political constitutions where one may say with equal truth that man does everything, yet does nothing.

XI

If anything be familiar, it is Cicero's analogy on the subject of the Epicurean system, which claimed that the world had been made from atoms falling randomly in space. I would rather believe, said the great orator, that letters thrown into the air would fall so as to form a poem. Thousands have repeated this thought and praised it. Yet as far as I know, no one has thought to give it the completeness which it lacks. Imagine that handfuls of printed characters thrown from the top of a tower should on landing make Racine's *Athalia*. What could one infer? *That a mind had directed their fall and arrangement.* Common sense will never find another answer.

XII

Let us now examine any particular political constitution, England's for example. It certainly was not made *a priori*. Her statesmen never assembled to say, *Let us create three powers, balancing them in such a manner, etc.* No one of them ever thought of such a thing. The constitution is the work of circumstances whose number is infinite. Roman laws, ecclesiastical laws, feudal laws, Saxon, Norman, and Danish customs; the privileges, prejudices, and pretentions of every segment of society; wars, rebellions, revolutions, the Conquest, the Crusades, every virtue, every vice, all sorts of knowledge, and all errors and passions; in sum, all these factors acting together and forming by their admixture and interdependent effects countless millions of combinations have at last produced, after several centuries, the most complex unity and the most propitious equilibrium of political powers that the world has ever seen.[33]

XIII

Now since these agencies, thus tossed into the air, so to speak, have arranged themselves so neatly, although no man among the vast multitude which acted in this vast world ever knew what he was doing in relation to the whole or foresaw the outcome, it follows that these agencies were guided in their course by an infallible power. Perhaps the greatest misconception in a century of follies was that fundamental laws could be written *a priori*, while they are obviously the work of n higher power, and committing them to writing long after is the surest way of proving that they are no longer valid.

XIV

It is quite remarkable that God, having condescended to speak to man, has Himself shown these truths in the two revelations His goodness has given us. There was a clever man who marked a sort of era in our century through the desperate conflict his works exhibit between the worst prejudices of the period, of sect, of habit, etc., and the purest intentions, the most sincere sentiment and the most valuable knowledge. He decided that *instruction coming directly from God, or given only according to His commands, should primarily certify to man His existence.*[34] Precisely the opposite is true. For the prime characteristic of this teaching is not to reveal God's existence or attributes but to suppose the whole already known without our understanding why or how. Therefore it does not state *there is* or *you shall believe in only one God, omnipotent and everlasting,* etc. It begins in purely narrative form: *In the beginning, God created,* etc., which assumes that the dogma was known before the writing.

XV

Let us pass on to Christianity, the greatest of all imaginable institutions, since wholly divine and made for all men and all ages. It, too, conforms to the general law. Its Author certainly was able to write Himself or to cause His doctrines to be written. Yet He did neither, at least not in a legislative form. The New Testament, posterior to the death of the Lawgiver, and even to the founding of His religion, contains narrative, admonitions, moral precepts, exhortations, commands, threats, etc., but nowhere a collection of dogma expressed imperatively. The Evangelists, describing the Last Supper, when God loved us *even unto the end,* had a fine opportunity to command our belief in writing, but they carefully refrain from declaring or ordaining anything. Indeed, we read, *Go, teach!* in their admirable history, but never *teach this or that.* If doctrine is found in the writings of a sacred historian, he is simply expressing it as something already familiar.[35] The symbols, which appeared later, are professions of faith, that it may be recognized, or for contradicting the errors of the moment. There, one reads *we believe,* never *you shall believe.* We recite them in private; we chant them in the temple with stringed instruments and organs[36] as true prayers because they are formulas of submission, confidence, and faith directed to God, and not ordinances addressed to man. I should like to see the *Concession of Augsburg* or the *Thirty-Nine Articles* set to music. They would certainly be amusing.[37]

The first symbols are far from containing the announcement of *all* our doctrines. Indeed, the early Christians would have considered the announcement of them *all* as a great sin. The same applies to the Holy Scriptures. There never was a more shallow idea than to seek the entirety of Christian dogma in them. Not a line in these writings declares or even hints at the plan of making from them a code or dogmatic statement of all the articles of faith.

XVI

Moreover, if a people possesses one of these *codes of belief,* we may be sure of three things:

1. Their religion is false.
2. They have written their religious code in a fit of delirium.
3. This people will soon scoff at the code, which can have neither strength nor durability. Such, for example, are the famous articles, "which are signed by more than read, and read by more than believe them.[38] Not only is this catalogue of dogma accounted next to nothing in the country which gave it birth, but it is also obvious, even to a foreigner, that the illustrious proprietors of this sheet of paper are greatly hampered by it. They would like to make it disappear, since it irritates the national good sense, enlightened by the passage of time, and since it recalls an unfortunate beginning. But the *constitution is written.*

XVII

Surely these same Englishmen would never have sought Magna Charta had not the nation's privileges been violated or unless these privileges had also existed before the Charter. In this respect, what is true of the State is true of the Church as well: if Christianity had never been attacked, it would never have determined dogma in writing. But whenever dogma has been fixed in writing, it is always because it existed previously in its natural state, *speech*.

The real instigators of the Council of Trent were the two arch-innovators[39] of the sixteenth century.[40] Their followers, having become more moderate, have since suggested that we expunge this basic law because it contains certain words which are disagreeable to them. And they have tried to tempt us by setting this price on a reunion which would make us accomplices without reconciling us. But this request has no justification in religion or philosophy. They themselves formerly introduced to religious language those words which now harass them. Let us hope that they may today learn to pronounce them. The Faith would be a thousand times more angelic if a sophistical opposition had not forced her to write. She weeps over these decisions which rebellion extorted from her and which always were evils, since they all suppose disbelief or attack and could only arise in the midst of the most dangerous disturbances. A state of war raised these venerable ramparts around the truth. No doubt they protect her, but they conceal her, too. They have made her unassailable, but by that very act, less accessible. Ah! That is not her desire. She wants only to hold all humanity in her embrace.

XVIII

I have spoken of Christianity as a system of belief. Now I shall consider it from the point of view of its governance [*souveraineté*] in its most extensive manifestation.[41] There it is monarchical as everyone knows, and this is as it should be. By the very nature of things, monarchy becomes more necessary in proportion as an association increases in size. It is not forgotten that an infamous person could nevertheless meet with approval in our time when he affirmed that *France was geographically monarchical.*[42] Indeed, one could scarcely express this incontrovertible truth better. But as the size of the French nation precludes even the thought of every other form of government, how much more must this sovereignty be exclusively monarchical which by the essential nature of its constitution will always have subjects on every part of the globe [that is, the Papacy]? Here, experience supports theory. This being established, who would not believe that such a monarchy would be more strictly defined and limited than any as to the prerogative of its leader? Yet the exact opposite is true. Read the countless volumes brought forth by "foreign war," and even by a species of "civil war," which has its advantages as well as its inconveniences—you will invariably see cited facts alone [and not an appeal to authority]. It is also remarkable, surely, that the Supreme Tribunal should steadily permit dispute over what appears to everyone to be the most fundamental question of the constitution without ever having wished to settle it by a formal law.[43] This is, unless I am greatly mistaken, because of the very basic importance of the question.[44] Some misguided fellows, bold only because of weakness, took it upon themselves to decide it in 1682 in spite of a great man,[45] and it was one of the most solemn imprudences ever perpetrated. Its monument, which endures,[46] is doubtless wholly to be condemned, but especially so for one feature hitherto unnoticed, although more vulnerable to enlightened criticism than any other. By writing, and without even apparent necessity (which carried the fault to excess), the famous declaration dared to decide a question which should invariably have been left to practical wisdom, enlightened by the universal conscience.[47]

This is the only point of view in harmony with the intent of this work. But it is quite worthy, in any case, of the contemplation of every just mind and upright heart.

XIX

In their general sense, these ideas were known to the ancient philosophers, who clearly perceived the faint—indeed, almost total—insignificance of the written word for great institutions. No one has ever realized or expressed this truth better than Plato, who invariably was first on the way to finding all great truths. According to him, the man who acquires all his education from things written *will never have more than the appearance of wisdom.*[48] The spoken word, he adds, is to writing as a man is to his portrait. The products of art appear as living things to us, but *if questioned, they maintain a dignified silence.* It is the same with writing, *which knows not what to say to one man and what to conceal from another.* It cannot defend itself if groundlessly attacked or insulted, for its author is never present to support it. Thus he who believes himself able by writing alone to establish a clear and lasting doctrine is a great fool. If he really possessed the seeds of truth, he could never believe that a little black liquid and a pen could germinate them in the world, protect them from harsh weather, and make them sufficiently effective. As for whoever undertakes writing *laws or civil constitutions* in the belief that he can give them adequate conviction and stability because he has written them, he disgraces himself, whether or no other people say so. He shows an equal ignorance of the nature of inspiration and delirium, right and wrong, good and evil. This ignorance is shameful, even when approved by the whole body of the common people.[49]

XX

After the wisdom of paganism, it will be instructive to hear Christian philosophy again. How much better it would be, said the most eloquent of the Greek Fathers, if we had never needed writing, but had the divine precepts been imprinted by grace in our hearts as they are with ink in our books. Since we have lost this grace through our own fault, we must follow the second-best course, without, however, forgetting the pre-eminence of our original condition. To the righteous of the Old Testament, God revealed nothing in writing. Seeing the purity of their hearts, he spoke directly to them. But when the Hebrew people sank into wickedness, books and laws became necessary. The same process recurred under the empire of the New Revelation, for Christ left not a single writ to *His* apostles. He commended them not to books but to the Holy Spirit: "He shall bring all things to your remembrance.[50] But because, in time, sinful men rebelled against faith and morality, books were again required.[51]

XXI

The whole truth is assembled in these two authorities. They demonstrate the profound idiocy (it is certainly permissible to speak like Plato, who never loses his temper), I repeat, the profound idiocy, of those unfortunate souls who imagine that legislators are men,[52] laws are paper, and nations may be constituted *with ink*. On the contrary, the latter show that writings are invariably a sign of weakness, ignorance, or danger and that the more nearly perfect an institution is, the less it writes. What is certainly divine [that is, the Church] wrote nothing at all in establishing itself, in order to make us feel that all written law is merely a necessary evil, generated by human frailty or malice, and which, moreover, has no authority except that received of a previous, unwritten sanction.

XXII

Here we must deplore the glaring fallacy of a system[53] which has divided Europe with such unfortunate consequences. Its partisans say: "*We believe only in the Word of God. . . .*" What a misuse of words! *We alone believe in the Word* while our *dear enemies* stubbornly persist in believing only *Scripture.* As if God could or would alter the nature of His creation and impart to Scripture the life and efficacy it lacks! The Holy Scripture—now then, is it not *a writing? Was it not formed with a pen and a little black fluid? Does it understand what to tell one man and what to hide from another?* Did not Leibnitz and his maidservant read the same words there? Can this writing be more than the *image of the Word?* However venerable it thus becomes, when we interrogate it, must it not *keep a divine silence?*[54] If it were attacked or slurred, could it defend itself in the Father's absence? Praise be to the truth! If the immortal Word [*la Parole*] does not give life to Scripture, it will never become *speech* [*parole*], that is to say, life. May the others invoke the silent word as often as they please. We shall smile peacefully at this *false god* while ever awaiting with tender impatience the time when its disillusioned partisans will throw themselves into our arms, which have for nearly three centuries been ready to embrace them.

XXIII

Each sensible person may become convinced on this point by a little reflection on an axiom as important as it is universal—that nothing great has great beginnings. All of history yields no exception to this law. *Crescit occulto velut arbor aevo*;[55] this is the motto of all great institutions. Therefore, any false institution writes voluminously, for it knows its weaknesses and seeks support. From this fact springs the indubitable result that no real and great institution can be based on written law, since men themselves, instruments, in turn, of the established institution, do not know what it is to become and since imperceptible growth is the true promise of durability in all things. A remarkable example of this sort is the power of the Popes, which I do not intend to discuss dogmatically here. Numerous writers since the sixteenth century have employed a prodigious amount of erudition to prove, by going back to the cradle of Christianity, that at first the Bishops of Rome were not what they later became. They took for granted that everything not found in primitive times is an abuse. Now I say, without the least spirit of contention or desire to offend anyone, that in this they displayed about as much philosophy and genuine learning as one who tries to find the dimensions of a mature man by measuring a babe in arms. This sovereignty I am speaking of here was born like others and grows as they do. It is lamentable to watch fine minds exhausting themselves to prove by infancy that manhood is a deformity. The idea of any institution full grown at birth is a prime absurdity and a true logical contradiction. If the enlightened and open-minded enemies of this power (and surely there are many such) examine the matter from this point of view, as I affectionately urge, I am sure all these objections derived from antiquity will vanish like a thin mist from before their eyes.

As for abuses, I should not concern myself with them here. However, since I have already mentioned them, I will say that there is much to be deflated in the oratory the last century had compelled us to read on this big topic. A time will come when every nation will consider the Popes against whom the greatest outcry was heard—such as Gregory VII[56]—as friends, guardians, and saviors of humanity, as the true Founding Fathers[57] of Europe. No one will doubt it when learned Frenchmen shall be Christians and English savants, Catholics—which must surely come to pass at last.

XXIV

But at this moment, what penetrating words can make us heard by an age infatuated with Scripture and so greatly at variance with the Word as to believe that men can make constitutions, languages, and even sovereignties? By an age for which reality is lies, and lies reality; which cannot even see what happens before its eyes; which feasts on books, seeking the equivocal lessons of Livy or Thucydides, while closing its eyes to the truth which shines forth in the newspapers?

If a humble mortal's prayers could obtain from Providence one of those memorable decrees which form history's great eras, I would ask it to inspire some powerful nation which had gravely offended it with the proud idea of constituting itself politically, starting at the bases. And if the ancient familiarity of a Patriarch were permitted me, despite my unworthiness, I would say: "Grant this people everything! Give them genius, knowledge, wealth, esteem, and, especially, an overweening self-assurance and that spirit, both supple and enterprising, which nothing can hinder, nothing intimidate. Extinguish their former government; obliterate their memories; destroy their affections; spread terror around them; blind or paralyze their enemies; set victory to guard all their frontiers so that none of their neighbors could intervene in their affairs or disturb their progress. Let this nation be illustrious in the sciences, rich in philosophy, intoxicated with human power, free from prejudice, from every tie and all higher influence. Supply all her wants, lest in time she should say, *I lacked this* or *that restrained me.* In short, let her act freely with this immensity of means, that at length under Thy relentless protection she may become an eternal warning to the human race."

XXV

It is true we cannot expect such a combination of circumstances, which would literally constitute a miracle. But similar though less startling events reveal themselves here and there in history, even in our times. Although they may not all have that ideal force, for example, which I wished for, they can still teach us valuable lessons.

Less than twenty-five years ago, we witnessed a solemn attempt to regenerate a great nation which was mortally ill. It was the first experiment of the great work and the preface, if I may so express it, of the frightful book which we have since been made to read. Every precaution was taken. The country's sages even believed it was their duty to consult the modern deity in its foreign sanctuary. They wrote to *Delphi,* and two famous Pontiffs solemnly replied.[58] The prophecies they announced on this occasion were not, as formerly, delicate leaves, the sport of breezes; they are bound

Quidque haec Sapientia possit, Tunc patuit. . . .[59]

It is only fair to acknowledge that in whatever the nation owed merely to its own good sense, there are elements we can still admire today. Certainly every qualification was united in the head of that wise and august person called upon to take the reins of government. Those chiefly interested in maintaining the old laws [such as the aristocracy] voluntarily made a noble sacrifice to the public, and in order to strengthen the supreme authority, they consented to a slightly different description of sovereignty.[60] Alas! All this human wisdom was at fault, and everything ended in death.

XXVI

Someone will say: "But we know what caused the failure of the interprise." How, then? Must God send angels in human form, commissioned to destroy a constitution? Secondary causes will always be necessary. What matter which they are? All instruments are effective in the Great Artificer's hands. But people are so blind that if tomorrow some constitution-monger should come to organize a nation and constitute them *with a little black fluid,* the crowd would hasten once again to believe in the miracle announced. Again they would say, *Nothing is missing, all is foreseen, all "written down,"* while precisely because everything could be seen, written, and discussed, it would be shown that the constitution was empty, offering only an ephemeral appearance.

XXVII

I believe I have read somewhere that *very few sovereignties are able to justify the legitimacy of their origin.* Let us allow the reasonableness of this assertion. Even so, objectionable acts which a chief may have committed will not tarnish his successors. The mists which would more or less conceal the origin of his authority would only be a disadvantage, the necessary consequence of a law of the moral order. Otherwise, it would follow that the sovereign could only rule legitimately by virtue of a deliberation of all the people—that is to say, *by the grace of the people.* This will never happen, for there are no truer words than those of the author of the *Considerations on France: The people will always accept their masters and never choose them.*[61] It is essential that the origin of sovereignty should show itself to be beyond the sphere of human power, so that even those men who appear to influence it directly are only circumstances. As for legitimacy, if its origin seems obscure, it is explained by God's prime minister in the province of this world—*Time.* It is nevertheless true that certain contemporary signs are unmistakable when we are there to observe them. But an expansion of this idea belongs to another work.

XXVIII

Everything brings us back to the general rule. *Man cannot create a constitution, and no legitimate constitution can be written.* The collection of fundamental laws which necessarily constitute a civil or religious society never has been or will be written *a priori.* Only when society discovers itself already constituted, not knowing how, can certain particular articles be made known or explained in writing. But almost invariably, these declarations are the effect or the cause of very great evils, and they always cost the people more than they are worth.

XXIX

To this general rule, that *no constitution may be "written or made a priori,* we know but one exception: the legislation of Moses. This alone was *cast,* so to speak, like a statue and written even to the smallest details by an extraordinary man who said, fiat! without this work ever after needing corrections, additions, or modifications by himself or anyone else. This alone has withstood time, from which it borrowed and expected nothing. It survived fifteen hundred years, and even after eighteen more centuries have passed since the great anathema which struck it on the fated day, we see it enjoying a second life and still binding, with some nameless and mysterious bond, the various scattered families of a people dispersed but not disunited.[62] Like magnetism, and with a similar force, it operates at a distance, making one whole of many widely separated parts. Evidently, to intelligent minds, this legislation surpasses the limits of human capability and is a magnificent exception to a general law which has only yielded once, and then to its Author. And it singlehandedly manifests the divine mission of the great Hebrew lawgiver much better than the entire work of that English Prelate, who, with the strongest mental powers and immense erudition, nevertheless had the misfortune to support a great truth by a miserable fallacy.[63]

XXX

Since the principle of every constitution is divine, it follows that a man can do nothing with one unless he seeks the aid of God, Whose instrument he then becomes.[64] Now this is a truth to which the whole human race has always strikingly witnessed. Examine history, which is experimental politics—there we shall inevitably find the Divinity always called to the aid of human frailty.[65] Fable, much truer than ancient history for those who are ready to understand it, further corroborates this demonstration. Always, it is an Oracle who founds cities. Always, this Oracle affirms heavenly protection and the heroic founder's success. Kings especially, heads of rising empires, are very often designated, almost branded, by Heaven in some extraordinary manner.[66] How many frivolous people have mocked the Saint-Ampoule[67] without ever dreaming that it is a hieroglyphic which one need only read to understand.[68]

XXXI

Consecration of kings springs from the same root. There never was a more meaningful and honorable ceremony, or more exactly, profession of faith. The Pontiff's finger has always touched the forehead of rising sovereignty. The many writers who have seen in these august rites only the workings of ambition, or even a deliberate conspiracy of superstition and tyranny, have spoken against the truth, nearly all even against their own conscience. This question deserves study. Sometimes sovereigns have sought consecration, and sometimes it sought them. Others have been seen to reject it as a sign of dependence. We are acquainted with sufficient facts to judge correctly on this score, but it would be necessary to distinguish carefully the men, the periods of history, the countries, and the forms of worship. Here it is sufficient to emphasize the general and eternal opinion which invokes the Divine Power at the establishment of empires.

XXXII

The most famous nations of antiquity, especially the more serious and wise, such as the Egyptians, Etruscans, Lacedaemonians, and Romans, were precisely those with the most religious forms of government. And the duration of empires has always been proportionate to the degree of influence the religious element gained in the political constitution. *The cities and nations most attached to divine worship have always been the wisest and longest lasting, just as the most religious ages have always been the most distinguished by genius.*[69]

XXXIII

Religion alone civilizes nations. No other known force can influence the savage. Without referring to antiquity's decisive proofs on this point, we can find tangible evidence in America. For three centuries we have been there with our laws, our arts, our sciences, our civilization, our commerce and luxuries. And what have we gained over the savage state? Nothing. We destroy these unfortunate beings with sword and alcohol. We gradually drive them into the middle of the wilderness until at last they wholly disappear, as much victims of our vices as of our callous superiority.

XXXIV

Has any philosopher ever thought to leave his country and its comforts to seek the savages in the forests of America for the purpose of arousing in them disgust for all the vices of barbarism and of giving them a moral system?[70] They have done much better. They have concocted fine books to prove that the savage is man in his *natural state*, whom we should all aspire to resemble. Condorcet has said that *the missionaries have carried nothing but shameful superstitions into Asia and Africa.*[71] With an inconceivable multiplication of folly, Rousseau has said that *to him, the missionaries seemed scarcely more moderate than the conquerors*[72] Indeed, their coryphaeus[73] has had the audacity (but what could he lose?) to cast the crudest ridicule upon these peaceful conquerors, whom the ancients would have deified.[74]

Nowhere else could you find more nonsense, indecency, and bad taste. Nevertheless, this book, of which few chapters are exempt from similar passages, this *showy geegaw*, some modern enthusiasts have unhesitatingly called *a monument of the human intelligence.* No doubt, like the chapel at Versailles and the pictures of Boucher.

XXXV

It is the missionaries, however, who have accomplished this marvel so far beyond human strength, or even human will. They alone have traveled the vast American continent from one border to the other to create men there. They alone have done what secular power dared not even imagine. But nothing of the kind rivals the [Jesuit] missions of Paraguay. There, the exclusive authority and ability of religion in civilizing men has been most marked. This wonder has been acclaimed, but not sufficiently. The spirit of the eighteenth century and another accomplice spirit have been strong enough to stifle partially the voice of justice and even that of admiration. Perhaps one day (for we do hope these great and generous labors will be resumed),[75] in the heart of a prosperous city founded on some old savanna, the father of these missionaries will have his statue. One might read on its pedestal:

TO THE CHRISTIAN OSIRIS
Whose emissaries have covered the globe

to snatch men from misery,
brutishness, and ferocity
by teaching them agriculture
by giving them laws
by teaching them to know God and to serve Him,
thus taming the unfortunate savage,
NOT BY FORCE OF ARMS
which they never required,
but by mild persuasion, moral chants,
AND BY THE POWER OF HYMNS,
so that men believed them angels.[76]

XXXVI

Consider this legislative order, reigning in Paraguay by the simple superiority of talent and virtue, never deviating from the humblest submission to the legitimate temporal authority, however misguided. At the same time, this order entered our jails, our hospitals, and our quarantine stations to brave the most vile and repulsive forms of poverty, disease, and despair. These very men, who hastened at the first appeal to lie down beside the indigent on their bed of straw, were at ease in the politest circles. They mounted the scaffold *to speak the last words* to the victims of human justice and from these scenes of horror hurried into the pulpit to speak vehemently before kings.[77] They held the paintbrush in China, the telescope in our observatories, Orpheus' lyre amidst the savages, and they exalted the entire age of Louis XIV. When now we realize that a despicable alliance of perverse government ministers, raving magistrates, and infamous secretaries has been able, in our day, to demolish this admirable institution and to congratulate themselves for it, we recall the imbecile who exultingly stepped upon a watch, exclaiming "I'll stop your noise!" But what am I saying? An imbecile is no criminal.

XXXVII

I have had to dwell principally on the formation of empires as being the most important subject. But all human institutions obey the same rule, being meaningless or dangerous unless they rest on the foundation of all existence. This principle being undeniable, what shall we think of a generation which has thrown everything to the winds, including the very foundations of the structure of society, by making education exclusively scientific? It was impossible to err more frightfully. For every educational system which does not have religion as its basis will collapse in an instant, or else diffuse only poisons throughout the State, *religion being,* as Bacon aptly says, *the spice which preserves the sciences from decay.*[78]

XXXVIII

The question so often asked, *Why a school of theology in every university?* is easily answered. *The reason is that the universities may exist and that instruction may not become corrupted.* Originally, universities were only schools of theology to which other *faculties* were attached, as are subjects around their queen. Established on such a foundation, the edifice of public instruction had lasted until our day. Those who have overturned it among themselves will long repent in vain. A mere child or a lunatic can burn down a city. But architects, materials, workmen, wealth, and above all, time, are necessary to restore it.

XXXIX

Perhaps equally much harm has been done to mankind by those who, while preserving the exterior forms of ancient institutions, are pleased to corrupt them inwardly. Already the influence of modern universities upon morals and the national character throughout most of Europe is quite familiar.[79] In this respect, the English universities have preserved a better reputation than the others, perhaps because the English know better how to keep silence or to praise themselves at the right moments, perhaps also because their unusually vigorous public opinion has there, more effectively than elsewhere, protected these venerable schools from the general curse. However, they must succumb at last, and already Gibbon's wicked heart has made us some strange disclosures on this point.[80] In brief, to continue with generalities, if we do not return to the old maxims, if the guidance of education is not returned to the priests, and if science is not uniformly relegated to a subordinate rank, incalculable evils await us. We shall become brutalized by science, and that is the worst sort of brutality.

XL

Creation is not man's province. Nor does his *unassisted* power even appear capable of improving on institutions already established. If anything is apparent to man, it is the existence of two opposing forces in the universe in continual conflict. Nothing good is unsullied or unaltered by evil. Every evil is repressed and assailed by good, which continually impels all existence towards a more perfect state.[81] These two forces are present everywhere. We observe them equally in the growth of plants, the development of animals, the formation of languages and empires (two inseparable things), etc. Probably, human powers extend only to removing or resisting evil in order to separate from it the good, which may then develop freely according to its nature. The illustrious Zanotti[82] has said: *It is difficult to change things for the better.*[83] This thought conceals a great meaning under the guise of extreme simplicity. It agrees perfectly with another thought of Origen which alone is worth a volume. *Nothing,* says he, *can be altered for the better among men* without God.[84] All men sense this truth, even without consciously realizing it. From it derives the innate aversion of all intelligent persons to innovations. The word *reform,* by itself and prior to any scrutiny, will always be suspect to wisdom, and the experience of every generation justifies this instinct. We know all too well the fruit of the most attractive speculations of this kind.[85]

XLI

Apply these general maxims to an individual example, the great question of parliamentary reform which has so powerfully stirred English minds for so long. Without being in a position to have a settled opinion, I am constrained to believe, from the mere consideration of the extreme danger of innovations founded upon purely human theories, that the idea of such reform is pernicious and that if the English yield too hastily to it, they will have occasion to repent. *But,* say the partisans of reform (for this is the classic argument), *the abuses are striking, undeniable; and can a formal abuse, a defect, be constitutional?* Yes indeed, for every political constitution has faults in its nature which cannot possibly be extracted from it. Moreover—and all would-be reformers should quail at the thought—these faults may change with circumstances, so that in showing that they are new, we have not yet proved them unnecessary.[86] What prudent man, then, would not shudder in setting to work? Social harmony, like musical harmony, obeys the law of *just proportions* in the *keyboard of the universe.* Tune the *fifths* rigorously and the *octaves* will be dissonant, and conversely. Since discord is inevitable, instead of eliminating it, which is impossible, we must moderate it by a general distribution. Thus, in all parts, *imperfection is an element of the perfection possible.* This proposition is a paradox in form only. *But,* one may still object, *where is the ride for distinguishing the accidental flaw from that which belongs to the nature of things and is impossible to exclude?* Men upon whom nature has merely bestowed ears ask such questions, while those who have a good ear shrug their shoulders in reply.

XLII

When abuses are concerned, one must be careful only to judge political institutions by their enduring effects and never by their causes, of whatever sort, which signify nothing,[87] still less by certain collateral difficulties which (if I may express myself thus) may easily preoccupy men of limited vision, preventing them from seeing the whole picture. Indeed, the cause should have no logical connection with the effect, according to the hypothesis, which seems already proved. Since the disadvantages of all inherently good institutions are only, as I just explained, *an unavoidable dissonance in the great keyboard,* how can institutions be ever judged by their causes and their faults? Voltaire, who spoke for decades on every subject without once penetrating the surface of any,[88] has argued facetiously about the sale of judicial offices in France, and perhaps no example would better illustrate the accuracy of my theory. *The proof that this sale is an abuse,* he says, *is that it originated in another abused.*[89] Voltaire does not err here in the way anyone is apt to. He errs shamefully, in a total eclipse of common sense. *Everything which springs from an abuse is an abuse!* On the contrary, one of the most general and obvious laws of the power, at once hidden and striking, which acts and makes itself felt on all sides, is that the remedy for an abuse arises from another and that the evil, having reached a certain point, destroys itself, as it should. For evil is only a negative quality having the dimensions and durability of the being to which it is attached and which it devours. It exists like an ulcer, which only terminates in self-destruction. But then a new reality will of necessity rush to fill the place of what has just disappeared, *for nature abhors a vacuum,* and good . . . but I digress too far from Voltaire.

XLIII

This great writer's error proceeds from the fact that *divided among twenty sciences,* as he himself somewhere confesses, and constantly occupied in communicating instruction to the world, he rarely gave himself time to think. "A sensual and dissipated court, reduced to the greatest want by its foolish expenses, devises the sale of judicial offices, thus creating" (what it never could have done freely, and with a knowledge of the cause) "a wealthy, irremovable and independent magistracy. In this fashion the infinite power, rejoicing in the habitable part of his earth,[90] employs corruption to create incorruptible tribunals" (as nearly as human frailty allows). Certainly nothing is so plausible to a true philosopher. Nothing is more consonant, by analogy, with that indisputable law which determines that the most important institutions are always the result of circumstances, never of deliberation. Here, the problem, once stated correctly, is nearly solved—the usual result with such problems. *Could a country like France be better judged than by hereditary magistrates?* If, as I suppose,[91] one answers in the affirmative, I must immediately propose this second problem: *The magistracy being necessarily hereditary, is there a more advantageous way first of constituting and then of recruiting it than one which fills the sovereign's coffers for the least cost and which simultaneously assures the affluence, independence, and even the nobility* (of a certain kind) *of the higher judges?* If venality be considered only as a means of inheritance, every fair-minded person is struck by this point of view, the true one. This is not the place to discuss the matter at length, but it is already demonstrated that Voltaire was completely unaware of it.

XLIV

Imagine a man like him at the head of affairs, uniting, by a happy chance, frivolity, incapacity, and rashness. He will not fail to act according to his scatterbrained theories of law and abuses. He will borrow at 7 per cent to pay off debts carrying a charge of 2 per cent. He will subvert the public by a flood of paid writings which will insult the magistracy and destroy public confidence in it. Soon, patronage, a thousand times more foolish than chance, will begin the endless series of its blunders. The distinguished man, no longer enjoying the right of inheritance for oppressive labors, will depart, never to return. And the great tribunals will be delivered into the hands of nameless adventurers, without prestige or fortune, replacing the venerable magistracy, in which virtue and learning had become as hereditary as the dignities of office, a true priesthood which other nations could envy until the moment when false philosophy, having banished wisdom from all her accustomed haunts, climaxed these noble exploits by driving her from the land altogether.

XLV

Such is the portrait of most reforms. For not only is creation beyond man's scope, but even reform is permitted him only in a subordinate capacity and with a multitude of formidable restrictions. Starting from these unquestionable principles, each man can judge his country's institutions with perfect certainty. Above all, he can evaluate all those *creators,* those *legislators* and those *restorers* of nations, so dear to the eighteenth century, which posterity will contemplate with pity, perhaps even with horror. Castles of cards have been built inside and outside Europe. The details would be odious to relate. But surely no lack of respect is shown anyone by a simple plea to look and judge by the event if he persists in refusing all other types of instruction. Man in communication with his Maker is sublime, his activities creative. The instant he separates himself from God to act alone, on the other hand, he does not lose his power, for it is a privilege of his nature, but his activity is negative and leads only to destruction.

XLVI

The history of all ages contains not one fact to contradict these maxims. No human institution can endure unless supported by Him who supports all—that is to say, unless it is specially consecrated to Him at its origin. The more it is permeated by the Divine essence, the longer it will survive. How strange is the blindness of men in our time! They boast of their understanding, yet they are ignorant of everything, since they do not know themselves what they are and what they can do. Unconquerable pride goads them incessantly to overthrow everything not made by themselves, and to effectuate new creations they abandon the source of all existence. Jean Jacques Rousseau has correctly said: *Vain little man, show me your power, and I shall show you your weakness.* He might just as truly have said, but to better advantage: *Vain little man, confess your weakness to me, and I shall show you your strength.* In fact, once a man has recognized his insignificance, he has taken a great forward stride, for he is quite close to seeking a support with which everything is possible. Exactly the opposite of this has characterized the century which just ended. (Alas! It has ended only in our calendars.) Examine all its enterprises, all its institutions whatsoever; you will find it always intent on separating them from the Divinity. Man has believed himself to be an independent being, and he has embraced what is really the practice of atheism, which is more dangerous perhaps and more reprehensible than that of theory.

XLVII

Beguiled by his vain sciences away from the only one which truly concerns him, man has come to believe that he has the power of creation, although he actually has not even the power of assigning names. He who cannot even produce an insect or a tuft of moss has thought himself the direct author of sovereignty, the most important, holy, and fundamental part of the moral and political world.[92] He has believed that a certain family, for example, rules because a certain people has wanted it to, while he is surrounded by absolute proof that every sovereign power rules because it is elected by a superior power. If he does not see these proofs, it is because he shuts his eyes or because he looks too closely. He believes that he himself has invented language. Again, he should realize that every human tongue is *learned* and never *invented* and that no conceivable hypothesis within the sphere of mortal powers could explain either the formation or the diversity of languages with the slightest plausibility. He has believed that he could constitute nations, in other words, *that he could create that national unity by virtue of which one nation is not another.* Finally, he has believed that because he was able to form institutions, he could all the more naturally borrow them from other nations, importing them ready made, with their original name, to enjoy of them the same advantages as had their first possessors. The French press has furnished me a curious example.

XLVIII

Some years ago, the French people took it into their heads to initiate certain athletic contests in Paris which in several contemporary writings were gravely called *Olympic Games.* The reasoning of those who invented or revived this high-sounding name was not complicated. *Men raced,* they said to themselves, *on foot and on horseback by the banks of the Alpheus. Men will race on foot and on horseback by the banks of the Seine. Therefore it is the same thing.* Nothing could be *simpler.* But without inquiring why they had not called these games *Parisian* instead of *Olympic,* I shall proceed to other observations. Before the *Olympic* Games were begun, Oracles were consulted, gods and heroes took part, nothing started before sacrifices had been offered and other religious ceremonies enacted. The games were considered the Popular Assembly of Greece, and nothing was more majestic. But before the Parisians instituted their contests, *revived from the Greeks,* did they go to Rome *ad limina apostolorum*[93] to consult the Pope? Before running their steeplechase for the amusement of shopkeepers, did they celebrate High Mass? With what great political aims were these races associated? What were the names of the High Priests? But enough. The most ordinary common sense instantly feels the emptiness, even ridiculousness, of this limitation.

XLIX

Yet in a journal written by intelligent men, whose only fault—or misfortune—lay in professing the modern doctrines, the following passage about these Games was written a few years ago with the most amusing enthusiasm.

I predict: The French Olympic Games will one day draw all Europe to the Champ-de-Mars. What frigid and insensitive souls are they who see in this only an athletic contest. As for me, I see a spectacle unparalleled since the pageantry of Elis, where all Greece could watch its own splendor. No, the Roman Circus and our own tournaments of chivalry could not hold a candle to it.[94]

As for me, I *believe,* indeed, *I know,* that no human institution is lasting without a religious foundation *and moreover* (I entreat the most undivided attention to this), *without a name taken from the national language, originating itself without any previous and public deliberation.*

L

The theory of names is yet of great importance. They are never arbitrary, as so many men *who have lost their names* affirm. God calls Himself *I Am,* and every creature calls itself *I am that.* The name of a spiritual being is necessarily relative to its action, which is its distinctive quality. Hence among the ancients, the highest honor for a divinity was polyonymy, that is to say, *having more than one name,* which indicates a variety of functions or a greater extent of power. Ancient mythology has Diana, still a child, asking Jupiter for this honor, and in the verses attributed to Orpheus, she is hailed with the title *Démon polynyme* (spirit of many names).[95] Essentially, this means that God alone has the right to bestow a name. He has *named* everything because he has *created* everything. He has named the stars[96] and the angels. The Bible mentions only three of the latter by name, but each relates to the purpose of these ministers. It is the same with men whom God has seen fit to name Himself, with whom Holy Scripture has acquainted us in considerable numbers. The names are always relative to the functions of these men.[97] Has He not said that in His future kingdom, He would give the conquerors *a new name*[98] proportionate to their *exploits?* Have men, *formed in God's image,* found a more solemn way to reward victors in battle than by giving them a *new name,* the most honorable of all in human estimation, that of the vanquished nation?[99] Each time that a man's life is supposed to change and take on a new character, thus often does he receive a *new name.* This is true in baptism, confirmation, enlistment of soldiers, entrance into a religious order, liberation of slaves, etc. In a word, the *name* of every being explains what he is, and there is nothing arbitrary about it. The common expression, *he has a name, he doesn't have a name,* is quite true and expressive. No man may be ranked among those *who in the time of assembly were called by name*[100] unless his family is marked by a sign which distinguishes it from all others.

LI

This also applies to nations. There are some *which have no name.* Herodotus remarks that the Thracians would be the most powerful people in the universe if they were united. *But,* he adds, *this union is impossible, for they all have a different name.*[101] It is an acute observation. There are also some modern people *who have no name* and others who have several. But *polyonymy* is as unfortunate for nations as antiquity could think it honorable for their deities.

LII

Since names partake of nothing arbitrary and originate, like all things, more or less immediately in God, we must not believe that man has the unrestricted right of naming even those things of which he has some right to consider himself the author and of imposing names on them to suit the ideas he forms of them. In this connection, God has reserved a sort of direct jurisdiction for Himself, which it is impossible to misconstrue.[102] *Oh my dear* Hermogenes! *Bestowing names is a weighty matter, which cannot be entrusted to a bad man, or even an ordinary man. . . . This privilege belongs only to a creator of names (onomaturgos), that is to say, to the legislator alone. But of all human creatures, he is the most rare.*[103]

LIII

Still, man loves nothing as much as giving names. This he does when he applies expressive epithets to things, a talent for which great writers—great poets especially—are distinguished. The just application of an epithet dignifies a noun, which becomes famous in this new guise.[104] Examples are found in every language. . .[105] Man will never forget his primitive privileges; in a certain sense, he will always exercise them. But how greatly has his degradation curtailed them! Here is a law as true as God its Maker:

Man is forbidden to give great names to works of his which he considers mighty. But if he has proceeded legitimately, the common names for the work will be ennobled by it and become great.

LIV

This rule is the same, whether it concerns political or material creation. For example, nothing is better known in Greek history than the word *Ceramicus.* Athens had none more magnificent. Long after it had lost its great men and its political significance, Atticus, then in Athens, wrote pretentiously to his illustrious friend: *The other day, finding myself in the Ceramicus,* etc., and Cicero teased him about it in his reply.[106] What is the intrinsic meaning of this famous word *Tuilerie?*[107] Nothing could be more ordinary. But heroes' remains mixed with this ground have consecrated it, and the soil has consecrated the name in turn. It is curious that at such a great distance in time and space this same word *Tuileries,* formerly famous as the name of a place of burial, should again be dignified under the name of a palace. The personage who arrived to inhabit the *Tuileries* did not attempt to give the building some imposing name to match its splendor. If he had made this mistake, there was no reason that the following day this place should not have been inhabited by prostitutes and thieves.

LV

There is another reason worth considering which should also induce us to mistrust any pompous name given *a priori.* Man's conscience almost always warns him of the imperfections of the work he has just produced. Rebellious pride, which cannot deceive itself, tries at least to deceive others by inventing an honorable name which implies precisely the opposite merit. This invention, consequently, instead of really attesting the excellence of the work, is a clear acknowledgement of the flaws which characterize it. The eighteenth century, so rich in every imaginable fallacy and foolishness, has supplied a myriad of intriguing examples of this point in the form of book titles, epigraphs, inscriptions, and other such things. At the beginning of one of the principal works of that age, for instance, one reads:

Tantum series juncturaque pollet:
Tantum de medio sumptis accedit honoris.[108]

Erase the presumptuous epigraph and boldly substitute, without even having opened the book and without the least fear of being unfair:

Rudis indigestaque moles
. . .
Non bene junctarum discordia semina rerum.[109]

Indeed, this book is the very image of chaos, and the epigraph eminently expresses what is wanting in the work to the highest degree. If you read at the head of another book *A Philosophical and Political History,*[110] you know without having read the history announced under this title that it is neither *philosophical* nor *political.* Besides which you will know after having read it that it is the work of a madman. Does a man have the effrontery to write beneath his own portrait *Vitam impendere veto*?[111] Do not hesitate to wager it is the portrait of a liar. Perhaps he himself will someday admit it to you when he may take a fancy to speak the truth. Who can see under another portrait *Postgenitus hic carus erit, nunc carus amicis*[112] without at once recalling that line, borrowed from the original itself, depicting him in somewhat different fashion: *I had worshipers but never a friend?* Indeed, never perhaps has there lived a man of letters less able to feel friendship and less worthy to inspire it. Works and enterprises of another land lend themselves to the same observation. For example, if in a famous nation music suddenly becomes an affair of state. If the spirit of the age, blind in every respect, grants this art a false importance and a false patronage, very different from what it needs, if in fact a temple is erected to music under the venerable and high-sounding title of *Odeon*[113]—it proves infallibly that the art is decaying. No one need be surprised to hear a famous critic in that country declare soon after, rather strongly, that nothing prevents hanging a "Room to Rent" sign above the entrance.[114]

LVI

But as I have said, all of this is only an observation of secondary importance. Let us return to the general principle, *Man has not, or has no longer, the right to name things* (at least, in the times referred to). We must realize clearly that the most respectable names have a plebeian origin in all languages. The name is never commensurate with the thing; the thing always glorifies the name. The name must *germinate*, so to speak, or else it is false. What did the word *throne* originally signify? *Seat,* or even *stool.* What does *scepter* mean? A staff to lean upon.[115] However, the *staff* of kings was soon distinguished from all others, and this name, with its new meaning, has subsisted for three thousand years. What is nobler in literature and more humble in its beginnings than the word *tragedy*? What has been more favored in our language than the almost repugnant word *drapeau* [flag], raised and ennobled by the warrior's lance? Many other names might be mentioned in corroboration—*Senate, Dictator, Consul, Emperor, Cardinal, Marshal,* etc. We shall conclude with the titles *Constable* and *Chancellor*, given to two eminent dignitaries of modern times. The first once meant merely master of the stable;[116] the second, *the man who stands behind a railing* (to prevent his being trampled by the crowd of suppliants).

LVII

Thus there are two rules for judging all human creations of any kind whatsoever: the *foundation* and the *name*. If the former is purely human, the edifice cannot stand. The more men who engage in its construction, the more deliberation, learning, and *especially writing*, they supply to it; in short, the more human means of every land, the more frail shall the institution be. Chiefly by this rule must we judge whatever has been attempted by sovereigns or assemblies of men for the civilizing, the founding, or the regeneration of nations.

LVIII

On the other hand, the more an institution's basis is divine, the more durable it is. For greater clarity, we should add that the religious principle is, by its nature, creative and conservative in two different ways. First, since it acts more strongly on the human mind than does any other element, drawing prodigious efforts from it. For example, if a man's religious beliefs convince him that it is greatly advantageous to him to preserve his body after death as nearly intact as possible without allowing any rash or profane hand to touch it, after exhausting the resources of embalming, this man will at last build the Pyramids of Egypt. Second, though the religious principle is so powerful in what it effects, it is infinitely more so in what it prevents because of the veneration with which it imbues everything under its protection. If a simple pebble is consecrated, there is immediately a reason why it will escape from hands which might misplace or defile it. The earth is covered with proofs of this truth. *The Etruscan vases*, for example, *preserved by the religion of the tombs, have come down to us, despite their fragility, in greater numbers than the bronze and marble monuments of the same epochs.*[117] If you wish, therefore, to *conserve* everything, *dedicate* everything.

LIX

The second rule, that of names, is no less clear or decisive than the first one. If the name is imposed by an assembly, if it is established by prior deliberation so that it precedes the thing, if it is pompous,[118] if it has a grammatical proportion to the object it is supposed to represent, lastly, if it is taken from a foreign language, especially an ancient language—all the signs of insignificance are found united, and one may rest assured that the name and the thing will quickly disappear. Contrary conditions indicate the legitimacy, hence the permanency, of the institution. We must take care not to pass over this subject lightly. A genuine philosopher must never lose sight of language, a true barometer whose variations infallibly predict *good and bad weather.* To confine myself to this subject, it is certain that the immoderate borrowing of foreign words, applied particularly to any sort of national institution, is one of the surest signs of a people's moral degeneracy.

LX

If the formation of every empire, the progress of civilization, and the unanimous agreement of all history and tradition do not suffice to convince us, the death of empires will complete the demonstration begun at their birth. As the religious principle has created everything, so has its absence destroyed everything. The Epicurean sect, which might be called *the skepticism of antiquity,* at first corrupted and soon after destroyed any government unfortunate enough to accept it. Everywhere, *Lucretius* was a harbinger of *Caesar.*

But all past experience fades in the light of the horrifying example supplied by the last century. Still intoxicated with its fumes, men are, at least in general, very far from being sufficiently composed to contemplate its real significance and, especially, to draw from this the necessary consequences. Thus it is crucial to direct the attention of all to this terrible scene.

LXI

There have always been some forms of religion in the world and wicked men who opposed them. Impiety was always a crime, too. Since there can be no false religion without some ingredients of truth, all impiety does attack some divine verity, however disfigured. *But only in the bosom of the true religion can there be real impiety.* From which it inevitably results that impiety has never produced in times past the evils which it has brought forth in our day, for its guilt is always directly proportional to the enlightenment which surrounds it. By this rule must we judge the eighteenth century, for in this respect it is unlike any other. It is often said that *all ages are alike and men have always been the same.* But we must beware of these general maxims, which are invented by the lazy and frivolous to spare themselves the trouble of thinking. On the contrary, every age and every nation has a special distinctive nature which must be carefully considered. Undoubtedly, vice has always existed in the world, but it can differ in quantity, essence, dominant characteristics, and intensity.[119] Although impious men have always existed, there never was before the eighteenth century, and in the heart of Christendom, *an insurrection against God.* Never before, above all, has there been a sacrilegious conspiracy of every human talent against its Creator. For this is what we have witnessed in our time. Vaudeville has blasphemed, as well as tragedy, and the novel, along with history and the physical sciences. Men of this age have prostituted genius to irreligion and, according to the admirable phrase of Saint Louis on his deathbed, "They have waged war against God with His own gifts."[120] Ancient impiety never becomes angry. Sometimes it reasons; usually it jests, but always without bitterness. Even Lucretius seldom descends to invective, and although his brooding melancholy temperament led him to see the dark side of things, he remains calm, even when he accuses religion of generating great evils. The ancient religions were not considered sufficiently important to enrage contemporary skepticism.

LXII

When the *good tidings* were first broadcast throughout the universe, the attack became more violent. Nevertheless, the enemies of Christianity always retained a certain moderation. They appeared in history at great intervals and invariably alone. They never formed a union or a formal society. They never abandoned themselves to such fury as we have witnessed. Bayle[121] himself, the father of modern disbelief, was unlike his successors. Even in his most reprehensible errors he does not show a great desire to proselytize, even less a mood of irritation or a factious spirit. He denies less than he doubts. He speaks on both sides. Indeed, at times he is more eloquent for the good cause than for the bad.[122]

LXIII

Not until the first half of the eighteenth century did impiety really become a force. We see it at first spreading in every direction with amazing energy. From palaces to hovels, it insinuates itself everywhere, infesting everything. It follows invisible paths, acting secretly but infallibly, so that the most acute observer, seeing the effect, cannot always discover the means. By an unimaginable delusion, it even wins the affections of those to whom it is most deadly, and the authority it is preparing to sacrifice embraces it stupidly before receiving the blow. Soon a simple scheme becomes a formal association, which by degrees rapidly transforms itself into a confederacy and at length into a grand conspiracy which covers all Europe.

LXIV

Then that species of impiety which belongs only to the eighteenth century discloses itself for the first time. It is no longer the cold tone of indifference, of, at worst, the malignant irony of skepticism. It is a mortal hatred, the tone of anger and often of fury. The writers of that period, at least the most distinguished among them, no longer treat Christianity as an unimportant human error. They pursue it like a formidable enemy. They oppose it to the last extreme. It is a war to the death. What would seem incredible, if our own eyes had not seen the sad proofs of it, is that several of these men, who call themselves *philosophers,* advanced from hatred of Christianity to personal hatred of its Divine Author. They truly hated Him, as one would hate a living enemy. Two men especially,[123] who will forever be covered with the anathemas of posterity, have distinguished themselves in this form of villainy, which seemed beyond the powers of human nature, however depraved.

LXV

Since, however, all Europe had been civilized by Christianity and its ministers had obtained high political prestige in every country, the secular and religious institutions had blended and, as it were, amalgamated in a surprising manner, so that one could with more or less accuracy say of every state in Europe what Gibbon has said of France, *that this kingdom was founded by bishops,*[124] It was inevitable as a result that the philosophy of the age would unhesitatingly detest the social institutions, from which the religious principle was inseparable. This is what actually occurred. Every government and all the institutions of Europe displeased it *because* they were Christian, and *in proportion as* they were Christian, an inquietude of belief, a universal discontent, invaded every mind. In France, especially, the philosophic frenzy knew no bounds, and soon a single powerful voice, formed from many voices in chorus, cried out in the midst of guilty Europe:

LXVI

"Depart from us![125] Must we then forever tremble before the priests, receiving from them such instruction as they are pleased to give us?

Throughout Europe, the truth is hidden by the fumes of burning incense. It is time that she emerge from this poisonous cloud. We shall no longer speak of Thee to our children. It is left to them, once they become men, to know if Thou exist, what Thou art, and what Thou ask of them. All that exists is distasteful to us, for Thy name is written over all. We wish to destroy everything, rebuilding it without Thee. Depart from our councils, our schools, and our homes. We can act alone; reason is all we require. Depart from us!"

How has God punished this execrable raving? He punished it as He created the light, by a single word. He said, "So be it!"—and the world of politics crumbled.

See, then, how the two kinds of proof unite to strike the least discerning eyes. On the one hand, the religious principle presides over all political creation. On the other, everything disappears as soon as it is withdrawn.

LXVII

Europe is guilty for having shut her eyes to these great truths, and she suffers on account of her guilt. Yet still she rejects the light and does not acknowledge the Arm which strikes her. Few men, indeed, of this materialistic generation are in a condition to recognize the *date,* the *nature,* and the *enormity* of certain crimes perpetrated by individuals, by nations, and by sovereignties. Still less are they able to understand the sort of expiation which these sins demand and the worshipful marvel which compels evil to purify with its own hands the place which the eternal Architect has already measured for His marvelous constructions. The men of this age have chosen their lot. *They have sworn to fix their eyes upon the earth.*[126] But it would be useless, even dangerous perhaps, to go into further detail. We are exhorted to *profess the truth in love.*[127] Moreover, on certain occasions we must speak it only with respect, and despite every conceivable precaution, this step would be slippery for even the calmest and best-intentioned author. Besides, the world still contains a countless horde of men so perverse, so profoundly corrupt, that if they should bring themselves to suspect the truth of certain things, their wickedness might redouble in consequence, making them, so to speak, as guilty as the rebel angels. Oh! May their brutishness become instead even greater, if possible, in order that they cannot become even as guilty as men can be. Surely blindness is a dreadful punishment. Sometimes, however, it can still recognize love. That is all that can be usefully said at this time.

Endnotes

Preface

1 Jean Paul Marat, *L'Ami du people*, no. 667, July 7, 1792, in Paul H. Beik, ed. and trans., *The French Revolution* (New York: Macmillan, 1970), 215–21.

2 The quotation is from Keith M. Baker, "Revolution 1.0," *Journal of Modern European History* 11 (May 2013): 200. The scholarship on the French Revolution is too vast to be discussed here in detail. For comprehensive overviews of the French Revolution, see in particular William Doyle, *The Oxford History of the French Revolution* (Oxford: Oxford University Press, 2018) and the still helpful (though dated) François Furet and Mona Ozouf, eds., *Critical Dictionary of the French Revolution*, trans. Arthur Goldhammer (Cambridge, MA: Harvard University Press, 1989). For particular resources on the significance of the flight to Varennes, see Timothy Tackett, *When the King Took Flight* (Cambridge, MA: Harvard University Press, 2003); on the Terror, the notion of "enemy of humankind," and the civic festivals, see Dan Edelstein, *The Terror of Natural Right: Republicanism, the Cult of Nature, and the French Revolution* (Chicago: University of Chicago Press, 2009); on the reinvention of Revolution, see Baker, "Revolution 1.0" and Dan Edelstein, "Do We Want a Revolution without Revolution? Reflections on Political Authority," *French Historical Studies* 35, no. 2 (2012): 269–89; on the relationship between religion and the Revolution and revolutionary ecclesiastical policies, see Nigel Aston, *Religion and Revolution in France, 1780–1804* (Basingstoke, UK: Palgrave Macmillan, 2000).

Helpful overviews of the historiographical debate on the Revolution are offered by Ronald Schechter, *The French Revolution: The Essential Readings* (Malden, MA.: Blackwell, 2001) and Paul Hanson, "French Revolution," in *Interpreting Early Modern Europe*, ed. by C. Scott Dixon, Beat Kümin (New York: Routledge, 2020): 443–70.

3 Russell Kirk, introduction to Edmund Burke, *Reflections on the Revolution in France*, below, 3.

4 Burke, *Reflections*, below, 234.

5 The scholarship on Gentz in English is scarce and dated, but a recent dissertation offers a helpful synthesis and evaluation of the available literature in English and German. Travis Eakin, "Between the Old and the New: Friedrich Gentz, 1764–1832" (PhD diss., University of Missouri-Columbia, 2019). Eakin reaches the conclusion that Gentz was an exponent of what could be called "reform conservatism," "rational conservatism," or "governmental conservatism." Gentz's skeptical outlook on the institutions of the Middle Ages and his top-down approach to politics were arguably a legacy of his education in Frederick II's Prussia and his Enlightenment and rationalistic formation. These elements of his political theory (and, perhaps, his religiosity, too) are elements that differentiate his reformist conservatism from Burke's.

6 For an alternative view of Burke, suggesting that he should be seen as a reformer rather than a conservative, and emphasizing the lack of contradiction between his judgment of the French Revolution and his espousal of what Kirk called "liberal causes" over the course of his career, see Richard Bourke, *Empire and Revolution* (Princeton: Princeton University Press, 2017).

7 For a comparison between the thought of Burke and Maistre, see Richard A. Lebrun, "Joseph de Maistre and Edmund Burke: A Comparison," in Richard A. Lebrun, ed., *Joseph de Maistre's Life, Thought, and Influence: Selected Studies* (Montreal: McGill Queen's Press, 2001), 153–72.

8 Burke, *Reflections*, below, 30.

9 Ibid., below, 137; Friedrich Gentz, *The Origin and Principles of the American Revolution, Compared with the Origin and Principles of the French Revolution*, below, 306. One could legitimately observe that, though acknowledging some faults in the French Old Regime, Burke and Gentz still held an overly positive view of the French monarchy,

nobility, and clergy, a perception of those institutions that was not shared by a large proportion of the French people in the 1780s.

10 The quotations are from Burke, *Reflections*, below, 44.

11 See Burke, *Reflections*, below, 69.

12 See Gentz, *The Origin and Principles*, below, 331. John Quincy Adams arguably held a view similar to Burke's, as is shown by a passage quoted in Kirk's introduction. See Kirk, introduction to Burke, *Reflections*, below, 3.

13 Burke, *Reflections*, below, 153.

14 This passage is not from the *Reflections* but from the "Letters on a Regicide Peace." Francis Canavan, ed., *Select Works of Edmund Burke* (*Indianapolis*, 1999), vol. 3, 182. It is also quoted in Kirk, introduction to Burke, *Reflections*, below, 9.

15 See, for example, Edmund Burke, "Speech on Conciliation with the Colonies" and "Speech on American Taxation," in Canavan, ed., *Select Works*, vol. 1 (Indianapolis, 1999).

16 Gentz, *The Origin and Principles*, below, 321.

17 See Joseph de Maistre, *Essay on the Generative Principle of Political Constitutions and Other Human Institutions*, below, 379. The emphasis is in the original.

18 For this view of the Old Regime in the writings of De Bonald, see, for example, *Louis Gabriel* Ambroise de Bonald, "On Jacques-Benigne Bossuet, Bishop of Meaux (1818)," in Christopher Olaf Blum, ed., *Critics of the Enlightenment: Readings in the French Counter-Revolutionary Tradition* (Wilmington, DE: ISI Books, 2003), 43–70.

19 Elisha Greifer, introduction to Joseph de Maistre, *Essay on the Generative Principle of Political Constitutions and Other Human Institutions*, below, 345.

20 Joseph de Maistre, *On the Sovereignty of the People*, in Richard A. Lebrun, ed., *Against Rousseau* (Montreal: McGill-Queen's Press, 1996), 87–89.

21 Steven Lukes, "The Meanings of 'Individualism,'" *Journal of the History of Ideas* 32, no. 1 (1971), 46. On Maistre's view of human nature, religious and political authorities, and the relationship between them, see also the helpful essay by Jean-Yves Pranchère, "Joseph de Maistre's Catholic Philosophy of Authority," in Lebrun, ed., *Joseph de Maistre's Life*, 131–50.

22 See below, Maistre, *Essay*, 350.

23 See Aristotle's *Politics*, bk. 3, ch. 16, sections 1286a–1287b, where he argues that the written law—like "reason without passion"—is made inevitably necessary by the complexity of human experience, though it should never contradict the unwritten law. See also Justinian, *Institutes* 1.2.1–3.

24 Maistre argued that God had communicated himself by *speaking* to the prophets, and that Jesus had put his disciples in charge of teaching his commandments without ever asking them to write them down. The Gospels and Epistles were an "accident"; "the Scripture was never part of the founders' primitive plan." See below, Maistre, *Essay*, below, 337. The *Essay* included some intensely anti-Protestant pages, where Maistre criticized what he regarded as an unhealthy Protestant obsession with the written word to the detriment of the wisdom of the Church. See ibid.

25 See the *Addresses to the German Nation* that Fichte delivered in the winter of 1807–1808 and that were published in 1808. The similarities between Maistre's discussion of the nation and language and Fichte's look particularly striking and paradoxical if one considers that Fichte's vocal support for the French Revolution in the 1790s had won him the reputation of radical Jacobin. Johann Gottlieb Fichte, *Addresses to the German Nation*, trans. Gregory Moore (Cambridge, UK: Cambridge University Press· 2008).

26 Maistre, *Essay*, below, 366.

27 Robert R. Palmer, *The Age of the Democratic Revolution*, 2 vols. (Princeton: Princeton University Press, 1959).

28 See, for example, Hannah Arendt, *The Origins of Totalitarianism* (New York: Schocken Books, 1951); Eric J. Hobsbawm, *The Age of Revolution, 1789–1848* (New York: Signet Books, 1962).

29 The relationship between conservatism and fascism is complicated. In *The Conservative Mind* Kirk quotes Robert Nisbet arguing against the widespread view of fascist movements as conservative. Russell Kirk, *The Conservative Mind: From Burke to Eliot* (Washington D.C.: Regnery Publishing, 1953), 486–87. While the point seems valid when applied to the Burkean strand of conservatism on which Kirk focuses in the book, other strands of conservatism, which shared Maistre's intransigentism, have flirted with nationalism and fascism. On this, see for example Graeme Garrard, "Joseph de Maistre and Carl Schmitt," in LeBrun, ed., *Joseph de Maistre's Life*, 221–38. In an Italian context, one

could look at the figure of Agostino Gemelli. Although I am not aware of any proof of a direct influence of De Maistre's thought on Gemelli, Gemelli is an example of how intransigent conservatism can lead to support of fascist regimes. For an excellent introduction to the Catholic debate over the crisis of the liberal state in the years leading up to Mussolini's rise to power, see Maria Bocci, *Oltre lo stato liberale: Ipotesi su politica e società nel dibattito cattolico tra fascismo e democrazia* (Rome: Bulzonni, 1999). See also Isaiah Berlin, "Joseph de Maistre and the Origins of Fascism," in *The Crooked Timber of Humanity: Chapters in the History of Ideas* (Princeton: Princeton University Press, 2013), 95–177 (which, however, is also a good example of the tendency—rightly criticized by Kirk and Nisbet—to conflate the Burkean and Mastreian strands of conservatism and see them both as part of the origins of fascism). Carolina Armenteros and Richard Lebrun, *Joseph de Maistre and His European Readers: From Friedrich von Gentz to Isaiah Berlin* (Leiden: Brill, 2011) makes a convincing case against a view of Maistre as a father of fascism and highlights the fact that he has attracted the interest of many non-Christian readers and readers on the left side of the political spectrum. While rejecting the notion that Maistre's ideas were somehow destined to originate fascist regimes seems sensible—and it seems important to highlight the conflict between Maistre's deep religiosity and attachment to Catholic dogma and certain aspects of fascist ideology that are absolutely incompatible with Christianity, and to remember that leaders like Hitler and Mussolini often appealed to Christianity only instrumentally and strategically—that does not refute the case that a certain intransigence fueled support for fascist regimes, or at least a sense, in many European critics of liberalism and socialism, that fascism was the only viable or the least-worst option.

30 Greifer, introduction to Maistre, *Essay*, below, 345.

Reflections on the Revolution in France

1 Psalm 149:6–8.

2 Dr. Richard Price, *Discourse on the Love of Our Country, Nov. 4th, 1789*, 3rd edition, pp. 17, 18.

3 "Those who dislike that mode of worship which is prescribed by public authority, ought, if they can find *no* worship *out* of the church which they approve, *to set up a separate worship for themselves*; and by doing this, and giving an example of a rational and manly worship, men of

weight from their *rank* and literature may do the greatest service to society and the world." Ibid., p. 18.

4 Ibid., p. 34.

5 1st Mary, sess. 8, ch. 1.

6 "That King James the Second, having endeavoured to *subvert the constitution* of the kingdom by breaking the *original contract* between king and people, and, by the advice of Jesuits, and other wicked persons, having violated the *fundamental* laws, and *having withdrawn himself out of the kingdom,* hath *abdicated* the government, and the throne is thereby *vacant*."

7 Dr. Price, *Discourse on the Love of Our Country*, pp. 22–24.

8 See Blackstone's *Magna Charta*, printed at Oxford, 1759.

9 1 W. and M.

10 Ecclesiasticus 38:24–25: "The wisdom of a learned man cometh by opportunity of leisure: and he that hath little business shall become wise. How can he get wisdom that holdeth the plough, and that glorieth in the goad; that driveth oxen; and is occupied in their labours; and whose talk is of bullocks?"

> **38**:27. "So every carpenter and work-master that laboureth night and day," &c.
>
> **38**:33. "They shall not be sought for in public counsel, nor sit high in the congregation: they shall not sit on the judge's seat, nor understand the sentence of judgment; they cannot declare justice and judgment, and they shall not be found where parables are spoken."
>
> **38**:34. "But they will maintain the state of the world."
>
> **I do not determine whether this book be canonical, as the Gallican church (till lately) has considered it, or apocryphal, as here it is taken. I am sure it contains a great deal of sense and truth.**

11 Dr. Price, *Discourse on the Love of Our Country*, p. 39.

12 Another of these reverend gentlemen, who was witness to some of the spectacles which Paris has lately exhibited, expresses himself thus: "*A king dragged in submissive triumph by his conquering subjects,* is one of those appearances of grandeur which seldom rise in the prospect of human affairs, and which, during the remainder of my life, I shall think of with wonder and gratification." These gentlemen agree marvellously in their feelings.

13 State Trials, vol. 2, pp. 360, 363.
14 October 6, 1789.
15 Tous les Evêques à la lanterne.
16 It is proper here to refer to a letter written upon this subject by an eye-witness. That eye-witness was one of the most honest, intelligent, and eloquent members of the National Assembly, one of the most active and zealous reformers of the state. He was obliged to secede from the assembly; and he afterwards became a voluntary exile, on account of the horrors of this pious triumph, and the dispositions of men, who, profiting of crimes, if not causing them, have taken the lead in public affairs.*xtract of M. de Lally Tollendal's Second Letter to a Friend*

> Parlons du parti que j'ai pris; il est bien justifié dans ma conscience.—Ni cette ville coupable, ni cette assemblee plus coupable encore, ne meritoient que je me justifie; mais j'ai à cœur que vous, et les personnes qui pensent comme vous, ne me condamnent pas.—Ma santé, je vous jure, me rendoit mes fonctions impossibles; mais même en les mettant de côté il a été au-dessus de mes forces de supporter plus longtemps I'horreur que me causoit ce sang,—ces têtes—cette reine presque égorgée,—ce roi,—amené *sclave,*—entrantà Paris, au milieu de ses assassins, et précédé des têtes de ses malheureux grades—ces perfides janissaires, ces assassins, ces femmes cannibales, ce cri de TOUS LES EVEQUES A LA LANTERNE, dans le moment où le roi entre sa capitale avec deux évêques de son conseil dans sa voiture—un *coup de fusil,* que j'ai vu tirer dans un *des carosses de la reine.* M. Bailly appellant cela *un beau jour,*—l'assemblée ayant déclaré froidement le matin, qu'il n'étoit pas de sa dignité d'aller toute entière environner le roi—M. Mirabeau disant impunément dans cette assemblée que le vaisseau de l'état, loins d'être arrêté dans sa course. s'élanceroit avec plus de rapidité que jamais vers sa régénération—M. Barnave, riant avec lui, quand des flots de sang coulaient autour de nous—lo vertueux Mounier* échappant par miracle à vingt assassins, qui avoient voulu faire de sa tête un trophée de plus: Violà ce qui me fit jurer de ne plus mettre le pied *dans cette caverne d' Antropophages* [the National Assembly] où je n'avois plus de force d'élever la voix, où depuis six semaines je l'avois élevée en vain.
>
> Moi, Mounier, et tous les honnètes gens, ont pensé que lo dernier effort à faire pour le bien étoit d'en sortir. Aucune idée de

crainte ne s'est approchée de moi. Jo rougirois de m'en défendre. J'avois encore recû sur la route de la part de ce peuple, moins coupable que ceux qui l'ont enivré de fureur, des acclamations, et des applaudissements, dont d'autres auroient été flattés, et qui m'ont fait frémir. C'est à l'indignation, e'est à l'horreur, c'est aux convulsions physiques, que le seul aspect du sang me fait éprouver que j'ai cédé. On brave une seul mort; on la brave plusieurs fois, quand elle peut être utile. Mais aucune puissance sous le Ciel, mais aucune opinion publique ou privée n'ont le droit de me condamner à souffrir inutilement mille supplices par minute, et à perir de désepoir, de rage, au milieu des *triomphes,* du crime que je n'ai pu arrêter. Ils me proseriront, ils confisqueront mes biens. Je labourerai la terre, et je ne les verrai plus.—Violà, ma justification. Vous pourrez la lire, la montrer, la laisser copier; tant pis pour ceux qui ne la comprendront pas; ce ne sera alors moi qui auroit eu tort de la leur donner.

* NB Mounier was then speaker of the National Assembly. He has since been obliged to live in exile, though one of the firmest assertors of liberty.

This military man had not so good nerves as the peaceable gentleman of the Old Jewry. See Mons. Mounier's narrative of these transactions; a man also of honour, and virtue, and talents, and therefore a fugitive.

17 See the fate of Bailly and Condorcet, supposed to be here particularly alluded to. Compare the circumstances of the trial and execution of the former with this prediction.

18 The English, are, I conceive, misrepresented in a letter published in one of the papers, by a gentleman thought to be a dissenting minister. When writing to Dr. Price of the spirit which prevails at Paris, he says, "The spirit of the people in this place has abolished all the proud *distinctions* which the *king* and *nobles* had usurped in their minds; whether they talk of *the king, the noble, or the priest,* their whole language is that of the most *enlightened and liberal amongst the English.*" If this gentleman means to confine the terms *enlightened and liberal* to one set of men in England, it may be true. It is not generally so.

19 Sit igitur hoc ab initio persuasum civibus, dominos esse omnium rerum ac moderatores, deos; eaque, quæ gerantur, eorum geri vi, ditione, ac numine; eosdemque optime de genere hominum mereri; et qualis

quisque sit, quid agat, quid in se admittat, qua mente, qua pietate colat religiones intueri; piorum et impiorum habere rationem. His enim rebus imbutæ mentes haud sane abhorrebunt ab utili et à vera sententia. Cicero, *De Legibus*, bk. 2, ch. 7.

20 Quicquid multis peccatur inultem.

21 This (down to the end of the first sentence in the next paragraph) and some other parts here and there, were inserted, on his reading the manuscript, by my lost son.

22 I do not choose to shock the feeling of the moral reader with any quotation of their vulgar, base, and profane language.

23 Their connexion with Turgot and almost all the people of the finance.

24 All have been confiscated in their turn.

25 Not his brother, nor any near relation; but this mistake does not affect the argument.

26 The rest of the passage is this:

Who having spent the treasures of his crown,
Condemns their luxury to feed his own.
And yet this act, to varnish o'er the shame
Of sacrilege, must bear devotion's name.
No crime so bold, but would be understood
A real, or at least a seeming good;
Who fears not to do ill, yet fears the name,
And, free from conscience, is a slave to fame.
Thus he the church at once protects, and spoils;
But princes' swords are sharper than their styles.
And thus to th' ages past he makes amends,
Their charity destroys, their faith defends.
Then did religion in a lazy cell,
In empty aëry contemplation dwell;
And, like the block, unmoved lay; but ours,
As much too active, like the stork devours.
Is there no temperate region can be known,
Betwixt their frigid and our torrid zone?
Could we not wake from that lethargic dream,
But to be restless in a worse extreme?
And for that lethargy was there no cure,
But to be cast into a calenture;
Can knowledge have no bound, but must advance

So far, to make us wish for ignorance?
And rather in the dark to grope our way,
Than, led by a false guide, to err by day?
Who sees these dismal heaps, but would demand,
What barbarous invader sacked the land?
But when he hears, no Goth, no Turk did bring
This desolation, but a Christian king;
When nothing, but the name of zeal, appears
'Twixt our best actions and the worst of theirs,
What does he think our sacrilege would spare,
When such th' effects of our devotion are?
"Cooper's Hill," by Sir John Denham

27 Rapport de Mons. le Directeur-Général des Finances, fait par ordre du Roi à Versailles. Mai 5, 1789.

28 In the constitution of Scotland, during the Stuart reigns, a committee sat for preparing bills; and none could pass, but those previously approved by them. This committee was called lords of articles.

29 When I wrote this I quoted from memory, after many years had elapsed from my reading the passage. A learned friend has found it, and it is as follows: "The ethical character is the same; both exercise despotism over the better class of citizens; and decrees are in the one, what ordinances and arrêts are in the other: the demagogue too, and the court favourite, are not unfrequently the same identical men, and always bear a close analogy; and these have the principal power, each in their respective forms of government, favourites with the absolute monarch, and demagogues with a people such as I have described." Aristotle, *Politics*, bk. 4, ch. 4.

30 Mons. Necker, *De l'Administration des Finances de la France* (1785), vol. 1, p. 288.

31 Ibid., vol. 3, ch. 8 and 9.

32 The world is obliged to M. de Calonne for the pains he has taken to refute the scandalous exaggerations relative to some of the royal expenses, and to detect the fallacious account given of pensions, for the wicked purpose of provoking the populace to all sorts of crimes.

33 See *Gulliver's Travels* for the idea of countries governed by philosophers.

34 M. de Calonne states the falling off of the population of Paris as far more considerable; and it may be so, since the period of M. Necker's calculation.

35 Travaux de charité pour subvenir au manque de travail à Paris et dans les provinces

	£	*s.*	*d.*
Livres 3,866,920	161,121	13	4
Destruction de vagabondage et de la mendicité			
1,671,417	69,642	7	6
Primes pour l'importation de grains			
5,671,907	236,329	92	
Depenses relatives aux subsistances, déduction fait des récouvrements qui ont eu lieu			
39,871,790	1,661,324	11	8
Total *Liv.* 51,082,034	2,128,418	1	8

36 This is on a supposition of the truth, of this story, but he was not in France at the time. One name serves as well as another.

37 Domat.

38 Speech of Mr. Camus, published by order of the National Assembly.

39 Whether the following description is strictly true, I know not; but it is what the publishers would have pass for true in order to animate others. In a letter from Toul, given in one of their papers, is the following passage concerning the people of that district: "Dans la Révolution actuelle, ils ont résisté à toutes les *seductions du bigotisme, aux persécutions, et aux tracasseries* des ennemis de la Révolution. *Oubliant leurs plus gânds intérêts* pour rendre hommage aux vues d'ordre général qui ont déterminé l'Assemblée Nationale, ils voient, *sans se plaindre,* supprimer cette foule d'établissements ecclésiastiques par lesquels *ils subsistoient;* et même, en perdant leur siège épiscopal, la seul de toutes ses ressources qui pouvoit, ou plutôt *qui devoit, en toute équité,* leur être conservée; condamnês à *la plus effrayante misère,* sans avoir été ni pu être entendus, ils ne murmurent point, ils restent fidèles aux principes du plus pur patriotisme; ils sont encore prêts à *verser leur sang* pour le maintien de la Constitution, qui va réduire leur ville à *la plus déplorable nullité.*" These people are not supposed to have endured those sufferings and injustices in a struggle for liberty, for the same account states truly that they had been always free; their patience in beggary and ruin, and their suffering without remonstrance, the most flagrant and confessed injustice, if strictly true, can be nothing but the effect of this dire fanaticism. A great multitude all over France is in the same condition and the same temper.

40 See the proceedings of the confederation at Nantz.

41 "Si plures sunt ii quibus improbe datum est, quam illi quibus injuste ademptum est, idcirco plus etiam valent? Non enim numero hæc judicantur sed pondere. Quam autem habet æquitatem, ut agrum multis annis, aut etiam sæculis ante possessum, qui nullum habuit habeat; qui autem habuit amittat? Ac, propter hoc injuriæ genus, Lacedæmonii Lysandrum Ephorum expulerunt: Agin regem (quod nunquam antea apud eos acciderat) necaverunt: exque eo tempore tantæ discordiæ secutæ sunt, ut et tyranni existerint, et optimates exterminarentur, et preclarissime constituta respublica dilaberetur. Nec vero solum ipsa cecidit, sed etiam reliquam Græciam evertit contagionibus malorum, quæ a Lacedæmoniis profectæ manarunt latius." After speaking of the conduct of the model of true patriots, Aratus Sicyon, which was in a very different spirit, he says, "Sic par est agere cum civibus; non ut bis jam vidimus, hastam in foro ponere et bona civium voci subjeiere præconis. At ille Græcus (id quod fuit sapientis et præstantis viri) omnibus consulendum esse putavit: enque est summa ratio et sapientia boni civis, commoda civium non divellere, sed omnes eadem æquitate continere." Cicero, *De Officiis*, bk. 2, sections 79–80, 83.

42 See two books entitled *Enige Originalschriften des Illuminatenordens* and *System und Folgen des Illuminatenordens*. München, 1787.

43 A leading member of the Assembly, M. Rabaud de St. Etienne, has expressed the principle of all their proceedings as clearly as possible. Nothing can be more simple: "*Tous les établissements en France couronnent le mulheur du peuple: pour le rendre heureux il faut le rénouveler; changer ses idées; changer ses loix; changer ses mœurs . . . changer les hommes; changer les choses; changer les mots . . . tout détruire; oui, tout détruire; puisque tout est à récreer.*" This gentleman was chosen president in an assembly not sitting at the *Quinze-vingt*, or the *Petits Maisons;* and composed of persons giving themselves out to be rational beings; but neither his ideas, language, or conduct, differ in the smallest degree from the discourses, opinions, and actions of those within and without the Assembly, who direct the operations of the machine now at work in France.

44 The Assembly, in executing the plan of their committee, made some alterations. They have struck out one stage in these gradations; this removes a part of the objection; but the main objection, namely, that in their scheme the first constituent voter has no connexion 'with the

representative legislator, remains in all its force. There are other alterations, some possibly for the better, some certainly for the worse; but to the author the merit or demerit of these smaller alterations appears to be of no moment, where the scheme itself is fundamentally vicious and absurd.

45 Non, ut olim, universæ legiones deducebantur cum tribunis, et centurionibus, et sui eujusque ordinis militibus, ut consensu et caritate rempublicam afficerent; sed ignoti inter se, diversis manipulis, sine rectore, sine affectibus mutuis, quasi ex alio genere mortalium, repente in unum collecti, numerus magis quam colonia. Tacitus, *Annals*, bk. 14, section 27. All this will be still more applicable to the unconnected, rotatory, biennial national assemblies, in this absurd and senseless constitution.

46 Qualitas, Relatio, Actio, Passio, Ubi, Quando, Situs, Habitus.

47 See *L'Etat de la France*, p. 363.

48 In reality three, to reckon the provincial republican establishments.

49 For further elucidations upon the subject of all these judicatures, and of the committee of research, see M. de Calonne's work.

50 "Comme sa majesté y a reconnu, non une systême d'associations particuliéres, mais une réunion de volontés de tous les François pour la liberté et la prospérité communes, ainsi pour la maintien de l'ordre publique; il a pensé qu'il convenoit que chaque régiment prit part à ces fêtes civiques pour multiplier les rapports et referrer les liens d'union entre les citoyens et les troupes." Lest I should not be credited, I insert the words, authorizing the troops to feast with the popular confederacies.

51 This war minister has since quitted the school, and resigned his office.

52 *Courier François*, July 30, 1790. Assemblée Nationale, Numero 210.

53 I see by M. Necker's account, that the national guards of Paris have received, over and above the money levied within their own city, about £145,000 sterling out of the public treasure. Whether this be an actual payment for the nine months of their existence, or an estimate of their yearly charge, I do not clearly perceive. It is of no great importance, as certainly they may take whatever they please.

54 The reader will observe, that I have but slightly touched (my plan demanded nothing more) on the condition of the French finances, as connected with the demands upon them. If I had intended to do otherwise, the materials in my hands for such a task are not altogether

perfect. On this subject I refer the reader to Mr. de Calonne's work; and the tremendous display that he has made of the havoc and devastation in the public estate, and in all the affairs of France, caused by the presumptuous good intentions of ignorance and incapacity. Such effects those causes will always produce. Looking over that account with a pretty strict eye, and, with perhaps too much rigour, deducting everything which may be placed to the account of a financier out of place, who might be supposed by his enemies desirous of making the most of his cause, I believe it will be found, that a more salutary lesson of caution against the daring spirit of innovators, than what has been supplied at the expense of France, never was at any time furnished to mankind.

55 La Bruyère of Bossuet.

56 "Oe n'est point à l'assemblée entiére que je m'adresse ici; je ne parle qu'à ceux qui l'égarent, en lui cachant sous den gazes séduisantes le but où ils l'entraînent. C'est à eux que je dis: votre objet, vous n'en disconviendrez pas, c'est d'ôter tout espoir au clergé, et de consommer sa ruine; c'est-là, en ne vous soupçonnant d'aucune combinaison de cupidité, d'aucun regard sur le jeu des effets publics, c'est-là, ce qu'on doit croire que vous avez en vue dans la terrible opération que vous proposez; c'est ce qui doit en être le fruit. Mais le peuple que vous y intéressez, quel avantage peut-il y trouver? En vous servant sans cesse de lui, que faites vous pour lui? Rien, absolument rien; et, au contraire, vous faites ce qui ne conduit qu'à l'accabler de nouvelles charges. Vous avez rejeté, à son préjudice, une offre de 400 millions, dont l'acceptation pouvoit devenir un moyen de soulagement en sa faveur; et à cette ressource, aussi profitable que legitime, vous avez substitué une injustice ruineuse, qui, de votre propre aveu, charge le trésor public, et par conséquent le peuple, d'un surcroît de dépense annuelle de 50 millions au moins, et d'un remboursement de 150 millions.

"Malheureux peuple! violà ce que vous vaut en dernier résultat l'expropriation de l'Eglise, et la dureté des décrets taxateurs du traitement des ministres d'une religion bienfaisante; et désormais ils seront à votre charge: leurs charités soulageoient les pauvres; et vous allez être imposés pour subvenir à leur entretien l." *De l'Etat de la France,* p. 81. See also pp. 92ff.

The Origin and Principles of the American Revolution, Compared with the Origin and Principles of the French Revolution

1 Thus, for example, among all the statesmen and literati, who spoke or wrote, either for or against the American revolution, there were only two, who even then foresaw that the loss of the colonies would be no misfortune to England: The one, Adam Smith, was at that time little read, and, perhaps, little understood: The other, Dean Tucker, was held an eccentric visionary.

2 So long as the colonists had found a paramount advantage in the *culture of the land,* they would probably have borne their dependence. But when the critical period had arrived, when in the natural progress of society, a considerable part of the capitals would have been employed in *manufactures,* the English monopoly would have become insupportable.

3 Lord North formally declared in parliament, that after what had happened, an entire repeal of all the new taxes could not take place, until America should be brought to the feet of Great-Britain.

4 This great man, who, faithful to the principles of ancient policy, and animated with the most unbounded zeal for the glory and welfare of his country, which under his administration had reached the zenith of her greatness, considered the separation of the colonies from England, as the greatest of all evils, said among other things, in a most impressive speech, with which on the 20th of January, 1775, he introduced the motion for withdrawing the troops from Boston: "I announce it to you now, my lords, we shall one day be *compelled* to repeal these oppressive regulations, they *must* be repealed; you yourselves will retract them. I pledge myself for it; I stake my reputation upon it; I am content to pass for a block-head, if they are not retracted."

It is furthermore very remarkable, that the disapprobation of the measures against America, was not confined to the then *opposition parties,* but was equally shown by several of the principal ministers. The duke of Grafton, who from 1776, to 1770, was first lord of the treasury, and afterwards, from 1771, to 1775, keeper of the seals, had at all times declared himself against the prevailing system; the same sentiments were ascribed to the earl of Dartmouth, secretary of state for America; lord North himself, who from 1770, was considered as first minister, is said to have manifested often in the deliberations of the cabinet, different principles from those he afterwards supported in parliament. But nothing can be more surprising, than that in one of the most violent debates, which took place in the house of lords, in February 1775, even lord Mansfield, a man in high consideration, and of great talents, but whom the whig party considered as an exaggerated partisan of the crown's rights, and as one of the most decided enemies of the Americans, carried away by the heat of the contest, formally declared, that the introduction of imposts, in the year 1767, was the most *absurd* and most *pernicious* measure that could have been devised, and had been the real cause of all the subsequent misfortunes.

5 Most of the colonies were founded before the middle of the seventeenth century, all before the revolution of 1688. The province of Georgia, the most southern of the colonies, and which was originally part of South Carolina, was the only one, which received her *separate* constitution since the beginning of this century (in 1732) and was likewise the only one for the settlement and cultivation of which the British government had been at any cost.

6 This is undoubtedly the greatest failing that can be objected against mixed governments. Fortunately, however, it must be acknowledged, that the probability of such a dissolution is more remote in proportion as the constitution approaches nearer to perfection. For the more easily one of the constituted authorities can resist the other, by its appropriate weight, the less will be the necessity of appealing to arms. On the other hand, the more imperfect the balance is, the greater will be the danger of a civil war. In this lies properly the decided superiority of the British constitution, above all other complicated forms of government, that ever were, or probably ever will be devised.

7 In many places the public officers appointed to collect the stamp-tax, were hanged up, or beheaded; but all, only in *effigy*.

8 Shortly before, the congress are said to have resolved upon a declaration, by virtue of which, the colonies offered, "not only for the future, in time of war, to pay extraordinary contributions, but likewise, provided they were allowed a free trade, for a hundred years, to pay an annual sum, sufficient in that period to extinguish the whole British national debt," and to have been deterred from giving their last sanction to this declaration, only by the account of new hostile measures of the parliament. This highly remarkable fact I mention however only upon the authority of a single writer, a very severe antagonist of the ministry,

though otherwise very well informed. Belsham's *Memoirs of George III*, vol. 2., p. 166.

9 I believe that in the first section of this Essay, I have completely shown the lawfulness of the American revolution upon legal principles; and yet in that analysis, it will be found, that the sphere of unalienable rights of man, and the sovereignty of the people, and the like principles, are not once touched upon.

10 The general opinion, and the unanimous testimony of all the known writers upon American affairs, leave scarce room for a doubt of this fact, though for the honour of the Americans I would most willingly call it in question. His "*Common Sense*," is a pamphlet just as contemptible, almost throughout just as remote from Bound human sense, as all the others by which, in later times, he has made himself a name. To appreciate the character and tendency of this work, which, perhaps, has never been judged as it deserves, and to obtain a full conviction that it was solely calculated to make an impression upon the mass of the people, and especially upon certain religious sects very extensively spread in America, the reader has only to remark the spirit of the author's favourite arguments, which are all drawn from the *Old Testament*, and the absurd reasoning, with which he attacks, not the king of England, but monarchy in general, which he treats as an *ungodly* invention. If such a *work* could have produced the American revolution, it would have been best for reasonable men to concern themselves no longer with that event. But it was certainly at all times, by the wiser and better men, considered, endured, and perhaps encouraged, only as an instrument to gain over weaker minds to the common cause. cause.

The difference between this writer and the great authorities of the American revolution, such as Dickenson, John Adams, Jay, Franklin, &c. will be still more apparent, if we remark a similar difference between the two parties in England, which accidentally concurring in the same object, but differing infinitely from each other in the choice of means and arguments, declared themselves there in favour of that revolution. Whoever compares, for example, the writings of Dr. Price (who notwithstanding his numerous errors, deserves not, however, to be put in the same class with Paine) with the speeches and writings of Burke during the American war, will sometimes be scarcely able to convince himself, that both were contending for one and the same thing. And, indeed, it was only nominally, and not substantially, one and the same thing, for which they argued.

Another indirect, but not unimportant, proof of the accuracy and necessity of the distinction here pointed out, lies in the unquestionable aversion of most of the great statesmen in America to the French revolution, and to all what since 1789, has been called revolutionary principles. A remarkable anecdote occurs, testified by a witness unobjectionable upon this point, by Brissot, a man afterwards but too famous; an anecdote which proves how early this aversion had taken place. In a conversation which, shortly before the breaking out of the French revolution, he had with Mr. John Adams, now President of the United States, this gentleman assured him he was firmly convinced, that France, by the approaching revolution, would not even attain the degree of political liberty enjoyed by England and; what is most important, he denied, in perfect consistency with his pure and rigorous principles, that the French had a *right* to affect such a revolution as they intended. Brissot attempted in vain by appeals to the *original compact,* to the imprescriptibility of the rights of the people, and the like revolutionary rant, to combat him. *P. Nouveau Voyage dans les Etats Unis de l'Amérique*, par Brissot, vol. 1, p. 147.

11 I purposely say, there was nothing of *itself* illegal in this alliance. For France found the independence of the colonies already founded, when she contracted an alliance with them, and might besides not shrink from the question as to the lawfulness of this independence. Nothing of *itself,* unnatural, or self destructive; for the principles of the Americans contained immediately nothing, which could in any manner be dangerous to the existence of the French monarchy: and the political and commercial interests of this monarchy seemed in a manner to force its taking a part in the American revolution.

All this however notwithstanding, I believe, with the most intimate conviction, that a more profound policy than that of the count de Vergennes, and a larger and more comprehensive view into futurity, would have prevented France from contracting that alliance. Not to mention the false calculation which burdened with a new debt of one thousand millions of livres, a state already very much disordered in its finances, in order to do its rival, in the most favourable contingency, an uncertain damage. The whole undertaking was resolved on without any real political regard to its remote consequences. The lawfulness of the American revolution, might be ever so clearly demonstrated to a man capable of judging of its origin, and of appreciating the grounds upon which it was supported; the time might come, when without regard to the particular situation of the colonies, the general indefinite principle of insurrection might be taken alone, from their revolution, and applied to justify the most dangerous crimes. The Americans might ever so cautiously keep within their rigorous limits; and neither maintain, nor care for the application of their principles to other states; at the first great commotion, those whom the French cabinet had sent into the republican school, might with the forms consecrated in America, put all the European governments to the ban, and declare lawful and even virtuous *under all circumstances,* what had been allowable only *under certain circumstances.* These possible consequences of the co-operation of France would not have escaped the penetration of a truly great statesman, and the world has paid dearly enough for their having been overlooked.

12 In no one point is the analogy between the conduct of the revolutionary leaders in America and in France, so striking as in this; yet it must not be forgotten, that the Americans failed partly from inexperience and partly from real necessity; whereas in France they knew very well what they were about, and opened and widened the precipice with design.

The history of the American assignats, is almost word for word, only upon a smaller scale, and not attended with circumstances of such shocking cruelty, as the history of the French ones. The sudden start from two millions to two hundred millions of dollars; the credulity with which the first assignats were received, the undeserved credit which they for a time enjoyed, their subsequent rapid fall, so that in the year 1777, they already stood with specie in the proportion of 1 to 3; in 1778, of 1 to 6; in 1779, of 1 to 28; in the beginning of 1780, of 1 to 60; fell immediately afterwards to that of 1 to 150, and finally would pass for nothing at all; the attempt to substitute a new emission of assignats, instead of those which were worn out, continued until at last it became necessary to establish a formal depreciation; the harsh laws made to support the value of the paper; the regulation of the price of provisions (the maximum) and the requisitions, which they occasioned; the general devastation of property, and disturbance of all civil intercourse; the wretchedness and immorality which ensued upon them—all this goes to compose a picture, which the French revolutionary leaders seem to have taken for a model. It is remarkable, that they closely copied the Americans only in two points, of which one was the idlest, and the other the most objectionable of any throughout their revolution; in the declaration of the rights of man, and in paper-money.

Essay on the Generative Principle of Political Constitutions and Other Human Institutions

1 Hence Burke was not inconsistent in defending the concrete English rights of American colonists while castigating the abstract French Rights of Man.

2 Romans 13:1.

3 It is unfortunate that Maistre never finished and did not publish his *Essay on Sovereignty,* his most systematic analysis.

4 See his letters to Bonald of January 21 and February 13, 1815, in *Oeuvres Complètes* (Lyon, 1886), vol. 13.

5 Maistre refers to his own *Considérations sur la France,* first published anonymously in 1796. See ch. 6.

6 Ibid.

7 Machiavelli is here appealed to as evidence: "A people accustomed to live under a Prince, should they by some eventuality become free, will with difficulty maintain their freedom." *Discourses on Livy,* bk. 1, ch. 16.

8 The great importance of this should be recognized in modern monarchies. Since all legitimate and sacred immunities of this kind must proceed from the sovereign, everything extorted from him by force is smitten with anathema. *To write a law,* as Demosthenes justly remarked, *is nothing. To make it wanted is everything.* (*Olynthiacs,* III) But if this is true of the sovereign's relationship to the people, what shall we say of a *nation,* that is to say—in the mildest language—of a handful of hot-headed theorists who would propose a constitution to the legitimate sovereign as one would propose a surrender to a beseiged general? That would be indecent, absurd, and above all, futile.

9 Machiavelli is again cited here: "It is essential that there should be but one person upon whose mind and method depends any similar process of organization." *Discourses on Livy,* bk. 1, ch. 9.

10 Maistre, *Considérations sur la France,* ch. 4.

11 Ibid., ch. 10, part 3.

12 Maistre's Preface was written in 1814, the year of Napoleon's downfall.

13 Proverbs 8:16.

14 Earlier, it should be recorded, Maistre had incurred some bad feeling at his court by seeking to treat with Napoleon.

15 Napoleon's "august rival" must be the Russian Emperor Alexander, at whose court Maistre was serving as Ambassador of Sardinia.

16 The sovereign and members of the royal family. The work referred to is Maistre's *Eclaircissement sur les Sacrifices,* ch. 3.

17 There is an untranslatable play here on the word *amitié. "Car . . . la bonne dame [amitié] est, dans certaines occasions, tant aussi aveugle que son frère [l'amour]."*

18 Jérôme Bignon, 1589–1656, lawyer, writer, and tutor of Louis XIII. The Salic law prohibited the accession of women to the throne.

19 Maistre is not quite accurate in his description of Locke's view of law. It is true that Locke uses the one word "law" for both natural law and positive law. It is further true that positive law requires the consent of society. (*Second Treatise on Government,* XI, 134.) But this does not mean that social agreement can make proper and legitimate a requirement not consistent with the law of nature (which is binding, since it derives from God's will). Recently published manuscripts, which were, of course, not available to Maistre, make this explicit. "Certainly positive civil laws are not binding . . . in any other way than in virtue of the law of nature." See John Locke, *Essays on the Law of Nature* (ed. W. v. Leyden, Oxford, 1954), pp. 119, 187 ff. The great difference between Locke and Maistre is not whether law is grounded in a higher obligation but, rather, how it is known and what it tells us. According to Locke, it is inscribed in the reason of men (not in their customs) and is as indifferent to the Stuarts as Maistre would have it partial to the Bourbons.

20 "Man in the state of nature had only rights. . . . Upon entering into society, I renounce my private will [*volonté particulière*] in order to conform to law, *which is the general will* [*volonté general*]." [This is the language of Rousseau, not of Hobbes or Locke. See *Social Contract,* bk. 1, chapter 6. Maistre, of course, considers all three writers of one piece.] *Le Spectateur Français,* vol. 1, no. 194, has deservedly mocked this definition. But it might have remarked further that this idea belonged to the period and especially to Locke, who has opened this century in such pernicious fashion.

21 Bergier [French theologian, 1715–1790], *Traité historique et dogmatique de la Religion,* vol., ch. 4 (after Tertullian, *Apologeticus,* 45).

22 Bergier, *op. cit.*

23 "The Church forbids its children, even more strongly than do the civil laws, from being their own judges; and it is by her spirit that Christian kings abstain from doing this and that they deliver up criminals to the judge, that they may be punished according to law and to the procedures of justice." (Pascal, *Lèttres Provinciales,* no. 14.) This passage is extremely important and ought to be more widely known.

24 I have often reflected upon this passage from Cicero: "The Senate repealed the Livian laws in one sentence and in a single moment." (*Laws,* ch. 2, section 6) By what right did the Senate take this liberty? And why did the people allow it? It is surely a difficult question, but what affair of this sort can astonish us? After all that has been written on history and Roman antiquities, it has been necessary in our time to write treatises in order to discover how the Senate was recruited.

25 See the *London Chronicle* for March 4, 1806. Notice that this word *Legislature* includes the three powers. It follows from this assertion that the King himself *is ignorant of the Privy Council.* However, I believe he has an inkling of it. [Maistre refers to the motion censuring the Chief Justice Lord Ellenborough's sitting in the Cabinet. In the debate on this motion, Fox argued that tradition, if not enactments, supported this double function of one person just as it supports the Cabinet, whose technical status is only that of a Privy Council. Maistre should have written "Cabinet," not "Privy Council."]

26 Jean Louis Delolme, 1740–1806, author of a widely read work on the English Constitution.

27 "The turbulent government of England" said Hume, "ever fluctuating between privilege or prerogative, would afford a variety of precedents, which might be pleaded on both sides." *History of England,* James I, 1621. Hume, in speaking the truth, does not at all lack respect for his country. He states what it is and must be.

28 Maistre probably refers to Necker, who was recalled to be Director-General of Finance in 1788, just before the French Revolution.

29 A couple, perhaps, or nobody. Persius, *Satires,* bk. 1, line 3.

30 Paine's view is that a constitution is not an unstated and merely implicit frame of government but an explicit act of the people "antecedent to government." Consequently, "whenever it cannot be produced in a visible form, there is none." Thus the English people "have yet a Constitution to form." *Rights of Man,* part 1.

31 This may serve as a commentary to Tacitus' famous epigram, *Corruptissima republica plurimae leges* [When the state was most corrupt, laws were most abundant] (*Annals* bk. 3, ch. 27).

32 From Amyot's translation of *Banquet des Sept Sages.*

33 Tacitus believed that this form of government would never be more than an ideal theory or a transient experiment. A mixed constitution [a blend of democracy, aristocracy, and monarchy] is "easier to praise than to create; and if created will not last long" (*Annals*, bk. 4, ch. 33). English good sense can, however, make it last a much longer time than one could imagine, by continually subordinating, to a greater or lesser extent, theory, or what are called the *principles,* to the lessons of experience and moderation, which would be impossible if the *principles* were written.

34 Maistre perhaps refers to the credo of the Savoyard priest in Rousseau's *Émile*, which must have seemed to him, if sincere, nevertheless lacking in orthodoxy.

35 It is quite remarkable that the Evangelists themselves did not take the pen till late, and mainly to refute the false tales circulated in their times. The canonical Epistles also originated by accident. The Scripture was never part of the founders' primitive plan. Mill, though a Protestant, has expressly recognized this (Prolegomena in *Novum Testamentum Graece*). And Hobbes had already made the same observation in England (*Tripos*, discourse 3).

36 Psalm 150:4.

37 Reason can only *speak.* It is love which *sings,* and that is why we chant our symbols, for *faith* is only *belief through love.* It dwells not only in the understanding, but penetrates further to take root in the will. With much truth and ingenuity, a philosophical theologian has said: "There is a difference between believing, and judging what it is necessary to believe." (Leonard Lessius [Flemish Jesuit theologian, 1554–1623], *Opuscula, De Praedestinatione* [Lyon, 1651], p. 556) [The Confession of Augsburg (1530) is the historic Lutheran confession of faith; the Thirty-Nine Articles (1571) states the Anglican views of certain dogmas.]

38 Gibbon, *Autobiography.*

39 I.e., Luther and Calvin.

40 One can make the same observation going back as far as Arius. The Church has never sought to write her dogmas. She has always been forced to do so by opponents.

41 That is, Papal authority in the Church of Rome.

42 This notion was a commonplace of the eighteenth century. See, for example, Rousseau, *Social Contract,* bk. 3, ch. 6.

43 The Vatican Council of 1870 later did enunciate the dogma of Papal infallibility in *ex cathedra* decisions regarding faith and morals.

44 I do not know whether the English have noticed that the most learned and ardent defender of the sovereignty here referred to entitled one of his chapters thus: *A mixed monarchy tempered by aristocracy and democracy is better than a pure monarchy.* [*Quod monarchia, aristocratia et democratia admixta, utilior fit in hac vita, quam simplex monarchia.*] Bellarmine [Cardinal] and Jesuit theologian, 1542–1621], *De summo Pontifice*, vol. 1, chapter 3. Not bad for a fanatic!

45 Bishop Bossuet, 1627–1704, who, caught between Rome and Paris, drafted as moderate a declaration as he could.

46 Napoleon, after signing a Concordat with Rome in 1801, further promulgated unilaterally an organic law which provided for the teaching of the Gallican Articles (see below) in all seminaries!

47 In 1678, Pope Innocent XI entered into the controversy in which his three predecessors had engaged with Louis XIV, a round in the perennial tension between Church and State. The subject was the King's claim to the conferral of all benefices in a diocese during the period between the death of its bishop and the nomination of his successor and to the granting of the investiture of bishops, who, during their ascension, were required to swear allegiance to the King as their liege lord. The King wanted to extend this right. Innocent opposed the King even more strongly than had those before him, and the quarrel at length became so severe that the Pope employed the threat of excommunication. The King then summoned the Assembly of Bishops, which met in Paris and unanimously adopted the famous Declaration of Gallican Liberties, whose four articles were as follows:

1. The Pope's authority is only spiritual and does not extend to temporal matters.
2. General Councils of the Church may overrule the Pope.
3. The liberties of the Gallican Church are inviolable.
4. In questions of faith, the decisions of the Pope are subject to amendment as long as they have not received the assent of the Church in a General Council.

A kingly edict further required that all French subjects accept these articles, which restated old claims, and not support contrary doctrines. The effect would have been to limit Papal sovereignty drastically. Louis had to back down when the Vatican withheld canonical acceptance of all new French bishops, but the policy expressed in these articles remained that which the French government unofficially followed thereafter. See also Maistre's *De l'église Gallicane*, ch. 3.

48 Plato's *Phaedrus*, section 15. [Maistre's use of Plato here is somewhat misleading. Plato is not opposing written laws. Instead, he merely says that writing a political treatise does not obviate the need for pursuing the truth dialectically. This may imply that philosopher-kings (when and if they exist) ought to rule without being bound by law, written or unwritten (cf. *The Republic*). But it is equally consistent with Plato's reformist zeal and constitutional tinkering (cf. *Laws*).]

49 Plato, *Phaedrus*.

50 John 14:26.

51 Chrysostom, *Homilies on St. Matthew,* Homily 1, section 1.

52 Among the multitude of wonderful things with which the Psalms of David sparkles, I single out the following: "Appoint, O Lord, a law-giver over them: that the Gentiles may know themselves to be but men." [Vulgate, Psalm 9:21]

53 That is, Protestantism.

54 Plato, *Phaedrus*.

55 It grows imperceptibly through centuries, like a tree. Horace, *Odes,* Ode 1, line 12.

56 Hildebrand, Pope at the beginning of the Investiture Controversy with the Emperor Henry IV, 1075–1122.

57 Maistre's term, *génies constituans,* is made to imply the contrast of the Pope with the "false" Founders, the members of the Constituent Assembly of 1789.

58 Rousseau and Mably (French political philosopher and historian, 1709–1785).

59 Whatever wisdom is here, lies open—apparently a ritual-statement of the Oracle.

60 A degree of the Constituent Assembly of 1789 changed the royal title to "Louis, by the grace of God *and the constitutional law of the state,* King of the French." (Italics ours.)

61 Ch. 9.

62 That is, the Jews.

63 The reference is to the *Divine Legislation of Moses* (2 vols., 1737–1741), by William Warburton, 1698–1779, Bishop of Gloucester. In upholding the divine origin of the Mosaic Law against the deists, the author employed arguments which landed him in controversy, arguments which were paradoxical, if not eccentric.

64 One can even generalize the assertion and declare that without exception, *no institution whatsoever may endure if it be not founded on religion.*

65 Plato, in an admirable and wholly Mosaic passage, speaks of a primitive age *when God had confided the establishment and administration of empires, not to men, but to daemons.* Then he adds, speaking of the difficulty of creating durable constitutions: *The truth is, that if God has not presided over the founding of a city, and it has a merely human beginning, it will inevitably suffer the greatest evils. Thus it is necessary to imitate the primitive procedure in every possible way; and reposing our trust in the immortal part of man, we must dedicate houses as well as States by consecrating as laws the will of the* (supreme) *intelligence.* [But Plato means that the rule of law as determined by reason—not tradition—is the best approximation of divine rule.) *If a State* (whatever its form may be) *is founded on vice and ruled by men who trample justice underfoot, no means of safety remains for it.* (Plato, *Laws,* bk. 4, 713–14.)

66 In controversy, much use has been made of the famous rule of Richard of Saint-Victor [d. 1173]: *"Quod semper, quod ubique, quod ad omnibus."* But this rule is general and may be expressed thus: *Every constant, universal belief is true, and whenever certain articles peculiar to different nations are separated from any belief and something common to all is left, this remainder is a truth.*

67 The Holy Ampulla was a vial containing balm used in the coronation ceremony at Rheims. According to legend, it had been brought by a dove during the baptism of Clovis, later King of the Gallic Franks, in 496.

68 By the very nature of things, each religion *puts forth* a mythology which resembles it. For this reason, Christian mythology is always pure, always useful, and often sublime, while (by a special exemption) it can never be confused with the religion itself. Consequently, no Christian *myth* can ever be harmful, and it often deserves full attention.

69 Xenophon, *Memorabilia*, bk. 1, ch. 4, section 16. [But modern authorities render the last sentence otherwise, that the "most thoughtful period of life is the religious."]

70 It is true that Condorcet has promised us that the philosophers would assume the unceasing responsibility for the civilizing and welfare of primitive nations (in his *Sketch for a Historical Picture of the Progress of the Human Mind*). We are waiting to see them begin.

71 Ibid.

72 Letter to the Archbishop of Paris[?].

73 That is, "leader," from the Greek *koryphaios*, "leader of the dramatic chorus."

74 "Well! My friends, why don't you stay at home? You might not have found more devils there, but you would have found just as much foolishness." (Voltaire, *Essai sur les Moeurs et l'Esprit*, introduction, *De la Magie*.)

75 The Jesuits were expelled from Portugal and her possessions in 1759.

76 Osiris, reigning in Egypt, rapidly elevated the Egyptians from impoverishment, misery, and savagery by teaching them to sow and plant, by giving them laws, by instructing them to honor and worship the gods. Afterwards, going throughout the world, he reclaimed it also without using any force of arms, but attracting and winning over most of the nations by gentle persuasion and remonstrances contained in songs and in every kind music. The Greeks thought he was Bacchus himself. (Plutarch, *D'Isis et d'Osiris*, Amyot trans.)

Recently, on an island in the Penobscot River, a colony of savages was found who still sang many pious and instructive hymns in their language to the music of the Church with a precision that one could hardly find in the best choirs. One of the most beautiful airs sung in the church of Boston comes from these Indians (who had learned it from their teachers more than forty years ago), although since that time these unfortunate people have had no benefits of religious instruction. (*Mercure de France*, July 5, 1806 [?].)

Father *Salvaterra* (a fine name for missionary!), rightly called *the Apostle of California*, went to meet the most intractable savages ever known with no other weapon than a lute, which he played quite skillfully. He began to sing: *I believe in thee, O my God!* etc. Men and women alike surrounded him to listen quietly. Muratori says, speaking of this extraordinary man: *this seems like the fable of Orpheus, but who knows whether he might not have failed in a similar situation?* [Maistre refers to father Salvatierra, 1648–1717, born in Milan of Spanish origin, a Jesuit missionary in Mexico.] Only the missionaries have understood that fable and demonstrated its truth. Plainly, they had discovered the sort of music worthy of being associated with these famous stories. They wrote to their friend in Europe: "Send us the songs of the great Italian composers, in order *to be most harmonious without the complicated accompaniment of violin obbligato*," etc. (Muratori, [1672–1750, Italian scholar] *Christianesimo felice* [Venice, 1752] ch. 12., p. 284.)

77 "I will speak of Thy testimonies before also kings, and will not be ashamed." (Psalm 119:46) This is the inscription which has been put under the portrait of Bourdaloue [1632–1704, a Jesuit preacher at Louis XIV's court] and which several of his colleagues have also deserved.

78 This argument is an appeal to the better judgment of one of Maistre's arch-enemies. In a lengthy *Examination of the Philosophy of Bacon*, published posthumously, he blames Bacon for considering religion and science "a bad marriage" and for thus causing the supremacy in the eighteenth century of the physical over the moral sciences. (See ch. 9.)

79 I shall not allow myself to publish here my own opinions, however valuable their exposition might be elsewhere. But I believe it is legitimate for anyone to reprint what has already been printed and to quote a German speaking about Germany—a man no one could accuse of infatuation with the old-fashioned ideas. He says this of the universities in his country: "All our German universities, even the best, greatly need a reform of morals. . . . Even the best are abysses in which a horde of young people are irretrievably losing their innocence, health and future happiness, and from which emerge creatures destroyed in body and soul, more a burden than a help to society, etc. . . . May these pages be a protection to the young! Let them read the following inscription on the doors of our universities: "*Young man! It is here that many of your fellows have lost their happiness along with their innocence*." ([Joachim Heinrich] Campe [German educationalist, 1746–1818], *Recueil de Voyages pour l'Instruction de la Jeunesse*, vol. 2, p. 129.)

80 See his *Autobiography*, in which, after several noble remarks about the universities of his country, he says in particular of Oxford: "She will as cheerfully renounce me for a son, as I am willing to disclaim her for a mother." No doubt this loving mother, sensitive as she should be to such

a declaration, has bestowed on him a magnificent epitaph: *Lubens merito.* ["Rightly willing," a formula used in making a vow.]

Sir William Jones [Anglican Divine, 1726–1800] in his letter to Mr. Anquetil, falls into a contrary excess, but it does him honor.

81 A Greek would have said: *πρὸς πανόρθωσιν.* One might say, towards *total restitution,* an expression which philosophy might quite fittingly borrow from jurisprudence and which in this new context would be wonderfully appropriate. As to the opposition and the balance between the two forces, it is readily apparent. "Good is set against evil, and life against death. . . . So look upon all the works of the Most High; and there are two and two, one against another." (Ecclesiastes 33:14–15.)

We may say in passing: thence arises the idea of *ideal beauty.* Nothing in nature is as it should be, but the true artist, he who can say *God is in us,* has the mysterious ability to discern the least disfigured features of beauty and to assemble them so as to form a whole which exists only in his mind.

82 Italian philosopher, 1692–1777.

83 *Difficile est mutare in melius.* (Cited in the *Transactions of the Royal Academy of Turin, 1788–1789,* 6.)

84 *A θεει,* or, to express this idea more tersely and free from grammatical license: *Sans Dieu, rien de mieux* [Without God, nothing better.] (*Origen against Celsus,* bk. 1, chapter 26.)

85 *Nihil motum ex antiquo probabile est.* [It is difficult to prove the need of any departure from custom.] (Livy, *History of Rome,* bk. 34, ch. 54.)

86 "*One must return,* they say, *to the fundamental and original laws of the state, abolished by an unjust custom;* and this is a game certain to lose everything. *Weighed on such scales, nothing will be just. However, the crowd is easily persuaded by such arguments.*" (Pascal, *Pensées,* part 1, article 6.)

Nothing could be truer, and yet—such is man!—the author of this remark and his loathsome sect [Jansenists] have incessantly played *this game, certain to lose all.* Indeed, *the game* has utterly succeeded. Moreover, Voltaire has spoken like Pascal on this point: "*It is a vain idea,*" he says, "*a futile labor, to attempt to justify everything by finding corresponding ancient institutions,*" etc. (*Essai sur les Moeurs et l'Esprit, etc.,* ch. 85.) Listening to him speak about the Popes further on, you will see how well he remembers his own maxim.

87 At least with respect to the institution's merit, for from other points of view it may be quite necessary to consider causes.

88 Dante said to Vergil, honoring him a bit too much, one must admit: *Maestro di color che sanno* [Master of those who know]. Parini [Italian poet and satirist, 1729–1799], although he had his head completely turned, has, however, had the courage to say to Voltaire, parodying Dante: *Sei Maestro . . . di coloro che credon che sanno*—an apt remark. [Maistre probably cites this from memory, in which case he is too kind to Voltaire. The 1801 edition of Parini's *Il Mattino* reads "those who *pretend* to know" (*se fingon*), p. 49.]

89 *Précis du siecle de Louis XV,* ch. 42. ["The other abuse" meant is the mismanagement of finances which produced the need to sell offices in order to raise revenue. See below.]

90 *Ludens in orbe terrarum.* (Proverbs 8:31) [Maistre continues to paraphrase Voltaire. Ibid.]

91 Here, in 1809, Maistre apparently feels obliged to defend every feature of the *ancien régime* in France. Earlier (1793), he could proudly compare his enlightened Savoy with the abuses of France. In Savoy, there had been no pecuniary privileges for the first two orders of society and no venality of either military or civil office. (See *Lettre d'un Royaliste Savoisien.*)

92 "(The) principle, which is noble in itself, and seems specious [implausible] . . . is belied by all history and experience, *that the people are the origin of all just power.*" (Hume, *History of England,* Charles I, ch. 59, year 1649.)

93 "To the abode of the Apostles." This phrase refers to the periodic visits of bishops to Rome.

94 *Décade Philosophique,* October, 1797, vol. 1, no. 31. This passage, seen together with its date, has the twofold value of being highly amusing and also thought provoking. In it one may see what ideas these children were toying with at the time and how much they knew about what man should know before all else. Since then a new order of things has sufficiently refuted these fine conceits. *And if all Europe today is drawn* to Paris, it is certainly not in order to see *Olympic Games.* (1814 [the year of Napoleon's defeat].)

95 See the note of Spanheim [German diplomat and classicist, 1629–1710] on the seventh line of Callimachus' *Hymn to Diana,* [ed. by Gravae, with commentary by Spanheim and others, 1697]. Cited by Lanzi

[Italian archaeologist, 1732–1810], *Saggio di Lingua Etrusca,* part 1, ch. 3. The Homeric Hymns are in reality only a collection of epithets which belong to the same principle of *Polyonymy.*

96 Isaiah 1:26.

97 Let us remember the greatest name divinely and directly given to man. The reason of the name was given in this case with the name, and the name expresses precisely the destination, or what amounts to the same thing, the power. [The name *Jesus* comes through the Greek from the Hebrew *Joshua,* meaning "Jehovah is salvation," and can be said to have been divinely imposed upon Christ, "for He will save his people from their sins." See Luke 1:31 and Matthew 1:31.]

98 Revelation 3:12.

99 This observation has been made by the anonymous but well-known author of the German book entitled *Die Siegsgeschichte der christlichen Religion, in einer gemeinnutzigen Erklärung der Offenbarung* [the author is Johann Heinrich Jung-Stilling, 1740–1817] (Nürnberg, 1799), p. 89. There is nothing which can be said against this page.

100 Numbers 6:12 [Vulgate].

101 Herodotus, *Therpsyc.,* v. 3 [Modern editions do not make the variety of names the cause of disunion. It is merely mentioned.]

102 *Origen against Celsus* bk. 1, ch. 18, 24, and *Exhortation to Martyrdom,* ch. 46. [Origen argues that words are not merely conventional but have a "natural" relation to the object signified. Hence the importance of calling God by His right names if prayer is to be efficacious. This is not to say that God has reserved "immediate jurisdiction" over all names. Rather, Origen held a view common to the Stoics and Plato. See below.]

103 Plato, *Cratylus,* section 390. [Names are not merely conventional for Plato, but the citation here may be misleading out of context. The law-giver is not, by virtue of political authority, entitled to fix names. Quite the contrary for Plato. Only to the extent he is guided by one who knows how to give correct or natural names—the dialectician—is the politician a true legislator.]

104 So that, as Dionysius of Halicarnassus has observed, if the epithet is *distinctive* and *natural,* it will weigh as much as a name. (*De la poesie d'Homère,* ch. 6.) One can even say that in a certain way it is worth more, for it has the merits of creation without having the flaw of neologism.

[This reference is a puzzle, since Dionysius wrote no work of that name. Furthermore, in his *On Literary Composition* he says (ch. 5) that there is no grammatical order prescribed by nature, emphasizing artistry over "nature."]

105 I recall no famous epithet of Voltaire—perhaps this is merely due to forgetfulness on my part. [The French idioms cited are untranslatable.]

106 In reply to your phrase, *finding myself in the Ceramicus the other day,* etc. (Cicero, *Ad Atticus*, vol 1, no. 10.) [In the Ceramicus, literally "pot maker," were statues of fallen heroes.]

107 With a certain latitude which still includes the idea of pottery or a pottery. [*Les Tuileries,* literally "tile works," was a royal palace in Paris. There is a garden there now.]

108 "Such grace can order and connection give, / Such beauty may the commonplace receive." (Horace, *Art of Poetry,* 242–43.) Epigraph on the title-page of Diderot's *Encyclopedia.*

109 A rough and disordered mass of things . . . ill-matched elements heaped in one." (Ovid, *Metamorphoses,* bk. 1, lines 7–9.)

110 The Abbé Reynal (1713–1796), *Histoire philosophique et politique des établissements et du commerce des Européens dans les deux hides.* This work, banned by the government, attacked both the monarchy and the Church as a violation of the first of the natural rights of man, liberty.

111 "To stake life upon the truth." (Juvenal, *Satires*, Satire 4, line 89.) This was a favorite motto of Rousseau's.

112 "Dear now to his friends, dear hereafter to posterity." This appears under a portrait of Voltaire.

113 Recalling an ancient Greek or Roman theater where poetry and music were performed.

114 "Music played in the *Odeon* fails to inspire the same emotion in me which I felt in the former *Theater of Music,* where I used to listen to the same pieces with rapture. Our singers have lost the tradition of this masterpiece (Pergolesi's *Stabat Mater*). It is written in an idiom foreign to them. They emit the notes without being acquainted with their spirit. Their execution is cold, soulless, unfeeling and inexpressive. Even the orchestra plays mechanically and so feebly that the effect is spoiled. . . . Ancient music rivals the noblest poetry, ours only the chirping of birds. Therefore, let our modern virtuosi desist from profaning sublime compositions . . . let them (especially) play Pergolesi no longer. He is too much for them." (*Journal de l'empire*, March 28, 1812.)

115 In the second book of the *Iliad,* Ulysses wants to prevent the Greeks from ignobly renouncing their enterprise. If in the middle of a tumult stirred by malcontents he finds a nobleman or king, he speaks gently to persuade him. But if he finds *a man of the people* in his hands (*δήμου ἄνδρα*), a noteworthy Gallicism), he beats him *with heavy blows of his scepter.* (*Iliad,* bk. 2, lines 186–201.)

116 Constable is only a Gallic contraction of *comes stabuli*, the companion, or the minister of the prince for the department of the stables.

117 *Mercure de France,* June 17, 1809.

118 Thus, for example, if any man but a sovereign calls himself *legislator,* it is a certain proof that he is not one. And if an assembly does call itself *legislative,* not only does it prove itself otherwise, but also, it has lost its wits and in a little while will be abandoned to the scorn of the universe.

119 One must be aware of the mixture of virtues, whose proportions have infinite variation. When the same sorts of vice have been discovered in different times and places, some men believe they have the right to conclude judicially that *men have always been the same.* There is no more common, no grosser sophism.

120 Joinville [1224–1317], *History of Saint Louis*, p. 145.

121 French critic and philosopher, 1647–1706.

122 For example, see with what powerful logic he attacked materialism in the article "Leucippus" in his Dictionary.

123 Many would qualify for this distinction, but Maistre certainly means Voltaire, and the second is probably Condorcet, whom Maistre elsewhere has called "the most ardent enemy of Christianity." See *Reflections on Protestantism,* written 1798 and later published posthumously.

124 Maistre omits Gibbon's characteristic flavor. The bishops were already wealthy and influential under the Roman Empire. "Their influence was augmented with the progress of superstition; and the establishment of the French monarchy may, in some degree, be ascribed to the firm alliance of a hundred prelates who reigned in the discontented, or independent, cities of Gaul." (*The History of the Decline and Fall of the Roman Empire*, vol. 1, ch. 38.)

125 Job 21:14. *Therefore they say unto God, Depart from us; for we desire not the knowledge of Thy ways.*

126 *Oculos suos statuerunt declinare in terram.* [Thev have set their eyes bowing down to the earth.] (Psalm 16:11.)

127 A *ληθεύ οντες ἐ ν ἀ γὰπη* (Ephesians 5:15) This expression is untranslatable. The Vulgate, preferring, with reason, to speak rightly than to speak Latin, says: *Facientes veritatem in charitate.* [Do the truth in charity.]